Encyclopedia of Human-Animal Relationships

Encyclopedia of Human-Animal Relationships

A Global Exploration of Our Connections with Animals

Volume 4: Liv–Z

Edited by
Marc Bekoff

GREENWOOD PRESS
Westport, Connecticut • London

Library of Congress Cataloging-in-Publication Data

Encyclopedia of human-animal relationships : a global exploration of our connections with animals / edited by Marc Bekoff.

p. cm.

Includes bibliographical references and index.

ISBN-13: 978-0-313-33487-0 (set : alk. paper)
ISBN-13: 978-0-313-33488-7 (vol 1 : alk. paper)
ISBN-13: 978-0-313-33489-4 (vol 2 : alk. paper)
ISBN-13: 978-0-313-33490-0 (vol 3 : alk. paper)
ISBN-13: 978-0-313-33491-7 (vol 4 : alk. paper)

1. Human-animal relationships—Encyclopedias. I. Bekoff, Marc.
QL85.E53 2007
590—dc22 2007016552

British Library Cataloguing in Publication Data is available.

Library of Congress Catalog Card Number: 2007016552

ISBN–13: 978–0–313–33487–0 (Set)
ISBN–13: 978–0–313–33488–7 (vol. I)
ISBN–13: 978–0–313–33489–4 (vol. II)
ISBN–13: 978–0–313–33490–0 (vol. III)
ISBN–13: 978–0–313–33491–7 (vol. IV)

First published in 2007

Greenwood Press, 88 Post Road West, Westport, CT 06881
An imprint of Greenwood Publishing Group, Inc.
www.greenwood.com

Printed in the United States of America

The paper used in this book complies with the Permanent Paper Standard issued by the National Information Standards Organization (Z39.48-1984).

10 9 8 7 6 5 4 3 2 1

For my parents, who always encouraged the animal in me.

Contents

Alphabetical List of Entries

Culture, Religion, and Belief Systems

List of Entries that Feature Specific Animals

This list includes those entries that focus on particular animals. Other entries also include information about these animals but not to the extent that the following essays do. Please see the index for all mentions of the large number of different animals that are included in these volumes.

Cats

Cats, Large (*See also* Tigers)

Cattle

Chickens

Chimpanzees (*See also* Great Apes; Monkeys)

Cockroaches

Corals

Cows. *See* Cattle

Coyotes

Dogs

Dolphins

■ *Living with Animals*
Famous Horses

Horses fit the human idea of a good animal primarily valued for their use. "Pleasure horses" are often providers of active companionship and develop a bond with humans. Historically, horses are known for their uses and their breed, and, especially during modernity and the current age, individual horses have achieved celebrity-hood. Horses rank high on Arluke and Saunder's sociozoologic scale of human assessment of worth, based on societal use and how they perform their assigned roles. Horses are assigned a high moral value and any abuse is likely to come to the attention of animal advocates.

The history of the horse is one of work for humans, although horses do not necessarily accept domestication and can revert back to the wild. In prehistory, horses are depicted in paintings in the Cro-Magnon period Lascaux caves of France. The descendents of these horses, thought to have existed in a line for 55 million years, have been found in Mongolia and named after their discoverer: "Przewalski's horse." Today, Przewalski's (pronounced pshuh-vahl-skeez) horse is an endangered species being bred and preserved in international zoos and protected in Mongolia in the wild, where they were re-introduced. It is possible to touch the past at the Gladys Porter Zoo in Brownsville, Texas, where pregnant mares are kept in a petting area for human contact.

The date at which horses were first domesticated has not been established in the archaeological record, but there is a record of objects that may have been used as the means of controlling them. In the La Marche cave, inhabited in Upper Paleolithic era, a carving dated to 15,000 years ago suggests a bridle, but there is no evidence of riding until 6,000 years ago, when horses became work animals (Anthony, Telegin, & Brown, 1991). The written historical record, whether of purported acts or myths, suggests that the horse is the most socially valued large animal in Western culture.

Western civilization developed with horses used for work, transport, and warfare. The Greeks valued horses, and their representation in sculpture on the Parthenon is illustrated in books and media. Xenophon's *The Art of Horsemanship* is the first known book on horses and is still in print. Pegasus, a winged horse, was a supernatural creature in Greek mythology and the name of a constellation of stars (Bulfinch and Manguel, 1998). One of the first individual horses to achieve historical immortality was Bucephalus (Byoo-SEFF-uh-luss), the favorite war mount of Alexander the Great and namesake of a Macedonian city.

The Romans prized horses, and chariot racing was a major sport. Nevertheless, the sacrifice of a horse from the winning team to appease the gods does not indicate pet-like companionate relations, although Roman bonding with fast chariot horses was found in the following graffiti about the horse Polydoxus: "Vincas, nonvincas, te amamus, Polydoxus" (Whether you win or lose, we love you Polydoxus). The mentally disordered Roman emperor Caligula was extremely fond of an individual horse, Incitatus, which means "spurred on." This horse had a gem-embellished collar, a royal purple blanket, oats dipped in gold, a marble stable, and was proffered human food, and Caligula gave the horse Roman citizenship and the status of a priest. Perhaps it was Caligula's high-consumption lifestyle that led him to individualize Incitatus and give him human favors. Early use of horses was for transport and warfare. Horse cavalries were used in battle and conquest (Keegan, 1983). Wars and conquests in which horse cavalry was important include those of the Greeks, Romans, Mongols, and Europeans in the Americas. The U.S. warhorse with the greatest fame was Comanche, the only survivor of Custer's last stand against Chief Sitting Bull and the Sioux. The connection between Native Americans and their "Indian ponies" is well known and a staple of childhood literature and, in a more menacing context, Hollywood film (Roe, 1955).

The horse was presumed extinct in the Americas at the time of Old World rediscovery. Horses that escaped from the Spanish and other colonizers became wild and are known as mustangs. Wild horses that were not recaptured by Native Americans remain loose in the American West and on isolated islands, such as Chincoteague, off the Virginia coast. The beef industry has claimed that horses compete for range grass with cattle. Although ranchers wanted to eliminate the mustang population, animal advocates were successful in legislating a ban against the slaughter of wild horses for use in pet food and for consumption overseas in horse-eating cultures, such as France and Belgium. This ban was temporarily lifted during the early twenty-first century Bush administration but is in place again. Wild horse round-ups still occur but the animals are adopted. Shy Boy became the most famous named mustang due to his taming by famed "horse whisperer" Monty Roberts.

There have been many epic rides. Tschiffeley's ride was undertaken in 1925. He sought to ride two hardy Criollo breed horses, Gato and Mancha, from Buenos Aires to Washington, DC, and succeeded. The account is documented in a children's book, *The Tale of Two Horses*, told from the humanly imagined perspective of Gato and Mancha.

Animals have been an object of fascination for children growing up during modernity and postmodernity. Children's books provide a socialization into the world of horses. *Horse Heroes: True Stories of Amazing Horses*, by Kate Petty, for grades two to four, targets horses whose names have been preserved by history. Among the various types of horses that gain public attention include (1) Hollywood horse stars; (2) thoroughbred race horses, standardbred trotting horses, and pacers, which are also the focus of a gaming industry; (3) large draft horses, such as the Budweiser clydesdales; (4) jumping, dressage, and other events horses; and (5) cowboy and rodeo horses.

The invention of the steam engine followed by the gasoline engine took work away from horses in the twentieth century. War, plow, draft, and ranch horse use greatly declined in favor of technological transport and machine heft. Social values of beauty, athleticism, and heroics changed the social construction of the horse's use toward pleasure and entertainment. Horses became stars with names that connected to their image. Hollywood horses have most often been connected to Westerns, films based on popular horse fiction, and thoroughbred racing. Roy Rogers's horse, Trigger, a golden Palomino with a white mane and tail, was known as very smart and learned sixty tricks. His most famous trick was rearing with Roy Rogers on his back. He starred in eighty-seven films and 107 television shows, living until age thirty-three. Trigger is still remembered in collectibles such as books, DVDs, and other fan memorabilia, including Breyer model horses. In addition, the Lone Ranger rode Silver, Tonto rode Scout, and Gene Autry rode Champion. Many movies have featured stunt horses. The 1960s fantasy sitcom *Mr. Ed* featured a horse that was trained to appear to be talking. *Fury* and *My Friend Flicka,* based on the book of the same name by Mary O'Hara, were both network programs that focused on boy and horse bonds and adventures. Socially, however, fame for individual horses matters only when they have a name the public can focus on.

Antedating Hollywood horses, the Lipizzaners are an all-white breed of horse developed for dressage and maneuvers in medieval warfare. Trained to perform special maneuvers on the field, the Spanish Riding School of Vienna, Austria, perpetuated the technique after the decline of use of horses in warfare following World War I. The most special movements are the airs above the ground and ballet sequences. The levade, in which a horse balances on his hind legs with rider, is followed by the coubette, a jump while balancing in levade. The capriole is a leap off the ground followed by thrusting the legs out behind while airborne.

Today, these maneuvers are viewed as dressage, but the purpose of the capriole in medieval warfare was to scare the enemy. Today, these horses tour the world for performances, but in World War II, General Patton rescued the horses and the Spanish Riding School in the advance of the Russian army. This was represented in the movie *The Miracle of the White Stallions* (1963).

In post-modernity, racehorses have become a vehicle of the gambling industry, and are mass-produced and mass-marketed. People do not have to visit racetracks and only the vehicle of celebrity or a famous race such as the Kentucky Derby brings high attendance and on-track betting. Celebrity racehorses are cherished and immortalized. The outstanding thoroughbreds so venerated include Man o' War from the 1920s, Seabiscuit from the Depression-era 1930s, Citation from the 1950s, Native Dancer, and Secretariat from the 1970s. There have been more horse-racing heroes since then, but the celebrity of these thoroughbreds has stood the test of time, although Seabiscuit was resurrected from obscurity by Laura Hillenbrand's award-winning best-seller, which spent more than one year on the *New York Times* bestseller list. The book gained popularity because, like all of the above horses, it is a story of social bonds between an animal and a group of people, all of whom, like the horse, overcame adversity.

In 2006, Barbaro, the Kentucky Derby winner, was the most famous thoroughbred race horse in the United States. This began by virtue of his stunning open lengths victory in the Kentucky Derby, the first step of the coveted but seldom obtained "Triple Crown." Sadly, his story turned into a tale of survival after a catastrophic mishap in front of the stands and on television. Diverted from watching the race, fans of the horse were horrified to see him standing on three legs, flexing his right hind leg to keep it off the ground. Barbaro was taken to the nearby New Bolton Animal hospital and found to have multiple factures in the major bones in the ankle of his right hind leg. Given a poor prognosis, Barbaro's tenacity on the track and in the process of attempted healing produced an outpouring of get-well cards and gifts, such as carrots and apples, that, as a horse, he could more reliably appreciate. Barbaro was treated as if he were a human patient. The owners, trainer, jockey, and others involved in the efforts to save him all emphasized that they would only continue the struggle if he was not in pain and enjoying life. Truly, public sympathy for Barbaro shows the extent to which Americans care about famous horses. Because of complications from his injury, Barbaro was euthanized on January 29, 2007.

See also

Language and Literature—*Children's Literature: Horses*

Further Resources

Anthony, D., Telegin, D. Y., & Brown, D. (1991, December). The origin of horseback riding. *Scientific American*, 94–100.

Arluke, A., & Saunders, C. R. (1996). *Regarding animals*. Philadelphia, PA: Temple University Press.

Barclay, H. B. (1980). *The role of the horse in man's culture*. London: J. A. Allen.

Bulfinch, T., & Manguel, A. (1998). *Bulfinch's mythology*. New York: Modern Library.

Hillenbrand, L. (2001). *Seabiscuit: An American legend*. New York: Random House.

Petty, K. (1999). *Horse heroes: True stories of amazing horses*. London: Doring Kindersly Limited.

Roe, F. E. (1955). *The Indian and the horse*: Norman, OK: University of Oklahoma Press.

Xenophon. (1987). (M. H. Morgan, Trans.). *The art of horsemanship*. London: J. A. Allen & Company.

Judith Ann Warner

Living with Animals
Feral Dogs and Humans

The adage that dogs are "man's best friend" would seem to imply that the reciprocal relationship is true. And as the providers of food and shelter to more than 50 million domestic dogs in the United States alone, humans are the closest thing to an interspecific buddy that dogs have. Fostering this relationship has taken time. The 400 or so recognized breeds that exist in the world today are the result of humans actively controlling dog breeding, primarily in the last three centuries, but building on a practice that began more than 15 millennia ago. Artificial selection, the process by which certain phenotypes are promulgated by allowing individuals with the desired traits to reproduce while preventing those with unwanted traits from doing so, has been remarkably successful at creating the domestic dog. We are the designers, the Dr. Frankenstein, if you will, whose creation sits in the living room waiting for a nod, a handout, and the chance to relieve itself on the neighbor's pachysandra.

Dogs' preeminence among pets lies in their ability to fit in to our lives, to become part of the social milieu we inhabit. No animal understands our verbal and nonverbal cues, our moods, our ways of living, better than dogs. Wherever humans are, dogs are too. This is the legacy of dogs' descent from wolves, the top-drawer predator that found it profitable to stick around pre-agricultural human settlements and make a living scavenging leftovers. Opportunism being what it is, some animals inevitably found themselves in nearly constant contact with humans, trading some of their independence for food and protection. With behavior that predisposes dogs to social life and, more importantly, to subservience (there is only one alpha male in a pack), the stage was set for an interspecific relationship that persists to this day and will endure far into the future.

But increasing numbers of dogs have found themselves out in the cold, abandoned by their former owners (I use the term "owner" advisedly since we frequently think of dogs as property. You may use the term "pack member" if you like). In the United States, every state has reported populations of feral dogs, and worldwide, feral dogs are a persistent problem in many countries where high human populations and low socioeconomic conditions permit large numbers of dogs to exist semiautonomously on the fringes of a town or village. That is not to say that most free-ranging dogs, or those with unrestricted access to public property, are feral. Free-ranging dogs are ubiquitous in many communities, urban and rural, and most are owned animals let loose for a time but still provided with shelter and food. Truly feral animals are rare and reasons for that underscore the relationship between dogs and humans.

Canids learn how to interact with their peers and to some extent, their environment, during a period of socialization that (for dogs) begins at about four weeks of age, peaks at about six to eight weeks, and extends to around fourteen to sixteen weeks of age. At this time, experience with their litter-mates, parents, and other members of the pack provides them with information about who is friendly and what a suitable pack-mate looks, sounds, and smells like. This is when exposure to unfamiliar environmental stimuli can be evaluated without bringing an immediate fear response. The pup sees which situations are good, which are bad, and how to respond appropriately. This process of socialization is the foundation of our camaraderie with dogs. The absence of positive social interactions with humans during the sensitive period will result in their being wild and unapproachable after the age of about fourteen weeks, a time when fearfulness and the tendency to flee unfamiliar individuals rises. Socialization beyond this age is very difficult since it must occur in the presence of the animal's subjective fear of the unknown. Of course, this does not preclude building social relationships with humans later in life, but such relationships will be more difficult to initiate, take longer to establish, and may not be as long-lasting. What does seem clear is that without continual reinforcement of the social bonds formed with humans, previously socialized dogs will regress or desocialize and ultimately become feral. If they live long enough.

A common misconception is that once a dog is released by its owner (or lost, abandoned, or escaped) into the wild, its instincts for survival will kick in and the animal will cope with its newfound freedom. It is back in nature, after all, so regardless of how easy a life Spot, the three-legged cocker spaniel, had as a pet, he should be able to shift into wolf mode, join the local pack or start his own, take down prey, and generally live the life he was born to have. Despite centuries of artificial selection, this animal still has over 99 percent of its DNA in common with *Canis lupus*, the wolf. So, while *Canis lupus familiaris* may look like a pug or a Chihuahua, its core is lupine. Having said that, the domestic dog behaves somewhat differently than wolves, largely as a result of development rates that have been altered because of artificial selection and the environment in which we now keep them. Opportunities to behave like wolves are usually limited. Thus, for those people contemplating abandonment of their dogs, belief in the "strength by virtue of inheritance" idea is certainly self-serving. But more than that, it indicates just how profound our ignorance is of our best friend. This became obvious when I had the opportunity to ask how dogs became feral.

While conducting a study of free-ranging dogs in Newark, NJ, I saw that some animals could be approached much more readily than others, while one or two were virtually unapproachable. The latter approximated a feral condition, but there really were not any feral dogs roaming the streets of Newark; they would not be tolerated for any length of time. The range of behavior was intriguing and suggested that the argument that feral dogs had somehow become "de-domesticated" could not be right. Domestication is an evolutionary process that cannot be undone in the sense that animals will revert to a prior state. Even if such a condition could be recreated, it most certainly would not happen in the lifetime of an individual. Therefore, it had to be an ontogenetic process that dogs went through to become wild, leading Daniels & Bekoff (1989) to propose that domestic animals undergo feralization when they fail to become socialized, or become desocialized, to humans and behave as untamed, wild animals.

Subsequent research on the Navajo Reservation in the southwestern United States not only bore this out but allowed me to ask some fundamental questions, such as: How common are feral dogs, where do they come from, and how difficult is it to become feral? The results were eye-opening and showed me firsthand how the pact we made with dogs those many thousands of years ago, when humans took on the role of species designer, has been neglected.

The Navajo Reservation is about 26,000 square miles of high desert scrub, forest, and canyons in Arizona, New Mexico, and Utah. Most Navajo living on the reservation reside in one of the 110 small communities, or chapters, that dot the landscape. An important feature of each chapter is that about a mile or so beyond the residential area is an open dump where household trash and other rubbish are discarded. Dumps are the place to be if you want to find feral dogs, and much of my time on the reservation was spent in and around one dump north of Window Rock, Arizona, the seat of Navajo government. Here, the harsh reality of feral dogs' lives unfolded as did all the aborted attempts at feralization that most dogs experienced. Dogs are commonplace on the reservation since many Navajo still own and herd sheep, have property they want protected, or like the company of dogs as pets. They tend to be free ranging because few homes have fences to confine the animals, and the community's isolation permits movement of the animals over large tracts of uninhabited land. When females whelp, pups may be kept, given away, or taken to the local dump to fend for themselves, often with the mother. Likewise, unwanted adults of either sex may be abandoned at the dump. Dogs were typically driven some distance to another community dump when being abandoned in order to avoid having the animal return to its former home.

Once at the dump, the clock is ticking. Every dog has a variable but limited amount of time to start its new life, to find shelter and food, to learn how to interact with its new neighbors, and to avoid being preyed upon by humans. Very young and very old dogs are at a distinct disadvantage for obvious reasons—they may not be efficient foragers or hunters and may be unable to adequately defend themselves from others. Body size often matters in nature, and larger dogs are afforded some leeway with regard to aggression from others, but even that is little defense against a pack of dogs. Starvation is a real threat to abandoned dogs at this time; dumps offer some food, but competition is tough and availability is unpredictable.

Three strategies were apparent. For pups abandoned at a very young age, success depends on having the mother present. These animals will never socialize to humans and therefore will naturally become feral if they can survive. With the mother as food provider and protector, there is some hope. However, if the mother is not up to the task, the outlook for the pups is bleak. In one case I observed, a pup's mother and entire sibship were wiped out one night by a hunter. That same evening, another female who was also abandoned with her own litter survived the slaughter, though her pups did not. The following morning, the interaction between the two—a pup with no mother and a mother with no pups—was sad. The pup attempted to suckle from the female whose own pups had already been weaned and which had no interest in the needs of an unrelated pup. Ultimately, the lone pup resorted to cannibalizing her own sibs before being adopted by a resident pack living in the adjacent canyon. This is hardly the norm, however, and most pups are not as lucky.

For adult dogs that were used to living with humans, a different course of action was seen. The proximity of the dump made it easy for them to go into the community and attempt to scavenge food from residents, possibly looking to find permanent shelter. Given the territorial behavior of many owned dogs in the community and the unwillingness of humans to feed the newcomers, this strategy rarely worked and the dogs frequently returned to the dump. Their survival then depended on food availability.

A number of abandoned dogs, particularly older pups around four to nine months of age, sat listless in the dump after their arrival. Their strategy, if it can be called that, was to stay in the area and make the best of it. There were no attempts to reconnect with humans in the community, and their actions in finding shelter and food could best be described as half-hearted. While I had no way of knowing their behavior prior to abandonment, it is hard not to think of these dogs as depressed in this new environment. Much of their time was spent sleeping, and they represented a segment of the population that either did not know what to do next or simply gave up. Their fate seemed to be preordained.

The outcome for pups born of feral parents on the reservation was not much better. Of the litters I observed, only one or two individuals survived to six months of age. Dangers such as predators, parasites, disease, and the difficulty of finding enough food to feed all the pups contribute to the high mortality rate. The social organization of feral packs is not as cohesive as that for nondomestic canids either, and this can impact survival. Boitani and Ciucci (1995), in a study of feral dogs in Italy, concluded that they had more ambiguous dominant-subordinate relationships and weaker social bonds among all group members than did wolves or dingoes. This, in turn, may pose an upper limit on the number of feral dogs that can effectively cooperate as a functional unit, as well as influence mortality and recruitment rates.

Consequently, when we ask how common feral dogs are in a particular place, the answer will usually be "not very common." The path to a feral condition is not easy, and most populations would probably go extinct without continued recruitment from free-ranging dogs outside the population.

Two competing pressures influenced the distribution of feral dogs relative to human presence on the Navajo reservation. Since recruitment of non-feral dogs into the feral dog population depended on proximity to human settlements, feral dog numbers tended to be highest on the outskirts of a community, much as it likely was in prehistoric times. But the rate of feralization, (i.e., how quickly individuals become feral) will depend on the behavioral changes needed (this will depend on the age of the dog and prior socialization), resource availability, and how completely the population is divorced from human influence. Without abundant prey or other food resources far beyond a community's borders, feral dogs were restricted to areas near the community. Similar findings have been reported elsewhere. Feral dogs in Romania, Turkey, Russia, Venezuela, and a number of other countries, for instance, are found in habitats with adequate food in the form of garbage, near towns or cities where the human population permits high dog numbers and conditions that support them. These habitats do not exist deep within wilderness areas. Only the development of water resources in wilderness areas of Australia allowed dingoes, the ultimate feral dogs, to move beyond the range of natural water resources. Thus, in an ecological sense we are dealing with populations of dogs whose range and lifestyle are controlled, at least indirectly, by the local human populace.

Unfortunately, our behavior has frequently initiated a set of actions with unintended consequences that negatively impact the local fauna. This can occur in three ways. First, feral dogs may compete with native wildlife and use food and shelter resources that are no longer available to other animals. The demise of two native Australian marsupial carnivores, the thylacine and the Tasmanian devil, on the mainland soon after the dingo's arrival about 4,000 years ago is attributed to competition.

Second, they may kill the native wildlife outright. Predatory behavior by feral dogs is often assumed to be more common than is warranted on the basis of data that have been collected. Numerous reports have suggested that feral dogs kill white-tailed deer in the United States, though several studies addressing the issue concluded that dogs were inefficient predators and did little more than harass adult deer. However, predation on ground-dwelling animals, whether they be mammals, reptiles, or birds, is fairly common in some places. Marine iguanas in the Galapagos Islands, for instance, have been under pressure from feral dogs since at least 1934, when the dogs were first reported on the coast of Sierra Negra, as have giant tortoises, flightless cormorants, and blue-footed boobies. Estimates are that dogs kill about one-quarter of the marine iguana population each year, a staggering number. In Venezuela, feral dogs are reported to prey on capybaras, while they may eat wombats and wallabies in Australia, wild turkeys in the United States, and an endangered golden langur in India and Bhutan. In Israel feral dogs are known to chase Nubian ibexes and rock hyraxes. The smaller the prey population, the larger potential impact dogs may have. Finally, feral dogs can introduce new diseases into the native canid population (that can spill-over into other carnivores) and/or reintroduce old diseases that may have been at low frequency. This will often be a function of dog density. The dhole (*Cuon alpinus*), a canid that was once distributed across Asia and now exists only in remnant populations as a result of competition, habitat loss, and disease, is one such example.

What does this say about our relationship with man's best friend? In a word, we have not lived up to our end of the bargain. With the creation of a new animal, at least morphologically if not genetically, comes an obligation to care for that animal. Problems with free-ranging and feral dog populations are linked directly to the local culture. Therefore, education that fosters responsible dog ownership must be a priority. Awareness of the problems that unregulated dog populations can cause and the health risks they pose (most rabies in the world is the result of dog bites) are a prerequisite for successful management programs. Furthermore, our obligation to care for the animals we created does not rule out taking steps to limit their numbers. Fertility control, while precluding actions that induce suffering in free-ranging or feral dogs, is justified logically and ethically. Such methods may not be feasible until dog numbers are brought below some threshold, however, and that remains an area of concern. But the scientific knowledge to achieve population control may be obtained before humans have the collective will to use it. In any case, we need to understand that imposing the burden of freedom on an animal that is unable to handle it may be imposing a death sentence.

Further Resources

Boitani, L., & Ciucci, P. (1995). Comparative social ecology of feral dogs and wolves. *Ethology, Ecology, and Evolution, 7,* 49–72.

Daniels, T. J., & Bekoff, M. (1989). Feralization: The making of wild domestic animals. *Behavioral Processes, 19,* 79–94.

Matter, H. C., & Daniels, T. J. (2000). Dog ecology and population biology. In C. N. L. Macpherson, F. X. Meslin, & A. I. Wandeler (Eds.), *Dog, zoonoses, and public health* (pp. 17–62). New York: CABI Publishing.

Thomas J. Daniels

Living with Animals
Fish and Humans

Fish have been of enormous importance to humans for as long as mankind has existed. Of the estimated 48,000 species of vertebrates, more than half—between 25,000 and 30,000—belong to the cartilaginous and bony fishes. Although a rather minor number of these species play a role in human nutrition, much of the interest in fish has centered on the question of how to maximize the yield of these species as a source of animal protein. The first attempts to maintain fish in ponds for the sake of joy were made over 2,000 years ago, when the Chinese began to selectively breed carp into today's popular kois and goldfish. Another big step forward in the study of fish was taken around 1850, when the predecessors of the modern aquaria were first built. This enabled enthusiasts to keep, and later also to breed, a variety of different fishes, including freshwater and marine species. Today, over 12 million households in the United States and approximately 60 million households worldwide maintain aquarium fish as a hobby. The development of aquaria, including sophisticated lighting, filtration, and heating systems, has also opened new vistas for scientists, as they became able to study fish in the laboratory. In the following, we will discuss two important aspects of these fish-human relationships in more detail—fish as a source of food and fish as model organisms in science.

Fish as a Source of Food

Global Data

Fish are a vital source of food. Overall, approximately 13 kilograms of whole fish are consumed per human per year, which accounts for roughly 16 percent of the global animal protein consumption. In countries with low income, the relative contribution of fish is even higher, often exceeding 20 percent of the total animal protein available. In recent years, the world production of fish has been between 120 and 130 million metric tons per annum. More than three-quarters of these fish are used for human consumption, whereas the remaining portion provides the basis for the manufacturing of fish meal and fish oil. The capture fisheries production contributes about 70 percent of this total world fish supply, whereas the aquaculture production accounts for the remaining 30 percent. Over 90 percent of the fishery catches come from oceans and seas, compared to less than 10 percent that originate from inland waters.

Capture Fisheries

Although the demand for fish supply will continue to increase in the future because of the rising world population, the capture fisheries production has reached, and in many areas of the world even exceeded, the levels of sustainability. In addition to the loss of natural habitats and pollution, this phenomenon is mainly due to overfishing. According to the United Nations Food and Agriculture Organization (FAO), 70 percent of the world's commercially important marine fish stocks are at present fully fished, overexploited, or even depleted. This not only endangers an important source of food for the world, but also leads to loss of jobs in the fishing industry and associated industries and presents a threat to marine biodiversity.

Aquaculture

One potential solution to overcome, at least partially, these problems is to increase the contribution of aquaculture to the global supply of fish. However, this will require careful selection and management of the species used. Carnivore and omnivore species are commonly fed on wild fish or compound feeds, partially based on fish meal. As a consequence, more fish biomass as feed is required than is produced. For example, for the production of 1 kilogram of marine fish (including flounder, halibut, sole, cod, hake, haddock, redfish, sea bass, congers, tuna, bonito, and billfish), an average of 5 kilograms of wild fish are fed, thus leading to an exploitation of the stocks of the latter species. Indeed, four of the five top capture species are used for feeder fish in aquaculture. Only a few of the most commonly farmed fish species require less fish as inputs than is ultimately harvested. Among them is carp, mainly produced in China for consumption by relatively low-income households.

Fish as Model Organisms in Science

The ability to keep, and in many cases even breed, fish in aquaria has stimulated researchers from a number of disciplines to study fish in the laboratory. In the following, we will take a closer look at four such areas of research that are important to humans: comparative genomics, developmental biology, ethology, and behavioral neurobiology.

Fish and the Vertebrate Genome

Several species of fish have played an important role in modern genetics, particularly in the area of comparative genomics. The latter studies the relationships between genomes (genome—the complete DNA sequence of an organism) of different species. A major goal of such studies is to discover new genes in humans and to learn more about the evolution of individual genes, or vertebrate genomes. This is achieved by identification of the entire set of genes in a given species and comparison with the human genome. One of the most intensively studied species used for these investigations is the Japanese pufferfish (*Fugu rubripes*), also known as Fugu fish, or blowfish. This fish has become popular as a Japanese delicacy that can be deadly poisonous if prepared improperly by the chef, since the liver and ovaries of this fish contain tetrodotoxin, an extremely potent neuroteoxin of which less than 1 milligram is sufficient to kill an adult human.

The fugu genome project was initiated in 1989 by Sydney Brenner (Molecular Sciences Institute in Berkeley, CA), Chris Tan (Institute for Molecular and Cell Biology in Singapore), Greg Elgar (UK Human Genome Mapping Resource Centre in Cambridge), and Lee Hood (Institute for Systems Biology in Seattle, WA). The fugu genome was chosen because it is only about one-eighth the size of the human genome, yet approximately three-fourths of its genes and regulatory sequences are shared with the human genome. The compact size of the fugu genome is largely due to rather short introns (noncoding DNA sequences) compared to those in the human genome. The similarity of the human and fugu genomes is, at first sight, surprising, considering that the lineages leading to the mammals and the ray-finned fishes diverged in the Paleozoic era, about 450 million years ago. On the other hand, since many cellular structures and body functions are virtually identical in fish and humans, the corresponding genes are highly conserved. This high sequence similarity can be used as a powerful tool by the researchers to identify homologous genes. Moreover, DNA motifs conserved during evolution usually represent genes, whereas nonconserved sequences tend to reflect "junk DNA." Thus, by comparing the sequences of humans and fugu fish, genes can be recognized that are difficult to identify in humans alone because they are buried in a huge amount of noncoding information.

A "draft" sequence of the fugu genome was published in 2002, thus making the fugu genome the second vertebrate genome sequenced, after the announcement of the sequencing of the human genome in 2000. In total, approximately 38,000 protein-coding genes have been predicted to exist in the fugu genome. By comparing the genomes of humans and fugu, almost 1,000 novel genes in the human genome were discovered, thus representing a milestone in the identification of the entire set of genes in humans.

Fish and the Embryonic Development of Vertebrates

Among the model systems employed to study vertebrate development, zebra fish have become one of the most prominent in recent years. The idea of using this just 3–4 centimeters long fish, a native to Indian rivers and frequently kept in aquaria, goes back to the work of George Streisinger, a prominent phage geneticist and fish hobbyist of the University of Oregon in Eugene, in the late 1970s and early 1980s. In contrast to the still widely used mice, zebrafish embryos are transparent and develop outside the mother. Thus, scientists can readily monitor the different stages of development, label individual cells and follow their fates, or perform grafting experiments.

The final breakthrough in the establishment of zebrafish as a model organism of developmental biology occurred after Christiane Nüsslein-Volhard of the Max Planck

Institute for Developmental Biology in Tübingen, Germany, and Wolfgang Driever and Mark Fishman of Harvard University in Boston, Massachusetts, initiated two large genetic screens in 1992–93. Chemicals were added to the water to generate mutants with developmental defects. The aim was to identify genes that had important functions in embryonic development. Using this and other approaches, an enormous advance in the cellular understanding of development has been made, including the discovery of many genes involved in human diseases. This approach has been possible because the development of organs such as heart, kidney, or brain is regulated by genes essentially identical in zebrafish and humans. Because of the short generation time, the large number of offspring produced, and the ease by which mutants can be identified, zebrafish have proven to be an excellent choice to identify such developmentally important genes—on a large scale and within a relatively short period of time.

Fish and the Study of Behavior

Fish have been premier model systems to study the principles of animal behavior since the beginning of ethology, the biological discipline that examines natural animal behavior. The most frequently used fishes are the three-spined stickleback (*Gasterosteus aculeatus*) of the family Gasterosteidae, the numerous (approximately 2,000) species of cichlids (family Cichlidae), as well as the guppy (*Poecilia reticulata*) and the swordtail (*Xiphophorus helleri*), the latter two members of the family Poeciliidae. The three-spined stickleback was introduced to ethology in the late 1940s and the early 1950s by one of the founders of ethology, Niko Tinbergen, then at the University of Leiden in the Netherlands. Cichlids have received major attention after publication in 1950 of a comprehensive monograph on the behavior of this family written by one of the first students of Tinbergen, Gerard Baerends and his wife Jos Baerends-van Roon. Gerard Baerends and associates also initiated the work on the guppy in the mid-1950s. Swordtails have been widely used for ethological studies, since Dierk Franck of the University of Hamburg, Germany, began his work in the 1960s.

Since these fishes are able to produce, under the seminatural conditions of the aquarium, a major portion of their entire behavioral repertoire, and typically a number of individuals can be kept together in a tank, they are particularly well-suited to study behaviors displayed in social interactions, such as those shown during aggression, courtship, and brood care. In addition, experiments can be run in which the behavior of the fish is manipulated to test certain hypotheses. Such experiments have the benefit of the rigor of the laboratory and are often impossible to conduct in the natural habitat. The results obtained by using this approach have led to the establishment of many of the key concepts of ethology. These concepts, in turn, have had a major impact on the development of modern psychology, and thus on the biological understanding of human behavior.

Fish and the Neural Mechanisms of Behavior

A major challenge in answering the question of how the brain controls behavior is to find a suitable model system. Such a model system should be based upon a biologically relevant behavior, yet simple and robust enough to be accessible at the neural level. Thus far, only a few vertebrate model systems fulfill these requirements. One of them is the electric organ discharge of weakly electric fish. There are two orders of teleost fish that generate such discharges: the mormyriforms from Africa and the gymnotiforms from South and Central America. The discharges, produced by a specialized electric organ in the trunk, are controlled by well-defined areas in the brain. The fish use these discharges, among others, for orientation and localization of objects in the closer vicinity ("electrolocation"), as well as for communication with conspecifics ("electrocommunication").

Because of the simplicity of the electric discharges, their robustness, and the ease by which they can be recorded, the electric behavior can readily be quantified and related to the activity of electric sense organs and nerve cells. Capitalizing on these advantages, researchers succeeded in identifying the entire chain of brain stations involved in neural control of one particular type of electric behavior, the so-called jamming avoidance response, in the gymnotiform fish *Eigenmannia* sp. This behavior involves a shifting of the frequency of the fish's own electric organ discharge away from a discharge of similar frequency. The elucidation of the neural mechanism governing the jamming avoidance response is mainly the merit of Walter Heiligenberg of the University of California, San Diego. Through the investigations of his group, important principles of processing sensory information and of motor control were discovered. Equally important, the work on weakly electric fish has stimulated the search for similar principles in other organisms, including humans.

Further Resources

Barlow, G. W. (2000). *Cichlid fishes. Nature's grand experiment in evolution*. Cambridge, MA: Perseus Books.

Bradbury, J. (2004). Small fish, big science. *PloS Biology, 2*(5), 568–72. Retrieved from http://biology.plosjournals.org/

Naylor, R. L., Goldburg, R. J., Primavera, J. H., Kautsky, N., Beveridge, M. C. M., Clay, J., Foke, C., Lubchenco, J., Mooney, H., & Troell, M. (2000). Effect of aquaculture on world fish supplies. *Nature, 405*, 1017–24.

Nelson, J. S. (2006). *Fishes of the world* (4th ed.). New York: John Wiley & Sons.

Taylor, M. S., & Semple, C. A. M. (2002). Sushi gets serious: The draft genome sequence of the pufferfish *Fugu rubripes*. *Genome Biology, 3*(9), 1025.1–1025.6. Retrieved from http://genomebiology.com/2002/3/9/reviews/1025

Zupanc, G. K. H. (1988). *Fish and their behavior* (2nd ed.). Melle, Germany: Tetra Press.

———. (2004). *Behavioral neurobiology: An integrative approach*. Oxford/New York: Oxford University Press.

Günther K. H. Zupanc and Marianne M. Zupanc

Living with Animals
Giant Octopuses and Squid

There are certain animals that we associate with danger to humans, and killing us is certainly an extreme form of human/animal interaction. We know that humans have been killed by such megafauna as sharks, grizzly bears, lions, tigers, crocodiles, and venomous snakes. Often, such human deaths are the result of careless trespassing in an animal's territory or careless handling of a wild or captive animal. If you are a circus performer, there is an inherent danger in putting your head between the toothy jaws of a tiger. Sometimes the tiger slips, no matter how well trained, and one runs the risk of winding up like Roy Horn of Siegfried and Roy's Las Vegas act—Horn was horribly bitten during his act by a tiger. Of course, the possibility of such a tragedy may be why we view such spine-tingling acts.

But the statistics of animal-caused human deaths show that we are more in danger from smaller animals than from lions, tigers, and bears. Mosquitoes kill thousands each year with their infected bites, which cause malaria and West Nile virus. Our allergic reactions to bee stings kill more people than sharks do. Third world countries are constantly battling schistosomiasis, trichinosis, tapeworms, and lungworms caused by invertebrates that bring about disease and death.

Tentacles of Death?

But there are several other invertebrates that grow large enough to possibly be dangerous to humans: giant octopuses and giant squid. Giant Pacific octopuses can grow to 180 kilograms with an arm span of over 9 meters. Giant squid can grow to 400 kilograms and be 20 meters long from the end of their body to the tentacle tips. Both animals have been vilified in novels and movies as man-eaters, terrorizing the shore and the open sea. But the truth is somewhat different from the fictional portrayals.

The evil reputation of octopuses probably started with the lurid novel *Toilers of the Sea,* published in 1866 by Frenchman Victor Hugo. The romantic novel of a seafarer was tremendously popular at the time, second only to his *Les Miserables* in popularity, although much less critically acclaimed.

Gilliatt, the hero of Hugo's novel, is stranded on an island near Guernsey, off the French coast, where he is salvaging a shipwreck. If he can accomplish this feat, he will win the hand of a beautiful maid in marriage. Unfortunately, before he accomplishes this Herculean task, a colossal storm ravages his supplies and renders him nearly destitute—he must live off seafood that he procures from the seashore. He follows a crab into a cavern shaped inside like a skull. Guess what is lurking inside! This is where the story really gets lurid and incredible, but readers of the time ate it up. Arms emerge from the creature "like a tongue out of monstrous jaws." Sucker cups attack his skin "as if numberless small mouths were devouring him at the same time." He was attacked by "gigantic hands . . . furnished inside with living blisters eating into the flesh." Luckily, Gilliatt has a knife, and after a heroic battle, he cuts off the head of the beast, killing it. Unluckily, after salvaging the shipwreck and its lost treasure, his beloved marries another suitor and he commits suicide by wedging himself in some rocks at low tide and waiting for the tide to come in, just as his former beloved sails by in a boat. This sounds like the subject of another opera by Andrew Lloyd Webber!

The Hugo narrative was tremendously popular in Victorian times. Newspapers of the age vilified the beast and debated its dangers. The novel affected people's perception of octopuses and probably increased their willingness to believe in monsters of gigantic proportions in other novels of that age, such as those described in *Moby Dick* or *Twenty Thousand Leagues Under the Sea* (and their subsequent movies).

According to biographer E. M. Grant, Hugo was not much of a seafarer. He never sailed on the open ocean, but spent some time observing on the coast of France. He could not have learned about large octopuses there, since European octopuses are small, rarely getting more than 5 kilograms. Grant postulates that Hugo probably learned of larger octopuses from the writings and illustrations of Pierre Denys de Montfort, who published a monograph on mollusks in 1802. De Montfort included the improbable illustration of an octopus attacking and sinking carrying down a sailing ship. Hence, Hugo was just putting pen in his novel to the erroneous scientific belief of the times.

The largest species of octopus is the giant Pacific octopus (*Enteroctopus dofleini*), from the Northern Pacific, and the truth about them is hugely different than the fiction. Although it has been reported to grow to over 100 kilograms, most at maturity are 20–30 kilograms, hardly large enough to sink a ship or even its dinghy. For the most part, they are shy and retiring beasts, living in a den and only coming out to look for food or a mate. At the end of their lives, males act differently as they are going through a stage called senescence, when they stop eating and their body organs begin deteriorating. Sometimes they even crawl out of the water onto the shore where they die, giving credence to the tale of octopuses crawling out looking for humans. But these animals have given up eating and cannot perform a directed activity because of the failing of their brains, and they certainly never attack humans.

There are several documented attacks on scuba divers by giant Pacific octopuses. Of course, there was no flesh eating involved and no deaths, but these could have been serious and could have resulted in tragedy. Typically, a large octopus of 20–30 kilograms envelopes a scuba diver that gets too close to its den. Perhaps it associates a diver with food or perhaps it is senescent. Individual octopuses have been proven to have different personalities and some are just more aggressive than others. The danger to humans lies in the possibility of losing a mask or regulator and the resultant panic. However, no divers have ever been killed by a giant Pacific octopus.

The real dangerous octopus is not a giant—just the contrary. It is the blue ring octopus and its relatives of Australia and Indonesia. Just the size of a person's thumb, this little beauty packs enough venom in its bite to kill ten people, and several people have died from it. It uses its venom to kill its prey, fierce mantis shrimp nearly its own size.

Giant squid on the other hand, are perhaps the best known, but the least understood, of all the cephalopods capable of being threats to humans. The giant squid is an enigma that many people have viewed in movies or on television or have read about in such potboiler novels as Peter Benchley's *Beast*. Who hasn't seen the fierce battle between Captain Nemo and the giant squid threatening his submarine *Nautilus* in Disney's "20,000 Leagues Under the Sea"? Authoritative books have been written about this monster, but even Ellis's definitive *Search for the Giant Squid* has only a slim chapter of what we actually know about it. We know they are big, we know they are not man killers, and we know that sperm whales eat them, but we know precious little else of their life style. Until one was finally spotted in December 2006 in Japan, no one had ever seen a live adult, despite several well-funded expeditions to find one, using manned submersibles, ROVs, and even cameras mounted on sperm whales.

What we do know about giant squid comes from their carcasses, washed up on beaches, trawled in nets, found floating on the surface, or dissected out of sperm whales (sperm whales are their main predator). According to Ellis, the first was described back in 1545 from Scandinavian waters. It was not named until Steenstrup described its genus as *Architeuthis,* which means "chief squid." Since then fifteen other species have been provisionally described, but Roper and his colleagues wrote "Many species have been named in the sole genus of the family *Architeuthis* but they are so inadequately described and poorly understood that the systematics of the group is hopelessly confused." Many researchers nowadays believe that there is only one species, *Architeuthis dux*, worldwide.

How big does the giant squid really get? Not as big as its legend would tell us. The largest known was 20 meters long, found off New Zealand in the 1880s. Its body was only 3 meters long and most of its length was from its two long tentacles. It was not weighed but was estimated to weigh about 500 kilograms.

These are large animals—the largest of the invertebrates. The largest octopus ever weighed was a giant Pacific octopus of 272 kilograms on the west coast of Canada, and these squid get considerably bigger. But there are no authenticated cases of giant squid ever harming a human. No boats have been pulled under by them. No humans have been eaten by them or even been pulled underwater by their long tentacles.

As a matter of fact, most scientists nowadays believe that the giant squid is somewhat of a weakling. This is all speculation again, but remember, we have few hard facts about the behavior of the beast. It uses ammonia for buoyancy to help it hang in the water without sinking. It has weak muscles in its mantle and small fins, thus indicating a poor swimming ability. Some scientists speculate that it may hang in the water, with arms and tentacles outspread and dangling down, waiting for a fish to swim into them. This method of catching prey is used by a jellyfish, of course, but also some of the other deepwater squids.

Giant squid have chitinous, toothed rings around the outer edge of each sucker on the arms and on the tentacle clubs. Other squids have fierce claws on the arms and/or suckers, but the giant squid does not, again an indicator that it is not the fierce predator that fiction would have us believe. The sucker rings undoubtedly help grasp its prey. They also leave circular scars on the skin of the sperm whales that eat them. Old-time whalers spoke of squid-sucker scars the size of dinner plates, leading them to speculate that there might be huge monster squid lurking in the depths that had not been seen yet. Some scientists on hearing the reported size of these scars thought that they might have been inflicted on small whales and that the scars grew as the whales did. However, the size of these scars has been greatly exaggerated as there is no hard evidence of any sucker scars larger than 5 centimeters across.

Although the war between giant squid and their sperm whale predators has been depicted as a battle royal, this appears not to be the case. Large squid are the primary food of sperm whales, and they eat many other species as small as 3 feet. There is no evidence beyond the sucker scars (and sperm whales have thick skin!) that sperm whales ever have much trouble eating a giant squid. Mariners have seen sperm whales bringing giant squid to the surface to eat them. Although they can stay down ninety minutes, whales have to breathe eventually. Such eyewitness reports typically recount that the whales were methodically munching their way through the squid with their muscular toothed lower jaw and swallowing them with ease.

Schools of the jumbo squid (*Dosidicus gigas*) sometimes wash up on the shores of California en masse. They can get up to 4 meters long. These strong, graceful swimmers are caught for food in the Gulf of California, where they are called "the red death." Fishermen are wary of them when they are caught, since they spray water and ink and they have both chitinous sucker rings and vicious claws on their tentacles. Divers have recently filmed them and proven their ruthless ferocity—pulling divers down, tearing their equipment off, and ripping wounds through thick dive suits. This is definitely a squid worthy of the reputation of a monster but again, no fishermen or divers have ever been killed by them.

The colossal squid (*Mesonychoteuthis hamiltoni*) might be the real monster worthy of giant squid reputation. It lives in the stygian depths near the Antarctic, over a kilometer deep. It gets big—10 meters long—but its body is larger than that of the giant squid. It has a larger muscular mantle and it has hooks on its arms and tentacles reminiscent of a velociraptor dinosaur. The largest specimen found was still a sub-adult—it was not mature yet. Although Roper points out that we know nothing of its growth, the possibility is still there for it to surpass the giant squid in size and weight and for it to possibly be a fiercer predator. However, there is no evidence that it ever comes to the surface, except in fishermen's trawl nets.

Thus we see that in the realm of relationships between humans and giant squid, the odds are highly in favor of humans in any encounter. The only human/giant squid interactions have been with tiny juveniles on the surface of the water or with dead adults. Although we still have not seen a live giant squid, the only way we are ever likely to see one is through the lens of the camera of an ROV or through the 15 centimeter thick glass of a submersible, which the squid could hardly affect or pose any kind of danger to.

Divers frequently see giant octopuses but have never been seriously harmed by them. In fact, just the opposite is true—humans have hunted giant Pacific octopuses for food for centuries on both sides of the North Pacific, as they have hunted common octopuses in the Mediterranean for millennia. More recently they are being harvested for long-line bait in fishing for halibut.

In the early 1960s giant Pacific octopus wrestling contests were held at Tacoma on Puget Sound, a long inlet off the North Pacific. Scuba divers competed to see who could bring up the biggest and most octopuses. The captured animals were forced out of their dens by noxious chemicals that were irritating to the octopuses (now deservedly banned!) and wrestled to the surface. In one contest 110 divers brought up twenty-five octopuses, the largest 20 kilograms, that were later released or donated to a local aquarium.

Today the mentality of scuba divers has changed from taking giant Pacific octopuses for food to observing these gentle giants in their natural habitats. Researchers have gleaned numerous facts about their lives from observing them, such as their elaborate mating behaviors, use of dens, and antipredator behaviors. In the laboratory we have also learned of their remarkable intelligence, for they are indeed intelligent animals. They can learn to run simple mazes, do target training, exhibit personalities and play behavior, and open screw-top jars to get at food inside. These types of human/octopus interactions, observing behavior in the wild and in the lab, are doing much to change our perception of these "monsters of the deep."

Further Resources

Ellis, R. (1998). *Search for the giant squid.* New York: Lyons Press.

Mather, J. A., & Anderson, R. C. (1993). Personalities of octopuses (*Octopus rubescens*). *Journal of Comparative Psychology, 107*(3), 336–40.

Roper, C. F. E., Sweeney, M. J., & Nauen, C. E. (1984). FAO species catalog. Vol. 3. Cephalopods of the World. FAO Fish. Synop., (125) 3, 277.

Roland C. Anderson

Living with Animals
Honeybee and Human Collaboration

Imagine a world without sweetness. Until cane and beet sugar became widely used, in the last five centuries, there was no sweetener available in substantial amounts other than that provided by the gentle honeybee. Gathering it from flowers, bees bring quantities of nectar into their home, the hive, where it is dried, cured, and converted into honey. The inhabitants of a colony, which might number as high as 60,000 bees in summer, will collectively fly 55,000 miles and gather nectar from more than 2 million flowers to make a pound of honey, with each bee contributing just a twelfth of a teaspoon to the communal food supply in her lifetime. Though we humans have benefited for centuries, bees actually make honey for themselves, not us. This fine golden liquid is a vital source of sustenance for the colony—it is the carbohydrate necessary for the growth of the young bees being raised in the hive. In winter, when there are no flowers or nectar available outside, bees eat the honey they have stored to sustain them through the winter.

Honeybees have produced their sweet sustenance for tens of millions of years. When *Homo sapiens* arrived, about 2 million years ago, the nutritional landscape was harsh, and man scavenged this precious sweet as often as he was lucky enough to find it. Without protection, and heedless of stings, early man would plunge his hand into a nest, pull out the heavy treasured combs, and gorge the sweetness on the spot. As humans became more settled and sophisticated, they developed the knowledge, tools, and techniques to keep the bees and their magical honey closer at hand. Starting in ancient Egypt, man realized he could have the sweetness on a more regular basis if he could convince the bee to live nearby and find a way to take the honey without harming the bees' home. Egyptian priests devised clay vessels to capture, transport, and house bees nearby, and random (and painful!) discoveries of honey turned into domesticated beekeeping. Inhabitants of temples, castles, monasteries, mansions, and humble homes throughout the following centuries all kept their source of household sweetness near at hand—bees housed in baskets, boxes, buckets, and bottles in the backyard.

"Domestic" is really the wrong word, though it is so often used. Bees are gentle and accommodating but never yoked, trained, or housebroken. No matter where they are "kept" (another inappropriate word) they are wild and untamed in their instincts and actions. In some ways, bees "keep" us, humoring us with honey and their divine presence if we maintain our good manners and behavior. The Egyptian priests seemed to have sensed this and harvested only the laden honeycomb, leaving the bees and their babies inside to thrive. The deal between a beekeeper and his (or her) bees since then has always been that the beekeeper gives them a nice home in which to live, with plenty of storage space, and in return he can empty some of this storage space of excess honey at certain times of the year.

Because bees were the providers of such magnificent and magical sweetness, the relationship between humans and bees has always been one of reverence. As they watched the bees among the flowers, ancient Egyptians assumed that bees were collecting or distributing honey that had rained down from the heavens and gods above. Consequently, the bees were seen as messengers and incarnations of the gods, who had bestowed honey from on high. In the fifth century BCE, Aristotle wrote that honey "is what falls from the air, especially at the risings of the stars, and when the rainbow descends." Three hundred years later, Virgil, another honey devotee, swooned that bees and honey were "heaven-borne, the gift of air." Admirers, philosophers, and sweet tooths all over the world still treat bees and honey with reverence.

Honey is the sweet distillate of nature, with as many varieties as there are combinations of flowers. Knowing this, ancient Egyptians loaded their hives onto barges and floated them up and down the Nile, chasing the wildflower nectar and the unfolding seasons. Beekeepers have also collaborated with bees to obtain certain very specific types of honey. In England, for example, where people are partial to heather honey, bees are carted out onto the moors in order to capture the treat. This is a "monofloral" honey, which beekeepers get by convincing their bees to forage nectar from a certain type of flowering plant. If bee colonies are transported to the middle of a eucalyptus grove, for example, the honey will have an aromatic, almost medicinal flavor. Hives placed in an orange grove will produce orange blossom honey, which is sweet, light, and full of citrus flavor.

An extremely important, often overlooked aspect of the importance of the honeybee to humans is its role in pollination. Bees gather plant pollen—which is almost pure protein—and bring it back to the hive to feed their young. In their constant quest for nectar and pollen, bees transfer genetic material from one plant to another and help promote the adaptation and development of the species. Many of our crops are wholly dependant on bees for pollination, and farmers across the country rent hives of bees to farmers to help produce garlic, apples, alfalfa, cauliflower, almonds, and clover. Bees are also beneficial, though not crucial, to dozens of other crops, including asparagus, coffee, endive, pears, strawberries, and tomatoes. Bees thus bring us our morning coffee and, by pollinating the alfalfa crop that produces hay and then meat and milk, deliver the cream we lace it with. It is estimated that a third of our food supply, directly or indirectly, comes to us by way of bee pollination.

The relationship between humans and bees is, or at least should be, collaborative and friendly. Bees generously provide us with the sweetness of honey and numerous other food and health benefits. Contrary to popular belief, they sting only when provoked. They are intensely loyal to their ruler, the queen bee, and will become aggressive when they feel she or the colony is threatened. Beekeepers may be stung many times, but it is usually because they did something clumsy in the hive, causing normally docile and sweet bees to feel unsafe. Usually, bees are gentle, playful even. For fun, some beekeepers smear honey across their jaw lines and necks and then secure the queen bee in a cage underneath their chin. Her loyal subjects crawl freely around, licking up honey, content to be near their ruler, and the beekeeper will sport what looks like a beard of bees. As a beekeeper, I have not tried this collaboration yet, but I have heard that it tickles.

See also

History—*Harvesting from Honeybees*

Further Resources

Crane, E. (1999). *The world history of beekeeping and honey hunting*. New York: Routledge.

Dadant, C. P., & Sons (Eds.). (1975). *The hive and the honeybee*. Hamilton, IL: J. M. Dadant and Sons.

Holley Bishop

Living with Animals
Honeybee Society and Humans

During the nineteenth century, in the so-called heyday of natural history, the natural theologians saw life lessons in all aspects of nature, including the behavior of animals. Now, two centuries later this penchant for extracting moral guidance from animals is still with us. Even a cursory search of recently published, popular books about animals reveals quite a number claiming that animals can teach us lessons about love, loyalty, heroism, parenting, getting along with others, and the nature of the divine, no less. This peculiar animal-human relationship in which people believe that they can derive guiding principles from their observations of animal behavior has two general effects. First, it brings one to see animals as more "natural" or "genuine" than are people and as possessing qualities that people either never had, or have lost. Such hierarchical views of nature impair our ability to study the behavior of animals *or* people in any reasonable way. The second effect is that this view of nature leads us to see some animals as "better" than others; that is, implicit in this view is the belief that animals that manifest "love," "loyalty," or "heroism" (dogs, perhaps) should be cherished and valued. Those that do not (rats, perhaps, and certainly most invertebrates) need not be treated with the same concern and, in some cases, may be exterminated at will.

It is difficult to extract ourselves from this peculiar relationship with animals when we are in the midst of it. Consequently, to gain perspective on how easily we can project our needs, points of view, or desires onto animals, it is often necessary to examine an example from which we have some historical distance. One especially instructive instance is the controversy over the genders and gender roles of honeybees that played out in the widely read beekeeping manuals published in Britain during the seventeenth and eighteenth centuries.

To understand this story, you need to understand a bit about the honeybee community. The honeybee colony is made up of three castes of bees. First, there is a single, large female, or queen, which is the sole reproductive member of the colony. The queen does no work other than laying eggs. Second, there are several hundred male bees, or drones, who have no stinger and who do no work in the hive. Third, there are up to tens of thousands of female workers, each armed with a barbed stinger. The workers do all of the work of the colony from building, defending, and maintaining the hive to foraging for food and making honey. Except under very unusual circumstances (e.g., the loss of their queen), the female workers cannot lay eggs and are often referred to as "sterile." During a single flight taken in late spring, the queen mates with a series of the hive's drones. The drones that mate with the queen die shortly thereafter.

The queen stores the drones' sperm in a special organ called the spermatheca until the next spring when she lays her eggs. The eggs hatch into grub-like larvae, which in turn, metamorphose into adult bees. As the queen deposits her eggs individually into the honeycomb cells of the hive, she applies sperm only to some. The fertilized eggs will become females. When the eggs hatch, the female larvae that are fed "royal jelly" (which is secreted by the workers) will become new queens and leave to establish new hives. The other female larvae become female workers. If an egg does not receive any sperm, it becomes a male, or drone. As midsummer approaches, the female workers kill and discard the drones remaining in the hive to conserve food stores for over-wintering.

The practice of keeping bees for their honey and wax was probably brought to Britain by the Romans. Once established in Britain, the practice itself did not change very much up until the sixteenth century, though its agricultural and economic importance increased dramatically. In addition to pollinating crops, bees produce wax (necessary for making candles for home and church) and honey (a staple sweetener). Consequently, people kept hives of bees as commonly as they did domestic birds. So, knowing how to care properly for one's bees and how to produce additional colonies were critical skills.

During the late sixteenth and early seventeenth centuries a middle class of prosperous farmers and gentleman landowners developed in Britain. These groups became a nearly insatiable audience for an ever-growing number of "how-to" books publish on a variety of topics, including beekeeping. Obviously, the commercial success of such manuals was directly related to the accuracy and usefulness of the information that they contained. So, to be successful, the authors of these books had to bring modern, accurate, practical information to their readers. However, abandoning ancient philosophical beliefs and folklore about bees and relying instead on the discoveries of contemporary entomologists was a two-edged sword. On the one hand, authors could sell more books if the information that they offered was accurate and up-to-date. On the other hand, many of the new entomological discoveries did not reflect the political opinions and moral lessons that the authors wanted to intermingle with their practical beekeeping advice. In fact, much of their collective energies over the next two centuries would be spent trying to reconcile the emerging, seemingly anomalous, discoveries of entomologists with socially acceptable moral lessons about sovereignty, class, and gender roles.

Beekeeping came of age in Britain during the first six decades of the seventeenth century, and several influential, original books on beekeeping were published during this period. Of these, the most important was Charles Butler's *The Feminine Monarchie* (1609). This very influential book (new editions were published well into the eighteenth century) came to be recognized as the first scientific book about honeybees and beekeeping. Butler's style was straightforward, clear, and critical. He acknowledged that the queen and the workers were female and his careful dissections confirmed that the drones were male. However, although Butler's book settled questions regarding the genders of the honeybee castes, the gender roles of each caste—including their manner of reproduction—remained controversial.

The first important practical beekeeping text to tackle the thorny problem of a supposedly "model" society run by females was Richard Remnant's *A Discourse or Historie of Bees* (1637). Remnant understood the hive to be a "female Monarchie" and accepted the fact that the females produce the drones, or males, only when they are needed. He also knew that the males do no work and are killed and discarded in the autumn. However, Remnant admittedly remained uncertain about the generation of the queen bee. He reasoned that if the hive represented a monarchy, the monarch certainly could not be born of a commoner. But, if one claims that the queen bee produces new queens, one is faced with the impossible task of finding her a royal mate. After all, the males of the hive are lazy, common drones; they simply are not appropriate husbands for a queen.

So Remnant postulated a common-sense view of procreation among the commoners (workers and drones must mate), but remained emphatically undecided about the origin of new queens. Remnant, then, was left with only a single anomaly to explain: Whether the existence of a feminine monarchy among the bees is an indication that "it is lawful for women to govern in a commonwealth [or] . . . in private houses and families" (p. 36). In the former case, Remnant answers that women may govern only when the "male sex is wanting; or secondly otherwise disabled by natural disability: as here [in the hive]; nature not having enabled the male to governe, the female doth it" (pp. 36–37). However, when it comes to the home and family, Remnant offers Francis Quarles' poetic warning: "Ill thrives the hapless family that shows,/A cock that silent and a hen that crowes./I know not which live more unnatural lives,/Obeying husbands, or commanding wives" (p. 38).

No new books on beekeeping were published in Britain until the Reverend Samuel Purchas' *A Theatre of Political Flying Insects* (1657). Of particular interest is the apparent conflict Purchas felt about the gender of the hive's monarch. Being as knowledgeable as he was, he could not deny her gender, but his text seems to indicate he could not accept it either. "Though a king in place and power," he says, "[the monarch] is in sex a female" (p. 28). Surprisingly, Purchas then goes on to refer to the queen with the pronoun "hee." Purchas carries the idea of the queen acting as a male to the extreme when, in discussing the reproduction of the royal caste, he claims the queen actually "injects a spermatical substance thick like cream" into the queen cells of the honey comb (p. 34). In contrast, when referring to the worker bees, Purchas uses the feminine pronoun: "A bee, like a man cannot live alone, if shee be alone, shee dies." (p. 17).

Agricultural beekeeping was temporarily depressed during the first half of the eighteenth century. However, the art flourished, kept strong by a ubiquitous fascination with science and nature, especially among the burgeoning middle class, which was a ready market for ambitious authors. These enthusiastic patrons sought more in their reading than the dry practicalities of agricultural textbooks but less than the esoteric entomological discoveries published in the journals of the new scientific societies, such as the *Transactions of the Royal Society of London*. In response to this market, a new spate of popular beekeeping manuals appeared, unrestrained by the limitations of experimental investigation and the demands of mutual agreement imposed by the institutionalized scientific journals, yet bound by the prior knowledge that their audience had about the basic biology and behavior of the honeybees.

In addressing this market, authors once again were caught on the horns of a dilemma. On the one hand, they sought continued use of the honeybee and its hive as a source of moral and social guidance. On the other hand, most of the established and virtually all of the emerging entomological discoveries about honeybee gender roles were not concordant with the pervasive social ideology. That is, by the beginning of the eighteenth century, definitions of male and female gender roles had become quite polarized. The division of labor between home and the workplace was growing increasingly more rigid, and restrictions were developing as to the availability of economic, political, and social options, especially to middle- and upper-class women (who, interestingly, were a very large segment of the audience to which the new beekeeping texts were directed). So, authors had to deny, distort, or explain away those facts about the honeybee community that did not fit the ideological messages that they wished to convey.

The first of the new generation of beekeeping texts to wrestle with these problems was Joseph Warder's *The True Amazons or Monarchy of Bees* (1722). In his opening chapter, Warder gives an accurate description of the female workers. However, he describes the drones not as idle freeloaders but as "noble little creatures," hard working and industrious in the tasks given to them by nature. Further, he contends, by tending to their putative chores, the males actually free the workers to attend to their appointed duties, "so that the Male-Bee is not only of great use but of absolute necessity, not only to the Being but to the well-being of the Colony of Bees" (p. 5). In defending the male bees, Warder makes it clear that their lack of a sting does not make them the emasculated, lazy creatures that some have accused them of being. Quite the opposite, he writes, their voices are loud and dreadful, at times, "causing Fear where no Fear is, especially to the fair and timorous Sex" (p. 6).

The True Amazons or Monarchy of Bees remained the standard work on beekeeping in Britain until 1744. It was superseded by *Melisselogia, or The Female Monarchy* written by John Thorley (1744). On the one hand, Thorley's anatomy was state of the art, and he settled for good the gender of the queen by reporting his observation of a queen laying eggs as she walked across his palm. On the other hand, Thorley saw in the bees profound lessons about life, especially for women. To those qualities usually attributed to the honeybees, Thorley added chastity. Ignoring virtually all that had been discovered and discussed over the last century and a quarter, Thorley referred back to Butler's claim that the bees actually do not copulate as do other creatures. "Another Virtue," he noted, "that . . . [is] a Pattern to all, especially the Female Sex . . . is their Cleanness and decency." The bees abhor all that is filthy and impure, he claimed. Their hive is always spotless and their dress always "neat to a proverb" (p. 31).

Thorley goes on, in quite a fascinating way, to make the roles of each honeybee caste fit just those selected facts that he wishes to include in his text. Because mating among the bees had never been observed, he argued that the drones actually serve no reproductive role. If they did, he says, the monarchy could not stand. No government could exist with dozens of pretenders to the throne. Certainly, if just a single queen can produce an entire colony, she does not need hundreds of males with which to mate. This idea, in Thorley's opinion, denigrates the queen, making her majesty "the most hateful and abominable whore, with Gallants by Hundreds." If the drones are the male reproductives, he asks, then "what has become of her so much boasted, admired chastity, wherein she appears such an eminent Pattern to the human Species?" (p. 93). So Thorley concluded that the drones are of neither sex and must have been created for some purpose other than reproduction.

In the same year that Thorley's book was published, an English translation of Bazin's *The Natural History of Bees* appeared in Britain (1744). This was the last major beekeeping text published in Britain that could turn its back on the growing consensus about the actual genders and gender roles of the hive's inhabitants. The way Bazin handles these issues is as unique and interesting as is Thorley's. Bazin's book is written as a dialogue between the characters Eugenio and Clarissa. Through Eugenio, Bazin explains that the hive consists of a single queen, which is the only female in the hive, 200 to 1,000 males or drones and 15 or more thousand worker bees of no sex. Instead of viewing the drones as indolent or lazy, Bazin reasons that their great reproductive honor actually exempts them from having to do any work in the hive. Although his explanatory task has been simplified somewhat by accepting the fact that only the queen lays eggs and naming the drones as her potential mates, he has created for himself the problem that Thorley was so anxious to avoid. That is, if the queen has gallants by the hundred, how can she maintain the virtue and dignity befitting a woman, especially a woman of her social rank?

Surprisingly, however, observations of individual bees in glass bottles revealed to Eugenio an appropriate, feminine demeanor on the queen's part at all times. When isolated with a drone, the queen must stimulate and caress the indolent, insensitive male into the act of love, and by choosing only one husband at a time, she maintains her virtue. Eugenio also found, much to his astonishment, that when a second, young drone is introduced into the same bottle (after the first has died of passion), the queen does not behave like a "brute" but rather like a virtuous wife. Remaining fixed to the body of her unfortunate spouse, she does not take a new husband until the following day. Although, at first, this may not seem like a long enough period of mourning for a respectable woman, Eugenio defends her actions. She should not be chastised, he explains, because, given the short life of a bee, a single day is likely a proper period of morning, as is a year for "one of our young widows" (p. 103). Although Clarissa is taken aback by much of this information, Eugenio assures her that the natural order is not, in actuality, violated at all. "You easily conceive," he points out, "what confusion, what a terrible situation it would be for a woman, to find herself in the midst and at the mercy of a crowd of active, petulant husbands, who would all be masters the same moment" (pp. 104–05).

Bazin's book was the last of its type. With the exception of a single, rather vitriolic text published in the nineteenth century (Robert Huish, *A Treatise on the Natural Economy and Practical Management of Bees,* 1815), practical beekeeping texts written after 1750 rapidly stopped using the hive and its inhabitants as models for English social life. Two major factors were responsible for this change, the most important of which was the publication of two highly influential papers about the bees in *Philosophical Transactions of the Royal Society of London* in 1750 and 1777. The first was Arthur Dobbs' accurate explanation of the function of the queen bee's spermatheca (the organ in which the queen stores the drone's sperm after mating). This bit of knowledge made the drones' role in reproduction and the timing of their emergence understandable. The second was an article by John Debraw that popularized and replicated the amazing discovery of A. M. Schirach, that a single, fertilized egg may yield either a worker or a queen depending solely on the larva's diet. This discovery put to rest debates about the bees that revolved around the rigidity of social class, for instance, who might be the "royal" mate to the queen, or whether the queen lays only "royal" eggs. Once it was accepted that a single egg could yield either a queen or common worker, the hive could no longer serve as a metaphor for class distinctions based on birthright.

The second factor that brought to a close this chapter of British beekeeping literature was a new sophistication on the part of the beekeeping public. Rapid dissemination of a growing body of scientific knowledge about the bees made it increasingly more difficult to distort scientific knowledge in the service of social ideology. As scientific discoveries about the bees became general knowledge, popular beekeeping books, with progressively fewer exceptions, came to contain the best of that knowledge and its practical application rather than the social and political ideologies of their authors. Perhaps such a scientifically well-informed perspective is necessary to maintain an appropriately sophisticated intellectual relationship with the animals around us.

See also

History—*Harvesting from Honeybees*

Further Resources

Fox Keller, E. (1985). *Reflections on gender and science.* New Haven, CT: Yale University Press.

Fraser, H. M. (1958). *History of beekeeping in Britain.* London: Bee Research Association, Ltd.

Prete, F. R. (1990) The conundrum of the honeybees: One impediment to Darwin publishing his theory. *Journal of the History of Biology,* 23, 271–90.

———. (1991). Can females rule the hive? The controversy over honeybee gender roles in British beekeeping texts of the 16th–18th centuries. *Journal of the History of Biology, 24,* 113–44.

Frederick R. Prete

Living with Animals
Horses and Humans: From Prey to Partner

For many thousands of years, the history of two species, humans (*Homo sapiens*) and horses (*Equus caballus*) has been intimately linked. No other animal, with the exception of the dog (*Canis familiaris*), has had such an intimate association with humans. Without horses, human civilization would have evolved very differently, since horses have played an integral part in the spread of human cultures throughout the world. Along with the historical, economic, and social bonds between human and horse, the horse's relationship to humans has itself evolved—from prey to pack animal to partner.

More than 5,000 years ago, the first interactions between humans and horses involved a predator-prey relationship. Based upon archeological and paleontological evidence, Stone Age humans hunted horses for meat, and, through overhunting, may even have helped drive horses to extinction in the northern hemisphere. By 3000 BCE, however, crops and domesticated livestock provided humans with enough food, so they could develop much different uses for horses. Although it is not known precisely how humans learned to tame horses, evidence suggests that horses were first used to pull carts, as oxen and other animals did. Riding seems to have come much later, almost 2,000 years after domestication. Inventions such as the saddle, stirrup, and bit were important cultural advances and allowed increased control of the horse and greater security for the rider.

Regardless of which came first, domestication of the horse opened up a world of new opportunities, and people could travel much greater distances—more rapidly—than they could on foot.

Once domesticated, horses became a vital part of the human lifestyle and were used in war, travel, and work. A horse's speed and agility made it indispensable during war, whether a person rode the horse or used it to pull a chariot. Horses were used as a major source of travel, and empires and cultures were built on their backs. Riding allowed people to hunt wildlife more efficiently. Given their great strength and stamina, people used horses to pack heavy loads over a long distance. Tending cattle and herding sheep and goats became much easier. Horses also worked on farms, but were often not as widely used, as they lacked the strength of, and required more expensive feed than, oxen.

Given the historical importance of the human-horse relationship, horse-centered cultures developed worldwide. The Mongols of Central Asia used horses in their devastating conquest of vast areas of land and identified with their tough, hardy ponies. The Mongols used them not only for transportation but also for food, and they used their horses' skin for tents and clothing. Native Americans in the United States used horses to expand their hunting grounds and interactions with other tribes. Modern cultures still identify with horses. Icelandic ponies were developed from Celtic and Germanic stock brought to Iceland in the middle of the ninth century. Offspring of these imports have lived in isolation for the past 1,000 years, and no horses have been imported into Iceland since the twelfth century. People in Iceland hold this breed in high esteem, treating them with respect and dignity, and they consider horse breeding more of an art form than a business.

The horse's importance to humans is reflected in art. From the earliest Paleolithic art, horses have been represented in multiple forms throughout the world. Cave paintings of wild horses at Chauvet, in France, are over 30,000 years old, and red and yellow ochre horses at Lascaux (also in France) are about 15,000 years old. Prehistoric artists in northern Africa drew horses on rocks around 1200 BCE. Iron Age artists fashioned horse jewelry from copper. Ancient Mesopotamians, Egyptians, and Greeks expressed their high regard for the horse in paintings, on coins, in sculptures, and in buildings and temples, including the masterful procession of horses and riders on the frieze of the Parthenon, surmounting the Acropolis in Athens. Horses have played an important role throughout the 3,000 years of Chinese history. One of the world's most impressive artistic equine creations was commissioned in 246 BCE by the first emperor of all China, Qin Shi Huang. His mausoleum, which took eleven years to complete, contains over 7,000 life-size figures of soldiers, horses, and chariots arranged in battle formations. In Germany, Albrecht Dürer's woodcarving shows The Four Horsemen of the Apocalypse (c. 1497–1498), a biblical image. Great cities throughout Europe display impressive sculptures of emperors and kings with horses, and rampant stallions grace coats of arms. In the United States, many people are familiar with Frederic Remington's early 1900 bronze sculptures and paintings of cowboys, Native Americans, and horses.

Although the internal combustion engine, still rated according to its horsepower, has replaced horses as the major source of transportation and work, they remain an important part of the culture of many industrialized countries, although in a much different way. The horse's role has evolved into one that provides mainly companionship and pleasure, instead of work. In this new role, horses continue to contribute to the quality of human life. Particularly in the United States, millions of people spend billions of dollars each year on horse-related activities. According to the American Horse Council, the horse industry's total economic impact equals $112 billion per year. With 6.9 million horses in the United States, the horse industry involves over 7 million people and provides almost 1.5 million jobs. What do all these people do with their horses? Several million participate in showing and racing, but millions more have horses simply for recreational purposes.

Horses provide more than entertainment and economic benefits, however. History is full of stories about the relationship between humans and their horses. In many countries and cultures, horses serve as symbols of freedom, strength, and loyalty. One of the most famous human-horse relationships developed between Alexander the Great and Bucephalus. As a twelve-year-old, Alexander rode the untamable stallion, named for his broad, bull-like head. While building his empire, Alexander rode Bucephalus thousands of miles through numerous adventures. Bucephalus died in Alexander's last battle, in 326 BCE, and Alexander founded the city Bucephala in honor of his horse. One of the world's most famous horsemen, a Greek named Xenophon (c. 430–335 BCE), wrote *The Art of Horsemanship*, in which he urged people to know the horses' mentality and treat horses with respect and understanding. Although thousands of years old, Xenophon's advice has found a receptive audience, in today's society, in the type of horse training called *natural horsemanship*. Natural horsemanship replaces brutal training methods—that subdue horses and break their spirits—with humane methods of training that the horses can understand. Several well-known natural horsemanship trainers, such as John Lyons, Pat Parelli, and Clinton Anderson, use their knowledge of horse behavior to effectively control the horse and produce a successful partnership between humans and horses.

Although there are many variations, natural horsemanship focuses on understanding and using a horse's natural behavior to achieve a desired result. Because horses are a prey species, they have evolved physical and behavioral characteristics—such as running, kicking, and biting—for self-preservation. Natural-horsemanship training is based upon gaining a horse's respect, understanding, and trust, so that the horse does not rely on its instincts when confronted with a new or scary situation. Natural horsemanship uses sensitization and desensitization techniques to teach the horse that the person is the leader of the herd and should be trusted and respected. It replaces the concept of force and punishment with gentle, firm leadership and leads not to a dominated horse, but to a partner.

Is the relationship between human and horse merely one of master and slave, or is there an emotional component to this relationship? Increasing scientific evidence suggests that many species—including horses—have rich emotional lives and are capable of some degree of fear, joy, anger, jealousy, and love. Many horses have formed strong bonds with their human caregivers. One ancient story describes the relationship between the Irish monk Saint Columba (521–597), and a white horse. The story tells how an aged Columba, aware that he was dying, sat down to rest. A white horse came over to him and leaned its head against Columba's chest, as though to comfort him. A servant tried to lead the horse away, but Columba stopped him, telling the servant to let the horse mourn.

Strong relationships also develop between modern horses and humans. Some horse owners build horse stalls that allow the horse to look through a window into the house. Horses have been taught to open refrigerators to bring cold drinks to people, or to ride in cars. People endanger their lives attempting to save horses stranded in floodwaters, on ice, or on busy highways. Firemen, rescue workers, and others gather to pull horses out of lakes or pools. In many communities, horse-rescue groups dedicated to rescuing starving and abused horses have been formed. Horses return affection to humans, and form attachments beyond the need for food or grooming. They will leave their herd to visit people or follow a favorite person. Some horses seem to know when a small child or handicapped person is riding them and will move slowly and carefully. Others will adjust their energy level to the ability of a rider, becoming gentle with a beginner rider, but spirited with a more advanced rider. Horses, too, have risked their lives protecting humans from danger, such as resisting a wild animal or standing over a fallen rider.

In many cases, the strong human-horse bond results in a complex, awe-inspiring partnership, with both participants seeming to read the other's mind. Horses perform intricate maneuvers—such as complicated reining patterns—receiving only very subtle cues from the rider. Many people have been thrilled by the spectacle of a horse and rider jumping through a hoop of fire, or a rider running at a full gallop on a bridleless horse. Some horses can separate a specific cow from a herd, with almost no directions from their riders, and other horses can conduct intricate dressage steps to music. Horses are the only animals that participate in the Summer Olympics and cooperate with their riders in negotiating difficult cross-country courses.

A new phase in the human-horse partnership emphasizes deepening the human-horse bond for the benefit of both species. For example, many old or slightly handicapped horses are donated to therapeutic riding centers. These centers use horses to provide physical and mental therapy to people with disabilities. People with spina bifida, mental retardation, and autism benefit from controlled-riding situations that help develop their muscles, flexibility, and confidence. The horses benefit by receiving a second chance at life, and are well taken care of and loved.

Through history, horses have served as symbols of desirable traits, such as freedom, strength, and loyalty. *Seabiscuit,* written by Laura Hillenbrand, tells the true story of a Depression-era racehorse and jockey that both overcome insurmountable odds, breaking race track records and becoming national icons. But the story is more than that of a horse and jockey; it's about the restoration of the American spirit, as the discouraged nation lifted itself out of the Great Depression. Many other books (*Black Beauty, My Friend Flicka, The Black Stallion*) have been written about the trials and triumphs of humans and horses. In real life, troubled humans learn from working with horses. To properly handle horses, a person must develop calmness, focus, respect, trust, and perseverance. For example, prison inmates learn patience, cooperation, and empathy through training horses. The traits people acquire from working with their equine partners can transfer into relationships beyond the human-horse bond, and family and friends benefit from this partnership.

Current issues challenge our modern relationship with horses. One of the major controversies surrounding the human-horse relationship is that of horse overpopulation and sending these excess animals to slaughter. In 2005, according to the Society for Animal Protective Legislation, more than 91,000 horses—many of them young and healthy—were slaughtered for pet food or shipment to other countries for human consumption. Some people feel there is no alternative to slaughter, although others believe that, given the unique history between human and horse, other alternatives should be utilized. Another issue challenging the human-horse bond focuses on the fate of the free-roaming mustangs in the American West. According to the Bureau of Land Management (the agency charged with care of federal rangeland and mustangs), there were approximately 27,000 mustangs and 3,500 burros in 2005 in eleven western states. To prevent overgrazing of arid grasslands, mustangs and burros are periodically captured and offered for adoption. To some people, these adoptions are necessary to prevent horse overpopulation and damage to the land. Others believe that mustangs should be allowed to live their lives in freedom, honoring the contribution of horses in helping shape the American west. Some other wild horses have been successfully protected and managed. Zoo managers and conservationists have protected and bred the Przewalski's horse (*Equus caballus przewalskii*), which became extinct in the wild. Now, conservationists are reintroducing this species to its natural habitat in Central Asia.

Through thousands of years, horses and humans have shared significant parts of their history. Despite an increasingly urban lifestyle in the United States and worldwide, horses play an important role in enriching many people's lives. The connection between humans and horses, evolving from predator and prey to partnership, reflects an increased understanding and enhancement of the symbiotic relationship between two very different species.

Further Resources

Anderson, C., & Hendrickson, A. (2004). *Clinton Anderson's downunder horsemanship: Establishing respect and control for English and western riders*. North Pomfret, VT: Trafalgar Square Publishing.

Chamberlin, L. E. (2006). *Horse: How the horse has shaped civilizations*. New York: Bluebridge.

Hillenbrand, L. (2002). *Seabiscuit: An American legend*. New York: Random House.

Irwin, C., & Weber, B. (2001). *Horses don't lie: What horses teach us about our natural capacity for awareness, confidence, courage and trust*. New York: Marlowe & Co.

Johns, C. (2006). *Horses: History, myth, art*. Cambridge, MA: Harvard University Press.

Lyons, J. (1991). *Lyons on horses*. New York: Doubleday Press.

Martin, P. S. (2005). *Twilight of the mammoths: Ice Age extinctions and the rewilding of America*. Berkeley: University of California Press.

Martino, T. (2004). *Horse nation: True stories about horses and people*. Troutdale, OR: NewSage Press.

Parelli, P. (2003). *Natural horse-man-ship: Six keys to a natural horse-human relationship*. Colorado Springs, CO: Western Horseman.

Heidi Marcum and Susan Bratton

Living with Animals
Hyenas and Humans

For most people, the term *hyena* is synonymous with the spotted hyena (*Crocuta crocuta*), rather than the three other extant hyena species—the striped hyena (*Hyaena hyaena*), the brown hyena (*Hyaena brunnea*), and the aardwolf (*Proteles proteles*). Although the relationship between humans and hyenas has mostly been shaped by the spotted hyena, the striped hyena has also played an important role in areas such as the Middle East and India, where spotted hyenas do not occur. The brown hyena, restricted to southern Africa, and the diminutive, insectivorous aardwolf have been of lesser significance.

The spotted hyena has appeared in folklore, literature, and art and has been the subject of much scientific research. Ecologically, it is the most important large carnivore in African savannahs. From an evolutionary perspective, the spotted hyena is renowned for the female "pseudo-penis," strong sibling rivalry in twin litters, female dominance, and a low level of aggression among competing males. For all these reasons, we will focus on this species. Prehistoric rock paintings of hyenas testify to the ancient relationship between humans and hyenas. It is likely that as long as humans have hunted, they have had to deter spotted hyenas from taking their quarry. The current widespread use of wire snares by African bushmeat hunters results in many hyenas being maimed or killed when caught by snares. The domestication of livestock has precipitated conflict between humans and hyenas, because of predation of stock. The three large hyena species have been systematically persecuted by farmers and government livestock officers, and this has caused a decline in hyena populations outside protected areas—and the extinction of some populations in the past one hundred years. Spotted hyenas have also been persecuted by managers of some national parks, nature reserves, and hunting areas. The use of insecticides has resulted in unintentional poisoning of aardwolves.

Occasional attacks on people, mostly by spotted hyenas and striped hyenas, have fostered a negative attitude toward hyenas. Hyenas most often attack children, people weakened by famine, and those sleeping inside insubstantial dwellings or huts without secure doors. In some areas of Tanzania, people place a banana seedling wrapped in a cloth at the hut entrance, because they expect a hyena, upon entering the hut, to grab the banana bundle at the door, rather than the children inside.

Spotted hyenas are proficient hunters, and, like many carnivores, they also scavenge for food. Striped hyenas and brown hyenas are accomplished scavengers, and all three large hyena species consume human corpses and will dig up buried bodies for this purpose. In some cultures, the scavenging of human corpses is considered to be evil, whereas in others, it is encouraged. The Maasai, in East Africa, cover their dead with fat to attract hyenas, because the failure of hyenas to consume a corpse indicates that the deceased person had a bad character. Several African cultures believe that spotted hyenas have fire in their stomachs, probably because their feces resemble ash. The spotted hyena has a very acid stomach, which is an adaptation for the extraction of nutrients from bone. Calcium carbonate from digested bone produces the ashen appearance of their feces.

Spotted hyenas have a penchant for wandering off with any interesting item they find, including car parts, plastic containers, cooking utensils, shoes, soap, and even the metal trays filled with formaldehyde solution set out by scientists as insect traps. Because of their habit of "stealing," they are known as thieves and are frequently blamed when items go missing. Some people believe that if a child is born when a hyena is calling, the child will become a thief. Footage of a "gang" of striped hyenas stealing items from a car was used in a television campaign in the United Kingdom to warn the public about thefts from cars. Because hyenas are nocturnal, the human imagination has cast them in a supernatural role. Their habit of eating corpses while yelling and laughing—and of prowling around houses at night—has probably helped to give the impression of evil intent. Although hyenas are often portrayed as being happy when they laugh, their laughter actually expresses submission and anxiety. Many African cultures believe that witches ride on the backs of spotted hyenas at night, and this is thought to explain why hyenas have a sloping back. Certainly witches in several areas of Africa keep live spotted hyenas as part of their paraphernalia for sorcery. It is also thought that witches consume hyena milk and use hyena "butter" to fuel their torches at night. These ideas are not too fanciful, given that spotted hyena milk is highly nutritious, because of its high fat and protein content (females nurse cubs for periods of up to two years). Even so, it is unlikely that witches regularly breed spotted hyenas to obtain milk and butter while they lactate. Some African cultures think that it is possible to determine the route taken by witches at night, because their flaming torches drip burnt hyena butter along their path. This idea probably arose because hyenas secrete a pungent, greasy scent, from a large anal gland, that they wipe on vegetation during a behavior termed *pasting*. In Africa and Asia, there is demand for body parts from spotted and striped hyenas for traditional medicine. For example, hyena tissue is thought to protect livestock and people from evil, and the genital organs are believed to improve virility. The latter belief may be because female spotted hyenas have an organ that mimics the male penis. The evolution and function of this appendage has been debated for centuries and led to the erroneous assumption, still held by some, that spotted hyenas are hermaphrodites. Interestingly, in the female-dominated social system of the spotted hyena, a male signal (an erect penis or pseudo-penis) is a frequently used social flag of submission.

In most cultures, it is an insult to call someone a hyena, because the creatures are seen as thieves, gluttons, lazy, stupid, sly, and ugly. Such negative attributes appear in many African folktales about hyenas and were rather heavy-handedly applied in the cartoon film *The Lion King*—where spotted hyenas were also portrayed as goose-stepping Nazis. One notable exception to the generally negative relationship between humans and hyenas is the association between hyenas and men from Harar, Ethiopia, who feed free-ranging spotted hyenas at night. This tradition has now developed into a popular tourist attraction.

Clearly, the general perception of hyenas is founded on superstition and prejudice, rather than fact. Even in the scientific realm, some aspects of hyena biology have been misinterpreted, because unsubstantiated assumptions appeared to make "common sense." For example, numerous scientific articles have suggested that female social dominance in spotted hyenas was achieved because adult females were considered to be awash with androgens, causing them to become larger than males and hyperaggressive. In fact, adult female hyenas have what can be viewed as "normal" androgen levels, similar to females in many other mammalian species, including humans. Furthermore, all natal females are socially dominant over immigrant males, even when they are considerably smaller than the males they dominate.

Young spotted hyenas and mothers at a communal den. ©Danita Delimont/Alamy

Further Resources

East, M. L., & Hofer, H. (2002). Conflict and cooperation in a female-dominated society: A reassessment of the "hyperaggressive" image of spotted hyenas. *Advances in the Study of Behavior, 31,* 1–30.

Glickman, S. E. (1995). The spotted hyena from Aristotle to the Lion King: Reputation is everything. *Social Research, 62,* 501–37.

Kruuk, H. (1972). *The spotted hyena: A study of predation and social behavior.* Chicago: University of Chicago Press.

Mills, M. G. L. (1990). *Kalahari hyaenas: The comparative behavioural ecology of two species.* London: Unwin Hyman.

Mills, M. G. L., & Hofer, H. (1999). *Hyaenas, status survey and action plan.* Gland, Switzerland and Cambridge, UK: IUCN/SSC Hyaena Specialist Group.

Marion L. East and Heribert Hofer

Living with Animals
Insect-Human Connections

Nearly one million living insect species have already been described by science. They comprise four-fifths of the animal kingdom and play significant ecological roles in terrestrial ecosystems. Besides that, they have caused—and continue to cause—sociological impacts in different human cultures, due to the almost infinite variety of colors, shapes, sizes, habits, and sounds they make, as well as because of their role in the dissemination of epidemics that, many times, have influenced the course of human history. Insect diversity is perceived by human beings through the vision, sound, smell, touch, and taste (and also extrasensitively by means of shamanic ordeals). The influence of insects in man's life can be felt in many culturally related connections, ranging from basic living needs such as food, medicine, and self-preservation (*entomophoby,* or fear of insects) to more humanistic uses such as aesthetics, arts, cosmetics, ethics (conservationism), mythology, religion, economics, and science. These connections, which will be briefly discussed in this essay, can be studied by the following research areas: applied entomology, cultural entomology, and ethnoentomology.

One of the oldest connections with insects is their use as food (*entomophagy*). This cultural connection has occurred since the Plio-Pleistocene, as shown by a study on several tools used by the *Australopithecus robustus* hominid, which has revealed that termites were part of his diet. Nowadays, more than two thousand species are regularly consumed by nearly three thousand ethnic groups in 120 countries. Out of the edible species, beetles make up the largest group (468 species), followed by wasps, ants, and bees (351 species), grasshoppers, locusts, and crickets (267 species), and caterpillars (253 species). Edible species contain high amounts of proteins and fats and are rich in sodium, potassium, zinc, manganese, magnesium, copper, phosphorous, calcium, and iron.

The connection with medicine and healing practices is also antique. Insects have been used live, cooked, ground, in infusions, in plasters, or as ointments, both in the curative and preventive medicines, as well as in magical-religious rituals. Scarabs, for instance, have been symbols of sexual vigor since ancient Egypt, and they are very efficient when used in love charms. The raw materials insects provide are used in the elaboration of traditional remedies that are recommended to treat a great variety of culturally diagnosed ailments. Insects have proven to be very important as sources of drugs to modern medicine, as immunological, analgesic, antibacterial, diuretic, anesthetic, and antirheumatic properties have already been found within their bodies. The word *medicine* owes its origin to the honey, since the first syllable has the same root as "mead," an alcoholic drink made from honeycombs and regularly taken as an elixir.

Because of their ubiquitous importance for humankind, insects began being depicted in rock art in ancient times. Even before that, insects made their debut in oral history (both spoken and sung). Later, they appeared in written literature, as characters in tales, novels, science fiction, and so on. Hieroglyphs and pictograms showing shapes of insects appeared in ancient Egypt (bees, scarabs, and grasshoppers were syllables of the alphabet) and also in the Mayan and Chinese texts. They have appeared in sacred books such as the Bible and the Quran. These animals are present in sayings, proverbs, parables, political and social satires, poetry, and prose. Epigrams and figures of speech using expressions with insects are very common in the vocabulary of many societies. Insect names are metaphorically used as synonyms for the seasons. Man-made products and public places (pubs, restaurants, department stores, etc.) are named after insects' common names, too. Insect images are even employed as advertising tools, attached to products and services.

The influence of insects can be viewed in modern music, where they are well represented in rock 'n' roll through the names of artists, titles of albums, and lyrics. They come in verses in metaphorical, humorous, literal, and appellant contexts.

Another interesting connection is through theater and movies. Insects and other arthropods have been onstage for more than two millennia, since Aristophanes wrote the play *Spheces* (*The Wasps*) in 422 BCE. Operas, such as *Madame Butterfly* by Puccini, and ballets, such as *Le Festin de L'Araignée* (*The Spider's Feast*) by Roussel, were also produced. Movies and television have depicted them as popular subjects—as "monsters" to be killed—such as the ectoparasites, household plagues, and venomous insects. Films rarely display positive images of arthropods.

Since the first Paleolithic paintings relating to the collection of honey, insects have served as inspiration for the arts. Frequently, they are considered as models for the production of jewels, ceramics, tattoos, sculptures, paintings, anklets, key rings, bracelets, necklaces, pendants, packing, labels, and textile models. They are also depicted in postal cards, phone cards, and stamps of different countries. Sometimes they are used alive, as the large beetles of the family *Cerambycidae* (wood-borers), which are painted and tied up to a small string or pin and used as a brooch in some parts of Mexico. As objects of amusement, insects are involved in many ludic activities. Cricket and mantis fighting became a very popular gamble and sport for people of all ages in Oriental countries. It is interesting to note that mantis behavior gave origin to one of the fighting styles of kung fu. In Asia, singing insects are kept in small cages so that their owners can enjoy hearing them.

As popular biological indicators, the appearance and behavior of certain kinds of insects in some cultures are interpreted as both beneficial and harmful events, as well as indicative of changing weather. According to the way people perceive and interpret these events, insects can be used to predict the following happenings: death, accident, money earning, rain, drought, summer, winter, a visiting person, abundance or scarcity of crops, and so on. From a scientific point of view, insects do indicate some man-made environmental disturbances, such as the aquatic dragonfly larvae that do not survive in polluted waters.

An amazing, indirect trophic connection is the employment of insects for hunting. The Bushmen from the Kalahari Desert use some beetle larvae of the *Chrisomelidae* family as hunting poisons, as they feed on the toxic leaves of *Commiphora*. People rub these larvae on the end of the arrows; the poison of just one arrow is capable of killing an adult antelope.

Some indigenous peoples around the world use insects as *entheogens*, which are psychoactive resources for spiritual and traditional use. Some examples are the beetles of the *Stenocentrus* and *Syllitus* genera that produce secretions of toluene in their mandibular glands as a mechanism of defense. This compound is a depressor of the central nervous system, and the exposure to low concentrations can cause mental confusion, fatigue, and weakness. Additionally, some young people have been using them as hallucinogens, too. Adolescents from Dubai, in the Persian Gulf, are "smoking" a kind of ant (sniffing the gases these little insects discharge when they are crushed). This practice of "ant-smelling" has become so popular among teenagers that a small package of *samaseem* ("ant" in Arabic) is sold for over US$135 in Abu Dhabi Emirate.

Other cultural bonds we might maintain with these animals are: the raising of insects as mini-livestock for several economic and personal purposes (like pets); insects as educational tools (all levels); forensic entomology; insects as war weapons; their use in philately, phone cards, and postal cards; and insects as sport mascots and other emblems.

In these general glimpse lines, we see that insects abound in our lives in a complex, varied, and multifaceted way. However, the negative aspects of the relationship with these animals predominate, due to attitudes of fear and disgust, especially in the Western cultures. It is certain that some species invade our houses and bodies, and others are truly a serious threaten to our health and well-being, because of their direct and indirect damages. But more than 99.9 percent of all species are directly beneficial to human beings—or, at least, do not harm them. If we want to survive on this planet, then we should have to search for more positive and harmonious attitudes towards these marvelous, creepy-crawly creatures.

Further Resources

Berenbaum, M. R. (1995). *Bugs in the system: Insects and their impact on human affairs*. Cambridge, MA: Perseus Books.

Hoyt, E., & Schultz, T. (1999). *Insect lives: Stories of mystery and romance from a hidden world*. New York: John Wiley & Sons.

Kellert, S. R. (1993). Values and perceptions of invertebrates. *Conservation Biology, 7*(4), 845–53.

Lauck, J. E. (2002). *The voice of the infinite in the small: Re-visioning the insect-human connection*. Boston: Shambhala Publications.

Eraldo Medeiros Costa Neto

Living with Animals
Killer Whales and Humans

At this point in our history, the human race has one of its most intriguing relationships with the animal known as the killer whale. More formally, this species is known as *Orcinus orca*, and we have come to know it as beautiful, graceful, and intelligent. Our relationship with the orca can be looked at from the perspectives of at least four different persons: the layperson, the businessman, the marine-mammal trainer, and the marine scientist.

The Layperson

Killer whales are, arguably, one of the most beloved species on earth. TV documentaries about their behavior are among the most popular in the nature genre. In millions of homes, posters, paintings, and sculptures of killer whales adorn the walls, and dozens of Web sites track the lives of individual whales. Millions of dollars are spent by tourists for just a glimpse of orcas from whale-watching boats, and hundreds of millions of dollars are spent by visitors to Sea World and other marine-life parks around the world. Perhaps it is the striking beauty of their brilliant black-and-white markings; perhaps it is the unique combination of grace and power that they possess; perhaps it is the intelligence and social complexity that they reveal to us. It is probably for all of these reasons. Regardless, one thing is clear: people love to love orcas.

The Businessperson

As a consequence of all that public interest, orcas represent great value from a business perspective. In the Canadian province of British Columbia alone, it is estimated that whale-watching generates more than fifty million dollars in annual revenue and employs thousands of people. In marine parks, orcas are indispensable centerpieces of large-scale operations that attract hundreds of millions of dollars. To understand this, simply visit a branch of Sea World on any day of the year and watch the people line up to pay the high admission prices. Now just imagine the same marine park, with all the same attractions—except for the killer whales. In that instance, some people would still come, but it would be a much smaller number. Because of this, each individual killer whale that is held in captivity has a market value that exceeds one million U.S. dollars. This means that, on a per capita basis, they are the most valuable animal species on earth. The point is simply this: if millions of people have orca posters on their walls, there is an opportunity for someone to make a great deal of money selling those posters.

The Marine-Mammal Trainer

The lucky few human beings who work with and care for killer whales on a daily basis, in the Sea Worlds and Marinelands across our globe, develop particularly close bonds with and very strong affections for them. This is all the more remarkable when considering the huge ecological and phylogenetic gap that lies between us. After all, killer whales live in an icy-cold, watery world, where vision is unimportant and sound predominates. Human beings require much warmer conditions, and we can barely function without our vision. Even more significantly, we are anchored to the land and nearly pathetic in the water. The human and the orca could hardly be more different as species and still share the common trait of being mammals. Orcas are streamlined, lightning-fast predators with the size and strength of elephants. We deal with our world via dexterous and gentle fingers, the likes of which they could never imagine. Yet, somehow, a bridge can be established. This is because the human and the orca share two very special traits: a high degree of sociality and a large-brained intelligence that searches for patterns in each other's behavior. The human learns to read the orcas' moods and feed their needs. Marine-mammal trainers search for just the right places on the tongues of the whales to tickle, and they bend over the sides of the pools in order to rub their giant animals anywhere that they may itch. They spend hours upon hours dreaming up whale-sized playthings to enrich the orcas' lives and playing games like hide-and-seek, deliberately popping in and out of view as the whales search for them. The whales, on their part, also devise games to play with the humans. For example, most whales in captivity are trained to retrieve objects from their pool when given the appropriate signals by a trainer. This writer once watched a killer whale rise up to hook a toy hoop on her dorsal fin. She then teased the trainer by bringing it to a point just beyond his reach. The whale went on for more than fifteen minutes, subtly shifting her position in a way that made the trainer move from place to place to reach the hoop—always thinking that he was going to get it at any moment, but always being kept just out of reach. If we could ever read a whale's mind, this one must surely have been laughing as it controlled and teased that human being on that day.

The Marine-Mammal Scientist

The popularity of these animals has also resulted in funding and logistical conditions that have enabled extensive scientific investigations of their lives in the wild. In much as the same way that Jane Goodall and other pioneering animal behaviorists have followed the lives of individual animals, there have been teams of researchers (such as Mike Bigg and John Ford) who have spent decades of their lives carefully documenting the behavior of each individual whale that lives in the northeast Pacific Ocean. This work has afforded us rich insights into the orca's nature, and it has made killer whales among the best-studied and most completely understood animal species on Earth. In this way, science has been afforded a priceless opportunity to test theories pertaining to the evolution of sociality and

Author and biopsychologist Michael Noonan working with a pair of orcas, or killer whales, at Marineland of Canada in Niagara Falls, Ontario. Courtesy of Michael Noonan.

the adaptive roles of kin favoritism. It has also allowed us to learn a great deal about the role of "culture" in the lives of complex animals like this. By following individual whales over many decades, scientists have learned that orcas live extremely long life spans (forty to seventy years), and that they do so in very stable family groups. Newborn killer whales come into a world that is dominated by mothers and aunts and populated by older brothers and sisters. They grow up in an acoustic world, surrounded by the sounds of their family calls. Every month or so, their groups intermix with other orca pods that consist of their first and second cousins and other, more distant relatives. These intermixings seem to be very pleasant times for the whales, with much amicable rubbing and playing. In other words, despite their alien environment, killer whales have developed lifestyles and social structures that have many parallels to our own. We have learned, for example, that different groups of killer whales specialize in different types of hunting strategies for different types of food. Not only that, but they evidently learn and utilize recognizably different vocalizations when they call to each other. In most respects, the parallel with human social learning and culture is quite striking, and the ability for us to observe these traits in a mammal that is distantly related is proving to be an enormous advantage, as animal-behavior scientists sort out the evolutionary origins of such things. It appears to be an example of convergent evolution in which two large-brained species have come independently to develop similar traits. For scientists, therefore, it means that the more we understand killer whales, the more insight we gain into the forces that have shaped our own natures, as well. To us humans, the killer whale embodies grace and beauty, and we are invariably inspired when we encounter them in person. Perhaps most significantly, the killer whale is a species that reminds us that the gap between nonhuman animals and ourselves is closer than we sometimes realize.

Due to intense public interest, orcas are indispensable centerpieces of large-scale operations that attract hundreds of millions of dollars, such as this beautiful whale at Marineland of Canada in Niagara Falls, Ontario. Courtesy of Michael Noonan.

See also

Conservation and Environment—*Whale and Dolphin Culture and Human Interactions*
Conservation and Environment—*Whale Watching*
Ecotourism
Zoos and Aquariums—*Marine Mammals and Aquariums*

Further Resources

Baird, R. W. (2000). The killer whale: Foraging specializations and grouphunting. In J. Mann, R. C. Connor, P. L. Tyack, & H. Whitehead (Eds.), *Cetacean societies* (pp. 127–53). Chicago: University of Chicago Press.

Ellis, S. (1995). Marine mammal behavior: Conservation through research. In E. F. Gibbons, B. S. Durrant, & J. Demarest (Eds.), *Conservation of endangered species in captivity: An interdisciplinary approach* (pp. 441–64). Albany: State University of New York Press.

Knudtson, P. (1996). *Orca: Visions of the killer whale*. San Francisco: Sierra Club Books.

Ridgeway, S. (1995). The tides of change: Conservation of marine mammals. In E. F. Gibbons, B. S. Durrant, & J. Demarest (Eds.), *Conservation of endangered species in captivity: An interdisciplinary approach* (pp. 407–24). Albany: State University of New York Press.

The Whale Museum. http://www.whale-museum.org. [Promoting stewardship of whales and the Salish Sea ecosystem through education and research.]

Michael Noonan

Living with Animals
Kiwis and Humans

The Nature of the Kiwi

All kiwis belong to the genus *Apteryx* and—along with the emu, rhea, ostrich, cassowary, elephant bird, and moa—are members of the order *Struthioniformes*. As well as being flightless, the *Struthioniformes* comprise the world's largest birds, although the largest of them—the elephant birds of Madagascar and moas of New Zealand—are now extinct. Kiwis are likely to have existed in New Zealand since the close of the Mesozoic, some sixty million years ago, and, as such, are the most ancient living bird group in that country. Based upon morphology, their closest relatives are likely to have been the extinct moas, although recent DNA work, based on moa's feathers, is yet to confirm this. The *Struthioniformes* are also known as ratites, an informal name for a group of birds that, although now very much a southern (or Gondwanan) phenomenon, appear to have originated in the northern hemisphere during the Mesozoic and migrated southward while becoming extinct in the north.

The kiwi is a relatively small, flightless, and nocturnal bird, about the same size as the domestic fowl. They are very unusual birds, however, with many very specialized and/or primitive characters. The kiwi has surprisingly poor vision for a nocturnal animal, and this can be seen with reduced pecten tissue within the eye; this tissue is a characteristic of reptilian and avian eyes and appears to be crucial in supplying oxygen and nutrients to the retina. However poor eyesight is complemented by an excellent olfactory sense

Apteryx mantelli, *the North Island brown kiwi. Courtesy of Shutterstock.*

(indeed, kiwis have an olfactory lobe some ten times that of other birds). The nostrils are placed at the end of a long, delicate, slender, downwardly curved bill; this arrangement is unique amongst birds, as nostrils are normally placed near the base of the upper bill. Kiwis have four toes, three forward directed and one backward (other birds have three in total); they lack a tail, although they do possess a pygostyle, or tail bone; their wings are vestigial, and although flight feathers are present on these, these differ little from kiwi feathers in general—for, unlike almost all other birds, kiwi feathers have no aftershaft or barbules, as in flying birds (the barbules are used to join individual feathers to make an effective wing). Instead, the feathers are very loose, their purpose being to keep the animal warm and perhaps to help with camouflage, although until the arrival of humans in New Zealand, there were few predators, except carnivorous birds. The fluffy, loose nature of kiwi feathers is an example of convergent evolution, where two very different evolutionary pathways have resulted in structures with similar purpose (i.e., kiwi feathers and mammalian hair).

Like other ratites, kiwis lack a keel bone, this being a subsequent modification in lieu of their flightless habit, as a keel provides attachment for the powerful flying muscles of flying birds. The kiwi female is some 20 percent larger than the male, and is unique amongst birds in having a single egg that is almost 25 percent of its body weight. On rare occasions, a kiwi will lay more than one egg, but irrespective of how many eggs are laid, it will be the male who incubates them, and this can vary from sixty-three to ninety-two days. The food of the kiwi comprises worms and arthropods (e.g., insects and crustaceans); it seeks these amongst forest litter with its extremely sensitive bill.

Prior to the arrival of humans, the kiwi had few predators—in their world there were no mammals except for bats and seals, and the only predators were avian. All this was to change abruptly some 700 years ago when the first New Zealanders, the Maori, arrived in the region. Human impact was disastrous for the bird, not only did the kiwi provide food and clothing for the Maori, it was defenseless against the mammals that came with them—rats and dogs. Numbers plummeted, and most species of kiwi are now listed with CITES as endangered.

From the above, we may conclude that the kiwi is a somewhat-primitive and specialized bird; it is certainly timid, as well as being flightless and almost blind . . . and it eats grubs.

Kiwis and the Nature of the New Zealander

The Maori greatly valued the kiwi for its feathers—which are both warm and decorative. White, red, and brown feathers were woven into a flax-based fiber to make wonderfully intricate and prized cloaks. However, the kiwi has a timid nature; in light of this, and the fact that it is a nocturnal bird, it was rather elusive to the hunter. The Maori captured them, however, by imitating the cry of the bird, to which the kiwi enthusiastically responded. Because of its secretive habit, the kiwi was known to Maori as *Te manu huna a Tane* (the hidden bird of Tane, the god of the forest). Surprisingly, the kiwi is a fast runner and can move through the forest more quickly than humans. Its running gait is erratic, however, with the head flicking from side to side. Although this gait is a function of the skeletal form and musculature, it may provide some opportunity for the bird to visually assess the proximity of any predator. This gait led to the name Maori term *whakakiwi*—given to somebody who gives sidelong looks or "shifty glances." In more recent times, dogs have been used in a benign way by the Department of Conservation to locate kiwis. The keen sense of smell that canines possess allows the birds to be located, in their burrows, during the day. This permits more effective population monitoring of this increasingly endangered bird.

The kiwi bird clearly lacks the characters one would normally associate with a national emblem; it is, nonetheless, the national bird of New Zealand, and is used widely to promote the country, its people, and its products. The kiwi is used as a quality mark, (both nationally and internationally) to market the very best of New Zealand produce—it is thus the quintessential New Zealand Made symbol—but this is only the beginning: it is widely adopted by clubs and sports teams (both officially, such as the New Zealand rugby league team, and unofficially, for overseas touring teams at all levels). New Zealand politicians have been shown to be more than proud to have been associated with the bird—one, longstanding Prime Minister Sir Keith Holyoake, was affectionately known as "Kiwi Keith."

The stylized kiwi adopted by the Buy NZ Made Campaign Ltd. and widely used to market New Zealand's products. (Reproduced with permission.)

When overseas, all New Zealanders, whether they are young New Zealanders on working holidays in Europe, old-age pensioners on ocean cruises, or soldiers fighting on distant battlefields, can be expected to be known as *kiwis*. One of the earliest uses of the kiwi in military badges was that of the South Canterbury Battalion (1886) and the Hastings Rifle Volunteers (1887).

The "kiwi" dollar, introduced as a golden coin in 1990. Courtesy of John Buckeridge.

The term *kiwi* is, however, perhaps most prominently known internationally in currency-exchange circles. Since 1967, when New Zealand changed to a decimal currency, the *kiwi* has been applied specifically to the New Zealand dollar. This was reinforced (visually) in 1990 when the New Zealand one dollar (then a paper note depicting a fantail bird) was withdrawn and replaced by a one-dollar coin with a kiwi and fern motif. The value of the kiwi dollar fluctuates somewhat, but, for much of its history, it has been worth approximately US$0.65.

The kiwi brand is not always what it seems: Many folk associate "kiwi" (and thus New Zealand) with shoe polish; indeed, Kiwi shoe polish is the world's most widely used brand. What is perhaps surprising is that this polish and the special opening lever associated with the tin were invented by Australians. Both the name and the logo were adopted by William Ramsay of Carlton, Victoria, in 1906. Kiwi shoe polish has never been a New Zealand company; indeed, it is now not even Australian, being owned (and manufactured worldwide) by the international conglomerate Sara Lee. What is interesting is why Ramsay chose the name, some one hundred years ago—perhaps it was simply the distinctive shape?

Perhaps the most unusual (and confusing) use of the term *kiwi* is not for an animal but for a small, relatively uninteresting fruit previously known as the Chinese gooseberry. A variety of this fruit was brought to New Zealand from the Yangtze region of China in the early twentieth century; through careful selective breeding, this nondescript fruit became the kiwifruit—or, simply, "kiwi." Kiwis (the fruit) are a rich source of vitamin C. They are also high in potassium, vitamins A and E, calcium, iron, and folic acid.

One of the first nurserymen who recognized the potential of the fruit was Hayward Wright, and it was the most popular variety that ultimately took his name (Hayward).

Wide adoption of the name *kiwi fruit* followed a very effective marketing campaign (commercial success in 1960s United States of America being deemed more likely if the politically unacceptable name "Chinese gooseberry" was avoided). Indeed, with a stretch of the imagination, the fruit looks a bit like the bird. However, the name was not patented and, as a consequence, is now used in many regions where the fruit is commercially grown (e.g., Australia, California, and Chile). The name *Zespri* has subsequently been adopted in New Zealand to distinguish the local product—from overseas competition, New Zealanders, and, of course, *Apteryx*.

Why the kiwi then, as the national symbol for New Zealand? There were other "grander" possibilities, such as the hawk, the mighty kauri tree, and, perhaps, the tuatara, an extraordinary living reptile that dates back some 200 million years. The kiwi, however, is special. It is strange in form and habit but nonetheless appealing. There is no other national symbol even remotely like it.

Further Resources

Miles, J., Potter, M., & Fordham, R. (1997). Northern brown kiwi (*Apteryx australis mantelli*) in Tongariro National Park and Tongariro Forest—ecology and threats. *Science for Conservation*. Department of Conservation, New Zealand.

Save the Kiwi. http://www.savethekiwi.org.nz/Home/

The Kiwi Bird Page. http://www.kiwi.bird.freeservers.com/

John Buckeridge

Living with Animals
Mountain Lions and Humans

Mountain lions, also known as cougars and pumas (among many other names), have roamed the western hemisphere for at least 100,000 years. They are the second largest species of wildcat in the Americas, being somewhat smaller than the jaguar. The extent of their geographic distribution, however, greatly exceeds that of the jaguar—or any other mammal in the hemisphere, except for humans. Mountain lions can be found as far south as Patagonia and as far north as the Yukon, living in a wide array of habitats, including rainforests and deserts, at elevations of from more than 11,000 feet to below sea level. This far-reaching range has brought mountain lions into contact with humans since people first crossed from Asia into North America. This essay discusses the relationship between mountain lions and humans throughout recorded history, with an emphasis on North America.

At the time of human arrival in North America during the last ice age, the mountain lion was only one of a number of large mammals roaming the landscape. There were several species of elephant, such as the woolly mammoth, as well as camels, llamas, horses, cheetahs, American lions, saber-toothed cats, and the now-extinct giant short-faced bear and dire wolf. Then, around twelve thousand years ago, North America was swept by a wave of extinctions in which about 80 percent of all mammal species on the continent disappeared, including the mountain lion. Some scientists believe these extinctions were caused by the continent's new human arrivals. They are, however, unclear as to whether mountain lions and other large carnivores disappeared because humans intensively hunted them and their prey or because of a "one-two punch" of human activity and climate change. Regardless of the cause, genetic research conducted by Melanie Culver and her associates has revealed that mountain lions in North America today are the descendents of several individuals that dispersed from Central America into the American southwest ten to twelve thousand years ago.

As far back as records go, the relationship between mountain lions and humans has been complex and has varied from culture to culture. In North America, for instance, mountain lions have been revered by many native cultures for their impressive nature and hunting prowess. They have played an important role in native mythology, particularly of those tribes living in the American southwest. Of course, not all native cultures viewed mountain lions as benevolent animals, and at least one considered them terrifying, flesh-eating monsters. Mountain lions were hunted by members of some tribes to display their hunting prowess as part of initiations into warrior clans, to access their power, to obtain their pelts, and, occasionally, to use for food. However, historians have found no strong evidence that hunting of mountain lions by native peoples was widespread or intensive, or that they tried to control mountain lion populations.

The relationship between mountain lions and humans in North America changed significantly with the arrival of Europeans. European settlers' perceptions of mountain lions and other large carnivores were dominated by fear and hatred, as they viewed these animals almost exclusively as predators of their livestock, competitors for the species they hunted for food, and threats to human safety. In the New World, virtually all predators were hunted relentlessly, and many colonies offered bounties for killing mountain lions and other predators. By 1850, the mountain lion was considered rare in the eastern two-thirds of North America and, by 1920, had been effectively exterminated from most states east of the Mississippi, with only a small population remaining in Florida.

As settlers pushed westward in the mid-1800s, they killed mountain lions and other large carnivores, as well as grazing animals, such as bison and elk, to clear the land for domestic livestock and farming. Beginning in the 1850s, many western states started offering bounties for mountain lions, wolves, and other carnivores. By the early 1900s, the federal government was paying professional hunters and trappers to exterminate mountain lions and other large carnivores. Sensationalized tales that depicted mountain lions as terrifying, cruel, supernatural, and even demonic creatures created fear and hatred amongst the public and bolstered extermination efforts. From 1907 to 1977 alone, according to records compiled by Ronald Nowak, nearly 68,000 mountain lions were reported killed in the western United States. Furthermore, according to mountain-lion researcher Ken Logan, more were likely killed when they fed on livestock carcasses that had been baited and laced with poison. Yet, even as the wolf and grizzly bear were extirpated from most of their historical range in the United States, the enigmatic and retiring mountain lion managed to survive in the rugged and mountainous areas of the American West.

The 1960s marked a turning point in the relationship between humans and mountain lions in North America. The change was precipitated by the development of the environmental movement, which opposed the wanton killing of predators and other wildlife, and by research on mountain lions in Idaho that dispelled the myth of these animals as rapacious killers and decimators of deer populations. As a result, state legislatures began rescinding the bounties and reclassifying mountain lions as game animals—a move that regulated the killing of the animals. The exception was Texas, where mountain lions are still classified as predators and have no protections. At the federal level, the Florida panther (a subspecies of mountain lion) was listed as endangered under the federal Endangered Species Act in 1973, and today is considered one of the most imperiled animals in the world.

Several opinion surveys indicate that the general public believes that mountain lions are an important component of the ecosystems, that mountain lions benefit their overall quality of life, and that humans have a responsibility to learn to live with mountain lions. Moreover, the public has shown increasing disapproval of traditional management practices, such as sport hunting of the mountain lion and, especially, the use of tracking dogs by hunters. Through the ballot initiative process, California voters permanently banned sport hunting of mountain lions in 1990, and Oregon and Washington voters prohibited the use of hounds to hunt them in 1994 and 1996, respectively. Still, more than 2,500 mountain lions are killed annually by sport hunters in the twelve western states that permit this activity. This is frequently justified as a technique to reduce mountain lion attacks on humans and on livestock, though there is no evidence to support these claims.

Mountain lions appear to be recolonizing parts of their former range in the eastern United States and Canada. Confirmed sightings in several Great Plains and Great Lakes states suggest that mountain lions are beginning to return to these areas and are likely dispersing from the Rocky Mountains and southern Canada. Though many state wildlife agencies maintain that sightings in the East are likely misidentifications or just wishful, the frequency of credible sightings has increased. This has stirred renewed and vigorous debate on the status and future of mountain lions in the East. Whether mountain lions are able to reestablish breeding populations in the East will depend primarily on public tolerance.

However, public sentiment remains inconsistent and changeable and can be influenced by conflicts between mountain lions and people. Attacks on humans, though exceedingly rare, usually increases public concern and may create negative attitudes toward mountain lions. Statistically speaking, mountain lions pose a far lesser threat than most perils faced by humans. For instance, each year in the United States, about 40,000 people are killed in car accidents, 5,000 are killed in work-related accidents, and 17 are killed by domestic dogs. In comparison, since 1890, sixteen people have been killed by mountain lions in North America. Even among the world's large cat species, including the tiger and leopard, attacks by mountain lions are extremely rare events. However, attacks are usually well publicized and are often reported in a sensationalized fashion that makes the likelihood of attacks seem greater than it is.

Expanding human populations and increasing human activity in mountain-lion habitat are also increasing the frequency of conflicts between humans and mountain lions. Even people who hold positive attitudes toward mountain lions may become less tolerant of mountain lions that frequent areas near their homes. In California, for instance, citizens who may support the ban on mountain lion hunting may not hesitate to request a depredation permit if a mountain lion attacks their cat.

Today, of North America's large carnivores—wolves, bears, and mountain lions—only the mountain lion persists in viable populations throughout much of the western United States. Mountain lions, like wolves and grizzly bears, are considered by conservation biologists to be top-level predators, because they sit at the apex of the food chain and play an important role in maintaining the health of the natural landscape through their interaction with their prey. By preying on deer, for instance, mountain lions help keep them from becoming too numerous and overbrowsing their habitat, which can negatively affect other species and even lead to extinctions. Some researchers have argued that, ecologically speaking, the mountain lion's wide distribution, adaptability to a wide variety of habitats, and superior predatory skills make it perhaps the most important large carnivore in the western hemisphere.

However, the long-term survival of the mountain lion in the American West, or its recovery in the East, is by no means assured. Citing concern over a declining trend in mountain lion populations across their range, due to persecution and degradation of mountain lion habitat and prey species, in 2002, the World Conservation Union (IUCN) upgraded the status of mountain lions to "near threatened." In the American West, the number of mountain lions killed by sport hunters and in response to conflicts between mountain lions and domestic animals reached all-time levels in the last decade. Moreover, the rapid growth of human populations in the West continues to drive new developments that destroy and fragment mountain lion habitat, isolating mountain lion populations and increasing their vulnerability to extinction.

Ultimately, humans will determine whether mountain lions are allowed to persist. There are still people who favor wholesale reductions or even complete removal of mountain lions. There are also some segments of the public that consider sport hunting of mountain lions to be great sport and a symbol of prowess and masculinity. Though they represent a minority, these views continue to hold sway over management decisions made by state wildlife agencies, which, for the most part, have not undertaken conservation planning for this species. In an effort to address the shortcomings of current management strategies, eleven of the world's leading mountain lion experts published the Cougar Management Guidelines, in 2005, that provides science-based recommendations for improving management and conservation efforts. In the end, if humans can overcome the historical obstacles and predator prejudice that have prevented us from developing sound, long-term conservation strategies for mountain lions, then humans can find ways to coexist with these magnificent animals and, in the process, preserve the natural and cultural heritage of the American landscape.

Further Resources

Clark, T. W., Rutherford, M. B., & Casey, D. (Eds.). (2005). *Coexisting with large carnivores: Lessons from greater Yellowstone.* Washington, DC: Island Press.

Cougar Management Guidelines Working Group. (2005). *Cougar management guidelines* (1st ed.). Bainbridge, WA: WildFutures.

Culver, M., Johnson, W. E., Pecon-Slattery, J., & O'Brien, S. J. (2000). Genomic ancestry of the American puma (*Puma concolor*). *Journal of Heredity, 91*, 186–97.

Hansen, K. (1992). *Cougar: The American lion.* Flagstaff, AZ: Northland Publishing.

Logan, K., & Sweanor, L. (2001). *Desert puma: Evolutionary ecology and conservation of an enduring carnivore.* Washington, DC: Island Press.

Murphy, K., Ross, I., & Hornocker, M. (1999). The ecology of anthropogenic influences on cougars. In T. W. Clark, A. P. Curlee, S. C. Minta, & P. M. Kareiva (Eds.), *Carnivores in ecosystems: The Yellowstone experience.* New Haven, CT: Yale University Press.

Nowak, R. M. (1976). *The cougar in the United States and Canada.* Department of the Interior. Fish and Wildlife Service, Washington, DC, and New York Zoological Society.

Papouchis, C. M. (2004). Conserving mountain lions in a changing landscape. In N. Fascione, A. Delach, & M. Smith (Eds.), *Predators and people: From conflict to co-existence.* Washington, DC: Island Press.

Christopher M. Papouchis

Living with Animals
Pesticide Effects on Honeybees

Honeybees have been many things to many people. We know them as pollinators and honey producers. What might not be so well known is their use as environmental monitors. They have been used as monitors in two ways: as biological detectors of pollution and as a device to sample material from the environment.

Bees can be used to monitor chemical compounds in the environment that have toxic effects on bees. Such compounds include pesticides that are used to control insect pests in agriculture, forestry, and management of human environment. In addition to pesticides, bees can be poisoned by air or water pollution. All toxic compounds can affect a honeybee colony, and individual bees are also at risk. Effects can also be observed to such industrial pollutants as sulfur dioxide, nitric oxides, and organic industrial gasses.

Some pollutants do not have any significant effect on colony or single-bee behavior but can be collected by bees. Heavy metals, radio nucleotides, and degradation products of pesticides that can be transported from the soil into flowers can be measured in collected nectar, pollen, and plant resins. Bees can also ingest pollutants through water collection. Volatile pollutants can attach to the body hairs of bees during foraging flights. Such pollutants can be measured through an analysis of hive air or sampling of returning foragers. Honeybees can also be used to monitor microorganisms during terror attacks.

A simple and efficient monitoring network was established in northern Italy during the 1980s. Hives were placed at contaminated areas, and if mortality exceeded a threshold of 500–700 bees a week, samples were obtained for chemical analysis. In recent years, the threshold was reduced to 200–250 bees per colony per week.

Many environmental studies of heavy metals and radio nucleotides have been performed on bee byproducts. This is a less expensive way to establish an environmental monitoring system. However, demands for better environmental monitoring have led to the development of sophisticated "monitoring hives" where an environmental scientist can collect physical and chemical samples of the hive environment and colony behavior. In addition to the analysis of dead bees and pollen loads at the hive entrance, digital counters are used to gather data on hive activity. Sensors are also placed inside the hive to measure temperature, humidity, and general vibration signals produced by bees. The hive is also placed on a scale to gather data on food intake, and samples of pollen, bees, and hive air can be taken automatically.

Further Resources

Bromenshenk, J. J., Henderson, C. B., & Smith, G. C. (2003). Biological systems (paper II), appendix S. In J. MacDonald & J. R. Lockwood (Eds.), *Alternatives for landmine detection* (pp. 273–83). Arlington, VA: RAND Science and Technology Institute for Office of Science and Technology Policy.

Celli, G., & Maccagnani, B. (2003). Honey bees as bioindicators of environmental pollution. *Bulletin of Insectology, 56,* 137–39.

DeVillers, J., & Pham-Delegue, M. H. (Eds.). (2002). *Honey bees: Estimating the environmental impact of chemicals.* London: Taylor and Francis.

Janko Bozic and Charles I. Abramson

Living with Animals
Pigs and Humans

Pigs have had a close association with humans for thousands of years. Indeed, this relationship can be so close that, in New Guinea, lactating women have been known to breast-feed needy piglets. Through co-evolution, we also share many common diseases.

For example, it is well known that the lifecycle of the pork tapeworm (*Taenia solium*) is dependent on the integral association between humans and pigs. Pigs are also thought to act as mixing vessels in the emergence of new variants of zoonotic influenza virus. The archeological record suggests that pigs were first domesticated from wild boar (*Sus scrofa*) around 9,000 years ago, and mitochondrial DNA evidence suggests that domestication has occurred on multiple independent occasions in different locations across Europe and Asia. Local breeds of domestic pigs may, thus, be genetically more similar to their local wild boar counterparts than to domestic pigs found elsewhere. Likewise, there have been multiple incidences of domestic pigs becoming feral and of wild boar being released in areas outside their original geographical range. As a result, pigs are now found throughout the world, in human-managed and wild-living populations.

Under human management, pigs have been artificially selected to enhance various traits useful to humans and, nowadays, can be found in a wide range of sizes, shapes, and colors, from prolific Chinese potbellied pigs to rotund, curly haired Hungarian Mangalica pigs; lean, black Iberian pigs valued for the flavor of their meat; fast-growing, large commercial-meat breeds; and diminutive minipigs and micropigs used in biomedical research. Human manipulation of pig genetics has been accelerating in recent years with the advent of technologies such as artificial insemination, embryo transfer, genome mapping, cloning, and transgenic animal production. Thus, pigs are currently being explored as a potential source of transgenic organs for transplantation to humans.

Our association with pigs, both wild and domesticated, is an uneasy one. We seek out wild boar as hunting targets but also fear them for their ferocity, retaining a healthy respect for their ability to kill us when provoked. We value—and farm—them as a tasty source of meat, yet monitor them closely as potential swine- and human-disease vectors. From an aesthetic perspective, we contrast the savage tusks and hirsute, muscular appearance of the adult wild boar with their elusive nature and the appealing striped coat of their young. Domestic pigs are prized mainly as a popular source of food, with pork accounting for 38 percent of total world meat consumption. They are also valued by some people for their truffle-hunting skills, recognized for their trainability, and adored as pets. Yet, domestic pigs also suffer the full gambit of insults from humans, ranging from individual abuse to industrialized neglect of their behavioral needs.

Feral populations of pigs, intentionally or unintentionally established in many parts of the world, have often taken humans by surprise through their invasiveness. Prolificacy—individual and social adaptability coupled with a prodigious omnivorous appetite and relative lack of natural predators in some areas—has prompted feral pigs to become notorious raiders of human crops or even predators of small livestock like newborn lambs, placing these pigs in direct conflict with humans. In places such as Hawaii and New Zealand, feral pigs are combated as deadly, native-wildlife-threatening pests. In addition, fear of their role as disease vectors has provoked often unsuccessful eradication efforts in some regions.

The increasing urbanization of human society and our distancing from nature and agriculture means that relatively few people today have ever actually met a pig. Hence, we may have rather unrealistic views about the nature of pigs, stemming from a combination of indirect sources of information. First, deeply rooted cultural attitudes may resonate in our current views. For example, in the Islamic and Judaic traditions, pigs are regarded as unclean animals and, in Christian thinking, the pig has been used as a symbol of gluttony and lust. Second, our views about pigs are heavily influenced by common parlance, which represents pigs—in different languages—as dirty, smelly, mean, treacherous, lazy, and contemptuous, but also as happy and satisfied animals. These attitudes may have arisen during the multipurpose, family farming period of agriculture, when a large portion of the public still had direct experience with pigs. Pigs were fed mostly human refuse once or twice a day, such that they devoured the food quickly, and they were usually held in small pens where they could not move around much or avoid being soiled by excreta. Their reputation has not been improved by the cannibalistic habits of some genetic lines, along with their role in disposal of human bodies in notorious murder cases. Third, these verbally transmitted attitudes are now compounded with pigs' portrayal as humanized characters in movies, cartoons, and books, such as Babe, Porky Pig, Wilbur in *Charlotte's Web,* Piglet in *Winnie the Pooh,* and Napoleon and Snowball in *Animal Farm.* Fourth, those who do come across pigs are most likely to do so in the context of intensive agriculture, where large herds of pigs are confined in limited, barren spaces, and their ability to express their natural behavior is restricted, making it easy to overlook their individuality. Last, a distorted and rudimentary knowledge about pigs may partially arise from our unwillingness to contemplate the link between the living animal and the pork on our plate.

Domestication has resulted in reduced fear of humans and decreased general agility, but the domestic pig retains the basic behavioral traits of the wild boar. This became clear to ethologists in the 1980s, through studies of domesticated pigs in the Edinburgh and

St. Anthony, whose followers lived among and cared for pigs. Illustration from Little Book of Piglets and Piglets *by Susan Fortunato. Courtesy of the Dover Pictorial Archives.*

A New Guinean mother, son, and daughter enjoy the shade with their pet dog and pig, ca. 1919. ©Corbis.

Swedish "pig parks." At the time, it was typical for people working in the pig industry to claim that domestic pigs had been so highly selected for intensive agriculture that they had lost their natural behavioral proclivities. The "pig park" studies revealed otherwise. The domestic pigs formed cohesive multigenerational matrilineal social groups as observed in wild boar. They exhibited long-term recognition of group members, synchronized their behavior, spent considerable time rooting and grazing, predated rabbits, wallowed to keep cool, and communicated with a rich array of vocalizations. Mother sows constructed nests adjusted according to the ambient temperature, and young pigs played extensively. This knowledge, in combination with more recent research into the cognitive and communicative abilities of pigs, has prompted a greater appreciation for the social complexity of pig lives.

In addition to their capacity to form long-term social bonds and motivation to engage in active exploration of their environment, pigs are noted for their intelligence, as indicated

A cartoon of a sow and piglets on trial in Lavegny, France in 1457, for killing and partly eating a child. From A Book of Days, *edited by Robert Chambers (W & R Chambers, 1869).*

by their relatively long memory, capacity for learning, and ability to adapt to a wide range of living conditions. Individual pigs also have distinct personalities and behavioral styles that are partly inherited and partly shaped through social experience during ontogeny. Sociality, adaptability, and trainability, coupled with individual behavioral distinctiveness, probably explains the current popularity of pigs as subjects of children's 4-H projects and of the smaller breeds of pigs as companion animals.

The discussion about welfare of pigs in intensive husbandry systems varies across the globe, from rudimentary in developing nations capitalizing on high levels of industrialized pig production to extensive in some countries where human living standards are high and a strong tradition of animal protection exists. Changes in people's attitudes toward commercially bred pigs and their living conditions are being sought in an intensified dialogue between all stakeholders. The possible contributions to this process include diversification into certified high-animal-welfare schemes by farmers, niche-marketing by retailers, informed choice by consumers, further provision of relevant knowledge about pigs' needs by scientists, and wise policy-making that includes education, legislation, and appropriate market tools. For instance, outdoor pig keeping has become the predominant method of pig production in Britain in recent decades, giving pigs more behavioral freedom and the public a greater opportunity to observe pigs—but also bringing new problems, such as increased piglet mortality and risk of infection with soil-borne parasites. Realistically, though, the major force driving pig husbandry worldwide is the human demand for mass, cheap pork production, and so it is questionable whether mainstream pig-industry practices will change, for the good of pigs, on a global scale anytime soon.

In comparison with several other domestic species, such as dogs, cats, cattle, horses, and camels, pigs have historically rarely been used as working or pet animals. The opportunity for affiliative relationships to develop between humans and pigs, either through genetic or cultural evolution, has, therefore, been limited. This, together with the above-mentioned projections of unpleasant human qualities on pigs, has resulted in less value being attributed and less concern given to pigs than to most other domestic animals. Thus, the human relationship with pigs can be seen as carrying both a natural and a historical handicap. As many societies in the world are now showing increasing appreciation for individuals or groups with a weaker position in society, perhaps a similar attitude could gain ground in our attitude toward pigs. There is a historical parallel for such change in the story of St. Anthony and his followers. St. Anthony, an early Christian hermit living in Egypt around the year 300, is said to have refused to retaliate toward a fierce pig that was sent to attack him as a part of sensual temptation. As a result, the pig was transformed into a docile porcine companion. His followers, monks of the order called Hospitallers of St. Anthony, were then renowned for taking care of "poor-doer" runt pigs, for their free-range pig raising and for traveling with bell-wearing porcine companions. Perhaps the message of this (hi)story is that a change, by humans, to a more knowledgeable and gentle attitude toward pigs will bring benefit to both species.

Further Resources

Choquenot, D., McIlroy, J., & Korn, T. (1996). *Managing vertebrate pests: Feral pigs*. Canberra: Bureau of Rural Sciences.

Gonyou, H. W. (2001). The social behaviour of pigs. In L. J. Keeling & H. W. Gonyou (Eds.), *Social behaviour in farm animals* (pp. 147–76). Wallingford: CABI Publishing.

Held, S., Mendl, M. T., Laughlin, K., & Byrne, R. W. (2002). Cognition studies with pigs: Livestock cognition and its implication for production. *Journal of Animal Science, 80,* E10–E17.

Larson, G., Dobney, K., Albarella, U., Fang, M., Matisoo-Smith, E., Robins, J., Lowden, S., Finlayson, H., Brand, T., Willerslev, E., Rowley-Conwy, P., Andersson, L., & Cooper, A. (2005). Worldwide phylogeography of wild boar reveals multiple centers of pig domestication. *Science, 307,* 1618–21.

Newberry, R. C., & Wood-Gush, D. G. M. (1986). Social relationships of piglets in a semi-natural environment. *Animal Behaviour, 34,* 1311–18.

Spinka, M., Illmann, G., de Jonge, F., Andersson, M., Schuurman, T., & Jensen, P. (2000.). Dimensions of maternal behaviour characteristics in domestic and wild x domestic crossbred sows. *Applied Animal Behaviour Science, 70,* 99–114.

Ruth C. Newberry and Marek Špinka

Living with Animals
Prairie Dogs and Humans

People have a love-hate relationship with prairie dogs. Some people love them, but others passionately hate them. Prairie dogs have been described by some as cute and cuddly and are kept as pets by a number of people; others describe prairie dogs as vermin, pests, and prairie rats that should be exterminated. Legends and myths abound that cattle and horses routinely fall into prairie dog burrows and break their legs and have to be killed, and that prairie dogs strip grasslands bare of every last blade of grass (Hoogland, 1995).

Prairie dogs are social, ground-burrowing squirrels that live in colonies (called *towns*) on the grasslands of western North America. They are found along a broad swath that extends from Canada to Mexico and from Arizona to the Dakotas. There are five prairie dog species: the black-tailed prairie dog (*Cynomys ludovicianus*), found in the western part of the Midwest; the Gunnison's prairie dog (*Cynomys gunnisoni*), found in northern Arizona, northern New Mexico, southern Colorado, and southeastern Utah; the white-tailed prairie dog (*Cynomys leucurus*), found in northwestern Colorado, Wyoming, and southern Montana; the Utah prairie dog (*Cynomys parvidens*), found in southeastern Utah; and the Mexican prairie dog (*Cynomys mexicanus*), found in central Mexico. Over most of their range, the distribution of the five species does not overlap.

About 100 years ago, prairie dog populations are estimated to have been around 5 billion animals. During their journeys in 1805, Lewis and Clark reportedly saw millions of prairie dogs, with towns stretching as far as the eye could see. Meriwether Lewis wrote in his journal on June 5, 1805, that, as the expedition traveled near the Marais River, Montana, they came upon a prairie dog town that stretched for about seven miles (Johnsgard, 2005). Another traveler in the American West, Captain Randolph Marcy, wrote on June 26, 1852, that, after observing a colony that he estimated was twenty-five miles long near the Red River in Texas, he thought that the population of prairie dogs was greater than any of the largest human cities (Johnsgard, 2005).

Today, their populations have been reduced to fewer than 2 percent of that number. A large part of that decline can be traced to poisoning campaigns. From the early 1900s, various branches of the federal government, including the U.S. Forest Service, the U.S. Bureau of Land Management, the U.S. National Park Service, the U.S. Fish and Wildlife Service, the U.S. Bureau of Indian Affairs, the U.S. Animal Damage Control (now called Wildlife Services), and the Biological Survey, have subsidized and sponsored prairie dog poisoning programs using taxpayer monies and conducting these activities on public land, including national parks. Normally, wildlife within the boundary of a national park is protected. However, the animosity toward the prairie dog has been so extreme that there was an exception that allowed the poisoning of "pests," as the prairie dogs were so named. State and local government agencies soon joined in the extermination campaigns, targeting prairie dogs on state lands. Some states even went as far as to *require* private landowners to poison and eliminate prairie dogs on their property.

Poisoning campaigns have been carried out because of the perception that prairie dogs compete with cattle for forage. In 1902, C. Hart Merriam, who was head of the U.S. Biological Survey, said that 256 prairie dogs eat as much grass as one cow, and 32 prairie dogs eat as much grass as one sheep (Merriam, 1902). The data that this was based on, if any, has never been established. However, this set the stage for the persistent perception that prairie dogs rob cattle of food and rob ranchers of their livelihood, and it provided the justification for poisoning campaigns that continue to this day.

However, the evidence that prairie dogs compete for food with cattle is not very clear (Detling, 2006). One study—in which some cattle were kept in paddocks that contained prairie dogs, and other cattle were kept in paddocks without prairie dogs—showed that, by the end of the study, there were no significant differences in the weights of the two groups of cattle, suggesting that prairie dogs and cows do not compete for food (O'Meilia et al., 1982). Another study that was based on computer simulations of the amount of grass eaten by different-sized populations of prairie dogs suggested that prairie dogs might diminish the amount of forage that would be available to cows by about 4 percent (Uresk & Paulson, 1988). To date, there have not been any studies that have conclusively shown that prairie dogs have a significant impact on the weight of cattle, (i.e., that prairie dogs and cows compete for food). This result might have been anticipated, because at least some species of prairie dogs coexisted without apparent competition for hundreds—if not thousands—of years with American bison (buffalo), and bison have food requirements that are similar to cattle (Detling, 1998).

Another source of prairie dog mortality at human hands is through recreational shooting. Shooting enthusiasts frequently use prairie dogs for target practice, often not even checking to see if an animal that they shot has been killed or simply wounded. The numbers of prairie dogs shot can be large. For example, in the years 1998–1999, the state of Colorado reported that 418,412 prairie dogs were killed by recreational shooters, and, in the year 2000, the state of South Dakota reported that 1,186,272 prairie dogs were shot (Reeve & Vosburgh, 2006). Shooting not only kills the prairie dogs but also disrupts the social system of these animals, who live in territorial groups and have complex social relationships. It also results in the deaths of pups whose mothers have been shot before the pups were fully weaned (Vosburgh & Irby, 1998). The shooting is condoned by federal agencies under the "multiple use" rule for public lands, and is an asset to state agencies, who benefit through the Pittman-Robertson Wildlife Restoration Act, which allocates money to state wildlife agencies from an excise tax on guns, bullets, and other hunting equipment.

Because of the decline in population numbers, efforts have been made to designate all of the prairie dog species as either endangered or threatened. The Mexican prairie dog was designated in 1970 as endangered in its entire range, central Mexico, under the provisions of the Endangered Species Preservation Act (a 1966 precursor to the Endangered Species Act of 1973), and in 1975 it was designated as endangered under the provisions of CITES, an international convention to protect endangered species. In 1973, the Utah prairie dog was designated as threatened over its entire range by the Bureau of Sport Fisheries and Wildlife (the precursor of the U.S. Fish and Wildlife Service). Subsequently, efforts have been made by various individuals and environmental groups to list the other three species under the provisions of the Endangered Species Act. The black-tailed prairie dog was designated as a Candidate Species for listing by the U.S. Fish and Wildlife Service in 2000, but was removed from that status in 2004 on the grounds that more prairie dog habitat was found than had previously been supposed. Efforts by concerned individuals and environmental organizations to list the white-tailed prairie dog and the Gunnison's prairie dog have been rejected by the U.S. Fish and Wildlife Service.

Despite the efforts to eradicate them, prairie dogs have a significant role to play in grassland ecosystems. Because they dig burrows with tunnels than can extend for long distances below the surface, they provide refuges for numerous birds, mammals, reptiles, amphibians, and arthropods. They are considered by many to be a *keystone* species, which is a species that has a disproportionate role in influencing the grassland ecosystem. Birds such as burrowing owls and mountain plovers nest in prairie dog towns; ferruginous hawks, swift foxes, and black-footed ferrets rely on prairie dogs for food; and small arthropods seek shelter from the midday heat inside the burrows. Some 208 other vertebrate species have been identified as having an association with prairie dogs in grasslands (Kotliar et al., 1999). Prairie dogs also modify the diversity of plants in the vicinity of their towns and, by clipping vegetation, cause resprouting of grasses and forbs that are then utilized by bison and pronghorn antelope, because the new sprouts are highly nutritious and lack some of the indigestible components of older vegetation. The burrows allow rainwater to percolate into underground aquifers, and the burrowing activity of the prairie dogs turns over nutrients in the soil by bringing up the soil to the surface, making those nutrients available to plants growing in the vicinity.

Some people who love prairie dogs keep them as pets. Until a federal ban on selling prairie dogs was implemented in 2003 because of fears of the monkeypox virus (which a few pet prairie dogs contracted from Gabon rats that were kept in the same cage during transport), the market for pet prairie dogs was thriving. Some estimates place the number of prairie dogs that were sold on a yearly basis as high as 90,000. These prairie dogs were sold worldwide. Owners of prairie dogs describe them as affectionate, intelligent, and relatively easy to train. The downside of the pet market is that prairie dogs have a very specialized diet that is sometimes difficult for people to provide, and veterinary care is sometimes difficult to obtain, because relatively few veterinarians are familiar with the diseases and physiological needs of prairie dogs.

Other people who love prairie dogs spend a considerable amount of time trying to save colonies from being exterminated. Organizations such as the Prairie Dog Coalition, the Rocky Mountain Animal Defense, and others have volunteers who spend hundreds of hours trying to transplant prairie dogs from development sites to new habitats where the animals will be relatively safe. Transplanting animals is a very time-consuming, labor-intensive job that requires weeks or months of effort (Truett et al., 2001), but the volunteers are united in their ethical concerns for these animals. Other organizations, such as the Southern Plains Land Trust, are buying land so that prairie dogs and other wildlife can live on their property without the risk of being poisoned or shot, and environmental organizations such as Forest Guardians are exploring legal means to save prairie dog populations.

Ultimately, the fate of prairie dogs lies in human hands. If the prairie dogs continue to be poisoned, shot, and displaced by development, their numbers can slip below what is required to maintain viable populations, and in the not-too-distant future, prairie dogs can become extinct in much the same way as the passenger pigeon. On the other hand, people can learn to coexist with prairie dogs and can set aside reserves where prairie dog towns will be safe from human intervention, in which case the prairie dogs will be with us for many more years to come.

Further Resources

Detling, J. K. (1998). Mammalian herbivores: Ecosystem-level effects in two grassland national parks. *Wildlife Society Bulletin, 26,* 438–48.

———. (2006). Do prairie dogs compete with livestock? In J. L. Hoogland (Ed.), *Conservation of the black-tailed prairie dog* (pp 65–88).Washington, DC: Island Press.

Hoogland, J. L. (1995). *The black-tailed prairie dog: Social life of a burrowing mammal.* Chicago: University of Chicago Press.

Johnsgard, P. A. (2005). *Prairie dog empire: A sage of the shortgrass prairie.* Lincoln, NE: University of Nebraska Press.

Kotliar, N. B., Baker, B. W., Whicker, A. D., & Plumb, G. (1999). A critical review of assumptions about the prairie dog as a keystone species. *Environmental Management, 24,* 177–92.

Merriam, C. H. (1902). The prairie dog of the Great Plains. In *Yearbook of the United States Department of Agriculture: 1901* (pp. 257–70). Washington, DC: Government Printing Office.

O'Meilia, M. E., Knopf, F. L., & Lewis, J. C. (1982). Some consequences of competition between prairie dogs and beef cattle. *Journal of Range Management, 35,* 580–85.

Reeve, A. F., & Vosburgh, T. C. (2006). Recreations shooting of prairie dogs. In J. L. Hoogland (Ed.), *Conservation of the black-tailed prairie dog* (pp. 139–56). Washington, DC: Island Press.

Truett, J. C., Dullum, J. L. D., Matchett, M. R., Owens, E., & Seery, D. (2001). Translocating prairie dogs: A review. *Wildlife Society Bulletin, 29,* 863–72.

Uresk, D. W., & Paulson, D. D. (1988). Estimated carrying capacity for cattle competing with prairie dogs and forage utilization in western South Dakota. In R. C. Szaro, K. E. Severson, & D. R. Patton (Eds.), *Management of amphibians, reptiles, and small mammals in North America* (pp. 387–90). Flagstaff, AZ: USDA Forest Service, Rocky Mountain Forest and Range Experiment Station.

Vosburgh, T. C, & Irby, L. R. (1998). Effects of recreational shooting on prairie dog colonies. *Journal of Wildlife Management, 62,* 363–72.

Con Slobodchikoff and Jennifer L. Verdolin

Living with Animals
Rabbits in Human Society

The rabbit-human relationship is among the most contradictory of all human-animal relationships. The history of rabbits in human society is a history in which rabbits have been worshipped, sacrificed, hunted, eaten, farmed, cherished, and experimented upon.

Few other animals are as simultaneously beloved and exploited as rabbits are, which tells us much about the importance of rabbits in human societies and even more about the treatment of animals by humanity.

Rabbits were originally domesticated by French monks for food in the first millennium CE; like cows and dogs, rabbits' social structure and eating habits make them well suited for living with humans, and their small size makes them relatively easy to handle, especially by women, who were typically charged with caring for small domestic animals. But rabbits had been a part of human society for millennia before then, and their use and representation tells us much about how humans saw and related to rabbits.

Rabbits (and hares) are one of the most common symbolic animals in the world, and representations of these animals have been found in the mythology and religious art of cultures on every continent, from ancient China, Egypt, Greece, and Rome to pre-Christian Europe, pre-colonization Africa, Meso-America, and Native America.

Rabbits' unique morphological and behavioral characteristics (such as their quickness, the fact that they live underground, their remarkable fecundity, and their ability to sleep with the eyes open) easily lend themselves to human interpretations, and for that reason they have played a prominent role in the magical, aphrodisiacal, and divinatory rituals of peoples around the world. But it is primarily the fact that rabbits were so well known for their sexuality that shapes the way that humans saw rabbits in the centuries before the time of Christ.

Rabbits are linked to sexuality—and in particular female sexuality and fertility—in the rituals, myths, and symbols of Ancient Greece and Rome [hares were sacred to Venus and Aphrodite (goddesses of love), as well as Diana (goddess of childbirth) and were often used in love spells, as aphrodisiacs, and to aid in fertility], Native American cultures, ancient Britain, Medieval Europe, China, and Japan. In eastern cultures as well as in Meso-America, ancient Europe, the Arab cultures, and Africa, the rabbit is also linked to the moon, which itself is linked to fertility and childbearing, with lunar goddesses commonly represented with or dressed as a rabbit or hare. Finally, thanks to the rabbit's fertility, rabbits are also used in myths and rituals to signify rebirth, explaining the rabbit's role in the symbols of Easter.

Rabbits' relationship with humans in ancient societies, then, was richly symbolic, and rabbits (or their body parts) were sacrificed to the gods, consumed or carried as aphrodisiacs, worshiped, and used in magical rituals and spells. Rabbits were also hunted as game and their skin used for clothing, but they were not yet raised as either food or pets.

After the advent of Christianity, rabbits lost their sacred associations in the Christian world and because of their links to sexuality and to pagan rituals were often demonized, becoming a common witch's familiar in Medieval Europe. Women who were accused of witchcraft, in fact, were often seen in the guise of rabbits, often leading to court trials and executions.

Rabbits are also found in the folklore and mythology of people in other areas of the world, especially among African and Native American societies, prior to colonization. Here rabbits figured prominently in the lives of many cultures, primarily as an animal to be hunted for food and clothing but also as an important part of the spiritual lives of many peoples. Rabbits play a part in the "just so" stories or explanatory tales of many African and Native American peoples, and their stories are also used to teach important moral lessons to children, imparting positive values such as humility, bravery, humor, and the value of quick wits over size and strength.

Representations of rabbits are still found in contemporary society, although they are largely stripped of their ancient symbolic meanings. For example, one of the most common ways that humans relate to rabbits today is not through real rabbits; rather, the enormous variety of rabbit-themed household kitsch—kitchenware, calendars, garden ornaments, figurines, and clothing—testifies to the importance of rabbit imagery in modern society, particularly to women, recalling the pre-Christian link between rabbits and women (a link also seen in the modern Playboy bunny).

Images of rabbits are also found in great abundance in the lives of children—in their literature, on their clothing, on their toys, and in the décor of their rooms. Rabbits seem to be (to those who have never lived with one) soft, sweet, childish, and cuddly, making them obvious choices to inhabit a child's world. But representations of rabbits are commonly found among children perhaps also because of their ancient associations with fertility and childbearing.

Some of the most popular literary renditions of rabbits have been inspired by real rabbits. For example, Beatrix Potter, nineteenth-century author and artist of the Peter Rabbit series of children's books, based her characters on her own pet rabbits, Benjamin and Peter. Richard Adams, author of the classic book *Watership Down,* on the other hand, based his realistic portrayal of rabbits on naturalist Ronald Lockley's *The Private Life of Rabbits*. *Watership Down* is a tale of a group of rabbits forced to find a new warren when developers destroy their home. It is both entertaining and educational in its accurate depiction of rabbit social life and the perils facing rabbits today. Unlike Beatrix Potter, however, Adams was no rabbit lover, advocating the killing of rabbits when necessary.

Throughout history, as we see, rabbits (and hares) have played a prominent role in human societies through their symbolic and ritual value; but what of real rabbits?

Clearly, the killing of rabbits for food is the oldest documented use of the rabbit and represents the earliest form of the human-rabbit relationship; from the hunting of rabbits for meat and fur on every continent, to the raising of a handful of rabbits in small gardens in the sixth century, to the raising of thousands of rabbits in large commercial breeding facilities today, the consumption of rabbits has been found in virtually every society. And although not a central feature of contemporary animal agriculture, rabbit meat plays a prominent role in small-scale farming as well as in third-world development projects aimed at providing poor villagers (mostly women) economic self-sufficiency.

The raising of rabbits for meat differs markedly from many of the commercial agribusiness practices used for more commonly raised animals, such as cows, pigs, and chickens. Although rabbits are often raised in large commercial "factories," in which rabbits are slaughtered by the thousands per week, they are still most commonly raised around the world in small backyard hutches or pens, an approach that is not that different from the way that rabbits have been raised for hundreds of years.

Because rabbits are often raised by small farmers, often by women (thanks to the ease of handling them and the low investment needed to begin raising them), and in quarters usually very close to the family home, a closer relationship has often developed between the farmer (or their family members) and the rabbits who are destined for slaughter. Many rabbit "growers" today, in fact, raise rabbits not just for meat but also as pets—both for sale and sometimes for their own families—a situation one would be hard-pressed to find among, say, cattle farmers.

Rabbits were almost certainly raised for fur since the time that they were originally domesticated for meat (it's unlikely that the early monks and farmers who raised rabbits for meat would discard their skins), but rabbits were not raised exclusively for fur until perhaps the sixteenth or seventeenth century; prior to that time most rabbit fur was from wild rabbits who were hunted or trapped. Today, rabbit fur is primarily produced in Europe and China and imported to the United States, where it is transformed into inexpensive fur garments and cat toys.

A relatively modern (since the nineteenth century) form of the human-rabbit relationship is the reliance on rabbits to act as a test subject for a wide variety of medical experiments and product testing procedures. We can thank the rabbit's small size, relatively gentle nature, and astonishing fertility for its popularity as research subject, coupled with the fact that rabbits are not as beloved as a pet animal as dogs or cats, keeping public outcry about their use to a minimum.

Yet even though rabbits are experimented on (to the tune of hundreds of thousands per year), the very same qualities that make rabbits a good test subject influence many researchers and research assistants to fall in love with them. Although many experiment protocols require that the animals be euthanized after the research is over (if they don't die in the course of the research), countless research assistants and animal care technicians have spirited away former laboratory rabbits, many of whom were lucky enough to become pets. Others find their way into farm animal sanctuaries, and at the time of this writing, a sanctuary dedicated to housing former laboratory animals is in the process of being established in Wyoming.

Putting aside the fact that the relationships embodied in the modern rabbit meat, fur, and vivisection industries are of a supremely one-sided nature—the rabbits serve the pleasure of humans, with very little, if any, return to the rabbits—we can also see the ways that those who work closely with rabbits have often moved beyond a strictly utilitarian view of them to one approximating friendship. Clearly, some unknown number of people throughout history charged with raising, using, or even killing rabbits have found themselves taken by the rabbit's charms, eventually leading to the idea that rabbits could be pets.

Even though rabbits were most certainly kept as pets by farmers' wives and children for centuries, as well as by hunters and gatherers who kept some game animals as pets, the idea of keeping rabbits as pets did not gain widespread acceptance until the eighteenth and nineteenth centuries. The development of the rabbit as a pet coincided, not coincidentally, with the rise of the commercial pet industry and the idea that keeping pets could instill positive values and behaviors in children; rabbits, thanks to their long association with women and children, became the ultimate "children's pet."

Originally, pet rabbits were acquired from farmers raising rabbits for meat or for fur, but eventually an informal industry developed to breed rabbits both for show and for pets. These "fancy" breeds such as lops, dwarves, and the like were seen as more suitable for pets than the meat rabbits, and the smaller breeds in particular were marketed as good children's pets.

But our understanding of pets, and certainly the understanding of rabbits as pets, has evolved to a considerable extent since the early days of the pet industry. Pet rabbits have, for hundreds of years, been most commonly kept as outdoor pets, living in hutches made of wood and wire. Fed and watered once a day, usually by the woman of the family, and occasionally taken out by the children to play, the human-rabbit relationship was hampered by the lack of close contact between human and rabbit. Furthermore, rabbits, like many other animals when living in a cage, tend to appear passive, reserved, and uninteresting, making it easy for family members to ignore them. Because they vocalize very rarely, their silence makes them easy to forget as well. On the other hand, because they do not readily vocalize, caged rabbits will often show their unhappiness through aggression, which generally leads to their continued confinement (or worse).

The pet rabbit-human relationship was then, for many years, almost as one-sided as the relationship found among rabbit meat producer and rabbit. Based on an incomplete and incorrect understanding of the animal (cute, soft, and sweet, with no real demands or interests), the relationship suffered due to a lack of knowledge about what rabbits are really like.

The rabbit-human relationship took a turn for the better in 1985 with the publication of Marinell Harriman's *House Rabbit Handbook*. Written to honor the memory of Herman, a stray rabbit who found her way into Harriman's backyard and then home, the book inspired tens of thousands of people to adopt rabbits as house pets and was the main factor in the establishment of House Rabbit Society, the first and only international rabbit advocacy group of its kind. In the twenty years since the first edition of the *Handbook* was released, the idea that rabbits could be treated on the same level as dogs or cats—that they could live indoors as part of a human family, that they could receive veterinary care, and that they could be spayed or neutered and live with companions of their own species—has gone from being laughable to being almost commonplace.

Tens of thousands of people who now live with house rabbits have taken the rabbit-human relationship to an entirely new level. Rabbits don't just share people's homes—they occupy an enormous part of their lives and have influenced the creation of an entirely new industry dedicated to providing for the needs of the house rabbit, from rabbit toy makers to specialized food and hay producers to rabbit condominium manufacturers to healthy snack companies.

Perhaps because rabbits have been domesticated for a much shorter period of time than dogs or even cats, rabbits are not the easiest animals to integrate into a human household. They chew, sometimes voraciously, leading house rabbit advocates to devise creative means of keeping phone and electrical cords, baseboards, walls, and furniture safe from sharp teeth. They are curious and spend more time than one might imagine climbing, digging, and jumping into and onto furniture, crevices, and counters, often causing much trouble in the process. Rabbits are willful and do not always come when called, obey their caretakers, or behave in an appropriate "petlike" fashion. They are intelligent, using tools such as toys, bowls, furniture, or cage bars to communicate their desires to humans and other animals. And they are messy, not so much with their waste (they are relatively easy to litter box train), but with their toys, as well as with whatever they choose to claim as their own.

Thanks to the work of House Rabbit Society volunteers and the ingenuity of thousands of rabbit lovers, problems like these are now managed through "bunny-proofing" the house, through purchasing and creating toys out of cardboard, wood, wicker, and wire, and through creatively re-imagining housing for rabbits inside of human homes. Rabbit veterinarians have learned how to safely treat rabbit illnesses and to spay and neuter them, allowing for the possibility of rabbit-rabbit relationships and making living with rabbits in the home a cleaner proposition.

The contemporary rabbit-human relationship, as it has been creatively reconfigured by house rabbit lovers today, appears to be moving away from not only the one-sided relationship represented in the meat rabbit business and through the old-fashioned child/hutch rabbit relationship but also from the typical human-pet relationship, which is marked at least in part by dominance and control. Although most people who live with rabbits still exercise at least some control over their rabbit companions, many are allowing their rabbits more freedom to be themselves than ever before and perhaps more than many pet lovers give to their dogs, cats, or birds. Some willingly live in a home in which hay is scattered on the floor, a litter box occupies the space in front of (or even inside of) the fireplace, cardboard boxes filled with newspaper are shredded and urinated on in the living room, and children's gates divide the house, forcing the human occupants to climb over them. Rabbit people often live like this, illustrating the great lengths to which many people will go to share their lives with an animal on as-close-to-equal terms as can be accommodated.

Beatrix Potter with one of her rabbits on a leash, photo taken in 1891. ©Penguin Group.

Many people who live with rabbits today go a step further and not only attempt to make their own relationship with rabbits as positive as possible but also use their love of rabbits to advocate for change for all animals. House Rabbit Society was formed out of one woman's love for rabbits, and countless other rabbit lovers now work to not only better the lives of rabbits but to improve the lives of other animals as well. Because of their use in the meat, fur, and vivisection industries, many animal lovers empathize especially with rabbits and use that empathy to try to secure better lives for all animals.

Rabbits, like many other animals, have been, for thousands of years, a blank slate on which humans project their own beliefs, desires, and interests. In pre-Christian societies, the human interests were combined with a partial understanding of the rabbit, leading to the symbolic and mythic uses of the rabbit seen in so many cultures. Ironically, those symbolic associations showed more of an appreciation of the "real rabbit" than is seen when the symbolic uses give way to the utilitarian, through the development of the modern rabbit industries. And still later yet, with the rise of the house rabbit movement, the subjectivity of rabbits has (re-)emerged, leading to the possibility of a human-animal relationship that is rich with possibilities—both for human and for rabbit.

Further Resources

Adams, R. (1989). *Watership down.* London: Avon.

DeMello, M. & Davis, S. (2003). *Stories rabbits tell: A natural and cultural history of a misunderstood creature.* New York: Lantern Press.

Grier, K. (1999). Childhood socialization and companion animals: United States 1820–1870. *Society and Animals: Journal of Human-Animal Studies, 7*(2), 95–120.

Harriman, M. (1985). *House rabbit handbook: How to live with an urban rabbit.* Alameda: Drollery Press.

Lockley, R. (1954). *The private life of rabbits.* London: Corgi Books.

Rowland, B. (1973). *Animals with human faces: A guide to animal symbolism.* Knoxville: University of Tennessee Press.

Smith, J. (2003). Constructing a "performance ethic": The discourse and practices of the house rabbit society. *Society and Animals: Journal of Human-Animal Studies, 11*(2), 181–97.

Margo DeMello

Living with Animals
Ravens and Humans

The northern raven, *Corvus corax,* is a bird of legend that is prominent in the folklore of people across the northern hemisphere, and one can hardly name another wild bird that has had more impact on the human imagination. I have previously explored the mythology of the raven in *Ravens in Winter* (1989), and, to reiterate here briefly, in various tribes raven is creator of the world—the earth, stars, sun, and people. Sometimes "he" is also a rascally folk hero, but he is never evil. In contrast, in European cultures he is a prominent symbol, if not an apprentice of, death. In Mecklenburg, Germany, from 1834–75 alone, 10,440 ravens were recorded as shot. In the New World, persecution continued by shooting and poisoned bait carcasses. The age-old traditions of our relationships with this bird continue to the present century. In northern Canada in some Native American towns ravens are as tame as hens. Whereas in central Europe and in Maine I have found him to be so shy that he flies off the moment someone looks in his direction. The interesting question is "Why?" Why is the raven credited in the mythology of many peoples variously (and sometimes simultaneously) as a trickster, creator of the world, a diviner if not apprentice of death, and a "presence" of uncanny intelligence?

The raven is both a generalist and a specialized scavenger. He is often a close associate of carnivores, especially wolves. In previous ages he was also a close associate with humans. In "recent" history he has been credited with clearing garbage from the streets of Old London and being a guardian of the empire by warning of enemy attacks. However, his ancient ties with European people have in recent centuries changed so that we now scarcely know him. But surely the raven as such has not changed, and I shall here explore raven-human relationships from the standpoint of psychological bonding, as opposed to a purely utilitarian perspective.

One of the dominant themes of biology is the interdependence of organisms. Most such interactions that evolve into stable associations depend on the interchange of resources. In the case of associations involving mammals and birds, it appears likely that proximate mechanisms of emotions would come into play because the emotions are the primary, in other words primitive, motivators as opposed to secondary or rational responses. For example, it is likely that wolves stay together as a pack and hunt as a group because they enjoy each other's company rather than that they behave only because they rationalize. Simply put, the emotions are reliable motivators in making, maintaining, and breaking complex social relationships because they provide constant internal prods that are compelling, if not also more reliable than reason, especially when the rewards are far in the future.

The strongest emotional attachments are usually found within the same species, particularly with offspring, mates, relatives, and associates. The different degrees of emotions attending these relationships in different species likely help establish and maintain life strategies such as polygyny, social versus solitary existence, and so on. In cross-species associations, one member almost invariably substitutes for the other's own species' mate, parent, offspring, or social companion. For example, both humans and dogs are pack animals, and allegiances transfer readily from one to the other. Similarly, young geese imprint on a human "parent" and become substitute "mates." The cross-species associations work because emotions that are adaptive in the "normal" context have become redirected to surrogate partners. More intellectually interesting are those cases of human-animal interactions where the above types of bonding are not so readily apparent, and I believe that the raven-human connection is one of them, although it is probably also adaptively rooted like any other.

Ravens form close trophic relationships with wolves and to some extent also with other large carnivores, so it seems unlikely that ancient human hunters would have viewed them as fundamentally different from wolves. Ravens actively follow wolf packs and feed alongside and literally underfoot with them at their kills. Even now (in Yellowstone Park) ravens arrive at wolves' elk kills within a minute on average, yet they do not come down to feed at fresh readily available elk meat for many hours, or even days. In short, they seek the wolves' company and take advantage of it if they can find it. Clearly, more than just proximate access to food is involved in the raven's association with wolves because they routinely fly over meat that is unattended by these carnivores. In effect, the ravens act as though they "like" the wolves; that is, they demonstrate an attachment to them. Inuit and other hunters routinely leave parts of their prey for ravens to feed from. Can the ravens' attraction be transferred to humans to create a raven-human relationship that (although ultimately utilitarian) is proximally based on mutual trust and attraction?

Any such potential association between wild ravens and humans, and *vice versa*, is not likely to be revealed in modern contexts. There is scarcely opportunity. Ravens have been relentlessly persecuted and extirpated over vast areas of their range since the advent of human agriculture, when herding of animals replaced the hunting culture. Herding has brought ravens death warrants because ravens feed on dead and dying domestic animals, and for this they have been widely accused of cruelty and causing the destruction of the herder's property. On the other hand, hunters revered them because they often formed a partnership with them by helping to find prey for mutual consumption.

In my studies of wild ravens in New England I have been impressed by these birds' shyness and caution. Most of the birds are almost impossible to approach. Their present shyness does not necessarily indicate continuing persecution now. Ravens have lifespans of a half-century or more and they culturally transmit behavior (such as fear of specific items or situations) from one generation to the next. Most of the information transfer occurs between parents and offspring in the short period after fledging. However, whatever alarms one raven in a group invariably spooks all of them. Conversely, what attracts one will attract others.

There are still areas of the world where ravens lack cultural fear of humans, although they are now quite indifferent to them. I cite an example that suggests what I think is the more "natural" raven-human relationship, one that is similar to that of their association with wolves (where the two partners of the relationship are not only tolerant of each other but also attracted to each other).

In November 2003 Dadre Traughber of northern California met a pair of ravens on a hike. She offered the birds some picnic lunch, and the pair came over to claim it, as ravens of populations that have not been persecuted often do. What followed, however, differed greatly. Traughber talked softly with the birds and continued to come back to the pairs' territory on numerous occasions, each time bringing treats and spending quality time with them. After a number of such visits the pair came to seek her out when she came near, often coming in noisily and doing impressive aerial displays as well. Eventually they stayed next to her for hours, fully engaged in displays to each other and to her, even in the absence of food. She says, "these bright birds have been my teachers and entertainers, and continue to do so."

She named the pair "Mobius" and "Sacagawea," or Mo and Sac. In 2004 the pair brought her their two clutches of two young each shortly after they fledged (subsequently the young disperse widely). As she continued to visit her friends in 2005 they again brought their two new clutches of young. In my studies of hand-raised birds I have discovered that young ravens fear anything new, but they have no fear of new things that their parents introduce them to. Similarly, at first the youngsters were a little shy of Traughber, but they quickly became as tame as the parents. I here describe in her own words her sixtieth meeting of the ravens (on May 11, 2005).

The family of four ravens came flying to Traughber from a distance, doing rolls in the air, and after landing Mo and Sac displayed in front of her. She reports: "Sac brought one of her offspring down, and once it came down itself it looked up at me. It was offered an almond and wasn't sure what to do with it! Mo flew to me as I was hiking away and came within ten feet of my head when he was attacked by red-winged blackbirds. I was able to shoo them away and Mo landed at my feet. He hung out with me for quite awhile. He walked around in circles overturning rocks. He was fed very few treats, but he just hung out, and then hunkered down in a resting position. I usually talk to him during these times and he seems to listen. Sometimes he talks back. Later on down the trail I went to a rocky outcrop to take photos, and Sac joined us. They began a long session of allo-preening, and then just hung out (no treats). Later on when hiking home Mo followed right behind me (for about a mile and a half) like a puppy."

About three months later the pair had fledged their second brood (of four young) that year (2005). (In the East and North they only raise one brood per year.) At that time the broods of young were banding up with each other in loose social groups while the parental bonds had loosened. On August 10, when Traughber visited the area (I will not reveal the location to protect the privacy of all parties concerned), the four young birds (easily identified by feather and mouth color) flew over to her and landed next to her. A tussle between them ensued, but even as they approached they begged from her as they do from their parents, by yelling and gaping. Sac and Mo were not present.

Apparently a tradition had been started. The young were unafraid, and they walked behind Traughber and sometimes flew up ahead of her, for a distance of about two and a half miles. She said: "The birds seemed to be very relaxed with me, more so than before.

I attribute this to my previous meetings with the parents and the time I spent hanging out with them." Precisely.

The amazing behavior of Traughber's ravens, which she has documented in hundreds of photographs, fit well with my years of controlled experiments and observations on Maine ravens. Anecdotes of ravens approaching people with no apparent purpose are legion, but to my knowledge most such meetings have not been followed up with systematic repeat visits, so that "relationships" did not have a chance to develop. Traughber's ravens approached no other persons when she brought others with her. Controlled experiments show that ravens are good at discriminating one individual from another, both other ravens and humans, and they recognize them from a distance, thus their relationship with one person will not be the same as with another, as among themselves as well.

Perhaps the most interesting question is why humans are attracted and often enamored by ravens, since the *material* assets appear to go only one way. People who meet ravens face to face almost invariably report feeling as though meeting a kindred spirit. Having come to know my own ravens individually, I confess to the same feeling. This begs the question of what qualities the birds project and whether their behavior of spontaneously approaching humans (as well as fleeing from them) is also derived from emotions that we can identify with. It may be far-fetched. But it makes adaptive sense: ravens who are *afraid* of humans don't get shot, and those who *like* to hang out with wolves get fed as regularly as Traughber's ravens now get fed by her. It is unlikely that ravens would attach themselves to large animals if there were not also benefits to that behavior, but hanging out with humans (or wolves) out of attraction will more reliably help to ensure those benefits on a long-term basis

Further Resources

Angell, T. (1978). *Ravens, crows, magpies and jays*. Seattle: University of Washington Press.

Heinrich, B. (1989). *Ravens in winter*. New York: Summit Books.

———. (1999). *Mind of the raven: Investigations and adventures with wolf-birds*. New York: HarperCollins.

Ratcliffe, D. (1997). *The raven*. New York: Simon & Schuster.

Stahler, D. R., Heinrich, B., & Smith, D. W. (2002). The raven's behavioral association with wolves. *Animal Behaviour*, *64*, 283–90.

Bernd Heinrich

Living with Animals
Rhesus Monkeys and Humans

Rhesus monkeys (*Macaca mulatta*) are one of twenty species of macaques (Genus *Macaca sp.*), closely related to the Japanese macaque, the crab-eating macaque of southeast Asia, the Bonnet and Lion-tailed macaques of south India, and the Barbary macaque of north Africa. Macaques are moderate-sized to large monkeys of the old world, terrestrial and arboreal in habit.

Rhesus macaques are notable among the macaques, and even among all species of nonhuman primates, for their degree of commensalism with people and for several other reasons of interest to people. First of all, although they are wild animals, rhesus are among the most *commensal* of all nonhuman primates in relation to humans; that is, they associate freely with people in our habitats and our behavior. Throughout their geographic range in Asia, they live commonly in and around villages, towns, cities, temples, parks, schools, market places, and other public areas. They thrive in agricultural lands, feeding on gardens, orchards, and field crops. They also inhabit forests—temperate, subtropical, and tropical—but the loss of forests in much of their range has forced many groups to invade human environments to a greater extent in recent years. This association is leading to more conflict with human populations, a topic to be explored later in this article.

Second, rhesus are notable among nonhuman primates as having the greatest geographic range of any monkey, prosimian, or ape. Rhesus are natural inhabitants of eleven Asian nations, stretching from northwestern Afghanistan, through Pakistan, India, Nepal, eastward to north central China and southeast Asia, to central Thailand, Laos, Cambodia, and Vietnam. India is the country of greatest rhesus abundance, however.

Third, rhesus have the broadest ecological range of any nonhuman primate, living in habitats as diverse as the tropical and subtropical forests of peninsular India, the deserts of Rajasthan, the crowded mega-cities of northern India, and the Himalayan mountains to elevations over 10,000 feet, reported at 3,600 meters in Nepal and 4,000 meters in the Qinghai province of China (Fooden, 2000).

Fourth, rhesus monkeys are famous as one of the most widely used primates in laboratory work in biomedical research, behavioral studies, vaccine development, and pharmaceutical testing. Rhesus have been used in research in immunology and infectious diseases, in vaccine development including polio vaccine, in perfecting many types of surgery including organ transplantation, in dietary studies, in the treatment of chronic diseases, and in safety testing of prescription medicines. In behavioral research, rhesus have been notable models for studies of animal learning, cognition, maternal care, and social aspects of behavioral development.

To meet this demand for laboratory and captive research on primates, India exported large numbers of rhesus monkeys to Europe, the United States, and other countries, primarily from the 1940s to the late 1970s. In some years, more than 100,000 rhesus were exported from India. This was controversial in India because monkeys are sacred in Hindu religion and philosophy, but an international agreement in the 1950s stipulated that India would export monkeys solely for humane biomedical and behavioral research, excluding space-related and defense-related research. Importing countries, notably the United States, violated these latter terms, using rhesus in both space and military research, and in 1978, Prime Minister Moraji Desai of India banned all export of rhesus monkeys. Rhesus are still used, however, for biomedical research and laboratory studies in India.

Populations of rhesus in India had been declining substantially during the 1960s and early 1970s due to excessive trapping for export and also due to India's food shortages and economic struggles during these years. Rhesus numbers stabilized in the 1970s, increased in the 1980s, and then expanded rapidly in the 1990s as trapping for export was prohibited and India's agricultural production increased. No scientific estimates of rhesus populations in India were available prior to 1959, but Sanderson (1957) expressed the conventional wisdom that "vast hordes of rhesus roam large parts of India," and he further indicated that the macaques of Asia and baboons of Africa "possibly exceed the total of two and a half billion or so human beings that now crowd the earth." This implied a gross overestimate of monkey numbers in India—more reasonable estimates based on field surveys in the late 1950s and early 1960s placed the numbers of rhesus in India in the range of one to two million, at a time when the human population of India was 380 million.

Nonetheless, the rapid depletion of rhesus populations due to excessive trapping for export in the late 1950s and 1960s, and also due to agricultural food shortages and poor economic conditions in India, led to the first nationwide survey of rhesus populations by the Government of India in the 1970s, in which a team of more than 30 field workers covered the rhesus range throughout India. They calculated a total population of only 183,000 rhesus in India (Tiwari & Mukherjee, 1983).

Since the export ban and the strong improvement of India's agriculture and economy, the natural population growth of rhesus, often 8 to 10 percent annually, has produced a remarkable increase in India's rhesus population, estimated to be 350,000 in the 1990s, and at least 500,000 by 2005 (Malik, 2005). This number may well be over a million, most of which are commensal. In the 1990s, over 60 percent of rhesus in India were in commensal habitats (villages, towns, and temples), 35 percent were in semi-commensal habitats (parks, roadsides, and canal banks), and less than 2 percent were in forest areas (Southwick & Siddiqi, in Biquand & Gautier, 1994). The rhesus populations of some cities, notably Delhi and Shimla, have increased manifold to become serious pest problems.

Rhesus commensalism has both positive and negative aspects. The positive aspects include the religious devotion of most Hindus toward monkeys. Monkeys are embodiments of the monkey God Hanuman, who in Hindu belief, played a key role in defeating the demon King Ravana, representing the victory of good over evil. In this belief, Ravana kidnapped Sita, the beloved wife of Rama, the reincarnation of Lord Vishnu, central in Hindu beliefs as the embodiment of virtue and wisdom. The evil Ravana abducted Sita to the island of Lanka, formerly Ceylon, now known as Sri Lanka. Hanuman and his monkey troop found Sita, enabled Rama to cross the straits to Sri Lanka, and the monkeys defeated Ravana in an epic battle. This story represents the ultimate victory of good over evil. It is celebrated in India every year in the festival Dussehra and the classic dance drama, the Ramayana. Hanuman, and his troop of monkeys, is portrayed in art, statuary, literature, and children's books throughout India. Hanuman is actually a langur monkey, a different species also common in India, but Hindus generalize and consider all monkeys sacred. Many Hindus feed monkeys as an act of devotion.

Monkeys are also a source of pleasure for families and children to watch. The infants and juveniles are cute and attractive, their play humorous and fun to observe. The care that mothers give their infants is appealing. Even their squabbles are amusing. Monkey groups in India are really a natural, enjoyable open-air zoo.

There are, however, a number of negative aspects to rhesus macaques in India, especially when they are too abundant. They tend to become very bold and aggressive, often snatching food from children and market vendors. Even worse, they can readily attack people, resulting in bites and severe injuries. Male rhesus have inch-long canine teeth that can cause serious wounds. Babies and even toddlers have been killed by rhesus attacks. Several behavioral situations commonly set the stage for attacks: when people tease monkeys or withhold food while feeding them; when a person inadvertently steps between a rhesus mother and her infant and the infant squeals an alarm or distress call; when a person turns his or her back to a subordinate male recently attacked by a dominant male, and the subordinate then seeks an object for re-directed aggression; or when one makes direct eye contact with an adult in an aggressive mood—the eye contact may be interpreted as a threat by the monkey.

Rhesus often enter homes, schools, businesses, and even hospitals and public buildings through open windows and doors, where they may attack if cornered.

Rhesus commensalism also has a negative effect from the standpoint of infectious disease. One reason rhesus have been valuable in biomedical research is that they have a disease spectrum similar to ourselves. Among their infectious diseases are tuberculosis, influenza, pneumonia, measles, bacillary and amoebic dysentery, tetanus, leptospirosis, leishmaniasis, hepatitis A, encephalitis, poliomyelitis, and a serious herpes virus infection known as Monkey B or Simian B virus. Monkey B virus causes only minor lingual lesions in rhesus, not a serious disease in monkeys, but it can be transferred in a monkey bite or scratch to humans, where it is usually fatal. Most rhesus in India show serological evidence of infection with Monkey B virus, but fortunately its transmission to people is rare due to a short intermittent viremia in the monkey. Nonetheless, no one knows how many people in India die annually from Monkey B infections, probably hundreds because monkey bites by rhesus are very common. Over thirty laboratory workers in the United States have become critically ill from B-virus after being bitten or scratched by a rhesus monkey, and 67 percent of them have died.

Rhesus also carry high infection rates of a retrovirus, or lentivirus, which is a close relative of HIV, the human immunodeficiency virus that causes AIDS. It is known as SIV, the simian immunodeficiency virus. SIV does not normally infect human beings, but it does cause an AIDS-like disease in monkeys. SIV provides a close laboratory model for the study of retroviral infections and the hope for an HIV vaccine as well as better treatments for human AIDS.

Another downside of excessive numbers of commensal rhesus monkeys in India is the damage they cause in agricultural crop loss. Even fifty years ago, before rhesus populations became a nuisance, many farmers, with orchard groves of mangos, papayas, apples, or bananas, considered rhesus a pest. That is true even more so now. Rhesus can be very destructive in orchards, gardens, and field crops. A group of 50 or 60 rhesus monkeys can easily devastate a small garden or orchard, or even fields of beans, corn, wheat, or rice as the crops ripen. Rhesus groups that feed in fields and gardens around villages sometimes number more than 100 monkeys. Traditionally, young children and elderly villagers are stationed in fields, gardens, and orchards as "chowkidars" to guard the crops from marauding monkeys, but usually the monkeys have ways of wearing down their patience or sneaking in for feeding when their guard is down.

A group of motorists stops to feed a group of rhesus monkeys. People often find the appeal of these monkeys hard to resist. Courtesy of Charles Southwick.

All of these factors lead to a "love-hate" relationship of the people of India with their monkeys. They love their close association with animals, they worship the oneness of all animal life and the sanctity of primates, but they hate the problems that too many monkeys, especially aggressive ones, inevitably cause. Frequent references to the "monkey menace" occur in newspapers, television, and e-mail. Clearly, management solutions are needed. These have typically involved trapping and relocation of problem groups to forest areas. There are, however, fewer and fewer forest areas available. Often they are just small patches requiring the monkeys to move to the nearest village and agricultural areas. Hence, relocation frequently metastasizes the "monkey-menace" to other areas. Relocation to forests also runs the risk of spreading dangerous disease pathogens to forest wildlife. Other solutions are needed, especially some form of humane birth control for monkeys.

Rhesus are by no means the only commensal monkeys that are sources of both cultural enjoyment and serious problems. Many other species are also notable examples: The Bonnet monkey in

A Buddhist monk throwing rice to rhesus monkeys in a temple setting. Courtesy of Charles Southwick.

Being one of the most commensal primates, rhesus monkeys live commonly in and around villages, towns, cities, temples, parks, schools, market places, and other public areas. Courtesy of Charles Southwick.

south India, the Japanese monkey, the long-tailed monkey of southeast Asia, the baboons and vervet monkeys of Africa, and even some of the New World monkeys of Central and South America (Paterson & Wallis, 2005). Many primate species are presently commensal, or will potentially become commensal with humans as we destroy, modify, or invade their natural habitats. A familiar example in the eastern and central United States is our white-tailed deer populations. In many states, deer are so abundant that they damage forest growth and regeneration in their own habitats, they feed on gardens and crops, and they contribute to the spread of Lyme disease.

Efforts in the direction of managing the detrimental aspects of primate commensalisms should emphasize both conservation and education. Conservation is needed to protect natural habitats. Education of people is needed to reduce artificial feeding and avoid conflict situations. Once serious problems of overpopulation have developed, current efforts of population reduction and birth control for monkeys have focused on fertility control of dominant males by means of vasectomy. This has been expensive and shown to be successful only in primate species such as Hamadryas baboons in Saudi Arabia, where single dominant males control mating in a "harem" group of adult females (Biquand & Gautier, 1994). It is not known if this approach will work with rhesus monkeys, where subordinate males are also active in mating.

New research and field studies are needed to find humane and feasible solutions to the problem of overly abundant commensal monkeys. Reasonable numbers of rhesus are desirable to maintain the close cultural connection of people and nonhuman primates; but excessive numbers, especially when the animals have developed destructive, aggressive, and dangerous behaviors, destroy this enjoyable and beneficial commensal relationship.

Further Resources

Biquand, S., & Gautier, J. P. (1994). Les Primates Commensaux—Commensal Primates. *La Terre Et la Vie: Revue D'Ecologie*. Tome XLIX, No. 3. Paris, France, pp. 193–319.

Fooden, J. (2000). *Systematic review of the rhesus macaque*, Macaca mulatta. *Fieldiana*. Chicago: Field Museum of Natural History.

Malik, I. (2005). *Rhesus in India*. New Delhi, India: Vatavaran.

Paterson, J. D., & Wallis, J. (2005). Commensalism and conflict: The human-primate interface. *American Society of Primatologists, Special Topics in Primatology, 4*. Norman, OK.

Sanderson, I. (1957). *The monkey kingdom*. Garden City, NY: Doubleday, Inc.

Southwick, C. H., Malik, I., & Siddiqi, M. F. (2005). Rhesus commensalism in India: Problems and prospects. In J. D. Patterson & J. Wallis (Eds.), *Commensalism and conflict: The human-primate interface* (pp. 238–57). Norman, OK: ASP Press.

Tiwari, K. K., & Mukherjee, R. P. (1983). Report on the population survey of rhesus macaques and hanuman langurs of India. Calcutta, India: Zoological Survey of India, Gov. of India.

Charles H. Southwick

Living with Animals
Sharks and Humans

Sharks are the most feared of the wild ocean predators. Unlike the rare sperm whale and the remote polar bear, sharks are both common and numerous in our surrounding seas. Yet sharks remain mysterious. More than grizzlies, lions, and snakes, sharks have become the most terrifying animal to many people. This fear even ripples to well-informed people in land-locked countries. Grizzlies are at least warm-blooded mammals. There are no "teddy sharks." Little sharks are not thought of as "cute"; they are wet and cold and they bite. As a consequence, humankind has had a difficult time conserving, managing, and otherwise relating positively to sharks. Do sharks deserve such loathing and calumny?

A diver films a blue shark. Courtesy of Harold Pratt.

In the Beginning: Humans Fear Sharks

Our first response to large predators is fear, and our anxiety of sharks is very old. Sharks became a distinct group on our planet over 400 million years ago, long before humans. We know from fossil records that prehistoric sharks were larger and stranger than any that swam in our oceans when man emerged. From that Pleistocene morning when a shark first approached a prehistoric human gathering mollusks in a shallow bay or stole a fish speared from the primeval shore, our relationship to sharks has been forged from fear. They were the enemy, along with lightning, the infected cut, the cave bear, and the tribe across the river that hunted on our territory. Some scholars think the biblical Jonah was more likely swallowed by a shark than a whale. The shark was the foundation animal to many early sea monster myths. These ancient feelings persist subliminally in humans of most races and cultures, although some Pacific islanders revere sharks and live in harmony with them. Many Hawaiian people regard certain wild sharks as "aumakua," guardian or ancestral spirits, and protest their slaughter. The recorded natural history of sharks began with the ancient Greeks. Aristotle knew sharks well and gave us the term claspers for their rodlike external sperm transfer organs. He made the first observations of shark reproductive behavior.

As human activity became more agricultural and then industrial, contact with sharks decreased. From the middle ages to the 1800s, European sea-going peoples had a nagging fear of large marine creatures, sea serpents, leviathans, and krakens. Watching the great whales at sea, and then witnessing a shark strike a hooked fish at the wooden rail of an early sailing ship, instilled a deep reaction that went quickly past awe to fear, dread, and amazing stories. "Man overboard" was usually a death sentence. It still brings anxiety and fear today, although drowning rather than shark attack was and still is the real danger.

Humans Eat Sharks

Today, people eat many more sharks than sharks eat people. According to statistics kept by the Food and Agricultural Organization of the United Nations, global fisheries for sharks and their cousins, the skates and rays, land 850,000 metric tons every year (1997–2003). Commercial shark fisheries have operated in the United States since the 1930s, but they remained small and localized through the 1970s, occurring mostly in the southeast. Around this time, a growing leisure class of boaters brought a wave of interest in recreational fishing for sharks. By some estimates, their landings approached the commercial catch. The U.S. commercial landings for 1979 were estimated to reach a high of 11,523 metric tons but have declined dramatically due to overfishing. By 1989 commercial landings reached only 7,122 metric tons. Jack Casey, an early visionary fishery biologist, established a NOAA-NMFS shark-tagging program in the 1960s that grew to involve sport and commercial fishermen. By 2002 over 160,000 sharks had been tagged. The program advocates the tagging and release of sharks to better understand their movements and biology as an alternative to landing sharks.

Prosperity in Asian countries in the 1980s and 1990s led to the widespread consumption of shark fin soup as a luxury and cultural item. Ironically, there is little food value from the shark fins in the soup. The shark ingredients are the cartilaginous supportive fin rays (ceratotrichia) from the dorsal and other large fins. Taste and nutrition come from other ingredients. The shark fin market draws from worldwide fisheries and selects for species with "superior" long fin rays, such as the great hammerhead, sandbar, and blacktip sharks. Because only the dried fin brings a high price, often twenty to thirty times the value of the flesh, which, unlike the fins, must be refrigerated, a fishery practice known as "finning" arose. The shark need not be boated, just "finned" at the rail and dropped alive, but mortally wounded, to endure a slow death on the sea floor.

The practice was slowed in 1993 by the first U.S. NOAA-NMFS fishery management plan for sharks of Western North Atlantic waters. Similar plans were adopted by U.S. western coastal states, Hawaii, Australia, South Africa, Canada, and New Zealand. Several other countries are drafting shark management plans. In the U.S. Plan, thirty-nine species of sharks were divided into three categories (large coastal, small coastal, and pelagic sharks) for the purpose of assessment and management. The groups are based on the fisheries that take these species rather than on the ecological characteristics of shark populations. The objective of the plan was to prevent overfishing, but by the time it was implemented the subject species were either fully exploited or already overfished. Management efforts have been refined and broadened, but because of their slow growth and low reproductive rates, signs of shark stock recovery in U.S. waters, even after decades of management, have been few. The blue shark, like many other species, knows no boundaries and swims in the open sea, on waters that touch many countries. International coordination and cooperation for worldwide fisheries conservation and management of sharks and other large pelagic animals, such as swordfish, tuna, dolphins, whales, and sea turtles, that share these large marine ecosystems is needed to manage these oceanic species.

Sharks Eat Humans

Although sharks capture the imagination and the fear of myriads of people, the number of humans that they actually maim or kill is minuscule. Statistically most humans die from many well-known medical conditions related to age and condition. Viruses and microorganisms also kill millions in third-world countries. In prosperous countries, early accidental death comes from motor vehicles and household accidents.

Peter Benchley's 1974 blockbuster book and subsequent movie "Jaws" changed the way we look at sharks today. The media is a great magnifying mirror. Books, television, and movies can bring our greatest fears to life. Sharks are a favorite subject for many people.

Before "Jaws," the sharks known by most seamen, divers, fishermen, filmmakers, and the military were the "requiem sharks," members of the Carcharhinidae, a large family that includes the tiger, bull, dusky, lemon, blacktip, and oceanic whitetip sharks but not the white shark. Benchley very carefully assembled his story around the few horrific but poorly understood attacks on humans by the white shark (*Carcharodon carcharias*), particularly the attacks in New Jersey in the summer of 1916. To this he added factual elements of the impressive size and aggressive behavior of some white sharks around boats gleaned from the popular and scientific literature and from his personal experience with Frank Mundus, a white shark hunter from Montauk, New York. With this solid base and excellent writing, Benchley changed the species of focus and galvanized the way we currently view sharks and shark attacks.

Shark attacks on humans are recorded in the International Shark Attack File (ISAF); the scientific record of worldwide shark attacks and fatalities administered by George Burgess at the University of Florida. The ISAF was a result of a Shark Research Panel that formed following a 1958 conference in New Orleans. The ISAF researchers have done an admirable job over the years with the task of putting sharks and attacks in perspective. According to Burgess, there are probably 70–100 shark attacks annually worldwide, resulting in 5 to 15 deaths. Statistics such as these are difficult to derive and authenticate because of poor reporting from third-world countries. Attacks have increased proportionally with human population increases. Where large shark populations conflict with human density in major residential centers such as Durban, South Africa, and Sydney, Australia, the likelihood of attack increases. Morbidity has declined significantly due to the advent of emergency services and improved medical treatment. Sharks play a minute role in accidental deaths when compared to vehicle accidents. In animal-caused deaths, sharks fall far behind snakes, dogs, and even deer!

Even though we are not on the menu, man has learned to protect himself from sharks in many ways. Chemical repellents have been around since the 1940s, and recent versions are showing promise. Several models of a diver-carried electrical field generator that irritates the shark's sensitive electromagnetic sensory systems also show promise. Less sophisticated but simpler in design are the chain-mail suits with kevlar panels and the old stand-by, the anti-shark cage. To date the most effective shark control method for beaches has been to "mesh" or net them with offshore semi-barrier nets. Their purpose is not to fence off the beach but rather to catch and kill the resident shark populations. This practice can upset the local ecology and cause undesirable fish and other species to flourish.

A New View of Humans and Sharks

Sharks are a natural part of the life of the oceans. They are not malicious toward man or other animals. To put sharks in perspective, we must first understand what they are and are not. Sharks are fish, large, awesome and carnivorous. But they are still fish with highly evolved, streamlined, and efficient bodies. Their life history strategies are more conservative than most fish, more like those of terrestrial mammals. The nearly 400 species of sharks grow slowly on average and live a long time. Unlike most fish, sharks do not spawn; they copulate and after a lengthy gestation, typically bear a small number of live fully formed young. They are not primitive. Like humans they are still evolving and becoming better adapted to recent conditions. For example, some sharks have warm bodies and larger brains that rival birds and insectivous mammals in body size ratio and learning ability. Working from Mote Marine Laboratories with the cooperation of Albion College, the author has discovered that some sharks have much more complicated lives than we ever expected. In our 14-year study of nurse shark reproductive behavior, we have seen

Worldwide Shark Attacks 1990–2004

Year	Total Attacks	Fatal	Nonfatal
1990	35	2	33
1991	33	3	30
1992	48	6	42
1993	41	11	30
1994	57	7	50
1995	67	10	57
1996	43	3	40
1997	49	9	40
1998	51	6	45
1999	56	4	52
2000	78	11	67
2001	68	4	64
2002	63	3	60
2003	57	4	53
2004	61	7	54

From the International Shark Attack File (N = 807)

mating females avoid specific males and perhaps choose others that are more fit. Adult male behavior is likewise complex. We have filmed older male nurse sharks as they sacrifice their chance at mating to cooperate with another male and help him procreate. Maternal females of many species, such as the sandbar and blacktip shark, travel hundreds of miles to seek out specific nursery areas at just the right time for giving live birth to their young in relative safety. Those who study ocean ecology have discovered that sharks play an important role in maintaining the healthy condition of other species in the sea by eating the unfit, the sick, and the wounded and by balancing trophic energy flow in tropical ecosystems. Sharks are an ancient, natural, and necessary part of the oceans.

The Future for Sharks and Humans

Our images of the future show us visions of life without rich biology. Popular science fiction adventures often depict life on starships with exploration crews or colonists who have hydroponic gardens, edible and attractive lush plants, and a few small cute pets. No sharks or grizzly bears are aboard. Science fiction stories don't usually include life support for predators. Ideal futures don't show wild carnivores as desirable components, quite the opposite. The outlook for sharks in the near future is not good either. Three factors directly diminish shark populations: direct human exploitation (overfishing), food web effects (catching shark prey), and environmental degradation (pollution and coastal development). As parttime carnivores ourselves, sharks and man compete directly for ocean food resources. Indirectly we deprive sharks and many other species of vital coastal habitat by dredging and developing wetlands and necessary shallow inshore nursery areas. Sharks live and reign at the top of a multi-dimensional trophic energy pyramid. They are sometimes referred to as apex predators. All life is interconnected. The top levels of the pyramid are subordinate to the health and prosperity of all of the levels. With humans in the equation, sharks are impacted both from below and above. For their very survival and our own, sharks need us to be effective and sympathetic stewards of our planet ocean.

Further Resources

Bonfil, R. International plan of action for the conservation and management of sharks. http://www.fao.org/documents/show_cdr.asp?url_file=/docrep/006/x3170e/x3170e03.htm.

Castro, J. I. (1983). *The sharks of North American waters*. College Station, TX: Texas A&M University Press.

Ellis, R. (1983). *The book of sharks*. New York: Harcourt Brace and Jovanovich.

FAO statistics are from: http://www.fao.org/fi/statist/statist.asp.

International Shark Attack File. Retrieved March 16, 2006 from http://www.flmnh.ufl.edu/fish/sharks/statistics/statsw.htm.

Pratt, H. L., Jr., & Carrier, J. C. (2001). A review of elasmobranch reproductive behavior with a case study on the nurse shark, *Ginglymostoma cirratum*. *Environmental Biology of Fishes 60*, 157–88.

Harold "Wes" Pratt

Living with Animals
Snakes and Humans

Few species evoke stronger emotions than snakes: People hate them, love them, revile them, and revere them. Efficient predators, snakes kill their prey mainly by constricting or using venom. The use of snake venom evolved primarily to capture prey and secondarily for defense; in fact, of the world's 2,500 species of snakes, only 500 are venomous. In the United States, approximately 20 venomous species belong either to the cobra family (coral snakes) or the viper family (cottonmouths, copperheads, and rattlesnakes). Although 7,000 to 8,000 people a year are bitten by venomous snakes in the United States, only about five die, and 20 percent to 30 percent do not receive any venom at all. Given the extraordinarily small chance of being killed by a snake, why do many people hate snakes and kill them on sight? Lynne Isbell, an anthropologist at the University of California, Davis, believes that a fear of snakes forced human ancestors to develop improved vision and larger brains to better detect venomous snakes. If a fear of snakes is a universal human trait, however, all snake-related stories should be negative. But, for every myth and symbol portraying snakes as evil, many other stories and myths describe snakes in much more positive terms.

Using snakes to symbolize fertility dates back thousands of years. Around 1600 BCE, the Minoans in Crete fashioned a statue of a goddess with several snakes entwined around her body. Aboriginal groups in Australia, as well as ancient Mesopotamians, believed snakes symbolized fertility and life, because they shed their skin and "renew" themselves. One of the oldest symbols in the world, the Ouroboros (or Oroboros), depicts a snake grabbing its own tail in its mouth, symbolizing eternity or immortality. The Caduceus, the modern symbol for healing and medicine, shows two intertwined snakes wrapped around a winged staff. A person born under the sign of the snake in the Chinese calendar is wise, enigmatic, self-confident and patient. Hindus in India have a particular reverence for snakes, even venomous species; they worship them as gods, have built temples for them, and hold festivals to honor serpents. Each year, Indians celebrate the king cobra in their festival Nagpanchami, and the Lord Shiva, the creator in the Hindu religion, is often depicted with a king cobra around his neck.

Snakes are also perceived as guardians or protectors. Lord Vishnu, the force that guards all that exists in the Hindu religion, is portrayed as reclining on a snake. Statues depict Wadjet, an ancient Egyptian goddess, as a cobra, ready to strike anyone endangering the pharaoh. The Indian queen of the snakes, Manasadevi, possesses special powers that protect humans from snakebite. Hindu worshippers pray to snake idols for knowledge and wealth, and Prussians and Lithuanians also believed in snake gods. In the Bella Coola, a Native American tribe in the Pacific Northwest, snakes can appear as spouses of humans.

Other cultures associate snakes with negative symbols. Ancient Greek mythology describes battles between mortals and Medusa, with snakes on her head instead of hair, and the Hydra, a fearsome monster with multiple snake heads. Cleopatra committed suicide by an asp bite. Despite some positive statements (Jesus telling his apostles to be "as wise as serpents" in Matthew 10:16), the Christian religion makes strong connections between Satan and snakes. In Genesis (3:14), the snake tempts Adam and Eve with the forbidden fruit, and God curses the snake. God sent "fiery serpents" to plague Moses's people in the desert, until Moses crafted a bronze snake on a pole that cured people of snake bites (Num. 21:5–9), and in Psalms 91 the psalmist says that God instructs people to trample upon cobras.

Living with Snakes

Today, people still interact with snakes, either intentionally or unintentionally, in the wild or in captivity. Some species of snakes make docile pets, particularly the smaller species, such as corn snakes, garter snakes, rat snakes, king snakes, and ball pythons. People also own larger species, such as pythons and boas, but these species are very hard to keep once they reach their full length. Unfortunately, people who can't keep these larger snakes sometimes release them into the wild, causing major problems for native snake species and wildlife that become prey.

Snake handling by some Pentecostal churches in the United States began in Tennessee around 1908. "Believers" can "take up serpents," (Mark 16:18) without being hurt (Luke 10:19). After the deaths of several handlers, snake handling was banned, but believers continue to challenge the ban on First Amendment grounds. Currently, snake handling occurs mainly in the Appalachian states. Snake charmers in India and Pakistan use flutes to "charm" venomous cobras in their roadside shows. Snakes do not respond to the music, they do not have a well-developed sense of hearing, but rather to the flute's movement or the tapping of the charmer's foot. Despite the scary sight of a rearing cobra, charmers have a low chance of being bitten because a cobra strike tends to be slow and predictable. Because snakes are treated cruelly (many are not fed, have their fangs removed, or have their mouths sewn shut), some places have banned snake charming.

Negative Attitudes to Snakes

A controversial treatment of snakes that is believed by animal advocates to be unnecessary and cruel involves rattlesnake roundups, held in Texas, Oklahoma, Kansas, New Mexico, Pennsylvania, Alabama, and Georgia. First used to reduce snake populations, roundups rapidly evolved into community fund-raisers. Eastern diamondbacks, western diamondbacks, timber rattlesnakes, and western (prairie) rattlesnakes are the favorite species for roundups. To collect rattlesnakes, people often illegally pour gasoline or other chemicals into rattlesnake dens, damaging not only rattlesnakes but also other species (turtles, frogs, snakes, burrowing owls, raccoons, opossums, and invertebrates) and the environment. Captured snakes are stored for long periods of time, often without food or water, in crowded containers, where half of them die, according to Bruce Means, a professor at Florida State University. Surviving snakes are used in competitions during the roundup, and they almost always die, often by decapitation, a particularly cruel way of killing snakes because their oxygen requirement is so low that body parts can stay alive for hours. Before death, snakes are "milked" of their venom, which supposedly is sold to companies to make antivenin, but critics say that the venom is gathered under such unsanitary conditions that no reputable company would buy it. The dead snakes are then eaten and their skins sold.

The impact of roundups on snake populations is enormous. Many areas have severely reduced snake populations, and conservationists blame rattlesnake roundups (along with the loss of habitat). Sweetwater, Texas, holds the nation's largest roundup, and more than 18,000 rattlesnakes were taken from the wild in one weekend, according to the Humane Society of the United States. Defenders of roundups maintain that snake populations can sustain roundups, that snakes are not mistreated, and that they educate people. Critics say that roundups deplete an area of snakes, the public is misinformed, and small towns can raise money through less cruel methods.

How do people justify their mistreatment and killing of snakes? Many people believe snakes are dangerous and aggressive; when they see a snake, they kill it. An estimated 50 percent of Americans have some degree of anxiety when they see a snake, and 20 percent are terrified even by snake pictures. This irrational fear, termed ophidiophobia, far exceeds the actual risk of getting bitten. John Stilgoe from Harvard University believes that people are afraid of nature because they are increasingly isolated from it, so they take drastic steps to reduce all risk, including never straying off of paved trails for fear of being bitten by a snake. The media also perpetuates myths and misconceptions about the danger from snakes. Most movies present snakes as dangerous, evil, and aggressive, such as in *Snakes on a Plane* (2006), the Harry Potter movies, and *Python* (2000), which involves a man-eating, impossibly large, python.

Fortunately, negative attitudes toward snakes are changing. The American Zoo and Aquarium Association and various zoos have condemned rattlesnake roundups and feature educational displays about the benefits of snakes. Some state wildlife agencies use their Web sites to describe the value of snakes in ecosystems. Pennsylvania outlawed killing snakes during roundups, and groups against roundups distribute flyers and lobby lawmakers to make them illegal. Educational programs aimed at children and adults use television and radio ads, written materials, and interviews to increase awareness of the value of snakes. Despite these positive first steps, much more needs to be done toward increasing the public's understanding and tolerance of snakes, a vital necessity if snake species are to be saved from persecution and possible extinction.

Further Resources

Greene, H. W. (2000). *Snakes: The evolution of mystery in nature*. Berkeley: University of California Press.

Kellert, S. R. (2003). *Kinship to mastery: Biophilia in human evolution and development*. Washington, DC: Island Press.

Manning, A. (1994). *Animals and human society: Changing perspectives*. New York: Routledge.

Menez, A. (2003). *The subtle beast: Snakes, from myth to medicine*. New York: Taylor and Francis.

Shepard, P. (1997). *The others: How animals made us human*. Washington, DC: Island Press.

Heidi Marcum

Living with Animals
Wildlife and Humans in the U.S. National Parks

When you think of wild animals what thoughts and feelings emerge in your mind and heart? For example, does a grizzly bear, large moose, or mountain lion image appear in your brain as a pleasurable reverie or a nightmare? Human relationships with wildlife are often part of any natural or cultural story preserved in the United States national parks. Visitor surveys have shown that observing wildlife is often the major reason to visit national parks. Being stuck in an "animal jam" while driving in many parks can quickly demonstrate how strong the desire is for most humans to encounter an animal in the wild. There is always some opportunity to encounter a member of the wild animal world in national parks either directly or indirectly. How we experience that encounter, both emotionally and intellectually depends upon many factors. As humans, we come from many different cultural, social, and economic backgrounds with diverse personal experiences with members of the animal world. Our interactions with animals usually differ if the relationship is with a wild, domesticated, or pet animal.

When we think about human societal and personal relationships with animals we most likely are referring to some level of value attached to a particular kind of animal. The value we attach to an animal often is related to the context within which we encounter it. In today's virtual world, it seems direct experiences with animals, certainly wild animals, is becoming a rare event. During our lives we have various indirect contacts with representations of animals in books, films, exhibits, zoos, and various other circuitous experiences that filter our perceptions of and values ascribed to animals. National parks are places where humans can develop, examine, explore, and discover personal relationships with members of the wild animal kingdom in natural surroundings. This entry will focus on the human relationships with wild animals contained within the U.S. national park system, recognizing that even in this setting, there is great variety in how individuals relate to the predator, the prey and species type. Although this entry focuses on the U.S. national parks, there are similar experiential possibilities in other parks and preserves in the United States and around the world.

Wildlife and National Parks: Some History

Managers of national parks are charged with protecting a variety of natural and cultural resources. Among resources to be protected and enjoyed by all of us is "wild life." Wildlife in national parks includes everything from large animals or "mega-fauna" such as bears and moose, to the tiniest microscopic creatures. It is important to understand that the park service mission is to protect these resources as well as provide opportunities for people to enjoy and experience them without compromising their continued existence, hence, their conservation.

The first national park was established by the Yellowstone Park Act that made Yellowstone the first national park in the world in 1872. This marks a significant event in the conservation and preservation of natural resources, including wild animals and their supporting habitats. It was an idea that would spread, but not without controversy, and included recreational and economic concerns as well as the protection of natural resources. Still, it was an important initial step and in part reflects a societal value placed on conservation of wild animals in their natural habitats. However, the value and perceptions of people toward animals during that period in history differed somewhat from those of today.

How wild animals were perceived and valued is reflected in how wild animals were managed in the national park system during those early years. Beginning in 1872, when national parks began to come into existence, there was no National Park Service. In fact, it was many years before the creation of the National Park Service we know today. It is important to understand that the National Park Service was established by Congress through the Organic Act of 1916, to preserve and protect the natural and cultural resources in national park units for future human generations. Specifically, the fundamental purpose of the national parks is "to conserve the scenery and the natural and historic objects and the wild life therein and to provide for the enjoyment of the same in such manner and by such means as will leave them unimpaired for the enjoyment of future generations."

Protection of animals in national parks is specifically part of the fundamental purpose of the parks but what animals and how they are to be protected is not really specified. In the early years of Yellowstone many animals such as bison, elk, grizzly bear, eagles, ravens, and wolves found good habitat in the region but were valued differently compared with today. In fact early public ranger programs portrayed predators, the wolf for example, as a "bad" animal and a threat to "good" animals such as elk. Predatory wolves were considered undesirable and systematically extirpated from park areas, whereas more preferential species were actively cared for. Despite increased ecological knowledge since learned that indicates the errors of this approach, such perceptions persisted until very recent times and are still controversial in some circles. Bear shows were staged in some parks, such as Yellowstone, Yosemite, Mt. Rainier, and Sequoia Kings Canyon. Bleachers were erected in Yellowstone near garbage dumps for visitors to observe bears feeding during the 1920s. Bison stampedes were staged for the enjoyment of visitors.

It was shortly after passage of the Organic Act that two scientists, Joseph Grinnell and Tracy Storer, published an article in *Science* magazine entitled "Animal life as an asset of national parks" that called for the study of how park resources, including animal life, should be studied scientifically. Management of resources could then be based on scientifically derived knowledge, provided such studies were undertaken. The point of this bit of history is to show how perceptions of animals and our relationships with them change over time. Most certainly our perceptions are influenced by understanding and appreciation of animal behavior and ecology.

It was during the late 1930s and early 1940s that National Park Service policies began to change reflecting the views that bear shows and the like were not only harmful and dangerous to both animal and visitor but also misrepresented the natural habitats and behaviors of wild animals. Regulations and educational campaigns were begun to minimize contacts between wildlife and people. Some animals once extirpated from national parks have now been returned, for example, wolves, otters, and condors. Indeed, societal perceptions of wild animals change over time and have been reflected in the policies of the national parks since the establishment of Yellowstone. It is an interesting history to explore and we have only briefly touched on it in this essay. Nonetheless, many of these new ideas about management and public access to wildlife remain controversial to this day as values and perceptions change and evolve.

Animal Encounters in National Parks

National parks provide humans with opportunities to discover many tangible and intangible meanings associated with animals. What feelings emerge as the howling of wolves reverberates in your very bones? Does a bobcat's shrilling cry cutting through an early morning mist bring a quiver to your skin? As a bald eagle, condor, or snowy owl glides across your path, are your senses transported to a different place and time? Maybe your humdrum random thoughts are startled by the appearance of a timber rattlesnake, orb spider, or delightfully colored snail. Perhaps some ancient memory stirs in your mind's eye at the sight of an alligator, a sea turtle, or a cave bat. Do you wonder how people depended on sea animals for their survival when you hover beneath clear ocean waters spying the life of a reef that seems indifferent to your presence? Maybe you experience a sudden chill of excitement when suddenly wild schools of fish jump and dart near the banks of mountain streams that break your pace during a hot summer hike. Do you imagine yourself in harmony with the world when you encounter a singing painted bunting, croaking tree frog, or squeaking prairie dog? Perhaps you feel in competition for your well-being when confronted with a twitching winged wasp, a sharp toothed barracuda, or snorting buffalo? Are you impressed by how young black bear cubs are tended by their mothers, or the community effort to protect hatchling birds by adult members of the colony. Are you shocked by the idea that newly hatched sea turtles must immediately scurry to the sea before being devoured by predators? Human relationships with wildlife are varied just as many other human relationships can be. These are just a few images that might be imagined and directly experienced in many national parks. It is challenging for all of us to explore, understand, and appreciate the diverse human values inherent in the wild animals that survive in national parks today.

Animals, Big, Small, Seen, Unseen, and Long Gone

The national parks protect many different kinds of habitats critical to many species of migratory birds, from large raptors such as eagles, hawks, and owls to scavenger birds such as the recently restored California condors in Grand Canyon National Park. Shorebirds and many kinds of aquatic birds can be observed in national parks along seashores, lakeshores, and rivers, and just about every park includes a plethora of small songbirds. In fact, national parks are among the best places to observe wild birds. Nearly every imaginable bird habitat, from arctic tundra to tropical rainforests, are represented, providing critical breeding, migratory stopover, and wintering habitat for a great variety of birds.

Research suggests that most visitors to national parks prefer to observe the large mammals and birds over the smaller and less observable mammals, reptiles, amphibians, and invertebrates. The site of a wild and free bull moose even from a safe distance can be an absolutely thrilling encounter. I have a vivid memory of such an encounter while visiting the Grand Teton National Park in Wyoming. I focused on his huge antlers as he grazed, periodically looking up and giving me a cautious glance. He allowed me to share the same relative wild space as long as I kept my distance. I stood motionless for close to an hour just watching this large animal carry out the simple task of eating. There are similar exhilarating experiences with much smaller creatures such as watching a solitary digger wasp busily excavate a tunnel in the ground and then provision the hole with captured insects as food for her larval offspring she will lay in the nest. Watching a land snail crawling along a trail side may at first appear quite uninspiring until one realizes that the bulky-looking shell is imperative for its survival much as my backpack provides me with some life protection in the wild. Sometimes just being in a space or habitat where animals are known to live, despite their cryptic behavior, offers us an opportunity to feel their presence even though we may never see them. You may or may not agree, but for this writer, just the knowledge that such animals are present fills me with wonder, and at times even a tinge of fear, but a good fear in knowing that animals such as the rattlesnake or mountain lion are free to roam and share the same space as I. Does this feeling awaken some deeply buried archetype that hides in the evolution of our psychology? Can just hearing the sounds made by an animal, smelling its musk, or spotting a lump of dung left behind, or even more exciting, spying a paw track or some other intangible evidence of an animal's presence, stimulates us to wonder, imagine, perhaps even appreciate our own freedoms to be who we are? Many animals are reclusive, very small, active only at night, and well camouflaged, and some are just too dangerous to see up close. The majority of animals, the all important species that constitute the base of the food chain, often go unnoticed but have value for us all to discover and understand.

There are many intangible relationships with animals that can be experienced in national parks. Some of our national parks, most notably Dinosaur National Monument, help us to make contact with the "wildlife" of the distant past. This park unit protects a large deposit of fossilized bones of animals that lived millions of years ago. The dinosaurs remains protected within this national park lived in the middle of the Age of Dinosaurs, about 150 million years ago. Since we can't see a live Apatosaurus or Allosaurus these days, we can only experience their tangible fossil bones and teeth and try to build an understanding and a relationship with these animals now long gone.

Opportunities to observe animals and animal signs in national parks can offer us experiences that can help us understand the human-animal relationships of people in the distant past. Oysters are a common site at low tide in the marshlands of the Timucuan Ecological & Historic Preserve and other similar parks. In the Timucuan Preserve, almost as common on the upland areas are ancient Indian shell middens, demonstrating how ancient Native Americans depended on these animals for survival. Native people who were living in the area at the time of first European contact are known as Timucua, whereby the Preserve derives its name. When I see an old oyster shell atop an ancient midden, I am transported back in time and realize the animal that occupied the shell lived long ago and succumbed to predation by an ancient human being whose relationship with that animal was different but at the same time similar to my relationship with oysters that continue to survive in the area today. Perhaps an ancient Indian wondered about the oyster's life as I have. Did the ancient Indian ponder the snapping noises emanating from the marsh muds that appeared to be made by the living oyster or some other sympatric species such as the snapping shrimp? Perhaps the ancient Indian was thankful for the source of food that would feed him or herself and the rest of the family. It is interesting to wonder about the relationships between ancient humans and the once living oyster.

National parks provide us all with opportunities to explore our personal relationships with animals as well as the relationships between animals and other humans both past and present.

Controversial Human Relationships with Animals in National Parks

Because of the diversity of perceptions among a diverse citizenry, the values and kinds of experiences humans seek in today's national parks are varied and often result in conflicts about how national parks manage wildlife and people. Some visitors appear to be unaware of how wild animals behave in their natural surrounding and either underestimate or overestimate the danger of animals when encountered. It is important for visitors to gain an understanding and appreciation for wild animal behavior. Some well-meaning visitors to national parks attempt to engage wild animals in their desire to relate to them. Unfortunately, attempts to touch or feed animals can trigger an aggressive response from the animal who does not understand the human intentions. Feeding or touching can also foster dependence on human sources of food that may not always be available. Human attempts to closely approach a wild animal can also cause the animal to become used to human presence. In the case of large predatory animals, such as grizzly bears, human interaction can lead to serious consequences for both human and animal. For many species, once an animal loses it natural caution or even fear of humans, the animal may become more aggressive. Experiences and educational programs in national parks can facilitate understanding and appreciation and can assist the visitor in building a personal relationship with wild animals without endangering the animal or the visitor.

Some national park units allow hunting and fishing. Hunting of wild animals and recreational fishing is valued by many people. This is certainly a controversial issue in many national park units that allow hunting or fishing during prescribed seasons. Public harvest (hunting or trapping) of wildlife in units of the national park system may be allowed only when hunting, trapping, subsistence use, or other harvesting is specifically authorized by statute or regulation and not subsequently prohibited by regulation. Where harvesting is allowed and subject to National Park Service control, the Service will allow harvesting only when the Service has determined that the harvesting will not unacceptably impact park resources or natural processes, including the natural distributions, densities, age-class distributions, and behavior of harvested species.

The objectives of fishing programs in national parks include the following: the management of aquatic resources as an important part of the ecosystem; the preservation and restoration of native fishes and their habitats; and to provide recreational fishing opportunities for the enjoyment of park visitors that is consistent with the first two objectives. Nonetheless, there are many people who believe that hunting or fishing is an interaction with animals that should not be condoned or allowed in national parks. How these particular human-animal relationships will evolve in national parks and in society remains to be seen.

There are many conflicting values and issues that impinge on human-animal relationships in national parks. A few other value conflicts can serve as examples. Snowmobile use is a popular though controversial means of winter transportation in many units of the National Park System. A concern is that increasing numbers of snowmobiles in the parks might be affecting wildlife, from large ungulates and carnivores to small mammals that burrow under the snow. Of particular interest are changes in animal behavior, mortality, susceptibility to disease, and population size that might be related to snowmobile use. For example, what impact do noises associated with human activities in parks have on the behaviors of various animals that exchange calls and other sound-producing mechanisms during mating season?

Some animals are considered pests because they threaten the survival of other animal or plant species, or threaten cultural resources such as historic structures, landscapes, and features. In many national park areas today there exists animal species that did not evolve or arrive in the area under natural conditions. Referred to as exotic or alien species, these animals may adversely impact park resources, including other native animal species. These alien species can be introduced by accident or purposefully by humans or by human-induced changes in the environment. The National Park Service itself in earlier times introduced species such as alien fish for the purpose of providing for visitor enjoyment (fishing) that have since impacted native species (for example, the introduction of Rainbow trout into the rivers of the Great Smoky Mountains National Park that severely impacted the native Brook trout). New National Park Service policies that direct removal of such detrimental alien species often become quite contentious when eradication or control programs are instituted. It depends on one's view with regard to the value of the alien species and/or what is being protected by the removal of the animal. Most agree however, that the animals be "removed" in a humane manner.

In some instances an animal species may present a public health threat. Integrated pest management (IPM) is a science-based, decision making process that coordinates knowledge of pest biology, the environment, and available technology to prevent unacceptable levels of pest damage while posing the least possible risk to people, resources, and the environment. Some microorganisms in parks cause disease that must be managed; however, native diseases may be part of a naturally functioning ecosystem protected within a park. Rather than attempting to eradicate all "bad" organisms that cause disease in animals (the way that "bad" predatory animals were eliminated in earlier times), park managers and National Park Service veterinarians try to preserve the health of entire ecosystems.

Volumes could be written about all the values conflicts that arise when considering human and animal relationships in national parks. We have only touched on some of the more salient issues. Our values of and relationships with animals are often as diverse as our ethnic, cultural, and experiential backgrounds. There is little doubt that our relationships with wild animals are important on many levels in the U.S. national parks. National parks have been places where people can experience animals in their natural surroundings. The kinds of experiences and interactions with animals that people desire in national parks have evolved and are reflected in some ways by National Park Service laws and policies. The laws and policies will continue to evolve and change as human-animal relationships change. It seems apparent that wild animals allowed to roam free and engage in their natural behaviors provide us all with opportunities to explore our own personal relationships with each animal. National parks provide a forum for experiencing and exploring many human-animal relationships and associated values, and perhaps is one of the most important reasons to protect the national parks and the wildlife therein.

Further Resources

Albright, H. M. (1929). Our national parks as wildlife sanctuaries. *American Forests and Forest Life, 35*, 505–7.

———. (1931). National parks predator policy. *Journal of Mammalogy, 12*, 185–86.

Bulbeck, C. (2005). *Facing the wild: Ecotourism, conservation, and animal encounters.* London & Sterling, VA: Earthscan Publications.

Calalane, V. H. (1961). Public hunting in the National Parks. *Atlantic Naturalist, 16*(3), 191–92.
Chase, A. (1986). *Playing God in Yellowstone*. Boston: Atlantic Monthly Press Books.
Grinnell, J. B., & Storer, T. (1916). Animal life as an asset of National Parks. *Science, 44*, 375–80.
McNamee, T. (1997). *The return of the wolf to Yellowstone*. New York: Henry Holt & Company.
Moulton, M.P., & Sanderson, J. (1997). *Wildlife issues in a changing world*. Delray Beach, Florida: St. Lucie Press.
Sellars, R. W. (1997). *Preserving nature in the national parks: A history*. New Haven & London: Yale University Press.
Wright, R. G. (1992). *Wildlife research and management in the national parks*. Urbana & Chicago. University of Illinois Press.
The U.S. National Park Service. http://www.nps.gov/
Other Web sites of the National Park Service: http://www.nature.nps.gov/biology/wildlifehealth/
http://www.nature.nps.gov/biology/ipm/
http://www.nature.nps.gov/biology/migratorybirds/

Daniel R. Tardona

Living with Animals
Wolf Emotions Observed

Wolves have been demonized for centuries, seen as bloodthirsty beasts haunting our nightmares. Determined to dispel this myth and to show the true nature of wolves as compassionate family animals, both playful and affectionate, nature filmmakers Jim and Jamie Dutcher lived six years in tented camps in the wilderness of Idaho among a pack of wolves, listening to them and earning their trust.

Jim and Jamie: When we began our study on wolves, there were only about fifty wild wolves left in the entire American West. Over the previous two centuries, more than two million wolves had been poisoned, shot, or trapped. One of the legendary noble creatures of the wilderness was headed straight for extinction.

Already cautious and elusive by nature, wolves have learned to fear and avoid humans, making it all but impossible to get close enough to observe and photograph their social behavior. A chance glimpse of this animal in its wild habitat is a rare and thrilling event.

Photographing wolves in the wild can also cause unsettling disturbances in their behavior and problems with their well-being. A wild wolf that has become habituated to humans doesn't have long to live—the next time someone points an object at that wolf, it might be a gun instead of a camera.

Jim: In filming the wolf, our goal was to observe not as scientists but as social partners. I knew from years of experience as a nature cinematographer that even seeing a wolf in the wild is a rare occurrence. Getting them to reveal their social structure, their manner of communication, and their intimate family life would require special conditions. I wanted to come as close as humanly possible to experiencing life inside a wolf pack. Although the politics, science, and history of wolves are fascinating subjects, my intention was to show their inner lives and inner workings and to understand their essence.

Adapted from "Living with Wolves" by Jim and Jamie Dutcher, published by The Mountaineers Books, 2005.

Jim and Jamie: Building on our previous experiences with wildlife and in consultation with biologists and wolf experts, our solution was to form our own pack of wolves. We acquired four pups that were ten days old from a wolf rescue organization in Montana. Acting as surrogate parents, we bottle-fed these newborn pups from the day they opened their eyes in order to establish a complete trust with them. We simulated a mother's care as best we could by using warm, damp rags to imitate her tongue and by holding the pups in blankets to replicate her body heat and fur. We fed the young wolf pups a specially modified canine puppy formula every four to six hours, and after a feeding the pups would fall asleep in our laps. With the help of our small, dedicated crew we worked in shifts so someone was with the pups at all times.

These intense sessions formed the basis for gaining the trust of the wolves—a relationship that grew into a lifelong bond. On the edge of the Idaho wilderness, we enclosed acres of streams, ponds, forests, and meadows, providing ample space and freedom for the wolves to live as a fully functional pack. For six continuous years, on an intimate level we camped among the wolves, observing and photographing their fascinating behavior, antic play, and complex social life.

For our own reference, we gave the wolves names, using the Lakota Sioux, Blackfoot, and Nez Perce languages to describe qualities that might characterize a wolf. Because the wolves were wild animals, we never tried to teach them their names. In any case, by nature the wolves would not respond to being summoned by name as a domestic pet would.

Jamie: Although we tried to remain pragmatic, we bonded with the wolves as much as they bonded with us. Our accounts are based on our feelings and experiences as filmmakers and as human beings. This perspective allowed us a range of speculation that might make a scientist uncomfortable. We were, however, extremely careful not to be swayed by fantasy or to make the wolves out to be more than they are. In the end, they are neither demons nor deities, but incredible and inspiring creatures in their own right. We set out to capture their lives on film and to show a side of them that is often overlooked by scientists and politicians. What we ultimately experienced went well beyond our expectations. They opened up their lives to us and accepted us as part of their world.

Jim and Jamie: Similar to a human being, a wolf bases its life on a social structure of family and community. Examination of the social behavior of wolves reveals a sophisticated and caring animal whose well-being results from an interdependent and complex social system.

Based on strong family ties and allegiances, the pack is held together by trust, instinct, and the DNA of thousands of years of evolved wolf society. A pack is an extended family of brothers, sisters, aunts, and uncles. Led by the alpha male and alpha female, pack life is ordered around a strictly enforced social hierarchy in which every wolf has a specific rank and role. The hierarchy among mid-ranking wolves seems fluid and prone to frequent shifts. On the other hand, the roles of alpha and omega—the top and bottom of the hierarchy—are usually fixed. They seldom change except under serious conditions such as the death or injury of another pack member.

A hierarchy with clearly established leadership also offers the best chance for a successful hunt, with each member playing a mutually supportive role. Over tens of thousands of years, wolves evolved this survival strategy of sustaining each individual by performing as a team. Not collaborating could mean a missed meal. And there is safety in numbers—an orchestrated attack with many wolves acting as one synchronized organism enables them to take down large game such as moose or elk and lessens the ever-present risk of serious injury.

However, the social hierarchy is about more than just competition and hunting strategy. Wolves develop trust in one another from lifelong bonds that reinforce a sense that they *belong* to a particular family and a specific pack. Cooperation extends into other aspects of their social life: rearing young, caring for injured members, defending territory.

The pack hierarchy generally has parallel lines of dominance for each sex. The alpha male dominates the entire pack. The beta, or second-rank, wolf dominates the mid-ranking wolves, also called subordinates. All adult wolves dominate the wolves in the lowest position—the omega male and omega female.

Although this social structure is strict, in that there will always be an alpha, a beta, and an omega—with numerous mid-ranking wolves—a wolf's specific position within the hierarchy can change with circumstances. An aging alpha with diminished health may be forced to retire, his once-confident demeanor replaced by sudden deference to a new leader. A scrappy and aggressive beta may then assume the alpha role and evolve more altruistic and relaxed traits befitting a leader. However, holding the beta position—"second in command"—does not automatically assure a wolf succession to the alpha role. In the Sawtooth Pack, for example, Matsi's beta rank was secure only as long as Kamots remained the alpha. The pack is an interdependent entity, and the reasons for position within the pack are complex and not always predictable or understood, except by the wolves themselves.

Jim: Whether by themselves or in the company of other pack members, wolves play with a variety of objects: branches, sticks, rocks, and clumps of hide can serve as toys. During filming, anything not nailed down was fair game—often never to be seen again or seen again in barely recognizable bits and pieces. Lens caps, gloves, tools, and, especially, my hat were all hotly coveted. Kamots the alpha was notorious for his stalking and stealthy confiscation of these prizes. Once in possession of the new treasure, he would prance about, playfully tossing and displaying the new item—daring people and wolves alike to "come and get it."

Jamie: Often, the omega wolf acts like a court jester to lighten the mood of the pack. Lakota the omega would grab a stick or an old bone, sometimes twirling it like a baton over his head, and race off into the meadow, inviting the others to chase him. The thrill of the game was usually enough to get the others to join in readily. Lakota often coaxed Kamots into a game of tag in which the alpha and omega both took turns being "it." Scientists might disdain the thought of assigning emotions to an animal, but since I'm not a scientist, I have no trouble calling it the way I see it. Witnessing scenes of play such as this, it appeared to me that the usual grimace of the beleaguered omega was replaced with what looked like a smile of pure joy.

Many years later, while filming through the open door of a small airplane, Jim and I watched a pack of wolves along the Yukon River. The wolves were engaged in a spirited game of tag, and I was caught in the reverie of similar moments with the Sawtooth Pack. As the wolves below chased and nipped each other's tails, I could imagine their expressions of joy. I knew that one of the wolves below me was the omega, keeping the tradition of the game alive.

Jim and Jamie: We decided to film the wolves in slow motion to better capture their grace and beauty. However, this technique ended up providing much more than just beautiful footage. Because many of the nuances of a wolf's behavior happen so quickly, they are difficult to see in real time, so filming in slow motion suddenly revealed swift gestures such as a quick cock of the head or a brief flash of fang. Reviewing these scenes frame by frame, we were able to examine subtle interactions that we had failed to notice earlier.

Wolves continually communicate with each other, sorting out their social positions and reinforcing the stability of the pack. For example, one wolf resting its head over the top of another wolf's back is a sign of affection, but it is also a gentle indication of dominance. Certain sounds or gestures find unmistakable parallels in human communication; others defy all attempts at translation.

The range of vocalizations, body language, facial expressions, personalities, and behaviors that we witnessed and recorded over the years coalesced to suggest an intricate and rich emotional component to the inner life of wolves. We believe that our experiences with the Sawtooth Pack provide not only a glimpse into the private lives of wolves but also a way for us to better comprehend our own humanity. The validity of interpreting the emotions of a wolf is, of course, open to argument, and a scientist may steadfastly resist this temptation. Most scientists will allow, however, that wolves do appear to express complex feelings.

The wolf hierarchy exhibits displays of care, empathy, and collaboration as well as contention. We observed and filmed ferocious behavior associated with establishing and maintaining pack hierarchy, but we also witnessed and recorded traits that humans admire, including the extremely affectionate and playful behavior associated with bonding as a family unit. Few animals on earth display the same intensity of commitment to family in the collaborative care of their young. Expressions of joy are evident at the birth of new pups, as are those of sorrow when a pack member dies. Play, complex in its rules and manifestations, is essential to the emotional stability of the pack.

Jamie: Jim often recalls how Motaki, the earliest pack omega was a submissive and sometimes fearful scapegoat of the pack. Yet she had an endearing ability to inspire the most spirited bouts of play. She seemed to organize games in part to deflect abuse away from herself. In any case, her role was critical to the cohesion and well-being of the pack.

One unforgettable morning, Jim made a terrible discovery. Motaki had been killed by a mountain lion that had managed to scale the fence and enter the enclosure. For the six weeks that followed her death, the pack did not play. What had been a daily occurrence stopped altogether. When the wolves passed through the aspen grove where she had been killed, they became quiet, their tails drooping noticeably. When they howled, Jim noted that the sound had an eerie quality; very different from the normal riotous pack rallies. Jim could come to only one conclusion: the wolves were in mourning.

Jim: All the wolves displayed great sensitivity and often acted with a unified mood. However, one particular pack member embodied all the qualities that humans find so admirable in wolves. This was Matsi, the ever-dutiful beta wolf.

As I reflect on our years of living with the Sawtooth Pack, Matsi, the beta, embodied all that was magical about them. Matsi patrolled their territory and took a central role in the care of the pups—almost exhausting himself keeping track of all of them and regurgitating half his food to keep them well fed. He maintained peace and order in the pack—and amid all this, he seemed completely content not to rule. Although competition among pack members is prevalent, Matsi always had the good of the pack in mind. Through Matsi, I realized that the workings of a wolf society are deeper and more complex than I could ever imagine.

Matsi possessed an intangible quality that is still difficult to describe. He always conducted himself with calm dignity. For Matsi, the well-being of the pack was paramount—the cohesion of the family was more important than anything. He wasn't terribly concerned with what we humans were up to, but he did seem to enjoy our company. Sometimes he would come and sit beside me—never actively soliciting my attention, never expecting anything, just spending time with a friend.

When I filmed the pack during the mayhem of feeding and then reviewed the many separate incidents in slow motion, Jamie and I began to see Matsi's role as peacekeeper and as a protector of Lakota, the omega. At first it seemed that Matsi was part of the pack jostling for meat and abusing Lakota in the process. When we viewed the film in slow motion, however, we could see that Matsi was actually forcibly inserting his body between Lakota and his aggressors. He was in effect "body checking" the other wolves out of the way, offering Lakota temporary protection and the opportunity to scramble for cover.

Jim and Jamie: We have not only seen this evidence with our own eyes but also heard similar scientific accounts of wild packs throughout North America. A biologist in Alaska told us of a wolf skull he had found that bore evidence of a broken jaw that had subsequently healed. A wolf with a broken jaw cannot bite, chew, or tear meat from a carcass, so how did this wolf survive? The biologist's only conclusion is that its pack cared for it until its jaw healed, regurgitating semi-digested food for it, as they would do for a pup. Another report in Canada tells of a wolf pack that lost a member at the hands of a poacher. The biologist who was tracking them reported that the pack moved in a figure-eight pattern for several days, howling frequently. His explanation is that they were searching in vain for their lost pack mate.

These scientific reports always stop short of attributing higher emotions to animal behavior. Given our experience with the Sawtooth Pack, however, we found it impossible to support the view that human beings hold a monopoly on elevated feelings such as empathy and compassion. In particular, this is the gift Matsi gave us, and it is also the most important message we can share about living with wolves.

See also

Conservation and Environment—*Coyotes, Humans, and Coexistence*
Conservation and Environment—*Wolf and Human Conflicts: A Long, Bad History*
Ethics and Animal Protection—*Wolf Recovery*

Further Resources

Dutcher, J., & Dutcher, J. (2005). *Living with wolves.* Seattle, WA: Mountaineers Books.

Jim and Jamie Dutcher

Media and Film
Advertising and Animals

In the United States particularly, advertising—calling attention to a product or business—is an important part of the economy. Many products are made familiar to the public specifically through creative advertising, and people respond by buying the product and ensuring the success of the business. Advertisers need to think of ways to catch people's attention. Since animals and nature are also important to a large part of our population, it is common to see ads with animals being the primary focus. Advertising with animals can make people think there is some connection with the product and nature.

Generally, there are three ways that businesses use animals in advertising: First, and most obvious, is representing animals as themselves. This is most common in an ad in which a very cute dog or puppy is used to sell dog food or cats and kittens are shown playing with some new cat product—clearly implying that if these cats and dogs like these things, then surely will your favorite pet!

Another way animals have been used in advertising is as symbols for something else. Many animals have become symbolic for qualities or attributes that are desirable. For instance, an automobile manufacturer shows a picture of a horse on a wide-open prairie. Next to the horse is an image of the car that is being advertised. The words written over the picture are "16 valves. Untamed freedom." In this instance, the company that is trying to sell its cars is equating horses with freedom—a common symbolic attribute of these animals. At the same time, the company is suggesting that if you drive this car, you will undoubtedly feel the same freedom that the horse represents.

The third and more recent addition to the way animals are used in advertising is by equating a concern for the environment with the product being sold. A recent ad for another automobile shows a picture of a zebra standing in the middle of a frame of a car. The car is situated on what looks like an African savannah. Expansive blue skies above with wispy clouds and a soft breeze blowing through the grasses punctuate this idyllic scene. The text reads, "Ingeniously designed to help protect the things that need protecting." The implication here is that just as the zebra and the environment need our protection, the auto manufacturer is interested in protecting the people who buy their cars.

Businesses use a variety of techniques to include animals in their advertising. Some of the ways that they have chosen to try to call attention to their products with animals include appealing to higher values, humor, peace, status, comfort, and using plays on words. The "freedom" in the ad mentioned above is an example of a value that might attract a prospective buyer. Another example of this type of value-laden ad is when a majestic elk is portrayed standing in the middle of a "sea" of peacocks. The words read "For 195 years. The Hartford has stood for dependability and strength. Now that is something to be admired for." In this ad, the company is stressing the qualities of strength and dependability—ostensibly attributable to the elk—as reasons to do business with them. They are also implying that admiration may come to a person who does business with them.

Many companies find that humor is a good way to sell their product. An airline company shows a picture of a silhouetted camel pulling a cart across a desert at sunset with the caption: "Day 4. Bought some clothes and jewelry and packed them in our SUV." In this ad the airline is referring to the cart in this faraway land as an "SUV" and clearly hoping to entice their prospective customers to want to travel on their airline. A bank that is interested in convincing consumers to save their money at their place of business shows a picture of a squirrel with his cheeks full and implies that you too can save for the future in their bank the way squirrels stash their food for the future.

An ad for a credit card company known for its travel expertise shows a picture of a man seated on a beach with his eyes closed, one arm around a dog seated with him and the head of a horse leaning down and touching its forehead to the man's face. This photo clearly depicts a picture of contentment, peace, and being in tune with nature. By implication, using their service will give you a similar kind of experience.

Advertisers target a particular group of people in their advertising and then try to impress them with the things that the company believes that group most values. A growing concern for the environment has induced companies to include more animals in their advertising because they can catch the attention of people who are interested in protecting the environment. Sometimes companies will differentiate their product not by their characteristics but by some "green" value attached to them. For instance, an ad may imply that, "because I am so fond of all wildlife, I use such and such a product." This product may have nothing to do with wildlife or nature, but the ad implies that if you use their product you, too, will be helping and caring for the environment.

There is however a *danger* in using any animal, or wildlife in particular, in advertising. Some people believe that the animals are not treated well, nor that the welfare of the animals is taken into consideration, when used in advertising. An example is a television

Motorists pass an anti-litter billboard showing animals' backsides along an expressway south of Chicago, May 1999. (©) AP Photo/Charles Bennett.

commercial showing a penguin waddling down the hall of an office building. Considerations arise such as: How was the penguin put there? How was it treated during the making of the advertisement, and what became of the penguin after the commercial was finished?

There are a few things to think about when one looks at an advertisement with animals in it. How is the advertiser portraying the animal? For example, does the image of the animal have any direct relationship to the product or is it symbolic? Why has the advertiser chosen to put this particular animal in the ad? Was the animal's welfare taken into consideration in the preparation of the ad?

See also

Conservation and Environment—*Advertising and the Endangered Saimaa Ringed Seal in Finland*

Further Resources

Bekoff, M. (Ed.). (1998). *Encyclopedia of animal rights and animal welfare.* Westport, CT: Greenwood Press.

Hart, A. (1992). *Understanding the media: A practical guide.* New York: Routledge.

Lerner, J. E., & Kalof, L. (1999). The animal text: Message and meaning in television advertisements. *Sociological Quarterly, 40* (44), 565–86.

Volpe, T. (2005). *The fast food craze: Wreaking havoc on our bodies and our animals.* Parks, AZ: Canyon Publishing.

Ritu Esbjörn

Media and Film
Animal Monsters in Film

Animal monsters are relevant to the relation between humans and other animals through various aspects. They are used to define "humanity" and "animality" and the relation between the two, and to offer warnings of "inaccurate" or "wrong" types of definitions and relations. Most commonly, animal monsters are born when animals get into the body of the human or gain control that usually belongs to humans. Thus, they break the human-animal boundaries and the relations that are considered appropriate. Here special attention is given to the Western animal monsters and their contemporary form.

History and Contemporary Presentations

Animal monsters have a long history in Western cultures. Animal-human hybrids, animal chimeras, and pure animal monsters can be found from, for instance, Greek culture (an example being the creatures met by Ulysses). The Bible talks of the "beast" and the "dragon." This gave room for the emphasis of demonic animal characters in the Middle Ages. Animals were at times seen as demons, which led to the view that witches could be identified through close contact with animals; at the same time the devil was often defined as an animal hybrid. Werewolves and dragons are part of various folklores, as are stories of monster-like wolves and bears. Today, this tendency still exists. For instance,

Hollywood cinema has used repeatedly all of these inventions in its animal imagery. King Kong has acted as the great animal monster of the Homeric type, and the *Omen* trilogy has identified dogs and crows as animals possessed by the devil. Werewolf films are still popular today, and predators such as wolves, snakes, and sharks are repeatedly described as monsters.

In the contemporary Western context, animal monsters exist primarily in popular horror film. They are constructed also in other fields, such as political discussion and the media. Wolves remain portrayed as dangerous and evil beings even in political decision-making processes; various types of animals (such as rats and snakes) are vilified as possibly dangerous and frightening "vermin" on the level of everyday practices; dangerous dog acts that emphasize danger and monstrosity of certain dogs find their ways into legislation; and the front pages of newspapers are often covered with stories of animals that have attacked humans or livestock, or pose a potential danger of doing so, and hence have become monstrous. However, the horror film is perhaps the most influential and commonly known form of construction of animal monstrosity, to a point of having a deep impact on how such monstrosity is built in other contexts (for instance, sharks became phenomenally vilified as a result of *Jaws* (Steven Spielberg, USA 1975).

Various different genres can be named. One is formed by domestic animals that gain power and turn against humans, thus becoming monsters. For instance, in *Man's Best Friend* (John Lafia, USA 1993), *Atomic Dog* (Brian Threnchard-Smith, USA 1997), and *Cujo* (Lewis Teague, USA 1983), dogs turn on humans, and in *Strays* (John McPherson, USA 1991) cats become monsters. Another genre is formed by wild animals that attack human communities. The shark from *Jaws*, the reptile from *Alligator* (Lewis Teague, USA 1980), and the snake from *Anaconda* (Luis Llosa, USA 1997) all present monstrous wild animals. A specific type between these two is formed by primates. The gorillas from *Congo* (Frank Marshall, USA 1995) and the primate from *King Kong* (Merian Cooper, USA 1933; remakes from 1972 and 2005) offer examples of wild primate monsters, whereas the ape from *Link* (Richard Franklin, USA 1985) portrays a domesticated primate monster, and the *Planet of the Apes* (Franklin Schaffner, USA 1968) conveys a civilization of manipulating and hostile apes. Further genres include films revolving around insects (such as those from *Arachnophobia*—Frank Marshall, USA 1990), prehistoric animals (such as those from *Jurassic Park*—Steven Spielberg, USA 1993), and alien animals (such as those from *Alien*—Ridley Scott, USA 1979). Also, human-animal hybrids form an important type of animal monsters (as shown, for instance, in *The Fly*—David Cronenberg, USA 1986). All of these genres construct animal monstrosity in a specific manner and follow different patterns of storyline and theme depending on what our relation toward the type of an animal in question is.

Animal-Human Relations

The animal monster serves often as the opposite of the anthropomorphic animal, although the two can also intertwine. Animal monsters describe the animals as "others," as beings who are opposites of humans. They portray characteristics that are very unlike those portrayed by what are understood as stereotypical humans, and hence aggression overtakes morality, instincts overtake reason, bodily functions overtake purity, etc. However, animal monsters may also include animals that behave similarly to human villains (for instance, cold intelligence and sociopathy are evoked). Thus, animal monsters are constructed as opposites of "good" human beings. As Andrew Tudor claims, monsters fall into anthropomorphic and alien, and as it comes to animal monsters, both types can be claimed to be "others" in relation to stereotypically good humans.

The interplay between animals and humans is brought to the fore in human-animal *hybrids*, in which the human and the animal are combined in the same body (as exemplified by Homer's sirens, which have the body of a bird and the head of a woman). Also *chimeras* (a word originally referring to a monster from Greek mythology), in which various animals are combined in the same body, are used (often, these chimeras are results of genetic engineering or nuclear radiation). A similar form is *metamorphosis*, in which the human and the animal take turns in possessing the body. An archetype of metamorphosis is the werewolf, which is at times fully human and at times fully animal. A fourth option is a full change from human into animal, as happens in *The Fly*. These interplays often revolve around dichotomies between humans and other animals. In the metamorphosis, the animal tends to signify the opposite of humanity, possessing negative character traits in comparison to the human counterpart. In the hybrids, the combination of humanity and animality as such tends to lead into horror: humans are not supposed to be entangled with animality. Thus, often the interplays concern maintaining borders between humans and other animals: combinations are seen as threatening and monstrous, and humans are to be not only kept distinct from other animals but also made into their opposites. It can be argued that in defining borders, they also define humanity: if wolves are immoral then humans are moral, etc. Still, it has to be remembered that human-animal interplay can also be seen as positive, as manifested in, for instance, the Greek gods who took animal forms (hence, animality can also be used as a sign of positive traits, such as strength, wisdom, etc.).

Monstrosity is commonly argued to be built around control: monsters are those beings who at the same time are to be controlled, and who seek to take control. A common example of a monster is a being that has been subdued but has become monstrous in her resistance to the control exercised over her. It has been argued to be the loss of control and the following helplessness at the face of another being that defines monsters. Following this, it can be claimed that animals become monsters when they gain control over humans, thus reversing the power relation between humans and other animals. Whereas traditionally humans hunt animals, when animals hunt humans, they become monsters. They are difficult to catch, kill, or even to visually identify, and they prey on people who become helpless victims. For instance, the shark from *Jaws* is nowhere to be found, cannot be killed by traditional methods, cannot even be identified, and kills people who have little means to defend themselves. Hence, the reversal of the power relation leads to helplessness, which causes horror and constructs monstrosity. Maurice Yocawar argues this helplessness to be an integral part of the natural and animal monsters. Loss of human control is at the core of animal monstrosity.

An important part of this aspect of control can be argued to be the independence of the monster. Monsters are beings often (albeit not always) defined by subjectivity, activity, independence, and strength. Whereas they might have been controlled and have thus been passive beings powerless to act, their monstrosity means that they now work independently of "normal" human beings and offer active strength against those that they dislike (or, at least, portray the potential to do so). As such, they pose a threat. A classic example is Frankenstein's monster, who breaks free of his creator's control. Also, many animal monsters follow this pattern. Whereas usually animals are seen as passive, subdued, and largely dependent upon the human actions toward them (even wild animals are "managed"), animal monsters become subjects with their own will and strength. A good example of this is King Kong, who seeks to break free from his controlled environment and status as an exhibition object. In this way, independence and strength of given animals in itself can lead into labeling these animals as "monsters."

According to Andrew Tudor, the sudden rise in the number of "natural nasties" in the 1970s points toward social reasons as a catalyst. The most important of these reasons

The famous fight scene between King Kong and dinosaurs, from Merian C. Cooper and Ernest B. Schoedsack's 1933 film, King Kong. *Courtesy of Photofest.*

is the birth of ecological awareness, since for the first time the limits and consequences of a modern way of living were brought to the fore. The control that humans had been thought to have became questioned, with nature "striking back" and with humans seemingly helpless at its hands.

The birth of the animal rights movement in its modern form also coincides with a growing interest in animal monsters (in fact, *Jaws* was made the same year as Peter Singer's ground-laying book, *Animal Liberation*). Animal rights question the power relation between humans and other animals and hence give reason for insecurity as it comes to the anthropocentric worldview. The claims of similarity between humans and other animals in both a descriptive and moral sense pose a threat and may lead to the construction of animal monsters. This element is often explicitly brought to the fore. In the movie *Man's Best Friend* an animal rights minded person, who has rescued a dog from a vivisection laboratory, comes to realize that the dog in fact is a monster.

Construction of Animal Monstrosity

A common definer of animal monsters is the element of being "out of place" with the ordinary. Harriet Ritvo argues that monsters are built on the incapacity to fit the "ordinary." They break existing categories that define what beings are and hence are seen as threatening. Noel Carroll claims that monsters are described by "un-naturalness": monsters do not fit into the reality as we know it and go against normality. Jeffrey Cohen argues that monsters refuse categorization and do not adapt to the "order of things." The fear toward and threat imposed by the monster follows this refusal. Hence, animal monsters can be argued to break categories of "normality" and to destroy existing definitions created out of reality. More specifically, it can be argued that animal monsters defy what "animals" and "humans" should be and what the relation between the two ought to be.

There are many methods in which the element of "being out of place" can be constructed. The first method concentrates on the physical body of the animal. Animals are oversize and come in overt numbers. Carroll talks of *magnification* and *massification* as terms referring to overtly large size and overt numbers of animals. King Kong serves as an example of the former, where as horror films such as *Arachnophobia* serve as examples of the latter. Next to this, we can talk of *specification* of a particular body part of the animal, so that it comes to signify the monstrosity of the animal (an example being *Jaws*, which creates icons out of the shark's mouth and fin). Also, *activication* is used, as the animal's actions (speed, way of moving, way of eating, way of killing, etc.) are emphasized. For instance, in *Anaconda* the snake's manners of eating whole bodies is underlined, and *Jaws* names the shark "an eating machine," concentrating on its manners of ripping apart human bodies. When the physical is emphasized, the animal's body often becomes a *spectacle*. The physicality of the animal is given significance in its own terms. Also the killing of the animal monster often follows this pattern, as it is made into a very visual, prolonged, and ritualistic event.

The second method is invisibility. Monstrosity is commonly defined through rendering the monster invisible to the human eye: it lurks in the dark where it cannot be seen. As is commonly argued, seeing and visualizing are important parts of the Western culture, and the denial of them potentially leads to fear, insecurity, and loss of rational explanation. Animal monsters are often held invisible, the archetype being again *Jaws*, in which the shark is seen only for a few seconds. Animal monsters are also often given the viewpoint, and hence the viewer is forced to perceive the world through their eyes, making the lack of one's own visual capacity even more pressing. In *Congo*, the monstrous gorillas even use the eye as a symbol, and literally rip off an eye from a human victim, thus in a very concrete manner taking away the capacity to see. In *Orca* (Michael Anderson, USA 1977), the eye of the animal is emphasized to great extent; for instance the hapless human victims are reflected onto the surface of the animal's eye.

The third method is characterization. Animals are given various psychological characteristics that define their monstrosity, ranging from aggression to immorality and sociopathy. Again, the shark from *Jaws* is defined through aggression, and the monstrous gorillas of *Congo* are seen as purposefully cruel; *Man's Best Friend* describes a dog that is determined by sociopathic need to kill people. In its extreme, demonization is used as a characterization. *Anaconda*'s snake is defined as a "devil," and it is a priest who tries to kill it. In *Rattled* (Tony Randel, USA 1996) the snakes are demonized as creatures that attack a suburb called Eden Valley, and in *Nightwing* (Arthur Hiller, USA 1980) bats are described as "the quintessence of evil."

Animals and Monsters

"Animals" and "monsters" are overlapping definitions. According to Jeffrey Cohen, monsters are understood through the need to define them and take control over them. As outsiders, monsters also determine who belongs to the community. Thus, monsters are beings that we seek to explain, take power away from, and that are used to describe the membership of, for instance, a moral community. These elements are again emphasized in *Jaws*, in which various efforts are made to understand what the creature in question is and how to take control over it while the shark attacks a small community from the outside waters. Monsters are also claimed to define humanity. Michael Uebel argues that monsters are defined as otherness, which paradoxically defines our sense of a self. Normality and humanity are reflected against what they are not, and hence as a negation, monsters help to build these elements. While doing so, they also determine what those creatures understood to be unlike us are defined as.

The aforementioned attributes are often found also from imagery concerning other animals. Science has, especially since the seventeenth century, tirelessly classified animals, thereby seeking to define them thoroughly—animals need to be explained. It has also helped to make better use out of the animals, and thus take firmer control over different species. In moral terms, animals are often defined as outsiders to the human community, and especially the moral sphere. Most importantly, humanity has repeatedly been defined through animality: humans are that which animals are not understood to be. Humans need the animals to define themselves, and the relationship is commonly seen as dichotomous.

Although to some extent simplifying, these correlations can be argued to help to understand why animals are easy to portray as monsters. The roles of animals and monsters have tended to be similar, and thus have given a ground for the construction of animal monsters. In order to read animal monsters critically, the mentioned cultural similarities are important to notice.

It is crucial to investigate the reasons for portraying animals as monsters. Cohen argues that monsters do not exist as subjects, but as text: they exist for the reader/viewer. As such they reveal presuppositions of the background culture. They tell about what we consider to be normal and what the categories and definitions concerning ourselves and other creatures are. Animal monsters reveal what we understand the nature of animals and humans to be and what the relation between these two ought to be according to our cultural context. Thus, they are a fruitful ground for analyzing how we define other animals in relation to ourselves. Steve Baker underlines how stereotypes especially tell us about cultural presuppositions: if animals are repeatedly described through certain understandings, these understandings are dominant or prevailing. As animal monsters emphasize otherness, and as we tend to describe animals as beings lacking important attributes often related with humanity, the prevailing imagery concerning animals can repeat the idea that animals indeed are rather mechanical beings and should remain passive, controlled, and outside the moral community.

David Ingram emphasizes the need for cultural reading of films concerning the environment and animals. This can also be applied to animal monsters. As animal monsters help to maintain and construct presuppositions concerning animals, which often have clear consequences, it can be argued to be elemental that underlying cultural imagery concerning animals be critically examined.

Further Resources

Baker, S. (1993). *Picturing the beast: Animals, identity and representation*. Manchester, UK: Manchester University Press.

Carroll, N. (1990). *The philosophy of horror: Or paradoxes of the heart*. London: Routledge.

Cohen, J. (1996). Monster culture (seven theses). In J. Cohen (Ed.), *Monster theory: Reading culture*. Minneapolis: University of Minnesota Press.

Ingram, D. (2000). *Green screen: Environmentalism and Hollywood cinema*. Exeter, UK: University of Exeter Press.

Ritvo, H. (1997). *The platypus and mermaid and other figments of the classifying imagination*. Cambridge, MA: Harvard University Press.

Serpell, J. (1986). *In the company of animals*. New York: Basil Blackwell.

Tudor, A. (1989). *Monsters and mad scientists: A cultural history of the horror movie.* Oxford: Basil Blackwell.

Uebel, M. (1996). Unthinking the monster: Twelfth-century responses to Saracen alterity. In J. Cohen. (Ed.), *Monster theory: Reading culture.* Minneapolis: University of Minnesota Press.

Yacowar, M. (1977). The bug in the rug: Notes on the disaster genre. In B. Grant (Ed.), *Film genre and criticism.* Lanham, MD: Scarecrow Press.

Elisa Aaltola

Media and Film
Animals in Film

There are three important interrelated aspects to the subject of animals in film. The first concerns the importance of the animal for the development of film technology, and the second concerns the nature of animal representation on film and how that has resonated with broader issues of the cultural status of animals. The third important aspect, which has an important bearing on the present, relates to television and the changing economics of the entertainment business.

The prehistory of animals in moving film begins, to some extent, with the optical devices and toys that gave the illusion of movement prior to the development of cinematography in the mid-1890s. These included a number of different machines such as the zoetrope, the phenakistoscope, and Muybridge's zoöpraxiscope, which he developed in 1879. It is important to note this because, although it is often remarked that the technology

Director Joe Johnston's 2001 film, Jurassic Park III. *Shown: Sam Neill (as Dr. Alan Grant). Courtesy of Photofest.*

of the cinematograph is a radically different development from what has gone before, the animal is a key visual object, a figure of continuity, especially in the shift from sequences of still photographs that depict movement to moving film imagery itself. Animals were an important driving force in the development of film, as well as often being its inspiration. Capturing animals on film presented technological challenges, which in turn reinforced the novelty of film via the animal's own potential for novelty and fascination. One can trace this theme historically from the photographic sequences of animal movement in the work of Eadweard Muybridge, Jules-Etienne Marey, and Ottomar Anschütz in the 1870s and 1880s to the "special effects" of stop-motion and models in groundbreaking films such as *The Lost World* (1925) and *King Kong* (1933). The animal continues to be a significant figure in later developments of film technology, especially in pioneering areas of special effects, animatronics, and computer generated imagery (CGI), both in fiction films such as *Jurassic Park* (1993) and in nature documentaries such as *Microcosmos* (1996) and the BBC's *Walking with Beasts* (2001).

One cannot write the history of the animal representation in the last 120 years without paying significant attention to film. This is in part because of the way film, in its constructions of the animal, intensifies already existing cultural responses to animals, whether these have to do with, say, sentimentality, brutality, aesthetics, or fascination. Furthermore, many of these constructions of the animal are subject to the conditions of mass markets. However, it is difficult to assess, through a lack of any in-depth historical investigation, the impact of animal film imagery on audiences in different parts of the world. Some assessment of this can be made by looking at popularity, or censorship debates, and the manner in which certain depictions of animals on screen have aroused controversy. Issues of animal welfare, especially in Britain, have been strongly determined by the changing status of the animal in public visual culture, most notably in the desire to render invisible such things as slaughter, animal experimentation, and public displays of mistreatment, especially since the mid-nineteenth century. This means that animal film imagery, as a visual medium, always has the potential for sensitive responses; it is never neutral.

From 1878, Muybridge used banks of cameras, the shutters of which were triggered by the horse's hooves breaking threads on the ground as it galloped past. Although this was radically different from the technology of moving film, it presaged a certain style of animal image that was almost a template for many of the earliest animal films. Most from the turn of the century were of animals in limited spaces such as zoo enclosures or bullrings, as well as parades past the camera, or horse races such as Birt Acres's film *The Derby* in 1895. Some of these films exploited animal combat of various kinds, such as *Mr. Delaware and the Boxing Kangaroo* of 1895. The killing of animals was not uncommon, as can be seen in Thomas Edison's *Electrocuting an Elephant* (1903), *Terrier vs. Wildcat* (1906), and the increasingly common genre of hunting movies such as Cherry Kearton's *Native Lion Hunt* (1909). However, animal film-making takes all manner of inventive directions from the first decade of the

From 1878, photographer Eadweard Muybridge used banks of cameras, the shutters of which were triggered by the horse's hooves breaking threads on the ground as it galloped past. Courtesy of the Library of Congress.

century. Percy Smith, for instance, explored the world of trick photography with his films of insects juggling or sitting on miniature chairs. One of the first animal adventure films, *Rescued by Rover* (1905), involved a dog finding and rescuing a kidnapped baby. To keep up with demand for exotic animal footage, Chicago film entrepreneur Colonel Selig kept a menagerie, as did Mack Sennett. In fact, Universal City had a zoo based on the lot for jungle dramas between 1915 and 1929. With the advent of sound it had to be closed down because it provided too much background sound for recording on neighboring sets.

All the recognizable strands of animal filmmaking—the rudiments of documentary, fiction films, use of special effects, and exploitation genres—were in place by 1910. Animal protagonists in animation became significant from 1913 with the release by Selig Polyscope of some experimental reels of the Doc Yak series about a goat. By 1914 animals began to play significant roles as the pets, sidekicks, or antagonists of main characters. The 1920s and early 1930s, however, saw a more ambitious realization of the possibilities of animal films including the wildlife films of Martin and Osa Johnson and Robert Flaherty's *Nanook of the North* (1922). Two important films, in terms of the way they were made, were produced by Charles Urban: *The Four Seasons* (1921) and *Evolution* (1926). The first of these, made by Raymond Ditmars, was compiled from footage filmed over a three-year period to show the lives of fauna and flora through the changing seasons of a single year. The second, epitomizing the composite method of much animal filmmaking, comprised a mix of models, animation, film material from the American Museum of Natural History and the Bronx Zoo, and other footage to depict the history of the universe. During the same decade Merian Cooper and Ernest Schoedsack made the spectacular documentary *Grass* (1925), at some personal risk to themselves, about the seasonal migration of the Bhakhtari nomads in what was then central Persia, and followed it up with the animal adventure film *Chang: a Drama of Wilderness* (1927), made in the jungle in northern Siam. In 1931, the adventure film *Trader Horn*, shot on location in Africa, included footage of animal fights and the killing of animals.

After World War II, Walt Disney's film series *True Life Adventures* (1948–60) brought a number of wildlife filmmaking strands together, linking scientific-educational themes with animal adventure narratives and comedy, underpinned by a particular version of pristine nature aimed, eventually very successfully, for a mass market. The first of these, *Seal Island* (1948), filmed in Alaska, led to many other films on subjects that either focused on lives of particular animals such as beavers and bears or concentrated on regions such as the desert, the prairie, or the Everglades. At the same time successful underwater documentaries began to be made with the films of Hans Hass, *Pirsch unter Wasser* (1940) and *Under the Red Sea* (1951), and from the mid-1950s the films of Jacques Cousteau. A list of other important non-Anglophone documentary filmmakers with an interest in animals would have to include Heinz Sielmann, Jean Painlevè, Bernhard Grzimek, Horst Stern, Jean-Jacques Annaud, Jacques Perrin, Luc Jacquet, and Werner Herzog.

Television also became a significant factor in animal imagery with Marlin Perkins paving the way in the United States, initially as a way of promoting the Lincoln Park Zoo, Chicago, in 1945. *Zooparade* was first broadcast in 1950, while in Britain the BBC broadcast its first wildlife programs with *Look* from 1953, with Peter Scott, and David Attenborough's *Zooquest* from 1954. This period in Britain also marked the beginning of a growing division between the skills of naturalist broadcasters, the disappearance of the combined amateur naturalist and filmmaker, and the emergence of a professional status for natural history filmmaking. Although the British programs would still continue with a strong studio component, the inclusions of wildlife footage pointed toward the more ambitious televisual documentaries in the coming decades, such as David Attenborough's groundbreaking *Life on Earth* (1979). Fictional animal adventures on television were usually highly sentimental, and they were a popular genre from the mid-1950s. *Lassie* went on air in 1954, *Fury*, an equine version of *Lassie* was launched in 1955, and later shows included Ivan Tors's *Flipper* (1964–67), *Gentle Ben* (1967–69), *Mr. Ed* (1960–65), and *Daktari* (1966–69).

The next major shift in animal filmmaking has been dominated by television's approach to animals in the 1980s and 1990s. The fragmentation of television audiences away from a few oligopolistic channels to smaller niche markets, via the expansion of satellite and cable and the inevitable cost-cutting, has led to cheaper formats such as reality shows. Nature documentaries have an advantage in that they can be rerun season after season, and wildlife footage can be archived, re-edited, and recycled in a different form for entirely new shows. The trends toward sensationalism in a highly competitive media environment saw an escalation of focus on scenes of predation and aggression in the 1990s. As a consequence of the arrival of Discovery Channel in 1985, National Geographic Television in 1995, and Animal Planet in 1996, animal topics became even bigger business, though their formats were and are governed by general shifts in strategy for all types of television programming rather than being necessarily determined by agendas specific to animal issues per se. Having said that there are still impressive, high-profile animal films being made such as *Winged Migration* (2001), *The Story of the Weeping Camel* (2003), *Kekexili: Mountain Patrol* (2004), *March of the Penguins* (2005), and *Grizzly Man* (2005). Important wildlife film festivals include the Wildscreen festival that takes place every two years in Bristol, UK, and the Jackson Hole Wildlife Film Festival, also every two years.

It is important to note that the range of animal filmmaking is not just limited to documentary-style fiction and sentimental family films, but also covers every aspect of human-animal relations. I will list some of the most important of these. Films such as Robert Bresson's *Au hazard Balthazar* (1966) and Ken Loach's *Kes* (1969) depict intensive relations between human and animal without anthropomorphizing or sentimentalizing the animal. Erotic or intimate relations with animals are explored in Nagisa Ôshima's *Max mon amour* (1986), about the relationship between a woman and an ape, and Ulrich Seidl's *Tierische Liebe* (1995) about pets. Films depicting animal slaughter and cruelty can be found in a range of films from animal rights videos distributed by campaigning organizations such as PETA (People for the Ethical Treatment of Animals), to documentary films such as Georges Franju's *Sang des bêtes* (1949) and Frederick Wiseman's *Meat* (1976). More outlandish versions of this kind of imagery can be found in Gualtiero Jacopetti's "shockumentary" film *Mondo Cane* (1962), which juxtaposes, among other things, rituals of slaughter and exploitation from different parts of the world, as well as a visit to a luxury pet cemetery in Pasadena, California. More meditative, artful explorations on human and animal identity can be found most strikingly in Bill Viola's *I Do Not Know What It Is I Am Like* (1986), while Chris Marker's *Sans soleil* (1983) uses animals to explore questions of cultural memory in Japan. A fictional counterpart to this, which explores political and historical shifts in Spanish history via the symbolism of animals, is Julio Medem's *Vacas* (1992).

Other important issues around animal filmmaking have concerned animal welfare, censorship, and in some contexts a considerable public sensitivity to certain kinds of animal imagery. The training of animals for film began as a haphazard affair, with most animals coming from circuses and zoos. The profession of animal trainers or wranglers in the film industry has a hazy history, although there were clearly individuals at work from very early on. A young Frenchman, Pierre Bourgeois, has been credited with starting the profession, training animals to repeat simple movements such as crashing through a window into a room. Animals were certainly considered expendable props up to the 1940s, with 150 horses allegedly killed during the making of *Ben Hur* in 1925. The riding of a horse off a 70-foot cliff during the filming of *Jesse James* in 1939 prompted the involvement of the

American Humane Association in film production, with the Hays Office giving the Association the right to review scripts and have a representative on set to supervise the filming of animals. In Britain the story is a little different because cruelty to animals was one of the grounds for censorship from the inception of the British Board of Film Censors (now the British Board of Film Classification, BBFC) from 1913 onward. The Cinematograph (Animals) Act of 1937 prohibited cruelty in the production of animal films. In many ways this Act was not fully implemented or effective until the 1980s. British companies specializing in providing trained animals for films slowly increased in number from the 1960s, and many of these now work under the auspices of the Animal Consultants and Trainers Association, founded in 1989, to regulate the fees and legitimize professional trainers. The British response to animal film imagery has also been marked by episodes that indicate a very particular cultural sensitivity. Examples include the BBFC's rejection of the *Island of Lost Souls* (1932), the film version of H. G. Wells's *Dr. Moreau's Island*, because of the theme of vivisection, and the controversy over whether to cut the dog fight scenes in *Amores Perros* (2000), on the grounds not just of cruelty but that they might encourage dog fighting.

Animal film imagery is always something of a composite. Live spontaneous footage is intercut with contrived shots, trained animals (and usually more than one for any individual character) are combined with animatronic models or CGI, and factual films are frequently underpinned by a contradictory combination of sentiment and a desire to see things such as predatory killing. In some senses, little has changed. The fascination with sharks and tigers, for instance, echoes the taste for hunting movies of a century ago. At one level, the way in which animal films are a combination of many different strands remind us of the complexity of animal representation and its extreme contrivance. Yet, at the same time, film addresses every single aspect of human-animal relations, making it the defining medium of modernity's engagement with the animal.

Further Resources

Bousé, D. (2000). *Wildlife films*. Philadelphia: University of Pennsylvania Press.

Burt, J. (2002). *Animals in film*. London: Reaktion.

Chris, C. (2006). *Watching wildlife*. Minneapolis: University of Minnesota Press.

Davies, G. (1998). *Networks of nature: Stories of natural history film-making from the BBC*. Unpublished PhD thesis: University College London.

Lippit, A. (2002). The death of the animal. *Film Quarterly, 56*, 9–22.

Mitman, G. (1999). *Reel nature: America's romance with wildlife on film*. Cambridge, MA: Harvard University Press.

Jonathan Burt

Media and Film
Cartooonists, Comic Strips, and Animals

Cartoonists by our very nature are animists. We see everything as being filled with a life force and having its own unique personality. We anthropomorphize all. Trees can talk and chairs can walk. Cartoonists, by definition, are also exaggerators. We make the lanky lankier, the cute cuter, the tubby tubbier, all for comic effect. So, how can cartoonists not be drawn to animals? They already run, crawl, swim, hop, and/or fly. Can a giraffe, a kitten, or a hippo be any more exaggerated? Mother Nature has done most of the job for us.

Take the family dog, for instance—a big-nosed, tail-wagging, long-eared, tongue-hanging ball of fur, filled with love, adventure, and innocence. Dogs are living cartoons. And they possess, as all animals do, an essential quality all daily comic strip characters need—the ability to see the world anew every single day. They live in the moment, greeting every walk, or meal, or belly-rub with such total excitement that you would think it was their very first. It is a quality cartoonists must emulate. It is not easy to stare into the white void of a blank sheet of paper every day with fresh enthusiasm, but seeing the world through your animal character's eyes makes it a whole lot easier.

The cartoonist/animal relationship is an evolving one. Animals have always been an integral part of the human psyche. They are our connection back to the Garden, back to the bliss. Animals have an innate understanding of the world that we struggle to achieve and that artists struggle to express. We have woven their spirits with our own throughout history, from the first cave drawings, to ritualized song and dance, to our mythologies and folklore, to our national symbols and cultural icons. So when the comic strip was originated around 1896 it was no wonder animals graced the first pages. (Swinnerton had his *Little Bears,* and R. F. Outcault's Yellow Kid shared *Hogan's Alley* with an assortment of city and farm animals.)

At the turn of the century America was still agriculturally based, and barnyard animals were portrayed in comics as often as household pets. Comic strip hijinks often involved goats, pigs, chickens, and other familiar barnyard animals. A few even had their own strip, such as Fred Opper's mule in *And Her Name was Maud.* Around the same time, the African safari was gaining in popularity, and in America's wilderness bear, fox, wolf, and other native species were still relatively commonplace. Exotic and wild animals captivated the public's interest and fueled the cartoonists' imagination. Their images filled the funny pages.

For the most part, early animal characters played supporting roles to humans. They were coconspirators or faithful companions or acted as the catalyst for comic mayhem. (Buster Brown had his pit bull terrier Tige; Little Orphan Annie, her shelter rescue dog Sandy; and Barney Google, his pony Sparkplug.)

As the comic strip evolved so did the animal characters. No longer just bit players, they took center stage. Cartoonists began giving them more human personalities and qualities—and a human consciousness. Animals now had a voice, but still enjoyed the protection of their inherent innocence—a powerful combination. Cartoonists used that voice not only to deliver punch lines, but also to express ideas, opinions, and emotions that human characters might have trouble communicating. Would the poetry of George Herriman's *Krazy Kat* have reached such heights if Krazy and Ignatz were burdened with only human sensibilities and form?

As the cartoonist/animal relationship continued to evolve, new interpretations of animal characterizations developed. The political cartoon, regulated to the editorial page, found its way to the comics section. The political cartoon predates the comic strip and historically used animal imagery to portray public figures and symbolize social issues, but it was not until *Pogo* that it became a strictly animal affair. Walt Kelly's ensemble of swamp critters in *Pogo* took political satire and social commentary, as well as zoomorphism, to new heights.

Another turning point in the history of animals in the comic strip was Charles Schulz's creation of Snoopy. When he first appeared in *Peanuts,* Snoopy acted like most neighborhood dogs, a family pet that simply barked and ran around on all fours. But then Charles Schulz let us in on a secret. Through Snoopy's "inner voice" he told us what our dogs were *really* thinking. Snoopy stood out from the rest of the animal cartoon pack because his thoughts were his own, shared only with the reader, and never with his human costars. He maintained a certain aloofness that is a part of every animal/human relationship. While Snoopy's vivid imagination (his fantasies of being a World War I Flying Ace, for example) was decidedly human, his nature was all dog.

Humor is a matter of perspective. Animal characters can give us an outsider's point of view, that unbiased observation of ourselves. It is a great tool for creating gags and an effective technique for expressing higher concerns. The early cartoonists' world was filled with a vast menagerie of creatures, and new and exciting variations were still being discovered. Extinction only referred to the dinosaurs, the dodo, and the passenger pigeon. The world has changed, and so has the cartoonist/animal relationship. Cartoonists have begun using their animal characters to give their real-life counterparts, and fellow fauna, a voice in the diminishing wilderness.

Bill Watterson's *Calvin and Hobbes* touched on animal and environmental issues. Berkley Breathed's penguin Opus took on the politics of animal rights, as did Gary Larson's collection of characters in *The Far Side*. Today, Dan Piraro (*Bizaro*), Dave Coverly (*Speedbump*), and Vic Lee (*Pardon My Planet*) regularly address animal concerns from the animal's point of view in their daily comic strip panels.

In my own strip, *Mutts*, which follows the friendship of Earl the dog and Mooch the cat, I decided to keep the animal characters' perspective as animal-like as possible. I wanted to capture on paper the spirit and joie de vivre of my real-life animal companions and in turn share the pure happiness I get from their exuberance. People cherish the special bond that they have with their animal companions. We walk, figuratively and literally, through life together. We acknowledge our shared emotions. We recognize our animal companions as precious not for the human qualities we impose on them but for their own unique being. In *Mutts*, I celebrate that human/animal relationship and try to extend the awareness that people have with their own animal companions to all living things.

Every day I sit at my drawing table looking out the window on a world of birds, rabbits, squirrels, and the occasional deer or fox. My dog Earl lies patiently at my feet, and my cat MeeMow is curled asleep atop my papers. For me, the cartoonist/animal relationship can be summed up in a single word—inspirational.

Patrick McDonnell

Media and Film
Planet of the Apes

Pierre Boulle's 1963 satirical French novel *La planète des Singes* spawned the 1968 film *Planet of the Apes* (*POTA*), as well as four sequels, two television series (one of them animated), a 2001 remake, several novel adaptations and comics, and a video game. These deviate from the original book and from each other in numerous ways, but all share the common basic premise of a dystopia ruled by talking apes who keep humans (with extremely varied cognitive and behavioral capacities) as slaves, pets, and laboratory subjects.

While the *POTA* extended universe involves various logical contradictions, continuity problems, and incoherencies (in the case of the films these frequently relate to time travel), it nevertheless provides a suitable fictional hypothesis for social commentary on *actual* human-animal relationships and discussion of important issues such as those of human self-righteousness, speciesism, Great Ape personhood, animal cruelty, and ethology in general. It makes us look at how we treat and stereotype others (be they apes, other nonhuman animals, or humans) by challenging common prejudices about the ways in which certain differences between creatures (considered both as individuals as well as members of various groups be they defined by race, species, or politics) should or should not matter socially, ethically, and legally. In the films, for example, it is offensive to call an ape a monkey because the latter are considered to be "further down the evolutionary ladder," and only "just above humans."

POTA also raises further questions about the interrelations between differences of sex, species, appearance, anatomy, age, size, neurology, mannerisms, strength, sentience, function, behavior, understanding, speech, language, psychology, emotion, thought, etc. To focus on speciesism for a moment, it helps motivate the idea that it is irrational—and immoral in a speceisist fashion—to do anything to animals that we are not willing to do to human orphans with identical abilities and potentials. But whereas the work of philosophers such as Richard Ryder and Peter Singer focuses on humans with ape-like abilities, *POTA* does just the reverse, in a world where anthropomorphized apes treat humans with similar abilities much as many of us treat nonhuman animals. This alone gives us cause enough to rethink our relationship with animals, but *POTA* goes even further, examining the possibility of various kinds of love that can exist between individuals belonging to different species, with activist apes frequently being accused of being "human-lovers."

Franklin J. Schaffner's 1968 film Planet of the Apes. *Shown from left: Kim Hunter, James Daly, Charlton Heston, Woodrow Parfrey, James Whitmore, Maurice Evans, Roddy McDowall. Courtesy of Photofest.*

"It's disgusting the way we treat humans" says one activist in Tim Burton's 2001 version: "it demeans us as much as them." Quite.

Further Resources

Boulle, P. (1963). *La planète des Singes*. Paris: Julliard.

Greene, E. (2006). Planet of the Apes *as American myth: Race and politics in the films and television series*. Jefferson, NC: McFarland & Company.

Ryder, R. (2001). *Painism: A modern morality*. London: Open Gate Press.

Singer, P. (1976). *Animal liberation* (rev. ed.). London: Jonathan Cape.

Constantine Sandis

Media and Film
Superhero Animals

Superheroic animals such as Bellerophron and Pegasus, not to mention the talking animals that populate Aesop's fables and various folktales from Africa, Asia, and Europe, have been with us since the dawn of literature. It was not until the nineteenth century, however, that artists such as John Macallan Swan, Sir Edwin Henry Landseer, and the French "animalier" sculptors (Antoine Louis Barye, Emmanuel Fremiet, Charles Paillet, Georges Gardet, etc.) began to depict heroic animals in semi-anthropomorphized form. Their works influenced early twentieth century artists such as Rembrandt Bugatti, but also helped form early "funny animal comics" such as George Harriman's daily comic strip *Krazy Kat* (1910), Sidney Smith's *Old Doc Yak* (1912), Pat Sullivan's *Felix the Cat* (1919), and Walt Disney's *Oswald the Lucky Rabbit* (1927), a predecessor of Mickey Mouse (1928).

Soon enough Mickey was joined by a host of friends such as *Pluto* (1930, the year the planet Pluto was discovered), Goofy (1932, then called Dippy Dawg), and Donald Duck (1934), who (with the exception of their pet Pluto) would all speak, think, act, and usually even dress like humans, thus enabling Disney to animalize certain human virtues and vices such as patience, bravery, laziness, gluttony, and stubbornness. Some, like Mickey, were natural heroes, but just like "real-life" heroic animals such as Rin Tin Tin and Lassie, they lacked the powers (supernatural or otherwise) to qualify as *super*heroes. Indeed the first twentieth-century *super*heroes and villains to have anything to do with animals were humans, such as Batman (1939), Catwoman (1940), and the Penguin (1941), who all adopted animal characteristics to varying degrees (though in the 1992 film *Batman Returns* Tim Burton rethought the Penguin as an animal-man "freak"). The first proper animal superheroes were combinations of funny animals and standard superheroes, such as 1943's Super-Rabbit, a Merrie Melodies Superman parody starring Bugs Bunny, though it would take another decade before things really began to fly. 1953 was the year of the mouse, witnessing the debut of both Al Fago's funny animal superhero Atomic Mouse and Warner Bros.' Speedy Gonzalez, who would star in his own Oscar-wining feature in 1955, also the year in which Paul Terry's Mighty Mouse was first introduced to the world.

The 1960s welcomed Spiderman in 1962 (another human with "animal" superpowers), Wonder Wart-Hog in 1962 ("The Hog is Steel"), Hal Seeger's Batfink from

1966 to 1967 (a parody of Batman), and Ward & Scott's Super Chicken who, somewhat controversially, gained his magic powers by drinking a Super Sauce that his butler would mix up in a martini glass. 1965's Asterix and the Banquet saw the first appearance of Dogmatix (Idéfix in the French original), a normal dog that gained super powers by drinking Getafix's magic potion and who, apart from becoming Obelix's pet, would soon star in over a dozen of his own adventures. That same year Goofy ate some magic peanuts and became Super Goofy, the first Disney character to lead an episodic double life as a superhero. Next up was Phantom Duck (1969), also known as PK (short for "Platyrhynchos Kineticus," which loosely translates as "Energized Duck"). PK, whose alter ego was Donald, had no supernatural powers but an array of gadgets created for him by his friend Gyro Gearloose. Soon after his lucky cousin and part-time foe Fethry also developed a superheroic alter ego. The Red Bat was occasionally joined by the Purple Butterfly (Fethry's girlfriend Gloria). The 1970s also saw the creation of Dave Sim's misogynist adult comic strip *Cerebus* (about an ambitious aardvark who eventually becomes Pope) and of a number of comics about super rabbits and hares such as Martin Greim's Thunder Bunny (1977). The most popular of these was Larry Hama's Bucky O'Hare (a green hare that captains a super-animal crew named The Righteous Indignation), who also had his own cartoon series, video and arcade games, and action figures.

The Righteous Indignation included Jenny (a super-cat) and Deadeye Duck (a pirate). Their main allies were Bruiser (a crazy baboon), Wolf, Rumble Bee, Digger McSquint (a mole engineer), Pitsop Pete (a pit bull space marine), Major Bottlenose (a dolphin cryptologist), The Secretary General (a pig), Grebb (a jackal), Chairman Harman (a walrus disguise operated by a newt), The Corsair Canards, and Kamikaze Kamo (a ninja duck). Their common enemy was an evil empire of toads, lizards, and crocodiles collectively known as The Toad Empire.

Another "bunny superhero" was Thomas and Shaw's Captain Carrot, created in the early 1980s for DC Comics. Carrot was from Gnu York but led a gang of anthropomorphic funny animal superheroes (his Amazing Zoo Crew) who lived in Los Antelopes, Califurnia, and were citizens of the United Species of America. With the exception of Carrot himself (who received his superpowers by munching cosmic carrots) and Little Cheese (a mouse student who gained his powers by eating from a piece of experimental cheese), all members of the Zoo Crew received their superpowers after having been struck by a meteor fragment. These included Alley-Kat-Abra (Mew Orleans), Pig-Iron (Piggsburgh), Rubber duck (Califurnia), Yankee Poodle (Follywood), and Fastback (a turtle with superchelonian speed). Their main enemies were Dr. Hoot (an owl), Jailhouse Roc (a giant flying vulture), Digger O'Doom (a mole who gained tremendous strength after eating one of Rodney's carrots), Frogzilla, and Dunbar Dodo.

During their short twenty-issue life the Zoo Crew gave birth to the fictional animal superhero team par excellence, the Justa Lotta Animals. This zoanthropic gang was a funny animal parody of DC's original 1960s superhero team the Justice League of America. Their main members were Super-Squirrel (who came from the planet Chipton and lived in Muttropolis), The Batmouse and Boyd the Robin Wonder, Wonder Wabbit, The Green Lambkin, The Crash, Aquaduck, The Green Sparrow, Stacked Canary, Hawk Moose, The Martian Anteater, Firestork, Zap-Panda, and The Rat Tornado. Their enemies included Feline Faust, Kanga Roo, Lex Lemur, the Porker, Hector Hamhock, The Weather Weasel, the Shaggy Dawg, and Amazo (an android composite of the parts of a dozen different animals).

The 1980s also witnessed the creation of numerous "furry fandom" animal superheroes for adults such as Cutey Bunny, Fission Chicken, Kitty, Doctor Whoot, and Mark E. Rogers' Samurai Cat. It was also a good decade for British superhero animals such as Roland Rat (an animal television puppet who drove a "rat mobile"), Welsh cuddly hero SuperTed (a defective soft toy given magical powers by Mother Nature), Danger Mouse (the greatest mouse detective in the world), and Count Duckula (an egotistical vegetarian vampire duck who hates the sight of blood). The last two spoke with the voice of acclaimed British actor David Jason (Duckula also featured the voice talents of Ruby Wax).

Meanwhile, across the Atlantic, Eastman and Laird's comic Teenage Mutant Ninja Turtles (TMNT; about four anthropomorphic teenage ninja turtles who live in the sewers of Manhattan) was spawning cartoons, feature films, video games, toys, and all sorts of other merchandise, not to mention a number of spoofs such as Adolescent Radioactive Black Belt Hamsters and Pre-Teen Dirty-Gene Kung Fu Kangaroos (Cold-Blooded Chameleon Commandos—not a parody but commissioned at the same time as TMNT by the same publishing company—were not quite as successful).

Characteristic of the speedy 1990s was Sonic the Hedgehog, (the "fastest thing alive"). Originally a Sega videogame character, he was soon given his own comic books, game books, and a number of television and novel series. Other 1990s animal superheroes include Astro City's Leopardman, various furry characters such as Buster the Amazing Bear, the Cyberkitties, the Extinctioners, Red Shetland (a parody of 1970s heroine Red Sonja), and 21st Century Fox, as well as the hugely popular fictional monster

Teenage Mutant Ninja Turtles. *Film poster. Courtesy of Photofest.*

species Pokemon and cult game favorites The Cheetahmen (three humanoid cheetahs whose enemies include a rhino, a hyena, and an ape-man). Things have come full circle in the twenty-first century, with the unlikely return of Pegasus as Barbie's horse.

Further Resources

Fingeroth, D. (2004). *Superman on the couch: What superheroes really tell us about ourselves and our Society*. Bristol, CT: Continuum.

Goulart, R. (2004). *Comic book encyclopedia*. London: HarperCollins.

Inglis, A. (2005). *Animals as superheroes in 19th century art*. Paper delivered at *Holy Men in Tights: A Superheroes Conference*. University of Melbourne.

Klock, G. (2002). *How to read superhero comics and why*. Bristol, CT: Continuum.

Misiroglu, G. (2004). *The superhero book: The ultimate encyclopedia of comic book icons and Hollywood heroes*. New York: Visible Ink Press.

Rodiss, H., Simpson, P., & Bushell, M. (2004). *The rough guide to superheroes*. London: Rough Guides.

Sabin, R. (2001). *Comics, comix and graphic novels: A history of comic art*. London: Phaidon Press.

Constantine Sandis

Mental Health.
See Animal Assistance to Humans; Health

Movies.
See Media and Film

Music, Dance, and Theater
Animals in Dance

Birds do it, bees do it, even educated ballerinas do it. Let's do it, let's dance. With apologies to Cole Porter, the language of dance is used to describe the movements of animals and objects, as well as that of professional human dancers. We describe a bird's movements as balletic; behavioral scientists speak of the communication among bees as the bee-dance; the coupling rituals of many animals are often described as a mating waltz. The connection between animals and dance (rhythmic and patterned human movement) is ancient and intrinsic. Human beings are hardwired to express themselves through dance movements, and the mimicry of animals is fundamentally connected with this expression. In his book *The Others: How Animals Made Us Human* (1996), Paul Shepard states that the imitation of animals is an inherent activity, part of an individual's development, and essential for our ability to participate in rituals and ceremonies. "In an evolutionary perspective," writes Shepard, "ritual has its roots in the imitative play of immature human mammals, goes on to the declared pretense of interspecies impersonation in child's play, and ultimately makes the play the thing" (p. 86).

According to Jean Clottes and David Lewis-Williams (1996), "from the beginning to the end," the first recorded art—the cave paintings of the Paleolithic period—"is an art of animal forms" (p. 41). The authors outline the numerous schools of interpretation of these early drawings but settle upon the explanation that most were representations of the shamanistic experience, a practice that was universal and transported the human shaman into the altered state of inhabiting other animals. The transformation into and imitation of animals and the power that they represented to early communities were part of the tribes' ritual presentations. The ubiquitous use of animal masks and imitative dances in these ritual ceremonies among native peoples is a strong indication that animal role-playing is a salient element in any community's ritual presentations. As early communities became more agricultural and their rituals and ceremonies more elaborate, the power of these animal representations took on a more complex and metaphorical context, but their importance remained constant. The rituals and ceremonies that would become the ancient Greek theater also pay homage to animal and dance movement. The word "tragedy" literally means "goat song," and is believed to derive from the practice of the chorus dancing around a goat, which would either be given as a prize or sacrificed.

From these initial excursions, humans developed all forms of participatory dance, including folk, ballroom, and social dancing. Imitation of animal movements still survives in a number of folk dances. One example may be found in Cameroon on the west coast of Africa, where the Bakweri tribe performs their Elephant Dance every year. The Bakweri believe that advanced members of the tribe can transform into an elephant, what they call their "elephant double." They perform this dance to attack and defeat their enemies while in the form of an elephant. In another example, the Chinese celebrate their New years with the Lion Dance. Although not native to China, lions are symbols of luck, joy, and happiness, and the dance is also used to consecrate temples and other buildings. For the most part, the animal legacy in ballroom and social dancing survives in certain dance names: Foxtrot, Turkey Trot, Bunny Hop, and Lame Duck to name a few.

Animal imagery and characters are more prevalent in performance dance. For a discussion of dance within a theatrical performance, such as musicals and opera, see "Animals in Theater" in this volume. Unlike the theatrical medium, there seems to be little attempt to realistically imitate the movement of animals in ballet and modern dance, the so-called concert dance forms. Perhaps the established metaphorical nature of dance itself eliminates the requirement to be lifelike, which is so prominent in the spoken theater. The goal is to create a beauty of movement by combining animal traits and the movement vocabulary of the specific style of dance, whether that be the formal strictures of ballet or the more modern styles: Graham, Limon, or Cunningham, for example.

There are a number of celebrated animal characters in the ballet repertory. The Mouse King and his army of uniformed mice are a seasonal favorite when *The Nutcracker* is performed. With music by Peter Ilyich Tchaikovsky (1840–93) and based on the E. T. A. Hoffman (1776–1822) children's classic story *The Nutcracker and the Mouse King* (1816), the ballet premiered in 1892 with choreography by Marius Petipa (1818–1910). *Swan Lake* (1877), also set to music by Tchaikovsky, is another classic animal ballet. Prince Siegfried falls in love with Odette, the queen of the swans, who is under the spell of an evil sorcerer (she takes human form at night but is transformed into a swan by morning). The ballerina who plays Odette also doubles as Odile, the sorcerer's daughter who disguises herself as Odette. One notable modern interpretation is the 1995 version choreographed by Matthew Bourne. Bourne's swans are male, as he was inspired by the physique of the real animal. He writes, "the strength, the beauty, the enormous wingspan of these creatures suggests to me the musculature of a male dancer more readily than a ballerina in her white tutu."

Other notable well-trod animal characters are the fawn in Claude Debussy's (1862–1918) *Prelude to the Afternoon of a Faun* and the mythological firebird in Igor Stravinsky's (1882–1971) *The Firebird* (1910). *Prelude to the Afternoon of a Faun* was originally choreographed by Vaslav Nijinsky (1890–1950) for the Ballets Russes and first performed in Paris in 1912. The work was inspired by the poem of the same name by Stéphane Mallarmé (1842–98). *The Firebird*, also produced in Paris by the Ballets Russes, is based on a Russian folk story of a magical glowing bird. In 1942 Stravinsky and choreographer George Balanchine (1904–83) were commissioned by the Ringling Brothers and Barnum & Bailey Circus for a ballet that would feature real elephants. *Circus Polka* premiered in New York City that same year and included fifty elephants, as well as Modoc, the principle pachyderm ballerina. Barbara Heninger quotes a contemporary New York Times review: "Modoc the Elephant danced with amazing grace, and in time to the tune, closing in perfect cadence with the crashing finale." A children's book by Leda Schubert with watercolor and ink illustrations by Robert Andrew Parker is based on the story.

Jack Anderson (1992) writes in his history of dance that the ballerina Anna Pavlova (1881–1931) was renowned for her portrayal of vulnerable birds and insects (p. 132). One such solo dance vignette was *The Swan* (1907), choreographed by Michel Fokine (1880–1942). Also known as *The Dying Swan* and inspired by the poem of that name by Alfred, Lord Tennyson (1809–92), the piece is set to the thirteenth part of the musical suite *Carnival of Animals* by French composer Camille Saint-Saëns (1835–1921). The complete *Carnival of Animals* was later used for an entire ballet. It calls for a variety of animal characters. The New York City Ballet version premiered in 2003. Choreographed by Christopher Wheeldon, it incorporated a new narration performed by actor John Lithgow.

On the modern dance side, a number of choreographers have incorporated animal movements, characters, and even animals themselves into their work. For *Sleepwalkers* (1968), *Crawling* (1974), and *Planet* (1976), Simone Forti studied animals in the Rome zoo. *Sleepwalkers* is based on sleeping flamingoes standing on one leg and the swinging head movements of polar bears. *Crawling* is taken from the movements of bees, flies, rabbits, brown bears, crows, elephants, and snakes. In *Planet*, Forti uses the character of a bird, lion, elephant, monkey, three bears, and two lizards. Sally Banes, author of *Terpsichore in Sneakers: Post-Modern Dance*, concludes that Forti connects her concept of a "dance state"—by which the choreographer means "the state of enchantment out of which Forti feels she moves" (1980, p. 34)—with that of the meditative state and ritual behavior of captive animals in cages.

Montreal-based choreographer Lucie Grégoire was inspired by birds and their ability to fly when she created *Azur* in 1988. Grégoire frequently uses the theme of nature with metaphorical links to animals in her work. A choreographer who took this one step further is New Yorker Martha Clarke. Her piece *Endangered Species* played at the Brooklyn Academy of Music in 1990 and featured human performers with live animals. Her desire was to show the connection between the fates of all earth's creatures. Hungarian choreographer and dancer Éva Magyar's intentions were less catholic with her 2001 work *House of Deer*. The work is based on a Hungarian folktale about a boy who turns into a deer. Magyar created a visceral piece about finding one's place and means of self-expression.

We have been imitating animals and dancing to their movements since before recorded history. This primal connection continues to captivate and inspire the minds and creative energies of contemporary choreographers from the traditional ballet and modern dances milieus. What we are left with is a better understanding of both ourselves and the animals we mimic.

Further Resources

Anderson, J. (1992). *Ballet & modern dance: A concise history*. Pennington, NJ: Dance Horizons.

Ardener, E. (1959). The Bakweri Elephant Dance. *Nigeria, 60*, 31–38. Available at http://www.bakweri.org/2004/02/the_bakweri_ele.html

Banes, S. (1980). *Terpsichore in sneakers: Post modern dance*. Boston: Houghton Mifflin.

Bourne, M. (2001). Interview with Matthew Bourne. Available at http://www.criticaldance.com/interviews/2001/mbourne9082001.html

———. Matthew Bourne's Swan Lake. Available at http://www.swanlaketour.com/

Buonaventura, W. (2004). *Something in the way she moves: Dancing women from Salome to Madonna*. Cambridge, MA: DaCapo Press.

Carter, A. (2004). *Rethinking dance history: A reader*. London: Routledge.

Clottes, J., & Lewis-Williams, D. (1996). *The shamans of prehistory: Trance and magic in the painted caves*. (S. Hawkes, trans.). New York: Harry N. Abrams, Inc.

Croce, A. (2000). *Writing in the dark: Dancing in the New Yorker*. New York: Farrar, Straus & Giroux.

Forti, S. (1974). *Handbook in motion: An ongoing personal discourse and its manifestations in dance*. Halifax, NS: Press of the Nova Scotia College of Art and Design.

Fraleigh, S. H. (1987). *Dance and the lived body: A descriptive aesthetics*. Pittsburgh, PA: University of Pittsburgh Press.

Gottschild, B. D. (2003). *The black dancing body: A geography from coon to cool*. New York: Palgrave Macmillan.

Grégoire, L. (1988). Azur. Available at http://www.luciegregoire.ca/htm/zaza_lgd00.html

Heninger, B. (2002). Igor Stravinsky: Circus Polka. Redwood Symphony Program Notes 2002. Available at http://www.barbwired.com/barbweb/programs/stravinsky_polka.html

Reynolds, N., & McCormack, M. (2003). *No fixed points: Dance in the twentieth century*. New Haven, CT: Yale University Press.

Schubert, L. (2006). *Ballet of the elephants*. (R. A. Parker, Illus.). Brookfield, CT: Roaring Brook Press.

Shepard, P. (1996). *The others: How animals made us human*. Washington, DC: Island Press.

Thomas, H. (2003). *The body, dance and cultural theory*. New York: Palgrave Macmillan.

Wheeldon, C. (2003). *Carnival of Animals*. Available at http://findarticles.com/p/articles/mi_m1083/is_9_77/ai_108114344

Andrew Cuk

Music, Dance, and Theater
Animals in Theater

Why are there animals in theater? Since the beginning of theatrical history, they have served as links to our human world. They provide a safe distance through which we may criticize ourselves and our culture. This is the most common reason we see animal characters or imagery on the theatrical stage. However, there are many instances that also reveal something about the animals themselves, and not solely as servants to the human endeavor.

The title "Animals in Theater" begs us to define both what we mean by "animals" and "theater." The latter may be interpreted broadly to suggest any live performance that has a semblance of narrative structure. This includes stage plays, musicals, opera, and many forms of performance art. It does not encompass music concerts, poetry and prose readings, circuses, stand-up comedy, and other forms of entertainment in which each portion of the work does not structurally depend on its previous and subsequent parts to relate a story. Although dance falls within our definition, it is discussed in the article "Animals in Dance" in this volume.

In defining "animals," the key consideration is the live nature of the theatrical medium. Does the title only refer to actual living animals performing on a stage, or is it the whole range of animal imagery—visual, oral, metaphorical—as it unfolds before an audience? Let us examine "animals" using the following categories:

1. actual living animals on stage
2. animals portrayed by elements of production
3. humans playing animals without human characteristics
4. humans playing animals with human characteristics
5. animal imagery and metaphors

Using real animals as performers is fraught with problems. Unlike film, which has the benefits of editing, camera angles, and special effects, it is very hard to control animals and get them to repeat the same movements throughout rehearsals and performances. Real animals tend to "steal the show" by their mere presence, and they pull the audience out of the established reality of the play. There are also the ethical considerations regarding the methods of training these animals receive.

Many theatrical works call for the use of real animals—whether one is employed is up to the individual production. Two of the most well-known examples come from the works of William Shakespeare (1564–1616). In *The Two Gentlemen of Verona* (1598), Launce enters with his dog Crab, and in the subsequent soliloquy reenacts the parting scene with his family. He uses his shoes, hat, and staff to indicate his various family members. When he must choose a stand-in for his dog, he says, "I am the dog. No, the dog is himself, and I am the dog. O, the dog is me, and I am myself" (II.3.20–22). This comical confusion demonstrates the very nature of stage illusion, how one thing can be made to signify something completely different by the verbal and nonverbal signs given to the audience. In the second Shakespearean example, Antigonus in *The Winter's Tale* (1610–11) is abandoning a baby in the desert. Shakespeare, who is usually quite stingy with stage directions, has him "*[E]xit, pursued by a bear*" (III.3.56). We do not know whether the author meant to have a real bear on stage, although entertainments such as bear-baiting were quite popular with Elizabethan crowds. One contemporary interdisciplinary performer who uses real animals on stage with both an aesthetic and political purpose is Los Angeles-based Rachel Rosenthal. Her intent in her performances is to make a pro–animal rights statement.

Real or mythological animals may be portrayed by the use of various elements of production. These may include constructions made by set, props, or costume technicians, and they may range from the most detailed realism to the mere suggestion of an animal or part of one. They may be static, operated by some sort of motorized apparatus, or—most likely—operated by stagehands. Animals may also be suggested by the use of lighting and/or sound techniques. Sound effects play a principle role in indicating the presence of an animal, usually off-stage—as in the sound of a dog barking or horses' hooves, for example.

A number of theatrical works demand that actors play animals that do not act like humans. These depictions have varying degrees of realistic animal behavior. Three examples from contemporary literature will demonstrate the broad range of these portrayals. *The Day They Let the Lions Loose* (1957) by Mexican playwright Emilio Carballido requires actors to play two lions as well as other animal characters. Carballido does not wish the lions to look realistic; however, they should be large like real lions, not cute or doll-like. Peter Shaffer, in his 1973 play *Equus,* also demands that a literal approach by the six actors playing horses be avoided. He goes further in his admonition that the actors should never bend forward or get down on all fours, but always "stand upright, as if the body of the horse extended invisibly behind them" (p. 15). The "animal effect," as he calls it, must be suggested mimetically with the face, neck, and limbs. For different reasons—Shaffer for dramatic effect and Carballido for a farcical one—both authors want to strongly suggest real animals without stepping into the trap of trying to create a realistic one—a task that rarely works in the theater. One author who has attempted to create the reality of an animal on stage is Mark Medoff. His play *Prymate* (2004) requires an actor to play a gorilla. Although he wishes the actor to mimic the sound and movement of a real gorilla, Medoff recommends that he not wear a gorilla suit. In the Broadway production, the actor playing the gorilla wore shorts, a t-shirt, and gloves. Medoff, Carballido, and Shaffer create real animals on stage but connect them directly to the humans in the audience, since we clearly see their humanness through the actors portraying them.

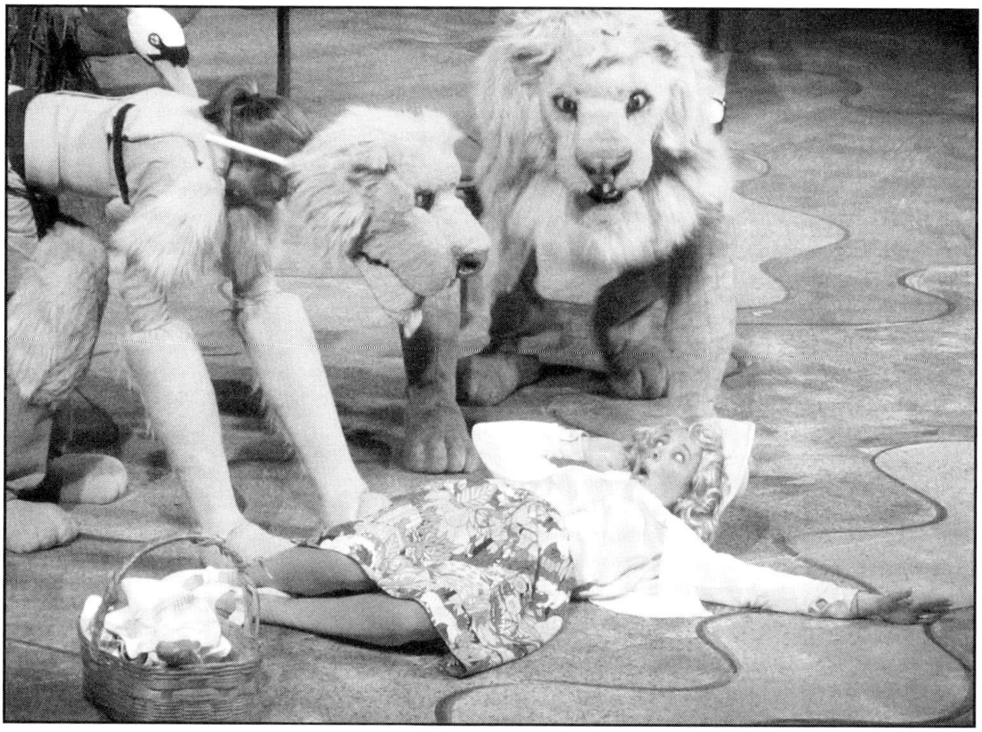

The Day They Let the Lions Loose *by Emilio Carballido, production at John Abbott College (Ste.-Anne-de-Bellevue, Québec), directed by Jason Howell and Andrew Cuk, costumes by Catherine. Performers: Jacinthe Briand-Racine with lions (l–r) Julia Haney and Jeremy Grauer. Courtesy of Andrew Cuk.*

Most likely when we see actors playing animals on stage, they have human characteristics: they talk, have human aspirations, and generally think the way we do. These representations vary from mere veneers of animality—animal characters whose actions as animals are limited or nonexistent—to more elaborate attempts to combine human and animal qualities. This is the predominant method in children's theater, where animal characters serve as conduits to a human moral. However, animals with human characteristics also appear in adult theater. One example that crosses the boundaries of children's and adult theater is the musical *The Lion King* (1997). Based on the 1994 animated Disney film musical, it incorporates over two dozen kinds of animals who speak, sing, and dance. The costumes and the actors' movements suggest the animals they portray, yet we see the faces and bodies of the human performers. Their visible expressions clearly show the connection between these animal characters and us. A similar example from opera is *The Cunning Little Vixen* (1924) by Leoš Janáček (1854–1928). One of Janáček's intentions in this opera about a fox family was to show the parallels between the human and animal worlds, and to this effect he changed the original happy ending from the novel by Rudolf Tésnohlidek (1882–1928) to a story ending with the death of the fox mother. John Tyrrell comments that this "turns the work from a light-hearted tale for children into a serious work, which, for all its comic touches, is able to include and comprehend death" (pp. 19–20).

Animals with human or anthropomorphic characteristics have appeared in dramatic literature since its inception in Western and Eastern cultures. One need only look at the fifth-century BCE Greek playwright Aristophanes, whose plays *The Birds*, *The Frogs*, and *The Wasps* use animal characters for political and cultural satire. In 1972, English director Peter Brook and writer Jean-Claude Carriere adapted the twelfth-century Persian poet Farid Uddin Attar's *The Conference of the Birds,* and future productions are encouraged to use imagination to determine the nature of the "bird form" of each avian character.

The largest category of the use of animals does not show animals on stage. There a many instances of animal imagery and metaphors in the theater: from common phrases, such as "she is as quiet as a mouse," to more elaborate symbols and references. The connection between humans and our animal counterparts may not be readily apparent in the simpler of these, but certainly many authors intend the link. Mexican author Elena Garro (1920–98), for instance, entitled her 1983 one-act play *The Dogs,* and although the dogs are predominant in the story and the play utilizes much dog and other animal imagery, the canines never appear. Garro wants the audience to equate the dogs with the mother and daughter of the play. We are meant to empathize and see the similarities of the tragic ending of these animals and women.

It is understandable that animals, who play such an important role in our daily lives, should have representation in our works of art. The theater is no exception, although the live nature of the medium tends to the metaphorical rather than the realistic.

Further Resources

Allen, M. (1983). *Animals in American literature.* Urbana: University of Illinois Press.

Aristophanes. (1962). *The complete plays of Aristophanes.* (Moses Hadas, Ed.). New York: Bantam Books.

Baker, S. (2000). *The postmodern animal.* London: Reaktion Books.

Carballido, E. (1971). The day they let the lions loose. In W. I. Oliver (Ed.), *Voices of change in the Spanish American theater: An anthology* (pp. 1–46). Austin, TX: University of Texas Press.

Carriere, J. C., & Brook, P. *The conference of birds*. Chicago: Dramatic Publishing Company.

Chaudhuri, U. Animal acts for changing times. Available at http://www.hotreview.org/articles/animalacts.htm

Cuk, A. (2004). *Animal imagery in contemporary Mexican theatre*. PhD Dissertation. University of California.

Disney Online. *The lion king*. Available at http://disney.go.com/disneytheatrical/thelionking

Garro, E. (1990). *The dogs*. In A. K. Stoll (Ed.), *A different reality: Studies on the work of Elena Garro* (pp. 68–80). Lewisburg, PA: Bucknell University Press.

Medoff, M. (2005). *Prymate*. New York: Dramatist's Play Service. Available at http://www.rachelrosenthal.org/

Sax, B. (1998). Bestial wisdom and human tragedy: The genesis of the animal epic. *Anthrozoös, 11*(3), 134–41.

———. (2001). *The mythical zoo: An encyclopedia of animals in world myth, legend, & literature*. Santa Barbara, CA: ABC-CLIO.

Scholtmeijer, M. (1993). *Animal victims in modern fiction: From sanctity to sacrifice*. Toronto: University of Toronto Press.

Shaffer, P. (1974). *Equus*. Garden City, NY: Nelson Doubleday.

Shakespeare, W. (1963). *The winter's tale* (F. Kermode, Ed.). New York: Signet Classics.

———. (1968). *The two gentlemen of Verona* (N. Sanders, Ed.). Middlesex: Penguin Books.

Shepard, P. (1996). *The others: How animals made us human*. Washington, DC: Island Press.

Tyrell, J. (1981). Leoš Janáček: *The cunning little vixen*. Liner notes, 13–27. *Leoš Janáček: The Cunning Little Vixen*, conducted by Sir Charles Mackerras. Decca Records.

Andrew Cuk

Music, Dance, and Theater
Interspecies Music

There is no doubt that humans have recognized the musical possibilities inherent in the sounds of animals for thousands of years, perhaps even longer than we have been able to speak. In his recent book *The Singing Neanderthals* (2006), archeologist Steven Mithen argues that Neanderthals had only a musical form of communication, using a kind of emotive structured cry with form and shape for its own sake, more like the songs of birds and whales than the syntax that defines human language and separates our vocal interaction more from the natural world. He then concludes that music for Neanderthals was much more important than it could ever be for Homo sapiens, because it was all the vocal communication they had.

Needless to say, this is a rather radical view that not all in his field would agree with, but it does point to an intriguing idea. Musical communication, as it is practiced by many in the animal world including birds, insects, whales, and wolves, may be more important to these creatures than it could ever be to us. Their music is clearly necessary and essential and has evolved over millions of years. They know the right song when they hear it; there is no need to endlessly search and experiment looking for the works of genius that just might endure. Human musicians have to struggle a lot more.

Why are these animal sounds music and not simply forms of language? Because the message in them is usually something similar and simple, with the males doing most of the singing. Attract a mate. Defend a territory. End of story? That is the function, the purpose, which says nothing about the inherent structure and beauty of the sounds, which evolution has so wonderfully produced. Natural selection is not really survival of the fittest, but survival of the interesting.

How to make sense of this animal music? Play along. Though it is common to look at whistling with canaries or talking to parrots as a kind of parlor trick or joke, it can instead be seen as a very serious activity indeed. Music, too, is a form of knowledge. By reaching out with beautiful sound we can touch the intelligence of other creatures in a way that is hard to measure but easy to appreciate. It is too easy to dismiss it all as wishful anthropomorphizing, but the musical approach is easier than imagining that animal sound is some alien language to decipher. Think instead of a foreign rhythm unfamiliar, but still a groove you can latch onto. Darwin wrote in *The Descent of Man* of the aesthetic sense in animals, and what better way to try to learn that sense than to take the leap and join in?

Thousand-year-old petroglyphs found in Russian Karelia may depict a man communicating sonically with beluga whales. Part of the traditional human way of living in a natural context includes the belief that all species listen to one another and respond as they are designed to do. It is simply not true that animals only respond to their own songs. It has long been noted in Indonesia that after a concert of gamelan music, all the insects will sing in an especially synchronized manner. Cicadas will fly at a loud ring of a gong, a sound very different from the ones they make themselves. For centuries European bird trainers have known that bullfinches, which only make a faint whistle in the wild, can be trained to repeat any simple melody within a several octave range. Why do they have this ability that they only use in captivity? No one knows, but in Germany during the eighteenth and nineteenth centuries, there were numerous bullfinch "academies" in which birds were taught to sing, and the best singers competed in public contests throughout the land. An early English collection of recorder tunes called *The Bird Fancyers Delight* includes pieces meant to be played specifically to starlings, chaffinches, and bramblings, all of which were observed to join in with melodies tailored to their aesthetic sense. There was even a small, high-pitched recorder called the "bird flageolet," which was recommended for such interspecies tutoring.

Birds are of course the most obvious singers in the animal world to have impressed human composers. Although Beethoven and Mozart each used specific bird songs in their music, they tended to laugh when asked about it—Mozart's elegy for his pet starling is entitled "A Musical Joke." Even Olivier Messiaen, the great twentieth-century French composer who spent years traveling the world transcribing the songs of as many birds as he could find in detailed, very abstract musical notation, never tried to jam along with these sounds. But in 1924, the world's first outdoor radio broadcast changed all that. British cellist Beatrice Harrison convinced the BBC to broadcast live from her garden at night, where nightingales sang along with her solo performances of Elgar's cello concerto and Londonderry Air. This radio program was heard by millions of listeners all over the world and was repeated live every year for twelve years with great success, thereby suggesting that listeners, if not composers, were certainly ready to admit the reality of interspecies music.

Late in the twentieth century the American jazz musician Paul Winter built his career upon the possibilities inherent in improvising with the natural world. His most successful wild experiments involved wailing on his soprano saxophone along with howling wolves, but he has also used recorded humpback whale songs as live elements in just about every concert he performs. Playing live with whales is much more difficult, but electric guitarist Jim Nollman has spent decades broadcasting his bluesy, feedback-tinged sound under the water so orcas and belugas can respond. Nollman offers some sage advice for those willing to try it: "Treat the music as an invitation. Visualize the bond of time and place as a sanctuary filled with music. Feel what it means to get on whale time. Don't try to communicate; remain humble to the fact that music—especially 'beautiful music'—is a judgment call. That rare bird known as the interspecies musician learns to meet the animal halfway, two species willing to play in the same band, if but for a moment. It frolics with our basic conception of what it means to be both human and animal." Both Winter and Nollman's music were tremendously important in building global support for saving the whales, resulting in a worldwide ban on commercial whaling in the 1980s. If they sing, and we can sing with them, how can we kill them off?

The rock musician Peter Gabriel, long a supporter of the intelligence of primates and a critic of the way these animals have been used in scientific research, began playing live with bonobo apes at the primate research center in Georgia in the 1990s. Recordings of these sessions are strangely melancholic, showing the famous ape Kanzi fingering a plaintive melody on an electric keyboard while Gabriel and bassist Tony Levin play along behind a protective glass. The song that resulted from this collaboration urges us to listen outward beyond the limits of humanity: "I didn't meet you in the jungle/Swinging from a tree/I sat down at the piano/You were playing with me . . . Intelligent life is all around us. . . . Talk to me now/I am listening . . . Communication with the animal nation/We are in communication with the animal nation."

The coming decades may see a much greater acceptance of the creative abilities of animals and our ability to interact with them intelligently. As human music grows to encompass ever more kinds of sounds and listens more sensitively to what is around us, there will be more interspecies music than ever before. It works best when the human musician welcomes the encounter with openness and respect, ready to take in the unfamiliar and genuinely learn something new, to change one's musical sense in the presence of new and exciting sounds. Approach the situation without too many expectations, and let us make music together that neither species could make apart. It is one more way for us to learn about and to appreciate the animal world.

See also

Communication and Language—*Similarities in Vocal Learning between Animals and Humans*

Music, Dance, and Theater—*Music as a Shared Trait among Humans and Animals*

Further Resources

Mithen, S. (2006). *The singing Neanderthals.* Cambridge, MA: Harvard University Press.

Nollman, J. (1999). *The charged border: Where whales and humans meet.* New York: Holt.

Rothenberg, D. (2005). *Why birds sing.* New York: Basic Books.

Rothenberg, D., & Ulvaeus, M. (Eds.). (1977). *The book of music and nature.* Lebanon, NH: Wesleyan University Press.

Schafer, R. M. (1977). *The tuning of the world.* New York: Knopf.

David Rothenberg

Music, Dance, and Theater
Music and Animals

There are two means of refuge from the miseries of life: music and cats.
—Albert Schweitzer

First off, do animal sounds qualify as music? My new Oxford American Dictionary defines "music" as:

1. the art or science of combining vocal or instrumental sounds (or both) to produce beauty of form, harmony, and expression of emotion.
2. a sound perceived as pleasingly harmonious.

If we remove "science" from the first definition, the sounds produced by at least some animals qualify for both definitions of music.

As our music is hugely varied in character, so too is the music of other animals, from the melodic songs of birds and the percussive clicks of fishes, to the buzzes and trills of insects, and the resonating anthems of whales. Some animal music is produced at too high a pitch and/or too fast a speed for us to detect or appreciate. The recently discovered songs that courting male house mice sing to females are spilled out in the span of just a fraction of a second and in the ultrasonic range. So too are the courtship songs of male sac-winged bats while they hover in front of females. At the other extreme, the deep rumbles of some whale sounds are too low for the human ear, and a single humpback whale song can span an hour and a singing session ten hours.

Are animals thinking about their music making? The skill with which certain birds mimic other sounds indicates a tuning in to the sounds of others and a capacity to shape one's own sounds to sounds that are probably not genetically preprogrammed. I have often listened captivated as a mockingbird rattles off an array of songs and calls of other bird species that inhabit his region. In suburban Maryland, I watched a mockingbird that in one brief session produced convincing renditions of Blue jay, Northern flicker, Eastern pewee, Eastern phoebe, Eastern kingbird, Killdeer, Tufted titmouse, American robin, Carolina wren, and European starling. In one night, two African Gray parrots recorded in Zaire produced more than 200 different motifs or songs, twenty-three of which were mimics of nine other bird species and one of a bat. Human sounds are also fair game for bird mimics. A male superb lyrebird filmed in Australia mimicked impeccably the sounds of a camera shutter, a camera with motor drive, a car alarm, chainsaws, and conventional saws. There may even sometimes be an element of humor in a bird's mimicry. There certainly is for us. Starlings have been known to disrupt European football (soccer) matches by mimicking the sound of the referee's whistle. A chaffinch in the London area learned to sing the sound of a phone ringing and appeared to use this as a prank to compel the master of the house to rush inside. We cannot be sure that the little bird found this comical, but he was perhaps entertained by the cause-and-effect dynamic.

Another facet of birds' musical sense is in their sense of timing. Some birds pack an incredible amount of complexity into short bursts of song, and it is only by recording these sounds at high speed and playing them back slowly that our own brains can process the compressed symphony within. Then there is the antiphonal calling of some species, in which two or more birds intercalate their calls, producing a unified sequence. In 2005, a team of ornithologists unofficially awarded the prize for most complex vocal performance by a nonhuman to the plain-tailed wren of Ecuador. Between four and seven birds gather to sing antiphonally with phrases alternating between the sexes. The resulting song is an amazing feat of coordination: although each sex has its own repertoire of about twenty phrases, the net effect is so perfectly synchronized that it sounds like a continuous allegro from a single bird.

The feelings we get in response to the sounds of other animals express our biological connection with them. The emerging field of biomusicology explores the idea of a "universal music," an intuitive musical sense shared by many animals, including humans. One's own response to a particular bird's song is personal and not easily described. But through music, many have expressed their admiration for the music of other beings. Mozart rewrote a passage from the last movement of his *Piano Concerto in G Major* to complement the song of his beloved pet starling. The solo piano piece *A Hermit Thrush at Eve,* by the American composer Amy Beach, was the result of an extensive musical dialog between the thrush, who sang his "lonely and appealing" songs over and over, and Beach, who wrote them down, revising with each repetition. So entranced was the American musicologist and humorist PDQ Bach by the tunes of a wood thrush emanating from the woods near his home that he composed a piece of music to it. Frederick Delius's *On Hearing the First Cuckoo in Spring* and Ralph Vaughan-Williams's *Lark Ascending* are among many more such examples.

The musicality of animal sounds other than avian also appeals to many of us. American musician Paul Winter has incorporated the sounds of many mammals and birds into his recordings, notably his 1994 *Prayer for the Wild Things*. Canadian musician Bruce Cockburn was obviously affected by the sounds of African frogs, whose ethereal chirps and trills grace several of the tracks on his 2003 recording *You've Never Seen Everything*.

We would be naïve to think that our music sprung spontaneously from our cultures, independent of the music that already filled the skies (and seas). Music resonates so well with our emotions, it feels organic. When I hear or play J. S. Bach's music, I feel as if it has existed for as long as the universe and that it was waiting for someone to write it down. It would also seem narrow thinking to assume that only we could derive pleasure from sound.

That other animals produce complex sounds associated with such emotive activities as courtship, mating, territory establishment, and social cohesion implies that for them, too, music can be a source of arousal and pleasure. As we understand more about the emotions of other animals, we may appreciate that their music, like ours, can be imbued with feelings. Some scientists, schooled to be skeptical of anthropomorphism, are reluctant to wade into the terrain of animal experience. Not so noted philosopher and ornithologist Charles Hartshorne, who recorded and analyzed the songs of hundreds of bird species over fifty years and concluded that birds sometimes sing because they are happy (Hartshorne, 1973). Musician David Rothenberg, in his 2005 book *Why Birds Sing,* reached a similar conclusion.

Through careful observation and study, we can begin to illuminate how a whale or a warbler might feel when they listen in on our music, or theirs. Several studies have shown that birds recognize and show preferences for human music. Java Finches learned to discriminate the music of Bach from that of Schoenberg played on the same instrument by the same performer. The trained birds could correctly identify pieces by these composers that they had not previously heard. They could also generalize to different composers, linking Bach to his Baroque contemporary Vivaldi, and Schoenberg to Eliot Carter. Some birds preferred the early music, others not. Pigeons can generalize from Bach to Buxtehude and Scarlatti, all Baroque composers, and among the modern composers Stravinsky, Carter, and Walter Piston.

This musical sense is not restricted to birds. Rats can also discriminate musical stimuli and performed better in a maze after being exposed to Mozart compared with Philip Glass. To my knowledge, neither frogs nor fish have been tested for a proclivity for the likes of Mendelssohn or Debussy, but studies show they can discriminate sounds on the basis of their harmonic structure, which suggests that basic aspects of human sound perception, such as pitch and timbre, are shared by all vertebrates.

An animal's response to the music of its own kind may depend on context. A resident male thrush probably feels quite different when he hears the song of another male intruding on his territory than does a nearby female. If it is not clear what aspect(s) of human or animal music an animals responds to, noninvasive experiments can be devised to examine this question. Starlings, for instance, have been found to recognize different chord types and rhythms. However, this still does not tell us about the bird's *experience* of music.

There is some evidence—mostly anecdotal—that farmed animals, including cattle, pigs, and chickens, respond favorably and selectively to the sounds of certain music. A nine-week study of a herd of 1,000 Friesian cows at the University of Leicester reported that milk yield rose by 3 percent a day when slow music, rather than fast music, was played. An unpublished study recorded 5.5 percent increased milk production in forty-two Holstein cows exposed to dramatic classical music, and a 6 percent reduction with rock music. Milk let-down has been shown to improve in relaxed cows, thus it is generally thought that increased milk yields reflect reduced stress and happier cows. But while positive milk production may reflect preference, it should not be assumed to reflect happiness, given that milked cows have had their calves taken away, which is an emotional upheaval for them.

Inevitably, there are disturbing aspects to the place of music in humankind's relationship to animals. How many birds have been imprisoned in tiny cages, unable to express their natural urge to fly or perform other motivated behaviors, because of the beauty of their plumage and voices? And how many naïve tourists have been hoodwinked into thinking that the swaying movements of defanged, half-starved, and sometimes blinded Indian cobras are in response to the sound, rather than to the swaying movements of the flute player?

Studies of animals' responses to human music suggest not only that birds and mammals may perceive music stimuli much as we do, they also demonstrate individual musical preference, which could also mean that our music has esthetic value for them. Neuroscientist Jaak Panksepp believes that human music triggers brain mechanisms evolved to respond to the crying of infants. Studies find that when parents and offspring reunite following a separation, chemical changes in their brains closely resemble those of other pleasure responses.

We must of course be guarded about reading too much into an animal's responses to music. In a study in which six cotton-top tamarins were given a choice in a V-shaped maze between consonant and dissonant tone interval sounds, the monkeys showed no preference. This study suggests that these monkeys at least may not be responsive to tonal sounds, though we must be careful about interpreting the behavior of animals in a context far removed from their natural milieu.

Ethologist and dog behavior expert Michael Fox once had a wolf named Tiny, who shared his life with Fox and his other canine companions for over a decade. According to Fox (personal communication, November 2005), Tiny demonstrated an acute musical sense in her reaction to his playing the Japanese shakuhachi flute. When Fox first raised the instrument and sounded a note, Tiny cocked her head and looked intently at both flute and Fox, raised her head and began to howl. Fox reports her note matched the one he was playing, and that she liked one particular note, which she would sing as soon as Fox found it on his flute. A visiting opera singer heard Tiny's singing and expressed astonishment at her musical sense. He also observed that she was "chording," singing two notes at the same time, as Tibetan monks do, and in perfect harmony with Fox's flute.

I am aware of anecdotal claims of birds singing in tune, including those of an accomplished American pianist who sent me written notes and a recording of birds singing during her playing of Bach, Mozart, and Schumann. Having listened to the tapes twice, I was unable to detect any clear or consistent tonal or temporal relation between the piano sounds and those of the birds (including captive finches and budgerigars and various wild species, including sparrows, doves, robins, cardinals, and crows). The pianist cautioned me that it takes some practice to concentrate on the birds' sounds, as our attention tends to gravitate naturally to those of our own species' music. Of course, if animals do not sing in key with human music it need not mean they are not relating to it on some level. The most tonally challenged of humans appear to enjoy music no less than do those with perfect pitch.

Anecdotes like these offer enticing suggestions that some animals may relate tonally to human music. An animal's ability to produce sounds in tune to music can certainly be tested scientifically using sound analysis equipment. What such responses might tell us of the animals' emotional experience is more elusive. We may never know just how another creature feels when listening to music, be it our own or that of their own kind. But we can be quite certain that music is emotive for them as it is for us. And as the emotional experiences of animals gain acceptance in scientific circles, we can hope that more insights can be gained from their study.

Further Resources

Balcombe, J. P. (2006). *Pleasurable kingdom: Animals and the nature of feeling good.* London: Macmillan.

Hartshorne, C. (1973). *Born to song: An interpretation and world survey of bird song.* Bloomington, IN: Indiana University Press.

Holy, T. E., & Guo, Z. (2005). Ultrasonic songs of male mice. *PLoS Biology, 3,* 386.

Rothenberg, D. (2005). *Why birds sing: A journey into the mystery of bird song.* New York: Basic Books.

Watanabe, S, & Sato, K. (1999). Discriminative stimulus properties of music in Java sparrows. *Behavioural Processes, 47,* 53–57.

Jonathan Balcombe

Music, Dance, and Theater
Music as a Shared Trait among Humans and Animals

Music is traditionally viewed as a method of communication between humans and other animals. Human music is said to "soothe the savage beast," and the songs of birds are often described as one of the most pleasing natural sounds. However, it is difficult to determine whether animals truly appreciate our music or try to reach us with theirs. It is also debated whether animal sounds that we interpret as musical are viewed in this way by the animals themselves.

It is often asserted that the creation of music is a uniquely human ability. As with other qualities (such as language, the use of abstract concepts, or insight learning), there are researchers and commentators that argue for and against the idea that music is a "humans only" ability, or whether human music has special qualities not found in animal equivalent. For example, human music is often assumed to have qualities other than functional goals (art rather than simply sending a message), whereas animal music is generally explained in terms of its purely functional goals even when it is demonstrably complex, structured, and flexible (e.g., whale song).

Researchers who study animals (called ethologists) are more inclined to say there is no clear distinction between how humans perceive and create music and how other animals do—making music a potential source of common experience and communication between species. However, some specialists in the musical sounds made by animals prefer to study animals without making comparisons with human behavior to ensure that they study the animal in its own right rather than assuming its actions are human-like (sometimes called "anthropomorphizing").

The debate about the equivalence of music between humans and other animals can be traced back to the writings of Darwin, who suggested that music is an ancient shared trait of humans and animals that stems from the desire to attract sexual partners, versus Spencer, who asserted music arose uniquely in humans from emotional speech (a debate summarized by Peter Kivy in the article "Charles Darwin on Music"). Herzog summarized what continues to be the position of many researchers of animal behavior in writing, "From a pure formal point of view, there seems to be no reliable criterion that would establish a fundamental difference between animal and human expression in sound."

This disagreement about the role of music continues today, with most musicologists inclined to believe that although the human ability to appreciate music has evolutionary underpinnings that leave humans and other animals with common skills and abilities to perceive music, both true music and true language are present only in humans. Ethologists commonly counter this assertion by demonstrating that the songs of some birds and whales show a degree of complexity and flexibility in performance that is equivalent to that found in human performances—and so it is difficult to point to any quantitative difference that prevents us from seeing animal music as directly equivalent to human music.

The Effects of Music upon Animals

It is not clear how other animals regard human music, but a range of studies suggest that it is beneficial to play music for animals captive in farms, zoos, and shelters. When music is played animals are often found to be calmer and more productive, with slow classical and easy listening often having more benefits than other musical styles. Similar positive effects have been shown on the behavior and productivity of farm animals such as dairy cows. This information may only demonstrate that music helps mask silence, sudden noise, and other unpleasant auditory states. However, it may also suggest that animals benefit from music emotionally.

Extensive research shows that some animals can respond to complex aspects of music in a way that suggests an ability to perceive the same qualities in music that humans do. Species including koi (fish) and pigeons have been shown to distinguish between musical styles and to recognize the style of novel musical pieces. Various species have been shown to be able to recognize the same piece transposed an octave. Although some studies have failed to find these abilities, their presence even in some animals suggests a widespread appreciation of music's basic qualities that is consistent with the idea that melodic music is as pleasing to many nonhuman species as it is to us. It has also been shown that animals have both innate and learned preferences between composers. For example, rats tend to prefer music by Mozart to pieces composed by Schoenberg, but they will also be biased toward music that they were exposed to when young.

Taken together this research indicates that animals' responses to music can be complex and subtle and form the foundation for personal likes and dislikes. Based upon this information, it is possible to see marked similarities between the way humans and other animals respond to human music. It is debatable whether this assumption is a solid support for the idea that music is a method for interspecies communication, but the idea remains plausible—and the basis for a burgeoning industry offering to sell CDs made specifically with your pet in mind (a dubious product unless the preferences of similar animals were studied in making the selections).

Humans in Animal Music

Many animals add sounds from the environment to their vocal range. Animals in the wild have been observed to mimic many human-produced noises, including cell phones. However, human-made noise also seems to disrupt and block communicative music—such as the effect of motor noise upon the distance whale song is able to travel through the oceans. Humans and birds engage in mutual mimicry of musical and language sounds.

Animals in Human Music

Most human cultures create music about animals, ranging from depicting animals realistically to using them as quasi-human figures or more abstract symbols. The role of animals in song shapes our beliefs about and relationship with this species. This is an ongoing process; one recent example is the growing movement among animal rights activists to develop songs that reflect their perspectives or replace songs for children in which animals are portrayed negatively or harmed (such as "three blind mice").

The appearance of animals in the music of specific cultures has been studied but received little in the way of general review. It appears that animal-related music tends to reflect the most important connections each culture or subculture has to animals. Examples range from the repeated attempts to portray the essence of animals in classical music (e.g., Camille Saint-Saens' *Carnival of the Animals*) to the use of animal calls in Native American songs (e.g., the "Kwakiutl Raven Song"). There are many modern musical recordings and performances themed around animals, often targeted toward children or families.

Human music often deliberately mimics the beauty of animal music, such as passages in Mozart's *Piano Concerto in G Major,* which is modeled on the call of a starling—and it is possible that animal music was a formative influence on human music and that the two have been connected from the very beginning. Some bio-musicologists argue that this ongoing connection between human and animal music is close to forming one set of principles, and which species composers and listeners come from is not a matter of prime importance.

The Mozart Effect on Humans and Other Animals

Some types of music are said to have a specific effect on both humans and other animals. Classical music, specifically Mozart, is said to improve performance on intellectually demanding tasks. As such it has been proposed that Mozart should be played to human infants. The evidence for this comes from two main sources. One is that listening to Mozart improves the performance of humans on some spatial tasks and on rats in the maze; however, this could be attributed to these subjects feeling relaxed by the slow tempo music and so calmer and more able to focus on the task. The other theory is that young children who learn to play music do better in their other classes—but this is a complex situation with many factors, including the fact that the children themselves chose to play music and so may have been different from the beginning. Overall there is not a clear demonstration that Mozart's music has direct effects upon the brain—although humans and other animals seem to have an innate preference for the work of this composer over many others, suggesting a special role for some types of music for a range of species and a potential shared experience.

In forming an opinion about how music creates a bond between humans and other animals, we must take into account that music's effects are often subtle, implicit, and difficult to appreciate. As Elizabeth Tolbert wrote, music is often vague in the content it conveys and so "not language," and yet we react to music so easily and intuitively that it is also considered a "universal language."

Subjective responses to music are hard to measure with animals since we do not share a common, unambiguous language. And music can have powerful effects without even the direct mechanism of conscious experience. For example, playing music to human patients was shown to improve recovery from hysterectomy *when played only while they were unconscious* under anesthetic in the operating theater.

When we use the scientific method we are often required to use the simplest explanation for any phenomenon (using a rule called Occam's razor or Lloyd Morgan's Canon). So in observing that dogs in a shelter become more relaxed when played music, the simplest explanation is that the musical sound blocks stressful sounds and breaks monotonous silence—but it remains possible that music communicates to animals on an emotional level, just as it does with us. The observation that bird and whale songs have roles in mate selection and territorial defense does not rule out the possibility that these animals sing for the sake of the music—and maybe even sometimes sing for us.

When it comes to finding a window into the experience of animals, we continue to have difficulty really knowing what animals intend by making their music and what they feel when hearing ours. People seem to divide into two groups. One feels that animals make and experience music and feel about music much as we do; one group declares that it is impossible to prove that this is true, dangerous to assume, and far too easy to make false assumptions when we see animals as "furry humans" rather than species with their own ways of seeing the world, which often diverge sharply from our own.

Nonetheless, many believe that if a human listener chooses to perceive animal musical sound as "music" or to share human music with animals, they allow for the possibility of a unique form of communication and bonding. The subjective intentions and experiences of animals remain as inaccessible to us except through indirect evidence and intuition.

See also

Culture, Religion, and Belief Systems—*Rituals of Humans and Animals*
Music, Dance, and Theater—*Interspecies Music*

Further Resources

Herzog, G. (1941). Do animals have music? *Bulletin of the American Musicological Society, 5*, 3–4.

Kivy, P. (1959). Charles Darwin on music. *Journal of the American Musicological Society, 12* (1), 42–48.

Nilsson, U., Rawal, N., Unestahl, L. E., Zetterberg, C., & Unosson, M. (2001). Improved recovery after music and therapeutic suggestions during general anaesthesia: A double-blind randomised controlled trial. *Acta Anaesthesiologica Scandinavica*, *45* (7), 812–17.
Tolbert, E. (2001). The enigma of music, the voice of reason: 'Music', 'language', and becoming human. *New Literary History*, *32* (3), 451–65

Emily Patterson-Kane

Pets
See Bonding.

Play
Human and Animal Play

Play is common in the young of many animal species, including humans. By understanding the nature of play in humans and other animals, we can better understand why play is important for the young of many species and learn to apply this knowledge to promote the well-being of the animals around us.

What Exactly Is Play?

Although researchers have not come up with a precise definition of play that everyone can agree on, most observers of animal (and human) behavior report that they "know it when they see it." Play differs from more "serious" forms of behavior because, at least on the surface, it appears to have no apparent function. Animals fight to gain access to mates, they flee to escape predators, and they forage to find food. But play behaviors (such as "fighting" with a littermate without inflicting harm or running in circles around a tree trunk) have no apparent purpose or goal. Play behaviors also look different—they usually are forms of functional behaviors (such as fighting or prey capture) that are exaggerated, reordered, incomplete, brief, repeated, varied in sequence, or inhibited in nature. A play bite, for example, is gentle and does not hurt the play partner.

Which Animals Play?

Although play is common in many mammals and some birds, Gordon Burghardt presents evidence that it may occur in some lizard, turtle, and fish species, as well. Playful species vary considerably in how much they play, but it is clear that primate and carnivore species are among the most playful. Individuals in playful species (including humans) show a similar course of play throughout development. Play begins in infancy, peaks in the juvenile years, and declines thereafter. In some species, play may continue into adulthood, but at much lower rates than in the juvenile period.

Scientists are beginning to identify some of the factors associated with the nature of play across species. In the case of play with objects, for example, primate species that show the greatest diversity and most complex forms of object play are those that: (1) are diurnal versus nocturnal (i.e., are active mostly during daylight hours); (2) are terrestrial versus arboreal (i.e., spend most of their time on the ground rather than in trees); (3) are bipedal versus quadrupedal (i.e., spend more time walking on two feet versus four); (4) have few or no natural predators; (5) have long periods of immaturity where they are able to manipulate objects long before they can independently move from one place to another; and (6) possess anatomical characteristics that support the visual and motor exploration of objects, including color vision, stereoscopy, opposability of the thumb and fingers, finger independence, tactile sensitivity, and large brains with well-developed visual and motor cortexes. That is, primate species showing the most elaborate forms of object play are those whose members are active during daylight, have hands that are not involved in competing activities (e.g., holding onto branches or walking), are not overly concerned about predators, have hands and brains that are well-adapted for object manipulation, and have extended infant and juvenile periods. Given these patterns, it is not surprising that humans engage in the most complex and diverse forms of object play of any primate species.

Why Do Animals Play?

The fact that play is more common in species with longer periods of immaturity has led researchers to speculate that extended opportunities to play with objects before maturity allows animals sufficient time to practice the survival skills that they will need as adults. Primates whose young engage in the highest levels of object play (e.g., chimpanzees, capuchin monkeys) often must engage in "omnivorous extractive foraging" as adults—that is, they sometimes must obtain plant and insect foods by such means as using stones to open nuts, using probes to access hidden foods, using leaf sponges to drink liquids, and peeling bark to get to insects. Object play for such species may provide young animals with the skills that they will need for effective foraging as adults.

The function of animal and human play has been the focus of much debate and has been difficult to study scientifically. Although the earliest functional hypotheses were that play provided animals practice in survival-related behavior (such as the example regarding object play above), there are little data to show that animals deprived of play are deficient in their survival skills. Animals deprived of play-fighting experience, for example, are not necessarily poorer fighters, and the amount of time that carnivores engage in prey-capturing play is not associated with later prey-capturing ability. Although play may be just a way that young animals burn off excess energy or kill time waiting to grow up, this seems unlikely. The young of many species devote considerable time and energy to play, often putting themselves at risk for injury and predation. As far as we can tell, play has a long evolutionary history, so if it serves no adaptive purpose, we expect that it would have disappeared from the behavior of young animals, due to natural selection.

More recent theories of play function focus on possible social functions—for example, facilitating the development of social bonds, helping animals learn to assess the fighting abilities of others, and facilitating cooperation and trust. Recent theories have focused on more subtle benefits of play as well—learning to cope with the unexpected, learning to regulate emotions, and cognitive stimulation. Such hypotheses have been offered and tested for both humans and other animals. It is likely that researchers will continue to pursue this issue for years to come.

How Does Animal Play Differ from Human Play?

Humans engage in all the major forms of play observed in other primates, including solitary object play, play-fighting, locomotor play (i.e., chasing and acrobatics), and social object play. Not surprisingly, the play of humans is most similar to that of our closest relative, the chimpanzee. Longitudinal studies of primates, for example, show that across species, young primates show very similar age-related patterns in the nature of their object play (although nonhuman primates go through the stages more quickly than humans).

Major differences in humans and other primates appear after twelve months of age, with humans engaging in more relational behaviors (such as tower building or putting a cube in a cup), more pretend behaviors (such as "drinking" out of an empty cup), and more playful sequences of action. Apes proceed to higher stages of object play than do monkeys, consistent with the greater biological similarities between apes and humans.

Although there have been virtually no empirical studies of locomotor play in humans (making comparison with the animal data impossible), studies of play-fighting in humans reveal many similarities with other animals. Children use similar play-fighting tactics as other primates (with the exception of the play-mounting and possibly play-biting), and, as in other species of play-fighting mammals, play-fighting in humans differs from serious fighting in specific ways. In both humans and other play-fighting mammals, play-fighting is accompanied by general amicable signals, is of reduced intensity, is of longer duration, involves "attacks" directed toward different body targets, is accompanied by role reversals and self-handicapping, rarely results in physical injury, and is terminated with the partners in close physical proximity. Play-fighting in both humans and other animals shows the same developmental course with age, and, like many other species, humans usually choose play partners of the same gender, and females are more likely than males to terminate play-fights with opposite-sexed partners. Finally, like many primates, males in both Western and non-Western cultures engage in more play-fighting than do females.

The main differences between the play of humans and other animals concern the roles of language and pretend. Unlike other animals, children in the preschool years spend a great deal of their playtime involved in fantasy play, and older children engage in structured, rule-governed games. Much of children's fantasy play involves acting out adult roles in a pretend context. Although researchers have recently identified examples of pretend play in chimpanzees and other apes, these are usually brief and infrequent.

When Do Humans and Animals Play?

Numerous studies show that play is most likely to occur when the child or animal has sufficient opportunities to play and when the individual is well-nourished, healthy, and not under stress. Surprisingly, some studies show that captive animals in enriched environments often show higher levels of play than animals in the wild. It appears that in these circumstances, the availability of play materials increases opportunities for play, little time must be devoted to foraging and finding food, and there is no threat from predators. Even in the absence of environmental supports, young animals will show great resourcefulness in creating opportunities for play. For example, although adult-child play is uncommon in many species, if age-mates are not available for play, young animals will initiate and engage in play with the adults that are present. Similarly, if no toys are available, children are often quite resourceful at finding objects, such as sticks and rocks, for their play activities. Studies consistently show that children or animals that are hungry, unhealthy, tired, or afraid are much less likely to play than individuals that are healthy and secure.

Implications for Human-Animal Relationships

Understanding the nature of play in humans and animals can help us promote the well-being of the animals in our communities. First, because we all know that play is enjoyable (and researchers such as Jaak Panksepp now have data that suggest that the brain pathways involved in play and laughter are common across mammals—human and otherwise), we should do what we can to provide animals with opportunities for play. Because, as mammals, we are equipped with much of the same play repertoire as our animal companions, this usually comes naturally—chasing or play-fighting with the dog, letting the cat bat around a roll of string, or even playing hide-and-seek with the rabbit. It is helpful to recognize that the types of play that animals like to engage in map onto their adult roles—for example, carnivores (e.g., cats) like play involving prey-capturing behaviors (e.g., stalking, pouncing, hitting), whereas group-living animals (e.g., dogs) like play-fighting.

Second, we can use our knowledge of play to develop enriched environments for animals—for pets, for animals in the zoo, or for animals in production environments. The simple fact that straw on the floor encourages social play in piglets can be useful information in designing animal environments. By understanding the nature of play for a particular species, the right kinds of environments can be created.

Finally, we can use our knowledge about play to help us assess the well-being of young animals. Although one can easily assess an animal's physical health, it is notoriously difficult to assess its psychological health. By observing animal play (especially in production and zoo settings), one can readily assess whether the environmental enrichments that have been put into place have been successful. As fellow animals who value play, we humans should recognize that encouraging play in our animal companions is beneficial to all.

Further Resources

Bekoff, M. (2001). Social play behavior: Cooperation, fairness, trust and the evolution of morality. *Journal of Consciousness Studies, 8* (2), 81–90.

Burghardt, G. (2005). *The genesis of animal play: Testing the limits.* Cambridge, MA: MIT Press.

Panksepp, J. (2005). Beyond a joke: From animal laughter to human joy? *Science, 308,* (5718), 62–63.

Pelligrini, A., & Smith, P. (2005). *The nature of play: Great apes and humans.* New York: Guilford.

Pellis, S., & Iwaniuk, A. (2000). Adult-adult play in primates: Comparative analyses of its origin, distribution, and evolution. *Ethology, 106* (12), 1083–1104.

Power, T. (2000). *Play and exploration in children and animals.* Mahwah, NJ: Erlbaum.

Scarlett, W., Naudeau, S., Salonius-Pasternak, D., & Ponte, I. (2005). *Children's play.* Thousand Oaks, CA: Sage.

Spinka, M., Newberry, R., & Bekoff, M. (2001). Mammalian play: Training for the unexpected. *The Quarterly Review of Biology, 76* (2), 141–68.

Thomas G. Power

Play
Humans, Animals, and Laughter

Laughter is a funny behavior. The philosopher Daniel Dennett writes of a curious "species of primate in South America, more gregarious than most other mammals": its members "often gather in groups, large and small, and in the course of their mutual chattering, under a wide variety of circumstances, they are induced to engage in bouts of involuntary, convulsive respiration, a sort of loud, helpless, mutually reinforcing group panting that sometimes is so severe as to incapacitate them. Far from being aversive, however, these attacks seem to be sought out by most members of the species, some of whom even appear to be addicted to them." He then notes that "the species is *Homo sapiens* (which does indeed inhabit South America, among other places), and the behavior is laughter," and asks, "What do we do better than we otherwise would do, thanks to the mechanisms that carry with them, as a price worth paying, our susceptibility to—our near addiction to—laughter?"(Dennett, 1991).

We can be poor ethologists of our own species. Because jokes offer the surest way of evoking laughter, even among strangers, we assume we can most easily discuss laughter in terms of preplanned humor. But most laughter in humans, when objectively observed in naturalistic settings, does not arise from jokes. Robert Provine reports that in his study of the triggers of laughter in normal human social situations, "Only about 10 percent to 20 percent of prelaugh comments were estimated by my assistants to be even remotely humorous" (Provine, 2000).

Other animals do not make jokes, unless we humans simply do not "get" them. Laughter can, therefore, seem to support human *exceptionalism*, the attitude that a vast gulf exists between our behavior and that of all other animals. But *do* other animals laugh? Does human laughter arise out of laughter or similar behaviors in other species? And how does human laughter relate to other human behaviors, like smiling and speech?

Laughter and sobbing are the earliest social vocalizations human children make. Unlike speech, they are relatively involuntary, socially contagious, and with a consistent emotional value, positive or negative. Like other primate social calls, they do not require fine articulation but only an "alternation of the presence and absence of vocal sounds, superimposed on relatively more stable mouth postures" (Deacon, 1997, pp. 250, 419). Their motor activity depends on midbrain and brain-stem circuits, rather than the higher speech centers. Like social signals in many species, human laughter and sobbing have evolved as a contrasted pair: laughter is produced by exhalation, also used in producing speech, and sobbing, by inhalation. Although chimpanzees can vocalize as readily in inhalation as exhalation, humans find it difficult, almost painful, to speak while inhaling. Sobbing captures and signals that pain; laughter makes the most of the relaxed effortlessness of our vocalizing while exhaling.

Because of the differences between the social calls of laughter and sobbing on the one hand and articulated speech on the other, we need to look for a deeper explanation for laughter than in jokes. Several competing biological theories of laughter confront the challenge. One proposes that laughter derives from aggression or mockery, as when chimpanzees hoot together at a common enemy, but neither for chimpanzees nor for children does laughter actually begin in intimidation or mockery. Another proposal suggests that laughter disarms aggression by serving as a signal of submission, but, as Robert Storey notes, one chimpanzee will never try to disarm another lurching ominously closer by greeting it with laughter. A third proposal views laughter as expressing relief at the passing of danger, or alerting others to the passing of a threat, but there is no evident selective advantage for such a signal. A fourth explanation, far more promising and seeing laughter in terms of play, has been most fully developed by the Dutch primatologist Jan van Hooff.

Van Hooff and Preuschoft locate the origins of laughter in the relaxed, open-mouth face that primates and other mammals (and even birds) display in play. Animal behaviors and expressions often become *ritualized*, stylized in a fixed and distinctive pattern that serves as a clear signal within a species, so that its members can understand each other and waste as little time, energy, and health as possible in friction or fighting or needlessly acting at cross-purposes. A ritualized behavior such as the widespread mammalian relaxed, open-mouth display, or human laughter, does not emerge simply as an expression of some internal state, but evolves gradually into a well-defined social signal, only because it is useful for senders to have receivers construe it in a certain way. Over time, minute differences of expression, gesture, and posture become intensified to the point where, say, signs of anger, such as bristling hair and tight lips, suggest to another: "Back off," while a smile suggests: "You may safely approach." Laughter and sobbing appear to have diverged in the same way, to be as distinct from each other as possible within our species.

If human laughter derives from the relaxed, open-mouth display common across many species, this display itself appears to derive, in turn, from the importance of play. Play has been observed in many animal species, including all mammals in which it has been looked for. We can expect play to have a biologically adaptive function, since it is so widespread within and across species, since it consumes valuable energy, and since it puts players at increased risk of predation or injury, yet remains eagerly anticipated, solicited, and maintained. Pleasure is nature's way of ensuring that creatures perform a normally beneficial activity, and animals, including humans, not only look as though they enjoy play, but their brains release dopamine when they anticipate or take part in it. Moreover, juvenile-play deprivation among both rats and humans strongly correlates with serious social malfunction in later life.

While most who study play agree that it must have an adaptive value, they disagree about what that value is. Among the many explanations proposed are training for later life and training for the unexpected—training for the expected versus training for the unexpected. *Both* in fact appear necessary.

Although running and frisking and cavorting can be performed solo, they can be dangerous in the wild, and animals rarely carry out such activities away from the vigilance of others of their kind. But a high percentage of play is social: chasing, mock-fighting, rough-and-tumble, tickling. Social play offers training in the unexpected moves of both evasion and defense, not only against predators but against aggressive competition with conspecifics.

But if such play is to be of benefit, it must not escalate into real fighting. Animals need to furnish very clear signals to each other that they are not attacking, only playing. The little nips that in many mammal species have been the main tools of play-fighting have to be distinguished, in advance, from real bites. The ritualized signal of the relaxed, open-mouth display has therefore evolved in species from rats and wolves to chimpanzees. The baring of the teeth before biting has moved away from the rigidity and tension of real aggressive biting toward the maximum looseness that tends to characterize all bodily movements and postures in play. At the same time, the breathlessness that results from the energy expenditure of intense play has been ritualized—in wolves and dogs and also in primates such as orangutans, gorillas, and chimpanzees—into a rhythmic pant, a volley of exhalations that, together with the play-face, seems the origin of human laughter. Even rats nipped behind the neck in their tireless play emit a joy chirp too high for human ears. In such play the active partner shows a play-face to signal that this is mock aggression, while the passive partner pants to indicate, "This is fun, keep going," as the roles rapidly switch back and forth.

Van Hooff notes two consequences of the play-face explanation for the origins of human laughter: first, that the idea that laughter originates in aggression cannot be right, since there is no evidence, either in closely related species or in human infants, for such an origin; and second, more surprisingly, laughter and smiling may have quite different roots. Smiling appears to derive from a fear grin, a baring of the teeth shown by a subordinate to a dominant, a nervous signal of submissiveness common in many species, including many parts of the primate line. That remote origin can still be detected in an embarrassed human smile of awkwardness, apology, or social deference.

In humans and in some other primate species, van Hooff observes, laughs and smiles, although they have different origins, tend to converge, so that a smile can seem like a weak laugh and a laugh like a strong smile. Some primate species, such as baboons and some macaques, are relatively despotic, and in these species the relaxed open-mouth play-face and the bared-teeth fear grin are very distinct. But other species, like other macaques and humans, are much more egalitarian; in such species, the two facial displays can converge as signs of lack of threatening intent and even friendliness.

How do the play-face and play-pant, as widespread animal social signals, explain human laughter in response to humor?

Minds are crammed with expectations preloaded through natural selection and updated by individual experience. Among the expectations that evolution incorporates in us, the most urgent of all is the expectation of danger, the unexpected manifestation of an expected threat. In play-fighting and tickling in animals (including humans) or in human peek-a-boo games, the rough form of a threat catches the attention and primes alertness, only for threat quickly to turn to opportunity. So long as a relaxed and trusting social atmosphere persists among animals that enjoy play-fighting and friendly nips or tickles, surprise movements produce the greatest vocal release and the greatest apparent pleasure—the unexpected within the context of harmless play. And in human laughter, we find the same.

Shared expectations that allow for surprises that catch us off guard, simulating risk and stimulating recovery, are the key not only to play of all kinds, but also to humor. If a would-be joke does not take us by surprise—if, as we say, we see the punch line a mile off—we will not find it funny. But surprise is not enough. Discrepancy alerts the right hemisphere of the brain to try to integrate new information with old. Those with damage in the right frontal neocortex often no longer understand humor. Knowing the association of humor and surprise, they tend to laugh at mere non sequiturs they think must be funny, when, to the rest of us, they are not. Only if a joke involves surprise *and* allows us to retrieve sense will it be funny, just as surprise moves by play-opponents that let us make quick recoveries will be especially rewarding.

Sociality regularly involves both cooperation and competition. Play prepares us for competition in a way that heightens cooperation, through its intrinsic pleasure and the common expectations that make it possible. Principles of fair play, turn-taking, and teamwork promote cooperation, while implicit or explicit rules and disqualifications punish cheating or aggression. Humor can also be used at the group level to promote cooperation—by its self-rewarding nature and by reinforcing the recognition of shared expectations—*and* to discourage or punish noncooperation or deviance. A sense of what is normal behavior within a group can be toyed with humorously, as a first sally of criticism, against those considered to violate common expectations. The few remaining hunter-gatherer groups, assumed to be closest to the evolutionary origins of human sociality, are all egalitarian. They police their egalitarianism, in the first instance, by ridicule of those who try to claim more than their share of goods or glory, and only later by censure, punishment, and even expulsion or death. From the hunter-gatherer, it is only a small step to the gentler, corrective joshing of the workplace or to satirical mocking of pretension, vice, and folly.

See also

Play—*Human and Animal Play*

Further Resources

Bekoff, M. (2002). *Minding animals: Awareness, emotions and heart*. New York: Oxford University Press.

Deacon, T. (1997). *The Symbolic species: The co-evolution of language and the human brain*. London: Allen Lane.

Dennett, D. (1991). *Consciousness explained.* London: Penguin.

Panksepp, J. (2000). The rat will play. In M. Bekoff (Ed.), *The smile of a dolphin: Remarkable accounts of animal emotions* (pp. 146–47). New York: Discovery Books.

Provine, R. R. (2000). *Laughter: A scientific investigation.* London: Faber & Faber.

Špinka, M., Newberry, R.C., & Bekoff, M. (2001). Mammalian play: Training for the unexpected. *Quarterly Journal of Biology, 76,* 141–68.

Storey, R. (2001). A critique of recent theories of laughter and humor, with special reference to the comedy of *Seinfeld. Interdisciplinary Literary Studies, 2,* 75–92.

van Hooff, J. A. R., & Preuschoft, S. (2003). Laughter and smiling: The intertwining of nature and culture. In F. B. M. de Waal & P. L. Tyack (Eds.), *Animal social complexity: Intelligence, culture, and individualized societies* (pp. 260–87). Cambridge, MA: Harvard University Press.

Brian Boyd

Rehabilitation of Animals
Rehabilitating Wildlife

Wildlife rehabilitators provide food, shelter, and skilled care to ill, injured, and orphaned wild animals. Once the animals have recovered (or matured) sufficiently to survive on their own, they are released into suitable habitat in the wild. Animals that are permanently disabled or otherwise unable to survive in the wild are considered nonreleasable. These animals are often kept in captivity as "animal ambassadors" that represent their species in educational programs for the public. Nonreleasable animals may also be used as foster parents for orphans of their species. In some instances, disabled animals that would have a low quality of life in captivity are humanely euthanized.

Wildlife rehabilitators (rehabbers) are certified by the International Wildlife Rehabilitation Council (IWRC), after satisfactorily completing a class in Basic Wildlife Rehabilitation. Rehabbers must also obtain permits from the U.S. Fish and Wildlife Service and their state fish and game agency. Local areas may also have permit and zoning regulations that apply to wildlife rehabbers. Some states restrict the rehabilitation of certain species or prohibit rehabilitation entirely.

Animals are usually referred to a wildlife rehabber by animal control agencies, fish and game agencies, veterinarians, or by the public. Individuals who find an ill, injured, or orphaned wild animal should contact a local wildlife rehabber for advice immediately. A wild animal should never be captured or handled without expert guidance, as they may cause injury or transmit disease.

Many animals that appear to be orphaned actually have a parent animal nearby and should be left alone. Attempting to raise an orphaned wild animal without the proper training, knowledge, and resources usually results in death for the animal, or, at best, a lifetime in captivity. Wildlife rehabbers have the skills to raise an orphaned animal to healthy adulthood, maintain the animal's wildness, nurture its survival skills, and release it into the wild to live free.

Wildlife rehabilitation is a complex field that requires knowledge in many disciplines. Most rehabbers choose to specialize and become expert in the care of certain species or types of animals. Although they must have basic veterinary knowledge, rehabbers can provide only basic first aid and support. They typically work closely with a local veterinarian who is willing to treat wild animals. Although there are a number of large wildlife rehabilitation centers in the United States, many rehabbers work out of their homes. It requires a significant commitment of time, money, and other resources to set up a wildlife rehabilitation program. For someone who is interested in getting into wildlife rehab, it is advisable to begin as a volunteer at an existing rehab facility. Experience at a rehab center would also be beneficial for anyone considering a veterinary or wildlife-related career.

Further Resources

Carlson, D. B., & Ruth, I. (1997). *Wildlife care for birds and mammals: Basic wildlife rehabilitation manuals*. Madison, CT: Bick Publishing.

Cuny, L. M. (1998). *Through animals' eyes: True stories from a wildlife sanctuary*. Denton, TX: University of North Texas Press.

International Wildlife Rehabilitation Council. http://www.iwrc-online.org/
National Wildlife Rehabilitators Association. http://www.nwrawildlife.org/
Stocker, L. (2000). *Practical wildlife care.* Ames, IA: Iowa State Press.
Wildlife Rehabilitation Listserv. http://LISTSERV.NODAK.EDU/archives/wlrehab.html
Wildlife Rehabilitator locator. http://www.tc.umn.edu/~devo0028/contact.htm

Carla Wakeman

Rehabilitation of Animals

Wild Bird Rehabilitation—Rare Intimacies: A Personal Essay

The human-animal bond extends beyond that of domestic pets or service animals. My research interests led me to Avian Haven, a wild-bird rehabilitation center created and managed by Dr. Diane Winn and Marc Payne. It was there that I began my research into the unique characteristics of the human-animal bond in wild-bird rehabilitation. More specifically, my interest is geared toward what I believe to be vast differences between that of an avian rehabilitator and a bird watcher.

The relationship we have with our wounded or orphaned birds is different from that of a companion-animal relationship, but perhaps not unlike that of a parent or physician. It is also quite different from that of the 70.4 million bird watchers who venture out of doors every year to engage in one of America's fastest-growing hobbies, one that is fueling a huge ecotourism industry. In my experience, the rehabilitation relationship can be deeply spiritual, due to the extended time we have to spend with the birds. At the very

Surrogate parents: barred owls and baby. Courtesy of Marc Payne.

least, it emphasizes the ecological role and sheer beauty and mystique of birds. It is a relationship that recognizes individuality beyond species.

Diane, who is also a professor of psychology, has noted various psychological aspects that emerge in wildlife rehabilitation which become apparent in a multitude of unexpected ways. Wild-avian rehabilitation is a practice of "letting go." In most cases, there is a goodbye. Whether it is a joyous—but anxious—release back into the wild or a euthanasia that we believe is a release from suffering, we learn to love and let go over and over. Keeping the heart open at the same time it is breaking is a deep spiritual practice. We never forget that birds are a part of the sky. It is where they belong. Birds are startling, elegant, strong, and fragile. We do grow fond of them. It is hard to say goodbye to many of them. But it is also joyous, this goodbye. The few times when there are not goodbyes fall under strict federal guidelines. We have a pair of beautiful barred owls that have made excellent surrogate parents. They seem to be happy and healthy and are fulfilled by having this important job to do. We have also had a crow who was a surrogate mom. Some nonreleasable raptors are allowed to go to facilities for purposes of education and training. There are rules to protect these special birds, and usually those rules are designed to ensure that they are not suffering in captivity.

A typical day at an avian wildlife center begins with feeding orphaned babies by syringe or tweezers in the infirmary, along with the other special-care birds. The birds range from American robins, mourning doves, Eastern phoebes, American goldfinches, blue jays, cedar waxwings, chipping sparrows, American crows, chimney swifts, rock doves, European starlings, English sparrows, various kinds of woodpeckers, barred owls, bald eagles, American kestrels, broad-winged hawks, and ospreys. In Maine, we also receive a number of herons, great horned owls, sharp-shinned hawks, loons, killdeer, and numerous other species—too many to remember. After working in the infirmary, staff and college interns are assigned to several outdoor aviaries to clean and feed the birds that still need hand-feeding. The excitement continues when we start flight training with the flycatchers or the raptors in the big flight-training facility.

The large flight compound is designed with a center group of housing cages surrounded by a circular continuous flyway, so that large birds that are ready to practice flying can fly in circles, nonstop, without coming to the end of a square cage. It is common to walk in and see crows or ravens circling around. Others in the middle area are housed until they, too, are ready to stretch their wings. To see an eagle flying laps, up close, is thrilling. There are also smaller raptors, such as the many kestrels we receive that will soon have their own flight-training facility. No less exciting is the small aviary, where the flycatchers learn how to catch insects in midair.

My beloved flycatchers have provided me with the strongest and most lasting bond of all the birds I have had the pleasure to work with. It is my favorite job to work in what is sometimes called "Sydney's Flight School." I stand in these aviaries for hours, with little insects at the end of tweezers, coaxing fledgling barn swallows, tree swallows, and phoebes to "come and get it." Opportunities to practice catching insects in midair will help them survive. So, as a dutiful surrogate mom, I coax and coax, and then comes that proud day when one of them makes a stab at it. Eventually, they all become ace pilots. They have to be, if they are going to get plenty to eat once they are released. I now see why this particular task is so fascinating to me and understand the psychological aspects that have led to this obsession. My father was killed in a midair collision when I was two years old. When I was four, a bird fell out of the sky and landed at my feet. I was absolutely hysterical. If Freud were here, he would say that I have a case of "displacement of affect." In other words, I could not grieve over my father, as I was too young to understand this loss at such an early age. At age four, I probably only knew he fell from the sky, and that is what killed him. When that bird fell at my feet, all I could think of was my father falling out of the sky.

I take my job very seriously. It is difficult to master letting go of the tweezers at the same time the birds get a good grip. Both of us must work together to get the process going in the right direction. The phoebes are the ace pilots of the group—they go straight to their target. The barn swallows are appropriately named, as they fly more like the old-time barnstormer airplane flyers, doing ballet-like loops and circles while on their way to get to the insects. But they always do get them after a few days of training. I find it amazing that wild birds would even respond to a human providing opportunities to practice skills that will later be important for survival in the wild. It never gets old or boring and never ceases to bring me great joy, delight, and awe. There they are, my little cadets, lined up in a row. At first, I can tell the difference between only the various swallows and phoebes. If I am lucky enough to be with the same group for more than a few days, I know each and every one of them and even give them names. Contrary to popular opinion, it is helpful to name them, as sometimes I need to let the next volunteer know that "Scruffy" or "Princess" isn't keeping up with the others and needs some extra coaxing.

Great attention must also be paid to keeping cages and feeding instruments clean. This is especially true when dealing with birds such as chimney swifts. A new batch of baby swifts just came in today. They look like naked reptilians, but to us, they are beautiful. Diane has a special connection to these birds. Her first year with baby swifts was heartbreaking. Diane and Marc lost almost all of them. In much grief, they found that these birds are susceptible to a mouth disease, and so they developed a preventative protocol that includes cleaning feeding instruments between each and every mouthful. When that terrible first season was over, Diane made a solemn vow to the

Phoebe flight training. Courtesy of Marc Payne.

swifts that she would never let them down if they gave her another chance. She got that second chance before the year was out—in September, after most swifts had already left Maine for Peru, she received one more very late nestling. By then, she had a pretty good idea of what had gone wrong and knew enough to care for that last bird of the season properly. She took that bird as a sign that the swifts had accepted her pledge. That fall and winter she read everything there was to read about swifts in particular (and insectivore nutrition, more generally). It was in that time period that she developed the songbird nestling diet that has since been published widely and is now used extensively in rehab centers all over the country. She contacted swift rehabilitators in many states and learned about their experience with this disease. Diane and Marc developed the prevention protocol that includes scrupulous feeding hygiene. Diane also learned what antibiotic is best to use if a bird comes in with this disease. That same winter, they designed a swift cage and built it in the following spring. The second season was a huge success. The last batch was ready for release after most swifts had left Maine, so Marc drove them to a release site they had scouted out in New Jersey—a huge, old chimney at a nunnery! The two of them talked on Marc's cell phone as he released those last three into a group of thousands in the sky. They have not lost a chimney swift to that disease in years. Needless to say, Diane is quite protective of them.

Chimney swift. Courtesy of Marc Payne.

Marc and Diane are now trying to find a way to help loons pass the lead sinkers that they pick up on the bottom of lakes, as they would do with gravel, in order to aid digestion. Sadly, most loons that come in with lead poisoning do not survive. Another project they are working on is a feeding protocol for newly hatched songbirds. Some of these orphaned birds have a difficult time surviving without their natural mothers. Others, such as killdeer, are amazingly resilient.

Two days ago, the killdeer were just pecking out of their eggs. Today they were hopping about on shaky long legs, often falling over one another. These little guys will give you a much-needed belly laugh when they try to catch up with each other, collide, crash, and get up again. They are considered precocial birds because they develop so very quickly. Their small lives are elegant and alive. And it is astounding how quickly they develop.

Diane had to euthanize a bird today. I understand the kindness of it. All the other ones, his buddies, were to be set free—and this one would never be able to be free because of his wing condition. It would have been cruel to let his mates go and leave him in a cage for the rest of his life, and the federal authorities would not allow it, anyway. I kept some distance, thinking it was a sacred moment. Later I asked Diane about it. I said it was nice that she could hold the bird while doing it in such a kind way. She does Reiki when they are dying, telling them that now they are really free to fly away, free from the pain, free from the danger, that they are loved. Diane's eyes teared up. I saw this bird's eyes. They were bright and attentive, and they did not show the terrible signs of unresponsiveness. But for this bird, how much more cruel to be kept in a cage to watch all his friends fly away into the wild.

Diane is a tender soul. She recently lost her mother to cancer, and her father died soon thereafter. Below, I will speak to her eloquent paper on the difficulty of euthanizing a bird shortly after her mother's death. Both of us agree that we worry more about suffering than death. Euthanasia is not the enemy, and death is not a failure. Allowing a bird to continue suffering is the cruelest of acts.

By far my most difficult moment was when a volunteer brought in a turkey vulture that had been shot with a BB gun. Pablo Neruda once called his dog's eyes "two moist question marks" (Neruda, 1994). This is the best description I can think of when I remember this vulture's eyes. He looked at us as though to ask, "Why did they do this to me?" I will never forget that bird. He had to be put down. Sadly, unkind people sometimes use birds for target practice. Moments like this, of feeling intense anger and sadness and love, are a prescription for compassion fatigue; if we forget that we saved this bird in a different way, we saved this bird from suffering. This is why most of us at Avian Haven have a strong need to bond with one another: it gets us through. Vultures are known to be some of the most accepting and playful birds. Lynn Marie Cuny, who runs a wildlife sanctuary, tells the story of an emu that was brought to the center and how the strange-looking bird was rejected by all of the avians except for the vultures. "One vulture who had his entire right wing shot off groomed [the emu's] large feet, then looked up at the huge, awkward bird who towered so high overhead, and made the perfect gesture of acceptance. . . . He selected a crisp, brown twig from among the sticks lying around, picked it up gingerly in his beak and walked over to the waiting emu. . . . The grand, old bird placed this perfect twig at the emu's feet and invited him to join the vulture clan" (Cuny, 1998, p. 11). Would we use such birds for target practice if we were aware, as young children, of such wonderful animal behaviors?

Diane speaks of her rehabilitation efforts as "trauma work." The work not only is about the birds' misfortunes—Diane shows how such work can remind one of one's own traumas. "Perhaps not many wildlife rehabilitators have been orphaned, kidnapped, shot, hit by cars, or attacked by cats, but death touches all our lives, and often in difficult ways" (Winn, 2002). I wonder, however, if many rehabilitators have not had some trauma that has effected the necessary empathy and passion needed to engage in this difficult work. I was orphaned at the age of ten years and have had my share of trauma, and I believe it is these very experiences that have resulted in my strong connection to and love for animals; Diane writes of her connection with her mother's recent death and the difficulty of having to euthanize a bird shortly after her loss. Liz Margolies writes from the perspectives of feminist therapies and attachment theory of the bond between women, animals, and maternal loss. Eisenstadt has written about parental loss and genius. This genius, while defined as a high degree of achievement and competence in certain fields, has also been seen in the many orphans who are gifted with special communication skills relating to animals.

Many of those who have dealt with multiple losses seem to develop a precocious morality and conscience with a strong sense of injustice and a desire to contribute to an ending of suffering. Animals have been treated unjustly for centuries, whether wild or domestic. Not all people can own animals, but they can devote time to wildlife rehabilitation. And there is something numinous about those who are wild and free and never lose touch with the sky. The intimacies we achieve with these birds are rare indeed. They stay with you forever.

Yesterday was one of those gorgeous Maine days, and I had the honor of picking up a ruffled and unresponsive barred owl at the local emergency animal clinic. Diane tucked him in on his side, with his glorious, feathered head on an elevated pillow and a heating pad underneath. It was dark and quiet, and he was given fluids and homeopathic remedies. There were no visible wounds or injuries, except his one eye kept closing—we think he may have been bumped by a car, a possible head injury.

It wouldn't be until October that I'd get the call I'd been waiting for; it was time for me to come pick up that barred owl and release him back into the forest where he was found. We checked his flight before boxing him up. The flight was smooth and silent, like a large moth gliding through the air. The veterinarian who helped stabilize him was invited to the release but could not make it. Still, he was thrilled to hear his work had made a difference. We rely on veterinarians a lot and owe them a huge debt of gratitude. To open up that box at dusk, to whisper to an owl that he is free again, and to watch him fly off gracefully is the best thank you Marc and Diane could give to those of us who work with them.

Although a lot of this work is fun, I cannot overemphasize the long, grueling hours of hard work, tears, anger, and frustration experienced during summers, when most people are basking in the lazy days and beautiful Maine weather. It takes a tremendously strong bond and love of birds to make this way of life a priority. There are those rare moments when we all have a nice lunch together. Often we are sitting outside surrounded by a paradise of birds and watching a "problem child" blue jay (who was inadvertently tamed before being brought here) sunning himself on the deck top right next to us. My bond to the birds extends to Marc and Diane. They are ever grateful for their volunteers, but it is I who feels indebted to them. I love it when Diane gives me a hug, along with a bag of fruit or an interesting article to take home. It amazes me that there is such warmth and optimism in a place where sadness is almost a daily occurrence.

Today will be my last full day until next spring. There I stand, looking at them, my babies, all of them in a row next to each other, mouths wide open. Their eyes seem to exude forgiveness. In most cases, the reason they are here is because of us. According to recent studies from the U.S. Geological Service, almost 25 percent of bird species in the United States alone are declining at a significant rate. This decline is attributed to the human species' destruction of natural habitats, human population growth, and the razing of stopover sites needed by migrating birds. Other reasons may include collisions with our windows, our poisoning of their food sources, and our letting our cats run wild outdoors. Yet here is this human, trying to help, trying to make it up to them, and their trusting eyes just break my heart. Of course, even after I am gone for the season, I keep track of the birds I've brought in. Below is a typical message from Diane, in response to my inquiry about a baby robin I had delivered. It is a beautiful summary of the bonds we have to each other and to our little charges.

> Hi, Sydney. The pigeon is absolutely fine, but the robin survived only a few hours after it arrived here. It was NOT your fault, nor that of the man who fed the bird sugar water, and it wouldn't have made any difference if it had gotten here immediately. To a more trained eye, the bird had central nervous system damage; its limb and head movements were random and uncoordinated, its eyes staring blankly. The mouth-opening was neither gasping for breath nor begging for food, but again, just random

movement. It may well have chirped occasionally and seemed to be perking up, but the damage had already been done in the fall from the nest. We got in another bird, a thrush, about the same age and size, shortly after this one arrived and of course put them together. The robin died cuddled up to what was essentially indistinguishable from a nestmate.

Like you, I try to absorb whatever lesson the universe had to offer in difficult experiences. One is that injured animals often die, no matter what we do. Another is that a comfortable and safe place to leave the body is a great gift to be able to provide. We try not to see deaths as failures, but (as described in the article I sent you) other kinds of releases. But I cry a lot over these birds, too.

The other day, I miscounted my swifts and had a horrible moment in which I thought one might have been clinging to a towel I'd put in the washing machine. I ran over, stopped the machine, and threw sopping wet towels all over the floor, in a desperate attempt to find the missing bird. Heather was great; she helped me sort through the towels and assured me that the bird was not there, nor in the water remaining in the machine. I went back and counted for the 10th time and found the bird behind something (that I'd checked previously, I thought). I went back to clean up the mess by the washer; Amy came in from outside and asked what had happened; I burst into tears and sobbed uncontrollably for about ten minutes.

These wonderful creatures are ever my best teachers.

Diane

I cannot think of a better way to end this encyclopedia entry. Everything I have tried to say and do is captured in this one kind note from Diane. The bond between us is strong because of our love for—and bonds with—these birds. And yes, they are ever our very best teachers.

Further Resources

Avian Haven. http://www.avianhaven.org/

Cuny, L. (1998). *Through animals' eyes: True stories from a wildlife sanctuary.* Denton, TX: University of North Texas Press.

Eisenstadt, J. (1978). Parental loss and genius. *American Psychologist,* 33, 211–23.

Karnicky, J. (2004). What is the red knot worth?: Valuing human/avian interaction. *Society and Animals, 12* (3), 253–66.

Margolies, L. (1999). The long goodbye: Women, companion animals, and maternal loss. *Clinical Social Work Journal, 27* (3), 289–304.

McElroy, S. (1998). *Animals as guides for the soul.* New York: Ballantine Publishing Group.

Neruda, P. (1994). *Odes to common things.* Boston: Bulfinch Press.

Oliver, M. (2003). *Owls and other fantasies.* Boston: Beacon Press.

Randour, M. (2000). *Animal grace: Entering a spiritual relationship with our fellow creatures.* Novato, California: New World Library.

Sibley, D. (2001). *The Sibley guide to bird life and behavior.* New York: Knopf Publishers.

Skutch, A. (1997). *Life of a flycatcher.* Norman: University of Oklahoma Press.

Thomas, S. (2002). Horrified fascination: Deciphering the Shiva dream. *Voices: Journal of the American Academy of Psychotherapists,* 15, 49–55.

Winn, D. (2002). Dealing [with] death: Psychological aspects of euthanasia in wildlife rehabilitation. *Journal of Wildlife Rehabilitation*, 25 (2), 22–25.

Sydney Carroll Thomas

Giant Octopuses and Squid

A giant Pacific octopus named Roxy at the Hatfield Marine Science Visitor Center in Newport, Oregon. Although giant squid and octopuses have been vilified in film and literature, no human deaths have been recorded as a result of contact with them. In fact, live giant squid are rarely seen, despite repeated efforts by marine biologists.

Courtesy of Shutterstock.

Living with Animals

Hyenas and Humans

Young spotted hyenas and mothers at a communal den.

© Danita Delimont / Alamy.

Living with Animals

Killer Whales and Humans

Killer whales, or orcas, are highly social and live in tight-knit family units that visit frequently with extended family groups. Orcas are intelligent and playful, enjoying games with trainers in captivity or cavorting with family members in the wild.

Courtesy of Michael Noonan.

Mountain Lions and Humans

Two mountain lions found on a hiking trail in California. Expanding human populations and increasing human activity in mountain lion habitat are also increasing the frequency of conflicts between humans and mountain lions.

Courtesy of Shutterstock.

Red Foxes in Urban Areas

Editor Marc Bekoff, who lives in the mountains outside Boulder, Colorado, has red foxes visit his house regularly. When it is extremely dry during the summer months and there are no sources of water nearby, Marc pours water on his hot-tub cover so that the foxes are able to drink.

Courtesy of Marc Bekoff.

Urban Animals

Zoos and Aquariums

Animal Welfare, Animal Rights, and Conservation at Zoos

Because of their large size, some animal advocates argue that elephants should be contained in sanctuaries of at least 10 acres rather in small zoo enclosures. Early onset of arthritis, neurotic behaviors, foot infections, and difficulty reproducing are purported to be the result of insufficient space.

Courtesy of Shutterstock.

Animal Welfare, Animal Rights, and Conservation at Zoos

Animals in captivity may exhibit unusual behavior, possibly because of a lack of stimulation in their surroundings. Dolphins occasionally ram their heads against the side of their pool until they die.

Courtesy of Shutterstock.

Reptiles and Zookeepers

The Cincinnati Zoo's Komodo dragon, Naga, eats a piece of steak as a homecoming meal at the zoo, 2002. Naga had been away from the zoo on tour visiting ten other zoos since 1995. At nine feet long, Naga is the largest Komodo dragon living outside his native Indonesia.

©AP Photo/Tom Uhlman.

Religion
See Culture, Religion, and Belief Systems

Research
Animal Experimentation in India

The history of animal experimentation in India in the twentieth century parallels that of the United Kingdom in the same period. However, after independence from Britain in 1945, there was a sudden rise in the number of animals used, with a much sharper decline in the conditions under which the animals were housed and experimented upon. India's first prime minister, Jawaharlal Nehru, gave a very high degree of importance to building scientific institutions which led to several animal-using laboratories being expanded.

In the late fifties, there was some amount of protest against the use of animals under conditions that many considered shameful. The initial cry was from Mrs. Rukmini Devi Arundel, who, as an independent member of the upper house of parliament, brought in a bill called the Prevention of Cruelty to Animals Bill. The government, realizing the importance of the measure, requested her to withdraw her bill and introduced an identical bill that, in 1960, became the Prevention of Cruelty to Animals (PCA) Act.

In 1959, a group that later registered as the Blue Cross of India in 1964 took up this issue very seriously. In March 1965, the Blue Cross held an international conference on the subject. The National Anti-Vivisection Society of the United Kingdom and the British Union for the Abolition of Vivisection sent a delegate, and the Scottish Society for the Prevention of Vivisection provided a large amount of literature and films for the conference. Rukmini Devi, who had been nominated by the government of India as the first chairperson of the Animal Welfare Board of India (a statutory body set up in 1962 under the PCA Act of 1960) presided over the conference. Under this pressure, the government of India set up the first Committee for the Purpose of Control and Supervision of Experiments on Animals (CPCSEA), whose members visited various animal-using institutions and met various stakeholders on this issue. The author and three other members of the Blue Cross were the first to depose before the CPCSEA, and their claims were met with disbelief—if not ridicule. It is pertinent to note that the chairman of the CPCSEA was Kamal Nayan Bajaj, a member of parliament, and most of the other members of the CPCSEA were the heads of animal-using, government laboratories. Yet, after visiting all the major labs over a period of a year, the CPCSEA came out with a paper on the issue that started out by saying:

> Vivisection, or animal experimentation, is one of the most inhuman cruelties against animals, which are being perpetrated in the world to-day. The object of these experiments is said to be in order to advance scientific knowledge, and to undertake research to save or prolong human or animal life and alleviate suffering. In the name of science, however, animals are made to endure the most barbaric tortures ever invented by the human brain, often lasting over long periods and without any sort of anaesthetic.
>
> Animals are frozen, boiled, have electric currents passed through their brains or are driven insane, all in an insatiable "quest for knowledge," which can do nothing whatever to benefit the human race. Many experiments which are successful with animals are a complete failure when applied to human beings. Vested interests, however, make it necessary for the experiments to continue, although what they are showing may be completely useless or already known.

> Not to be outdone by the rest of the world in cruelties, we perform them here in India on a smaller scale, but no less horrible, as can be seen in the photograph on the facing page. In this Calcutta experiment, several monkeys were given experimental dropsy leading to their death in one to four months. In the various research laboratories and institutions of India, experiments are performed on certain animals like buffaloes, horses, sheep, goats, dogs, cats, monkeys, rabbits, guinea-pigs, mice, frogs and fowls. Apart from experimenting upon them here, the export of monkeys from India for experimentation in other countries provides a handsome source of income, especially in dollars, as a monkey which fetches about Rs.10 in India costs more like 7 pounds or 8 pounds in the U.K.
>
> Rhesus monkeys in large numbers in the Northern Indian State of Uttar Pradesh are trapped, stuffed into cages and carried on shoulder-poles to Lucknow. A train journey of 260 miles takes them to New Delhi whence a transport plane carries them the 4,000 miles to London Airport. From London they may be flown another 3,000 miles across the Atlantic to New York from where they travel on for a further 700 miles in trucks to Okatia Farms in South Carolina. Here the Rhesus monkeys of India are caged with other hordes of 'Java' monkeys from the Philippines. After twenty-one days of rigorous health check, they are d[i]spatched to laboratories in Toronto, Pittsburgh, Detroit and Berkeley, California. It is disturbing to note that although the Okatia Farms may receive 5,000 monkeys a month, the supply never catches up with the demand but is rather on the increase all the time.
>
> The above gives a small idea upon this vast subject which to deal with adequately is far beyond the scope of this small hand-out. (CPCSEA)

With typical bureaucratic efficiency, the CPCSEA then abdicated its responsibility by saying:

> Much might be done towards alleviating the suffering of animals held for experimental purposes, through personal contacts with Medical Students and the Staff of Medical Colleges. It should be made more generally known that a very large proportion of painful experiments serve no useful purpose, and instances are known in which treatment successfully made on animals, when applied to humans proved disastrous. Seminars organized to discuss the subject with doctors and students might well prove profitable. Failing all else, there is nothing to prevent airing our views wherever possible and denouncing the cowardice of gaining human benefits at the expense of animals which are entirely at our mercy and unable to protect themselves. The Government of India have now set up a committee for the purpose of regulating animal experimentations. (CPCSEA)

In the meantime, the Blue Cross carried on with its campaign. In 1966, the World Coalition Against Vivisection, headquartered in Geneva, started its India office with Captain V. Sundaram as its president and S. Chinny Krishna as its honorary secretary.

The attitude of the scientists who constituted the bulk of the members—with the odd civil servant thrown in—can be judged by the fact that, over the next three decades, the CPCSEA was reconstituted three times and met precisely twice. Even the reconstitution was done only after numerous letters were sent by the Blue Cross and the Animal Welfare Board. In 1990, the Indian National Science Academy (INSA) brought out its Guidelines for Animal Experimentation. These guidelines remained totally ignored by the scientists.

In 1996, Mrs. Maneka Gandhi became the Minister for Environment and Forests, Government of India. Her first move was to reconstitute the CPCSEA with herself as chairperson. The author was also nominated as a member. Many of the other members were from animal-using laboratories. With a great deal of difficulty, rules were formulated, based on the guidelines issued in 1990 by the Indian National Science Academy. Realizing that these rules were finally going to be effectively implemented, the scientists literally took to the streets in protest. Dozens of identical letters of protest were sent to the prime minister, alleging that implementation of these rules would set back India's scientific progress. A small committee of five was set up by the prime minister, with the condition that Mrs. Gandhi could not be on this committee. Three animal-using scientists, the director of the Animal Welfare Division of the Ministry of Environment and Forests, and Dr. Chinny Krishna were given the task of addressing the objections raised by the scientists and drafting suitable rules. A fresh set of rules were then drawn up, considered by the CPCSEA, and passed, after following all required procedures.

For the next two years, over 500 laboratories and research institutions were inspected. Conditions were found to be deplorable in most of the places. Photographs were put up on the CPCSEA website. Realizing that the government meant business, government and private institutions began to implement the rules regarding registration, housing, and treatment of animals.

By 2002, serum and vaccine manufacturers, breeders, and animal users were not averse to following the rules, since they had begun to realize that they were obtaining better and more dependable results. The vast majority of the larger institutions were registered. Things were looking much better for the millions of animals bred and used in experiments each year. (CPCSEA)

In mid-2002, some scientists were able to have Maneka Gandhi removed, first as minister and then as chair of the CPCSEA. The CPCSEA was also purged of Dr. Sultan Ismail, Dr. P. Y. Guru, and Dr. S. Chinny Krishna, all of whom were strongly in favor of "good" science and proper regulations. The Ministry of Health took control of the CPCSEA, but the reforms had been set in motion, and much of the progress was irreversible. The implementation is not as effective as it could have been, but the law is there now to protect the animals. (Blue Cross)

Further Resources

The Blue Cross. http://bluecross.org. [See PCA Act and Rules for the legal provisions.]

Committee for the Purpose of Controlling and Supervision of Experiments on Animals. *Animal Experimentation*. (1965). Government of India, Ministry of Agriculture.

CPCSEA. Ministry of Environment & Forests, Government of India. http://CPCSEA.org

S. Chinny Krishna

Research
Animal Models and Animal Welfare

Animals serve in research-and-testing laboratories as models of human biology and medicine. Controversy exists as to whether such use is scientifically sound, in which case it could not be ethically justifiable. Furthermore, there is controversy over whether animal use would be justifiable even if the science is "good." Consumers can try to minimize their use of cosmetics and some other products that have been safety-tested on animals. In contrast, few medicines and no surgeries are developed without use of animals as models.

Animal modeling is more complex than it at first would appear. Animals cannot be thought of as miniature people, identical in every way but size and language. Not even humans' closest relatives, the great apes, can be seen as "substitute people" in every aspect. Rather, animals must be carefully chosen to model some particular aspect of human biology—not the *whole* of human biology. Data extrapolated from animals must be interpreted in this limited context. Overinterpretation of animal data invites criticism.

A bewildering array of animal species is pressed into service as models. Rodents, rabbits, and primates may first come to mind, but horses, roundworms, fruit flies, zebra fish, songbirds, and many, many others model some aspect of human biology. Woodchucks, for instance, are susceptible to a woodchuck hepatitis virus similar in many ways to the virus causing human hepatitis B. Leprosy can be produced in nine-banded armadillos but in few other animals. Labrador retrievers develop a hip dysplasia that resembles human osteoarthritis. Squid nerve axons transmit nervous signals much as human nerves do. These are but a few of the thousands of ways in which animals are used as models for normal and diseased human biology.

Advances in techniques to grow isolated cells or larger tissues and organs in culture media have made some of the uses of animals obsolete. After all, why use an animal as a model when actual human cells can be grown in the lab and studied? Typically, scientists use tissue-culture systems to study events at the cellular and subcellular levels. For example, tissue culture may be the best route to study which types of cells the human immunodeficiency virus is capable of infecting, what cell-surface molecules it binds to to gain entry to the cells, and what events occur in the cell that eventually kill it. But when research requires studying the interaction of many different cells and tissues, such as how the immune system protects or fails to protect the brain from the effects of the AIDS virus, or how nutrition or medications will affect this relationship, then scientists may turn to whole-animal models.

Many factors influence the choice of model. Animal-welfare regulations require scientists to consider using less-sentient species when possible (such as fruit flies instead of mice, or fish instead of monkeys). Cost considerations push scientists to choose smaller animals with shorter life cycles for many studies. Data may be most easily obtained and analyzed from smaller, simpler organisms than from larger ones; thus, zebra fish are chosen for studies of organ development, because the embryo is largely transparent, develops in an egg outside of the mother's body, and is easily accessible and visualized. On the other hand, larger size may be required if large tissue samples or large organs are desired, such as when surgical techniques are being developed and taught to human surgeons. To best analyze data and interpret it in the light of what is already known, scientists will often choose the animal models most common to their fields, whether that original association was somewhat arbitrary (such as use of rats rather than hamsters in psychology experiments) or based on unique biological attributes (such as studies of vitamin C in guinea pigs, one of the few nonprimate mammals to require dietary vitamin C the way humans do). Increasingly, research requires knowing an animal's genetic makeup, so well-studied and easily modified species, especially mice, zebra fish, and fruit flies, have become more widely used.

Controversy exists over just how useful animal models are. Certainly no drug is marketed in the United States without having been studied in animals. Is this because there is always a biological need to use animal data to develop drugs, or simply because the law requires animal safety data to be submitted before a drug can be licensed? Some scientists believe that animal modeling can provide useful information about human health and disease only if the strengths, weaknesses, and limitations of a given model are recognized in interpreting experimental findings.

Models may be classified in many ways. This essay looks at three broad categories of animal models: testing for product development, skills development, and induced and spontaneous models of disease.

Animal Models in Safety Testing

Using animals to test the safety of drugs, cosmetics, and environmental chemicals is what most people think of—and criticize—first. The crudest version of safety testing is to apply a compound to an animal—either acutely at high doses or at lower doses over a longer period of time—and watch for reactions (see figure below). The reactions may be eye irritation, skin irritation, fetal deformities, development of cancer, or a host of other toxicities. To move beyond a simple "Safe/Not Safe" determination, scientists developed more measurable practices, such as the Draize test for eye irritation or the Lethal Dose 50 (LD50) test. Both are ways of quantifying how much of a compound leads to what degree of injury. Both are still used today, though less than in the past.

This crude approach to safety testing may be criticized both for the suffering it inflicts on animals and for how reliably this information, especially the quantitative information, really applies to people. There is no guarantee that a compound that causes

Rows of rabbits held in stocks for contact-irritancy (Draize) testing. ©Michael Rougier/Time Life Pictures/Getty.

cancer in mice will do so in people, or that one that is safe in mice will not cause human disease. Moreover, small animals have much faster metabolisms and may have differences in their enzymes that process chemicals, so the amount of compound that is safe or dangerous may be different for a mouse than it would be for a person.

Safety testing does not usually generate truly new biological information, and, for this reason, replacing animals in safety testing is a more realistic goal than replacing them in original research. The Center for Alternatives to Animal Testing was started in 1981, at Johns Hopkins University, to develop alternatives to these types of testing. It is necessary that animal alternatives, such as development of an artificial skin to replace guinea pigs in testing for contact irritation, be evaluated scientifically and validated as useful before regulatory agencies, such as the Food and Drug Administration or the Environmental Protection Agency, will consider them an acceptable replacement for animal studies.

Animal Models for Skills Development

Animals have been used in classrooms for years. Sometimes, they have been used to teach students anatomy or to demonstrate physiological functions, such as how the heart beats. In addition, animals have been used to allow human and veterinary surgeons-in-training to develop their manual skills before working on actual patients. For surgeon training, dogs and pigs have often been chosen, because their size more closely approximates a human patient than that of other animals. For microsurgical training—such as learning to repair blood vessels or nerves—smaller animals, such as rats, are often used. For most such training, healthy animals are used and then killed or euthanized at the end of the training session.

As with safety testing, animal models are still used, but their classroom use has been decreased, because of greater reliance on alternative methods and models. Many medical schools have phased out animal use during the four-year MD curriculum, though animals may still be used in advanced surgical-residency training. Many veterinary schools allow students to opt out of classes that would require medically unnecessary surgeries to be conducted on healthy laboratory animals. Human and veterinary surgeons-to-be can acquire many of the basic skills of cutting tissues and placing stitches via the use of artificial (plastic, foam, etc.) models—and through practice on *cadavers* of animals euthanized for other purposes. An imitation rat is marketed for developing microsurgical skill. Skills development is furthered by assisting practicing surgeons performing real surgeries, gradually taking on more and more of the operation under guidance.

Surgical research differs from surgical training. Although large (humanlike) sizes may be useful for surgical training, they are less relevant in researching surgical concerns such as organ-transplant rejection, surgical infection, or healing processes. For these studies, rats and genetically modified, transgenic mice are commonly used.

Induced and Spontaneous Animal Models of Disease

There is no field of human medical, surgical, or psychiatric research that does not include some use of animal models. Animals are used to study the normal, healthy biology relevant to disease processes, as well as to study the diseases themselves. How animals are used depends on what the scientist is trying to learn. For example, a scientist may cause a cancer in an animal by implanting some cancer cells into the animal's body. This will tell little about what causes cancer in people (people don't typically get cancers from transplanted cancer cells), but may be useful in studying some approaches to treating already-developing cancers. Conversely, a study on how influenza is transmitted may yield valuable information for preventing an epidemic, but may tell nothing about how to treat the infection once it has developed.

Spontaneous animal models of human disease are those that develop more or less naturally, possibly by genetic mutation. A single-point mutation in the gene on the X chromosome that codes for a molecule called *dystrophin* knocks out that molecule's function, resulting in Duchenne muscular dystrophy in dogs, people, mice, and possibly other species. Though mutations arise spontaneously, and many times, in these species, they may also be propagated when the affected or carrier individual has offspring. In this way, colonies of dogs or mice with a predisposition to muscular dystrophy were developed for research. Other spontaneous animal models for study could include infections that develop and spread in wild, pet or food animal populations, or accidents, injuries and poisonings that might occur outside of the laboratory. Laboratory animals may be maintained into older age to study the conditions known to naturally arise in geriatric animals of a particular species or strain. *Induced animal models* are those that start with healthy animals and then cause a disease in the laboratory. Cancers may be induced by exposure to chemicals, by irradiation, or through transplant of tumor cells. Infections may be caused by directly exposing an animal to a virus, bacteria, prion, or fungus. Psychiatric conditions may be caused by manipulating an animal's environment, by subjecting an animal to shocks or other stressors, or through injection of chemicals. Some conditions may be caused by surgically altering an animal, say, by creating an abnormal blood flow through an organ or removing some organ or gland entirely, such as in early studies of diabetes mellitus that involved removal of the pancreas from previously healthy laboratory dogs. An increasingly active approach to animal modeling is through genetic modification of mice, zebra fish, rats, and other species. Genes may be introduced that will cause disease. One example is the "oncomouse," developed at Harvard University, into which a cancer-promoting oncogene was inserted, making the animal more prone to cancers. The opposite is to "knock out" a gene to cause disease: removing a functional gene, such as one that encodes for cell's insulin receptors, leading to diabetes in those mice unable to respond to their body's own insulin. Even more complicated is the ability to turn added genes on, or to knock out a gene's function, at any point in an animal's life, simply by feeding it a special chemical in the diet that the gene binds to. *Negative models*, in which an animal fails to respond as a human might, can also be useful. Scientists find value in studying the small number of animals capable of being infected with HIV and susceptible of developing an AIDS-like condition. But there can also be reason to study animals (most apes and monkeys, for example) that are resistant to that virus, in order to figure out why they are resistant and to see what lessons that might hold for preventing human HIV infections.

Further Resources

LaFollette, H., & Shanks, N. (1996). *Brute science: Dilemmas of animal experimentation*. London: Routledge.

Quimby, F. (2002). Animal models in biomedical research. In J. G. Fox, et al. (Eds.), *Laboratory animal medicine* (pp. 1185–1219). Academic Press: New York.

Rowan, A. N. (1984). *Of mice, models, and men: A critical evaluation of animal research*. Albany: State University of New York Press.

Zurlo, J., Rudacille, D., & Goldberg, A. M. (1994). *Animals and alternatives in testing: History, science, and ethics*. New York: Mary Ann Liebert, Inc.

Larry Carbone

Research
Animal Models in Health Research

Over 150 years ago, animal models were introduced to study the causes, cures, and nature of human diseases and health. The animal-model rationale is based on the evolutionary theory of common descent. That is, because of the genetic relationship between animal species and humans, it is possible to learn about human diseases and disorders by studying nonhuman species.

Relationship between Animal Models and Biomedical Science

Animal models may be developed by private industries, such as drug companies, to study therapeutic agents. Before any drug can be marketed to humans, it must first be tested on animals. Consequently, virtually every drug on the market had to be tested on an animal model at some point.

Another important place where animal models are developed and used is on university campuses. The models are typically developed using funds from public (federal) sources. In the United States, the bulk of public funding for animal models has come from the National Institutes of Health (NIH), and as NIH funding for medical research has increased, so has the number of scientific articles introducing animal models (see figure). The number of scientific articles published in the previous ten years that use "animal model" as a keyword phrase has averaged about 10,000 per year. This number probably severely underestimates the total articles published using animal models, because implicit in most nonclinical biomedical research is the use of an animal, at some point.

Every vertebrate class has been represented in animal models, including lampreys, zebra fish, frogs, turtles, finches, primates, rodents, and carnivores (see Table 1). Many invertebrates are also used, including cockroaches (in locomotion studies), sea hares (in learning and memory studies), snails (in feeding studies), and nematodes (in genome studies).

Four different animal model types are used: induced, negative, spontaneous, and orphan. The induced model experimentally induces an animal with the disorder or disease under investigation. These models are often used to study disease progression and to develop therapeutic agents. Negative models study resistance to diseases. Often times, the negative models are used to understand how a given species' unique attributes serve as a potential defense against disease. The hope is that if these same unique attributes could be artificially induced or mimicked in humans, then humans could be provided with resistance to the disease as well. Models used to study viral infections are examples of induced and negative model types.

The spontaneous model exploits a given species' genetic predisposition toward developing a disease, in order to study congenital conditions. These models can provide genetic explanations for diseases, and the promise is that either direct genetic manipulations or other therapeutic agents can be provided to humans, in order to prevent the disease. A recent example of this model type is the dog-genome project, which has sought to understand the cause of hip disorders in certain dog breeds. The promise is that both dog breeds and humans may, ultimately, benefit from this research.

The orphan model presents a disorder in a nonhuman species that has not yet been observed in humans. The orphan models provide a watchtower for the discovery of previously undetected disease in humans. Often, these models become important for the basic scientific insights they provide, as opposed to the insights into medical conditions. They may also provide important veterinary benefits to the selected animal species as well.

Table 1. Number of articles published in biomedical journals ("medsearch" database) using "animal model" and the animal group name as keywords, 1965–2005.

Group	Number of articles
Amphibian	98
Bird	398
Cat	3,031
Chipmunk	1
Degu	9
Dog	12,549
Fish	1,081
Guinea pig	7,103
Mouse	100,482
Pig	10,657
Primate	2,962
Rabbit	16,231
Rat	98,256
Sheep	3,511
Shrew	104
Tadpole	28
Turtle	35
Wild mouse	71
Invertebrate	161
Vertebrate	729

Each type of model has its advantages. Any animal model is likely to develop out of an understanding of some distinct feature that an animal species shares with humans. One species may have a certain anatomical, physiological, or behavioral feature that it shares with humans. Another species may manifest a condition in a way that makes the condition easy for investigators to evaluate, even if the condition's appearance is very different from its appearance in humans. Yet another species may show immunity or resistance to a disease that occurs in humans, making it worthwhile to understand what unique features exist in the animal that do not exist in humans. Whatever the case, there is always an important relationship between the animal model and humans, which makes the medical or scientific comparison between the two species worthwhile.

Relationship between Animal Models, Scientists, and Society

Obviously, the use of animals to study diseases and their cures is controversial. The animals pay a heavy sacrifice—in the form of stress, pain, discomfort, and death—to provide scientific knowledge. As a result, the NIH and other funding agencies have made an effort to search for alternative models for studying disease. University animal-review boards have become stricter in the allowable animal research. They attempt to get investigators to stop seeing their animal subjects as expendable objects. There is an emphasis to reduce stress, discomfort, and pain; to reduce the number of animal subjects required to produce conclusions from a given study; and to require investigators to search for alternative methods and models before a study involving animals is undertaken. These changes, fueled in large part by people concerned with the treatment of animals, will probably continue to reshape animal-model development in the decades to come.

There remain many facets of animal research that could be improved. For instance, housing facilities are designed primarily for the convenience of animal caregivers. The facilities make bedding, food, and water easy to change, thus creating a clean and sanitary housing environment that is easy to maintain. But these environments are also likely to induce stress, boredom, and other negative side effects in the animals. It is probable that ignorance of, or inattention to, ecologically and ethologically relevant factors in animal care and housing induces numerous ill effects that alter important scientific results. For instance, it is possible that stress and boredom could slow or inhibit the therapeutic actions of drugs and treatments. This could lead to negative results that would have been positive ones if the animal subjects had been housed in enriched environments. The negative result would lead to an otherwise-effective drug being scratched from further investigation or development.

Thus, it behooves future scientists to provide insights in these areas, because such insights will improve the quality of both biomedical studies and the lives of animal subjects. Future findings may also lead to alternative means of studying diseases and of developing treatments. It is important to emphasize that it is possible, through appropriate scientific discovery and argument, to have most scientists come to appreciate the lives and well-being of their animal subjects more fully. The impact would be to have an effective change in the relationship between medical science and animal research.

Further Resources

Hau, J., & Svedsen, P. (1994). *Handbook of laboratory animal science, volume II: Animal models*. Boca Raton, FL: CRC Press.

Hau, J., & Van Hoosier, G. L. Jr. (2003). *Handbook of laboratory animal science, volume III: Animal models*. Boca Raton, FL: CRC Press.

Parker, H. G., Kim, L. V., Sutter, N. B., Carlson, S., Lorentzen, T. D., Malek, T. B., Johnson, G. S., DeFrance, H. B., Ostrander, E. A., & Kruglyak, L. (2004). Genetic structure of purebred domestic dog. *Science, 304,* 1160–64.

Geoffrey E. Gerstner and Keith Heller

Research
Animal Use by Humans in Research and Experimentation

Despite over a century of animal rights and antivivisectionist protest, scientists, regulatory agencies, and others have remained convinced that experiments on animals yield important scientific and medical discoveries. At this time, animal experimentation is not only permitted by American laws, it is actively required; for example, before most drug studies can proceed to clinical trials in human patients, animal data must first be collected. Animal use still seems to be increasing, despite its high cost, tight regulation, and the availability of cell cultures, advanced imaging procedures, and other technologies that replace some animal studies.

A very wide variety and large number of animals serve in experiments. Great apes, such as chimpanzees, are used in small numbers in laboratories. *Drosophila* fruit flies, *Caenorhabditis* nematode worms, and other invertebrates are also common laboratory inhabitants. Also numerous are mice, rats, zebra fish, frogs, and others. Numbers of laboratory animals are difficult to come by in the United States. The United States Department of Agriculture publishes its annual report, including the numbers reported for the handful of species covered by the Animal Welfare Act. In 2004, they reported the use of 1,101,958 dogs, cats, primates, and other "covered species" (http://www.aphis.usda.gov/ac/awreports/awreport2004.pdf). This number excludes the vast number of mice, rats, fish, and frogs for which there is no required reporting. This author has estimated that some 80 million to 100 million mice and rats are bred for use in laboratories annually. Comparing these numbers to vertebrate and invertebrate animals used for human food is difficult. This author has estimated that approximately one hundred mammals or birds are killed for food each year in the United States for every one laboratory mammal or bird, but this is a very, very rough estimate.

The variety of animal species in the animal laboratory comes from a variety of factors, including how well a given species corresponds to a particular aspect of human biology; how unique a species is in some aspect of its biology; size; cost; ease of maintenance in the laboratory; availability; status as an endangered species; status as a species covered by law; and many other factors. Increasingly, genetic factors (how fully the species' genome has been mapped and how easily the species' genetics can be re-engineered in the laboratory) drive the choice of species.

All things being equal, scientists are under an ethical and regulatory obligation to choose the least-sentient species that will serve the scientific purpose. This is rarely the sole criterion in choosing an experimental animal, however. Fruit flies, for instance, might generally be considered better for genetic studies than chimpanzees or mice, because they are thought to be less sentient, but their shorter life cycle, simpler genetic make-up, small size, and the ease with which they are kept in the lab are all also points in favor of choosing fruit flies for genetic studies. For genetic studies of uniquely mammalian traits, mice, rather than chimpanzees, would be chosen to replace the fruit flies, not because they are less sentient than chimps, but because they are small and cheap, have short generation cycles, have a well-defined genome, can be easily genetically re-engineered, are not an endangered species, and are less-thoroughly regulated by the government. Despite the challenges and expense of working with them, however, chimpanzees' and monkeys' genetic closeness to human and complex mental abilities sometime make them a scientist's first-choice study animal.

The overwhelming majority of animals used in laboratories are bred for use in laboratories. Laboratory-bred animals, in general, are less likely to carry infections, are less likely to be distressed by life in the laboratory, and may be more genetically uniform. Most of the exceptions to this general rule raise ethical concerns. Laboratory-bred *Xenopus* African clawed frogs are the most numerous frogs used in laboratories, but wild-caught frogs of other species are also used, and over-collection of species causes conservation problems. Wild-caught nonhuman primates are used in some laboratories, raising concerns about conservation of species, as well as welfare concerns in capturing these highly social animals and removing them from their group. Farm-raised pigs and sheep may be found in laboratories without inciting much controversy. Overwhelmingly, the most controversial acquisition of laboratory animals is the use of so-called random source dogs and cats. The 1966 Laboratory Animal Welfare Act was passed largely to prevent theft of companion animals for sale to laboratories. People who work in laboratories (such as this author) believe companion-animal theft for laboratories to be rare; nevertheless, purchase of "random source" animals is still permitted in many states, and these can include former household animals that were rescued by or donated to animal shelters.

Animal Research: Critiques and Defenses

Animal research has long been controversial. Criticism comes in two main forms. First, there is the scientific claim that studies on animals are not only useless, but downright misleading. Critics claim that information gleaned from animal studies rarely applies well to humans, and that it is difficult to tell when the information would apply and when it would not. They further warn that animal studies may falsely find a dangerous human drug to be safe in animals or, conversely, that animal studies may lead a scientist to abandon a particular line of research, because animal studies show it to be useless. Critics point out that if the development of penicillin relied on guinea pigs (for whom it is often fatal), it would never have been developed. In other words, animals are too different from people to serve as models of human health and biology.

The other criticism is more clearly moral: whether or not animal studies are scientifically valid, it is wrong to inflict illness and pain on sentient animals solely for human benefit. Critics holding that view would say that even if a cure for a devastating disease could assuredly be found by harming a small number of animals, it would still be immoral to conduct that research. Most such critics focus on traits humans and animals share, such as some degree of consciousness, sentience, or the ability to feel pain and suffering as the basis for arguing that if it would be wrong to do something to a person, it would likewise be wrong to do that thing to an animal. In other words, animals are too much like people for us to justify using them in experiments.

The two arguments against animal research often work together. If moral critics believe it would take an extraordinary effort to justify some limited animal research but are convinced that the science of animal studies is weak, they will, of course, conclude that most animal research should be stopped.

Defenders of animal research tend to argue that animals are sufficiently different from people that it might be acceptable to use them in studies, as long as scientists are careful to do their best to limit the pain and distress in the laboratory. These research defenders mostly argue that animals may feel pain but do not have sufficient consciousness and self-awareness to be placed on a moral level with people. On this side of the argument there are also extreme views, such as the view that humans have no duties to animals whatsoever, and that, while animals are similar enough to humans to make research worth doing, they are too dissimilar to raise qualms about harming them.

The most consistent defense of animal research is that in the eyes of most scientists, it *works*. Virtually every modern medical and surgical advance has involved some use of laboratory animals in its development. That claim is not necessarily the same as saying that there could have been no other route to these advances, one that did not involve animals. That argument also, more importantly, does not rule out the day when medical advances will no longer require animal studies. Science would not stop if animal use—or even only harmful uses of animals—stopped, but it might be very different. Many projects might not be able to be accomplished. Others might be done in different ways. Some might be largely unchanged.

At this point in time, the compromise position, as represented by laws such as the Animal Welfare Act, is that animal research is permitted by law, and even sometimes required by law, but with systems of oversight to try to minimize the amount of pain and distress animals in laboratories experience.

Scientists, animal-care-and-use committees, regulatory agencies, and funding agencies all perform some sort of comparison of costs and benefits in using animals. The benefits are most often seen in terms of medical advances for human health. It is important to recognize that these are potential benefits, and that not all experiments will lead to cures for human diseases. If scientists knew in advance the results of their experiments, there would be no reason to do the research. Even experiments that yield hoped-for results must be seen in their humble context, where any one finding is just part of a very large puzzle of how the body works. It would be incredibly rare to be able to say, "This is the crucial experiment that eradicated Disease X."

Just as the human benefits of animal research are potential and hard to predict, likewise, there can be uncertainty in the cost of such research—cost measured in terms of animal suffering and death. Veterinarians and others must predict the degree of pain and distress anticipated, make recommendations on ways to decrease the pain (by changing how the experiment is done or by adding more painkillers for the animals), and then make their best assessment of how the animals are actually faring.

See also

Research—*Animal Models and Animal Welfare*
Research—*Animals Models in Health Research*
Sentience and Cognition

Further Resources

Carbone, L. (2004). *What animals want: Expertise and advocacy in laboratory animal welfare policy*. New York: Oxford University Press.

Institute of Laboratory Animal Resources. (1996). *Guide for the care and use of laboratory animals*. Washington, DC: National Academy Press.

Orlans, F. B. (1993). *In the name of science: Issues in responsible animal experimentation*. New York: Oxford University Press.

Orlans, F. B., Beauchamp, T. L., et al. (1998). *The human use of animals: Case studies in ethical choice*. New York: Oxford University Press.

Rowan, A. N. (1984). *Of mice, models, and men: A critical evaluation of animal research*. Albany, NY: State University of New York Press.

Russell, W. M. S., & Burch, R. L. (1959). *The principles of humane experimental technique*. London: Methuen & Co.

Stevens, C. (1990). Laboratory animal welfare. *Animals and their legal rights*. Washington, DC: Animal Welfare Institute.

Larry Carbone

Research
Animal Use in Science

The use of animals in science and medical research is very controversial. Most people focus on the *ethics* of using animals. Animal advocates state humans do not have the *right* to use sentient nonhumans for selfish purposes. Animal users claim, among other things, that without using animals in medical research we would no longer see cures and treatments for diseases. In this essay, I will attempt to present the various ways animals can be used in science and the relative merits of each.

Animals are used for scientific purposes in roughly nine different ways.

1. Animals as models for human disease
2. Animals as models for testing drugs destined for humans
3. Animals as spare parts
4. Animals as factories or bioreactors
5. Animal tissue to study basic physiological principles
6. Animals for dissection in education
7. Animals as a modality for ideas (heuristic)
8. To benefit other animals, such as veterinary research
9. Knowledge for knowledge's sake

When people think about the use of animals in medical research they usually think first of using animals to model human diseases and, second, using animals in drug testing and development. But these are the very areas that are currently being questioned by many scientists. Some acknowledge that using animals for these two purposes is probably no longer viable.

What makes a drug good or bad? Most things, including water and oxygen, may be good for you provided they are given in the proper dose at the proper time. In the sixteenth century, this concept led Paracelsus to say: "The dose determines the poison." The same is true today. But today we should add a corollary: "The genetic makeup also determines the poison." We cannot rely on a totally different species to predict what is good or what is bad for us. We cannot even consistently rely on members of our own species.

Of ten medications withdrawn from the U.S. market between 1998 and 2001, eight were withdrawn secondary to side effects that occurred primarily in women. Were these drugs good or bad?

RotaShield was a vaccine against rotavirus, a virus that causes roughly 500,000 deaths per year. Worldwide, one child out of 200 dies from rotavirus, which suggests that it is a much needed vaccine. But one child out of 2,500 in the United States suffered the side effect of intussusception, a potentially lethal bowel condition. Furthermore, not many children in the United States die from rotavirus. Outside of the United States, the risk benefit ratio was very favorable. In the United States the risk benefit ratio was judged unfavorable. Because the vaccine could not be sold in the United States it was judged by the manufacturer to be cost ineffective and discontinued. Millions of children worldwide died as a result of not having the vaccine available. Was this a good drug or bad?

Troglitazone, also known as Rezulin, was very effective for many in controlling diabetes. But in others it caused liver failure. Thalidomide caused birth defects in thousands but today is used as a cancer treatment for some. Aspirin causes life-threatening allergic reactions in some patients, but for most is an excellent anti-inflammatory drug. Penicillin, likewise, causes a life-threatening allergic reaction in some but has saved millions of lives. Cisapride, also known as Propulsid, was an effective drug for gastrointestinal disorders, but some patients suffered heart rhythm abnormalities and died. Are these good drugs or bad? The answer depends on who is getting the drug. No drug is always good or always bad.

Allen Roses, worldwide vice president of genetics at GlaxoSmithKline, a pharmaceutical company, said fewer than half of the patients prescribed some of the most expensive drugs derived any benefit from them and that more than 90 percent of drugs are effective in only 30–50 percent of the people.

These examples give us a hint as to why many scientists think using animals to model human disease and test drugs is no longer a viable way to do things. Today we know that sometimes you cannot even predict how a woman is going to respond to a drug or disease based on how a man responded. If we cannot do that, obviously we cannot predict how one species is going to respond based on another species.

But if the animal model was at least somewhat useful in the past for studying disease and testing drugs, what has changed in the last few decades that renders it obsolete? Mainly two things. First, the level of examination has changed since the eighteenth and nineteenth centuries. As our examination of living systems has become increasingly fine-grained, we have found that subtle differences between organisms tend to outweigh gross similarities when it comes to explanations of biologic activity. Science could use animals to shed light on shared functions when we were struggling to understand things such as organs; the functions of the liver and heart are similar between species. But today we are studying drug response and disease at the level that defines not only a species but also in many cases the individual.

Second, our knowledge has increased. Today, science studies human disease and drug response in light of complexity theory, evolutionary biology, gene expression, and gene regulation. If I had to single out one thing that has led to the demise of the notion of trans-species extrapolation it would be the concept of gene regulation and expression.

The mouse and human genomes do not appear to be qualitatively very different. They both contain about 30,000 genes, with mice having 300 humans do not have and vice versa. Humans and mice both have the genes that in mice result in a tail. In humans, the gene is turned off, whereas in mice it is turned on. It is the same gene but regulated differently. The difference between the species lies in the regulations of the same genes. Gene regulation also determines drug reaction and disease response. Because of differences in gene regulation, even identical twins may respond differently to disease and medications.

Conversely, animals can still be useful in science, and people who promote animal use often focus on the uses in numbers three through nine in the previous list. Number three involves the use of animals for spare parts. For example, many people have had an aortic valve from a pig placed in their hearts to replace their own aortic valves. There is no doubt that pig valves function adequately in humans, and hence this is a scientifically viable use of animals.

Number four is that animals can be used as factories. For example, for decades insulin was harvested from cows and pigs at slaughter. Hepatitis B and C viruses and other viruses were grown in nonhuman primates and other animals so scientists could have a convenient reservoir of the virus for study. This was before the viruses could be grown in culture. More recently, mice have been used to produce monoclonal antibodies. Use number five is that researchers frequently use tissues obtained from animals to study basic physiological processes. Most people are familiar with dissecting animals, number six, as it occurs in schools. Dissecting animals will reveal some principles that teachers want students to learn, such as that nerves, arteries, and veins usually are found in proximity.

Some researchers admit they do not use animals as models of humans because animals are not good models for humans, but instead they use animals only as number seven, a heuristic device or as a source from which to get new ideas. Of course, if a veterinarian or scientist wants to learn about diseases of cats, he or she can study cats as in number eight. And the final area, number nine, is knowledge for the sake of knowledge alone. Many scientists state this as a reason to do research on animals: not to cure human disease but simply to seek more knowledge.

Numbers three through nine are scientifically acceptable ways to use animals in science. The animal protection community, however, objects to the use of animals in such a fashion and you may hear them speak of alternatives for these uses. For example, aortic valve replacement can be performed with artificial or synthetic valves instead of obtaining them from pigs, and physicians no longer prescribe insulin from pigs and cows because human insulin can be synthesized. Instead of using animal tissue to study basic physiological processes, human tissue is plentiful and better if what the scientists actually want is more knowledge about humans. These are all alternatives to using animals and are also scientifically valid.

Arguments about ethics have been around for centuries. Ethics is somewhat subjective, but science should be less so. Scientific questions are eventually answered with more or less unanimous agreement. Such is the nature of studying the material world. In the final analysis, society will have to decide what role animals will play in scientific pursuits, indeed in all pursuits. There is hope that all sides will be able to agree on the scientific principles outlined previously and use that knowledge to make intelligent decisions.

Further Reading

Greek, J. S., & Greek, C. R. (2000). *Sacred cows and golden geese: The human cost of experiments on animals*. New York: Continuum.

———. (2002). *Specious science: How evolution and genetics explain why medical research on animals kills humans*. New York: Continuum.

———. (2004). *What will we do if we don't experiment on animals? Medical research for the twenty-first century*. Victoria, BC: Trafford Publishing.

LaFollette, H., & Shanks, N. (1996). *Brute science*. New York: Routledge.

Ray Greek

Research
Animals in Space

Before human beings ventured into space, American and Russian scientists launched animals with the aim of testing both their rocket engineering and the living conditions of the space environment that they would eventually encounter. When humans finally traveled to space, they still took animals so as to conduct further biological experiments, a practice that continues to this day at the International Space Station. Animals and insects that have been launched on either orbital or suborbital flights include chimps, dogs, monkeys, cats, rabbits, mice, rats, turtles, frogs, spiders, crickets, and swordtail fish. Over the years, many countries have issued stamps commemorating them.

The first five animals to be sent into space, collectively known as the *Albert Series*, all boarded V-2 Blossoms from White Sands, New Mexico, not long after the end of World War II. Albert I was a rhesus monkey who on June 11, 1948, was launched with virtually no publicity or documentation. Three days later another lab monkey (Albert II) reached an altitude of 83 miles, but died upon impact. In August that same year, an anesthetized mouse (Albert III) was the first astronaut to return alive. He was followed in December 1949 by Albert IV, a monkey who died on impact after a successful flight.

In May 1950 the last of the Alberts (Albert V) was launched; this mouse survived impact and was photographed in flight.

Next came the animal astronauts of the Aerobee missile flights, launched from Holloman Air Force Base, New Mexico. First up, on September 20, 1951, were Yorick (another monkey) and his eleven copassengers (all mice). The 236,000-foot missile flight was successful and Yorick became known as the first monkey to survive a flight to space. On May 22, 1952, he was followed by Patricia and Mike (two Philippine monkeys) and Mildred and Albert (two mice), who were all placed in different positions (the last two inside a drum where they could "float weightlessly") and shot 36 miles up at an average speed of 2,000 mph in order to test various effects of rapid acceleration. They were all recovered safely by parachute.

Meanwhile, back in the USSR, Soviet scientists began experimenting on rats, mice, rabbits, and eventually, dogs. The latter were chosen with the ultimate aim of designing a human space cabin (monkeys were thought to be too fidgety). Between 1951 and 1952 the Soviets launched at least nine stray female dogs (always in pairs; some dogs flew twice) on at least six of their R-1 series rockets (the precise facts are disputed among researchers). The first pair of hounds, Dezik and Tsyganka (Gipsy) were launched on August 15, 1951, and were successfully recovered by parachute. Next came Dezik and Lisa, who in September that year tragically died in an unsuccessful flight. The third pair, Smelaya (Bold) and Malyshka (Little One) were launched successfully, despite Smelaya's brief escape on the eve of their mission. The fourth launch (carrying a pair of dogs whose names remain unknown) was as tragic as the second, but the fifth (also carrying two anonymous strays) was successful. Finally, on September 15, 1951, the last pair of R-1 canines was launched successfully, though only after one of the original crew (Bobik) escaped and was replaced at the last minute by a dog found near the local canteen, which they named ZIB (the Russian acronym for "substituting missing-dog Bobik"). Other dogs associated with this series of sub-flights include Albina (Whitey), Dymka (Smoky), Modnista (Fashionable), and Kozyavka (Gnat).

Four years later, on November 3, 1957, Sputnik 2 famously orbited with a small stray dog named Laika (Barker, though her real name was Kudryavka, which means "little curly"). Two other dogs had been trained for this flight: Albina, who was the first back-up, and Mushka, upon whom the life support and instrumentation were tested. The dogs were all kept in increasingly smaller cages for periods of two to three weeks.

Shortly after the launch the Soviets caused public outrage by announcing that Laika would almost certainly die in space (at that time there was no recovery method for orbital flights). For a long time, they persuaded the world that she ate and barked for about a week before dying painlessly in orbit. However, in 2002 Dimitri Malashenkov of the Institute for Biological Problems in Moscow revealed that she died from panic and/or overheating a mere five to seven hours after take-off. The dead dog then circled the earth more than 2,500 times before burning up in its atmosphere. She did prove, however, that a living organism can survive in weightlessness for a long time, thus paving the way for the human astronauts of the 1960s. In 1988 Oleg Gazenko (one of the leading Soviet scientists involved in their animals-in-space program) announced that he regretted sending Laika into space: "The more time passes, the more I'm sorry about it. We shouldn't have done it. . . . we did not learn enough from this mission to justify the death of the dog."

The year after Laika's death, the United States launched a series of mice as part of their disastrous Mouse in Able (MIA) project. In July, MIA-1 was destroyed along with the rocket (Reentry 1). Laska (MIA-2) also died, and later that same month Wilkie (MIA-3) was lost at sea. In another mission, fourteen mice were destroyed along with their Jupiter rocket.

On December 13, 1958, another Jupiter rocket was fired, this time carrying a south-American squirrel monkey named Gordo, who, after a fifteen-minute (1,800 mile) flight, also died when a parachute failed to open. The naval medicals concluded that his heartbeat and respiration showed that humans could survive a similar trip. However, the American Society for the Prevention of Cruelty to Animals (ASPCA) complained that only inanimate objects should be used for such tests, and The British Royal Society for the Prevention of Cruelty to Animals (BRSPCA) expressed "grave concern and apprehension."

Able, an American-born rhesus monkey, and Baker, a female spider monkey from South America, were launched on May 28, 1959, aboard an Army Jupiter missile. They traveled 300 miles into space at speeds that at times exceeded 10,000 mph and were recovered unharmed, becoming the first living creatures to survive a space flight. The flight lasted fifteen minutes, during nine of which the monkeys were weightless. The mission was criticized by various animal welfare groups, such as the League Against Cruel Sports, who called the mission "scientific devilry," and the Conference of Anti-Vivisection Societies (made up of twenty-nine animal welfare groups), who stated that "cowardly acts such as this can never be justified on the grounds of expediency and all thinking people will be disgusted to learn of this latest misuse by scientists of defenseless animals." Able died June 1 from effects of anesthesia. Less than a month later, on June 3, four mice were launched from Vandenberg Air Force Base on Discoverer 3 as part of the Corona program of U.S. satellite spies. According to the CIA, the first try at launch failed when before the flight the mice were found dead after having eaten the krylon that had been sprayed on their cages. The second try was delayed because they realized the humidity sensor couldn't distinguish between water and mouse urine. When the rocket was finally launched, it fired into the Pacific Ocean, and the back-up crew of mice died.

Squirrel monkey Baker rode a Jupiter missile from NASA into space in 1959. Courtesy of NASA.

One of the better known "space-monkeys" was a rhesus called Sam (an acronym for the U.S. Air Force's School of Aviation Medicine), launched on December 4, 1959, with the aim of testing the launch escape system of a Mercury spacecraft. The experiment was successful, and Sam was recovered a few hours later (he lived a healthy life until 1982). His mate (a rhesus monkey named Miss Sam) was launched in a similarly successful test on January 21 the following year.

Soon after, the Soviet Union began testing on more dogs. On July 2, 1959, Otvazhnaya (Brave One) and Snezhinka (Snowflake) made a successful high altitude test, accompanied by a rabbit called Marfusha (over the next year Otvazhnaya was to participate in five more similar experiments). A few weeks later, on July 28, Bars (Panther) and Lisichka (Little Fox) were launched on a Korabl Sputnik 1; both dogs died when the booster exploded. On August 19, 1960, Belka (Squirrel) and Strelka (Little Arrow) boarded Korabl Sputnik 2, accompanied by forty mice, two rats, a grey rabbit, and fifteen flasks containing plants and fruit flies. The flight was a success and Strelka later gave birth to

Belka and Strelka, part of the Russian Space Agency. ©Bettmann/Corbis.

six puppies of which one was presented to President John F. Kennedy as a gift for his children. Korabl Sputnik 3 was launched in December that same year, carrying Pchelka (Little Bee) and Muska (Little Fly), along with more mice and insects. They all burned up upon re-entry. The next attempted Korabl flight was aborted after reported failure in the upper rocket stage. The intended crew (two more stray dogs called Damka and Krasavka) were recovered safely. Next up were Chernushka (Blackie), who was accompanied by a guinea pig and some mice aboard Korabl 4 on March 9, 1961, and Zvezdochka (Little Star), who less than three weeks later successfully tested Korabl 5 on a lonely flight in which she was only accompanied by the simulated Ivan Ivanovich.

Arguably the most famous animal astronaut of all was a four-year-old West African chimpanzee called Ham (his name was an acronym for Holloman Aero Med), who, having been chosen from a short list of six astro-chimps, on January 31, 1960, donned his spacesuit and boarded the Mercury Redstone rocket at Cape Canaveral to become the first chimpanzee in space. Reaching a record speed of 5,857 mph and an altitude of over 155 miles (both due to technical problems), Ham was weightless for 6.6 minutes of his 16.5-minute flight. He landed dehydrated and fatigued to a reward of one apple and half an orange but went on to live a healthy life until 1983 (his body was preserved by the Smithsonian Institute, who have permanently loaned it to the International Space Hall of Fame in Alamogordo, New Mexico). Without Ham, America would not have been able to launch its first human astronaut, Alan B. Shepard, Jr., on May 5, 1961, though by then the Soviets had already orbited Yuri Gagarin around the

Ham was the first chimpanzee in space, 1960. Without Ham, the United States would not have been able to launch its first human astronaut, Alan B. Shepard Jr., on May 5, 1961. Courtesy of NASA.

earth for almost two hours on April 12 that same year, following their successful Kotabl dog launches. Although the Soviets had chosen dogs over monkeys for their experiments (because they fidgeted less), the Americans preferred chimpanzees over dogs because they were more similar to humans.

Some of the technical defects that occurred during Ham's flight were not corrected until November 1961, when a chimpanzee named Enos orbited the earth twice (the mission plan had called for three orbits but the flight was terminated early due to technical difficulties, which included a thruster malfunction). Without this further animal testing John Glenn would not have been able to orbit Earth in 1962. That year Enos was reported to have died at Holloman Air Force Base from a case of dysentery unrelated to his space travel. Equally unfortunate was Goliath, a squirrel monkey killed on November 10, 1961, when the Atlas E rocket he was launched in was destroyed within 35 seconds.

On October 18, 1963, the French launched and successfully recovered Felix, the first cat to make it to space. A second cat launched six days later could not be retrieved. On February 22, 1966, the Soviets launched two more dogs, Veterok (Breeze) and Ugoyok (Little Piece Of Coal), in order to test the prolonged effects of radiation caused by the Van Allen Belt during space travel. Their twenty-one days in space remain the canine record to this day, surpassed by humans only in 1974. On September 15, 1968, Soviet scientists launched a number of turtles, worms, flies, and bacteria on a one-week mission to orbit the moon. The re-entry capsule was successfully retrieved. A similar mission on November 10 that same year was unsuccessful.

Between 1966 and 1969 the United States launched three missions in the Biosatellite series. The first of these carried insects and frog eggs, as well as various micro-organisms and plants; it was never recovered. The second, launched in 1967, had a similar cargo but was recalled early, whereas the third, launched in 1969, carried a male monkey named Bonnie. This mission's main purpose was to investigate the effect of space travel on numerous functions and abilities including behavior, cognition, and metabolism. Eight hours after his recovery, Bonnie died of a heart attack caused by dehydration.

After the successful human landing of Apollo 11 on the moon, the use of animals in space was mainly restricted to biological experiments. Popular subjects included turtles, rabbits, fish, and insects. On July 28, 1973, two spiders named Anita and Arabella were to make headline news by spinning their webs in space. Between then and 1996 the Russians launched a series of life-science missions (involving various monkeys, rats, tortoises, insects, frogs, fish, newts, and quail eggs) in cooperation with a number of countries and organizations, including the Commonwealth of Independent States, the European Space Agency, and the United States. A monkey named Multik died the day after his recovery from one such two-week mission (Bion 11), bringing ethical questions relating to animal experimentation back on the agenda and causing NASA to back out of participating in subsequent Bion missions. Other life-science experiments have included Spacelab missions (1983–present day) experimenting on both humans and animals. The environment within the animal enclosure modules used in these missions meets most of the recommendations of the *NIH Guide to Care and Use of Laboratory Animals*, with the exception of its increased ambient temperature and housing density. On April 17, 1988, a record number of over two thousand creatures accompanied the seven human astronauts of Shuttle Columbia (STS-90) on a sixteen-day Neurolab mission.

The 1990s saw China launch guinea dogs and Japan launch newts, while the United States extended their menagerie to include snails, sea urchins, moths, crickets, carp, and oyster toadfish. More recently, in December 2001 twenty-four mice boarded the Space shuttle Endeavour as part of an experiment on a bone-regulating protein called osteoprotegerin, whereas in January 2003, Space Shuttle Columbia carried bees, ants, silkworms, and Japanese killifish, all part of various international high school projects. The United States, Russia, China, Japan, and France all continue to fly animals into space.

Further Resources

BBC. *On this day.* http://www.bbc.co.uk/

Borkowski, G. L., Wilfinger, W. W., & Lane, P. K. (1995/1996, Winter). Laboratory animals in space: Life sciences research. *Animal Welfare Information Center Newsletter*, 6(2–4).

Cassidy, D., & Hughes, P. (2005). *One small step: America's first primates in space.* New York: Chamberlain Brothers.

Tara, G. (1988). *A brief history of animals in space.* Available at http://history.nasa.gov/animals.html

Constantine Sandis

Research
Experimental Psychology

The relationship between humans and animals as described within experimental psychology is closely tied to the development of psychology as a scientific discipline. Studies using animals have been of two main kinds: experimental physiological work that oriented toward illumination of human psychological phenomena, and research focused on the animals themselves. The latter is known as animal psychology or comparative psychology. A brief overview of its history seems appropriate.

The new psychology, experimental psychology or scientific psychology, as it has commonly been referred to, began in the mid-nineteenth century, from the convergence of philosophy on one hand, and the natural sciences (especially physiology, physics and astronomy) on the other. Before 1860 there were no scientists that called themselves psychologists. Philosophers have always been interested in the problems of the mind and knowledge of reality. They have asked whether animals have a mind and, if so, to what degree it differs from the human mind. The answer has been dependent above all on social influences, particularly those of religion. However, it has also depended on the curiosity of individuals that led them to make detailed observations of nature, and even on their audacity to oppose the mainstream ideas of the time. For most of the classical Greeks, inclined toward the observation of nature (though not to studies involving intervention), animals were regarded as rational beings. Aristotle (384–322 BCE), who believed functions of the mind were situated in the heart, thought "In the great majority of animals there are traces of psychical qualities" and that the difference between humans and animals in this respect was only a question of degree. Later, Galen (c. 129–99 CE) made an important advance, locating the mind in the brain and distinguishing between sensory and motor nerves, though he believed that nerves were passive conductors of the animal spirit. It could be said that modern science began only in the seventeenth century. In the Dark Ages (c. 500–1200) and Middle Ages (c. 1200–1500), western civilization was dominated by theological dogma.

The philosophy of R. Descartes (1596–1650) had a great influence on the subject at hand. He believed that animals lacked moral qualities and reason. They were dissected in anatomic and physiological studies, then, without considering any ethical problems such studies posed. As they had no soul, even vivisection was permissible. Frogs, newts, and snakes were commonly used in early experiments. Soon, natural sciences began to complement each other. By 1780 L. Galvani (1737–98) found that a frog's leg would move when brought into contact with metals and concluded that animal tissues generate electricity. The Voltaic battery (A. Volta, 1745–1827) led later to physiological studies of the nerve impulse. Rabbits, dogs, and monkeys were used for the systematic study of effects of electrical stimulation of the cerebral cortex. J. Müller (1801–58), considered by many the father of experimental physiology, maintained that the velocity of the nerve impulse was comparable to the speed of light. This idea was in agreement with the philosophy of the time, which considered that the mind could not be assessed experimentally, but only by introspection, that is, by the verbal report of a person's own experience. But by 1850 L. F. von Helmholtz (1821–94) measured the rate of conduction of the nerve impulse in a frog's leg and found it to be even slower than the propagation of sound. By 1820 the astronomer F. W. Bessel (1784–1846) suspected errors of observation when different persons estimated the transit of a star. Comparing the measurement made by different people, he established what is called "the personal equation" and also its variability, which later led to the search for psychophysical explanation of the phenomenon. Later studies and discoveries allowed the calculation of the time between the observation of a signal and the reaction to that signal. E. H. Weber (1795–1878) in 1846 and G. T. Fechner (1801–87) in 1860 described the relationship between the intensity of a stimulus and the magnitude of the resulting subjective sensation. In sum, the important discoveries were (a) nerve impulses and their propagation at a measurable speed, (b) the existence of personal differences in human reaction times, and (c) the indirect measurement of subjective experiences. These discoveries introduced rigorous methodologies for making measurements that left no doubt that mental processes could be subjected to experimental control and analysis.

J. Locke (1632–1704) is regarded as the philosophical parent of experimental psychology. For him, ideas were the units of mind, and his doctrine of association is based on the combination of ideas. He also argued that there was a continuum between animals and man. Other empiricist philosophers, those that argued that knowledge is grounded on experience, such as D. Hartley (1705–57) and D. Hume (1711–76), also accepted that animal and human natures had much in common. Later, the evolutionary associationism of H. Spencer (1820–1903) proposed a hierarchy, going from instincts formed out of reflex actions to cognition evolved from instincts. In the mid-nineteenth century, conditions were ripe for the emergence of psychology as an independent discipline.

W. Wundt (1832–1920) is called the main founder of experimental psychology. He is believed to be the first to call himself a psychologist. In 1867 he gave his course the name "Physiological Psychology," which later became the basis for his famous book. Because philosophical psychology and physiology were the parent disciplines, that seemed to him an appropriate name for the new science. In 1879 he established, in the University of Leipzig, the first formal psychological laboratory. Wundt spoke of a scientific psychology and his books included the recently developed methods for the measurement of mental processes. For him, scientific meant experimental. However, he argued that this was not the only appropriate method for psychology. The higher mental processes, he believed, must be studied through the history of human nature. The majority of the first American experimentalists were trained by him. At the same time, the ideas of Spencer and Darwin (1809–82) contributed to the emergence of animal psychology, and this later became formally experimental with E. L. Thorndike (1874–1949). The Darwinian theory of evolution made logical and fundamental the extension of the concept of mind to animals.

Before much work began in academia, there were a great deal of writings about animal behavior both as simple experiments and field observations. The study of animals became interesting for its own sake. J. Romanes (1848–94), a writer friend of Darwin, wrote the first book on comparative psychology by combining scientific with anecdotal accounts of behavior. C. Lloyd Morgan (1852–1936), a professor at Bristol, described the methods and "basal principles" that should guide the scientific study of the discipline. They appeared in his book *Introduction to Comparative Psychology*, published in 1894. The most famous of his rules is known as "Lloyd Morgan's canon." He formulated it as a restriction on interpreting behavior in terms of a higher psychical process when it can be explained by a lower one. Careful observations of how his pet fox terrier pup Tony learned to carry correctly his stick led him to formulate that it was learning by trial and error that accounted for the behavior, not the perception of relations. Thereafter he used these observations to back up his canon. Besides methodological principles, the book contains detailed descriptions of his own controlled experiments on the pecking behavior of Blackie, one of his chicks, among other investigations. He expressed his expectations about the future of the discipline as follows:

> I believe that there is here . . . an, extensive field open to experimental observation. Is it too much to hope that in connection with some university in Great Britain there will some day be founded a Chair of Comparative Psychology, with an experimental station attached, where animals may be reared under test conditions and under foster-parents, so that the development of their intelligence may be carefully studied?

Comparative psychology, though, was to flourish first in America. At the beginning of the twentieth century America already had an important group of outstanding experimental psychologists, and the new discipline began to subdivide. E. B. Titchener (1867–1927) argued that psychology should be concerned only with the generalized, conscious human mind, as Wundt did. American psychologists, however, began formal work on animal, child, abnormal, and applied psychology, stressing an organism's adaptation to its environment. The renowned historian E. G. Boring (1886–1968) tells us that, when in 1895 Thorndike took W. James's (1842–1910) graduate course "The Relations between Physiology and Psychology" at Harvard, he was not allowed to incubate and hatch chicks in his bedroom. James tried to get him space at the University but did not succeed. James then took Thorndike and his chicks to the cellar of his own home. He began there his famous works on intelligence in chicks, and later went to Columbia carrying them in a basket. He used labyrinths made of books to study their behavior. Fish and monkeys were also studied. He constructed a "puzzle-box" for cats and dogs, where a hungry animal was confined and had to learn to escape by pulling a cord or pressing a lever. These much-cited works were published in 1898 and 1911. He developed a theory on the nature of learning by association. The following paragraphs illustrate his thinking:

> The main purpose of the study of the animal mind is to learn the development of mental life down through the phylum, to trace in particular the origin of human faculty. . . . It is so useful, in understanding the animal, to see what it does in different circumstances and what helps and what hinders its learning, that one is led to an intrinsic interest in varieties of behavior as well as in the kinds of consciousness of which they give evidence.

Thus, he admitted the possibility of drawing inferences about the mind from the observation of behavior, something regarded as useless by J. B. Watson (1878–1958) some years later.

R. M. Yerkes (1876–1956) is also a good representative of the comparative psychology paradigm, partly because he worked with worms, crabs, turtles, frogs, doves, crows, rats, pigs, monkeys, apes, and men, but also because he, together with W. Köhler (1887–1967), found the way to introduce a new concept to the discipline, the "insight" issue. Around 1916 they independently described the behavior of apes confronted with situations where the path to food was restricted. Different tools were provided, and the apes had to find the appropriate solution if they were to reach the food. After unsuccessful attempts some of the animals became inactive and then later performed the chain of actions correctly. They were interpreted as having solved the problem by insight, that is, by a sudden perception of relations during the period of inactivity. Sultan, one of the more skillful of Köhler's chimps, appeared to have solved the problems this way. However, the period of inactivity was for I. P. Pavlov (1849–1936) in 1934, "mere extinction and nothing else." A statement surely not at all shared by Yerkes, especially when describing Prince Chim, a bonobo whose sensitive behavior caused the pioneer scientist to wonder whether he was in front of a new primate species, as later turned out to be the case.

By 1904, Pavlov wrote that "the physiology of salivary glands had revealed the so called psychical phenomena." He discovered the conditioned reflex. With a simple operation he brought "to the exterior, on the skin, the normal opening of a salivary gland excretory canal." Fixing a funnel to the canal end, he could "observe with precision the gland activity." He noted that what he at first called "psychical secretions" flowed when the operated dog anticipated food. When an external agent, as a sound, was temporally paired with food the salivatory response could be elicited by the sound. He immediately realized that he had a means to study behavior objectively. Dogoniai and Krasavets were two of the many dogs studied by his group of collaborators. Watson, whose doctoral thesis was *Animal Education: The Psychical Development of the White Rat* (1903), endorsed Pavlov's work and appealed to the study of behavior without any reference to mind. By 1913 Watson wrote that in psychology the "theoretical goal is the prediction and control of behavior." The proposition was later promoted by B. F. Skinner (1904–90), who developed the operant conditioning technique to study behavior. He constructed what is called the Skinner box, a cage with one or more windows to present stimuli (when visual), an operandum (a bar for a rat to press, or a key for a pigeon to peck at), and a mechanism to present food. The box may also have additional devices for the automatic recording of responses. The operant conditioning is established when a response is followed by a reinforcing stimulus, usually food. His book, *The Behavior of Organisms* (1938), provides a system where the environmental conditions are rigorously controlled and behavioral variables are measured as response strength. Conditional reflex and operant conditioning both provide a kind of language that builds up a communication canal between animal and experimenter. As Boring noted, "When an animal learns to avoid a shock, he is using his new-found language of conditioned response—not purposively, it is true, yet he is using it—to tell you that he does not like the shock, that he knows it is coming, that he knows how to avoid it. . . . His discriminations are his words."

The middle of the twentieth century was a productive time with strong controversies about the nature of animal behavior. The important question was whether animals are relatively passive beings shaped by the environment or whether cognition and motivation underlie their behavior. E. C. Tolman (1886–1959) developed a system that was overlooked during the period of mainly stimulus-response oriented work, though present animal cognition studies incorporate his views. His work *Cognitive Maps in Rat and Men* (1948) summarizes his thinking. Action would be the product of knowledge about goals and of purpose to meet them. He found clear evidence that rats in a maze learn about their environment without performance, and this was interpreted as the acquisition of a cognitive map. With adoption of this tradition, currently the emphasis is not only on what animals do but also on what they know and how they know it.

At present, experimental comparative psychologists worldwide have left aside extreme schools of thought and work on a variety of topics, bringing together causation and function, description and explanation, physiological, behavioral, social, and environmental levels of analysis, and studying the spectrum from honey bees and fishes to dolphins and elephants. Work on perception now also takes into account motivation and attention and has broadened its scope to information processing. Reaction times of pigeons are measured as they search for a specific symbol, and electrical changes occurring in the brains of cats are followed during the presentation of external signals. Those who work on learning and memory now recognize species-specific constraints on the detection and association of certain stimuli. Frogs, for example, have a predisposition to respond more to blue than to other colors, and for a rat it is easy to learn an association between taste and subsequent gastrointestinal illness. Current studies on play, individual differences, personalities, and emotional responses of animals emphasize the significance of adaptive functions. Pattern recognition, internal image, concept formation, ability to manipulate symbols, language, thought, intentionality, and consciousness are phenomena that can be represented on a scale that ranges from the widely accepted to the wildly controversial. Nevertheless, they all are important topics for the understanding of the processes of knowledge, historically always the subject of psychological science.

Not many disciplines have undergone such deep transformations in their subject matter and methodology as experimental psychology has. Nor have many traveled their road in the company of so many animal species. One must credit in particular such cooperative beings as rats and pigeons, which have collaborated in such abundance, usually unnamed, and identified only by a number.

As a final note, it rarely has been explicitly acknowledged in psychology that "experimental" has long had two distinct meanings. As in most other sciences, its oldest sense is simply as a synonym for empirical. Historically, any empirical study or observation carried out to answer a question or test a hypothesis has been labeled an experiment, in contradistinction to theoretical or philosophical analyses. Under the influence of the field of statistics over the last century, however, the term experimental also has been given a much narrower meaning, that of pertaining only to controlled, comparative, or manipulative experiments, that is, studies designed to assess the effects of some experimenter-manipulated treatment factor, experimental variable, or external stimulus on a subject or other type of experimental unit.

Further Resources

Bekoff, M. (Ed.). (2004). *Encyclopedia of animal behavior*. Westport, CT: Greenwood Press.

Bekoff, M., & Jamieson, D. (Eds.) (1996). *Readings in animal cognition*. Cambridge, MA: MIT Press.

Green, C. D. (Ed.). (2000). *Classics in the history of psychology*. Available at http://psychclassics.yorku.ca

Hearst, E. (1979). The first century of experimental psychology. Florence, KY: Lawrence Erlbaum Associates.

Celia M. Lombardi

Research
A Honeybee Model of Alcohol-Induced Behavior

One of the novel uses of invertebrates is in the study of ethanol- or alcohol-induced drinking behavior of humans. Although invertebrates may seem unlikely subjects, several previous attempts have been made to explore the effects of ethanol consumption on invertebrate behavior. The first attempt was described anecdotally in 1888, when the naturalist John Lubbock fed "spirits" to ants and observed how intoxicated individuals interacted with nest mates. As Lubbock noted,

> The sober ants were rather puzzled; but after examining the intoxicated individuals, they picked up the strangers and threw them into the ditch, while they carried their own friends into the nest, where no doubt they slept off the effects of the spirits.

Since Lubbock's initial observation, there have been other attempts to develop ethanol models using invertebrates. The first of these used the sea hare *Aplysia californica* to examine both tolerance and neurophysiological effects of ethanol exposure at the cellular level. Most recently, ethanol intoxication in the fruitfly *Drosophila melanogaster* was described, as was a mutation sensitive to ethanol-induced loss of postural control. The honeybee (*Apis mellifera* L.) is also a suitable animal for ethanol research and has much to recommend it.

Consider, for instance, that honeybees are inexpensive to procure and maintain. Moreover, as with vertebrate models and those using *Aplysia* and *Drosophila*, much is known about the natural history, physiology, genetics, and behavior of honeybees. Automated and unautomated techniques are available to study a wide range of honeybee behavior, including learning and locomotion. Unlike most other animal models, honeybees are social, and therefore the effects of ethanol exposure on such advanced behaviors as the "dance language" and social caste interactions can be studied.

The initial goal of research exploring the use of honeybees to study ethanol-induced behavior is to produce a catalog of similarities and differences in the ethanol-induced behaviors of bees and humans. This comparative approach differs substantially from that used in fruit fly (*Drosophila melanogaster*) and nematode (*Caenorhabditis elegans*) models of alcoholism. In these models, more attention is paid to molecular and biochemical effects of ethanol than behavior.

Research has discovered several effects common to ethanol consumption in vertebrates and honeybees, including disruption of learning and of decision making, decreased locomotion, and the ability to self-administer ethanol. Of special interest is that honeybees will consume 100 percent ethanol and will drink large quantities of an ethanol solution. For example, at a single feeding, bees will drink the equivalent of 11 liters of wine! Moreover, application of the emetic disulfiram reduces ethanol consumption in honeybees, although, as in humans, there are large individual differences.

Experiments in which honeybees fly to artificial flowers containing ethanol reveal that animals given a choice between a 1 percent ethanol solution and sucrose show no aversion to an ethanol solution. Honeybees given a choice between a 5 percent ethanol solution and sucrose-only show no overall differences in the initial choice of artificial flowers, but some bees do switch over to flowers containing sucrose. It is also known that drinking a 2.5 percent ethanol solution disrupts the ability of honeybees to make complex decisions associated with choice behavior.

Experiments designed to study the preferences of bees to commercially available ethanol products consumed by humans indicate that bees will not consume bourbon but will consume various wines, schnapps, liquors, and beers. The relationship between the amounts consumed is not directly related to the sugar content in the drinks. In general, however, bees prefer more sweet drinks with less alcohol.

It has been known for some time that ethanol is associated with several types of aggressive behavior in humans, nonhuman primates, and rodents. Exposure to ethanol also influences aggression in honeybees. A unique aspect of this work was the use of Africanized honeybees. The so-called "killer bee" is known for its aggressive behavior as compared to the more docile European honeybee. The results of experiments in which "killer bees" drank from an artificial flower containing 20 percent ethanol clearly showed that aggression, as measured by the number of stings on a leather patch, increased compared to a colony receiving a 1.8 milliliter sucrose solution. The bees became so aggressive that the experiment had to be terminated.

The comparison of ethanol-induced behavior among honeybees and humans also extends to social behavior. Bees foraging at artificial flowers containing a 5 percent ethanol solution stopped communicating with their nestmates upon returning to the hive. Not only did they stop sharing food with their nestmates, the drunken bees also stopped communicating by the waggle dance. Instead of the well-coordinated movements of the waggle dance, the bees switched to a "tremble" dance. This tremble dance reminds an observer of the uncoordinated movements associated with a human who has consumed too much ethanol.

The work on the social insect model of alcoholism is only in its beginning phase. It is expected that as the model progresses, the honeybee will become an important part of research efforts to understand how ethanol influences human behavior.

Further Resources

Abramson, C. I., Place, A. J., Aquino, I., & Fernandez, A. (2004). Development of an ethanol model using social insects: IV Influence of ethanol on aggression of Africanized honeybees (*Apis mellifera* L.). *Psychological Reports, 94,* 1107–15.

Abramson, C. I., Sanderson, C., Painter, J., Barnett, S., & Wells, H. (2005). Development of an ethanol model using social insects: V: Honeybee foraging decisions under the influence of alcohol. *Alcohol, 36,* 187–93.

Abramson, C. I, Stone, S. M., Ortez, R. A., Luccardi, A., Vann, K. L., Hanig, K. D., & Rice, J. (2000). The development of an ethanol model using social insects: Behavior studies of the honeybee (*Apis mellifera* L.). *Alcoholism: Clinical and Experimental Research, 24,* 1153–66.

Moore, M. S., deZazzo, J., Luk, A. Y., Tully, T., Singh, C. M., & Heberlein, U. (1998). Ethanol intoxication in Drosophila: Genetic and pharmacological evidence for regulation by cAMP signaling pathway. *Cell, 9,* 997–1007.

Rothenfluh, A., & Heberlein, U. (2002). Drugs, flies, and videotape: The effects of ethanol and cocaine on Drosophila locomotion. *Current Opinion in Neurobiology, 12,* 639–45.

Wolf, F. W., & Heberlein, U. (2003). Invertebrate models of drug abuse. *Journal of Neurobiology, 54,* 161–78.

Charles I. Abramson, Janko Bozic, and Harrington Wells

Research
Laboratory Animal Welfare

Around the world, millions of animals are used in laboratories. Scientists may use animals to test toxic chemicals or to develop new surgery techniques. They may cause cancers and infections in animals to study them and develop cures. They may kill the animals to collect tissues and study their cells. Despite the animal death and pain that these acts can bring, there are ways to limit animal suffering in the laboratory.

The principle that underlies most regulation of laboratory animal use is that it can be justifiable to harm animals for science, but that animal pain and distress must be limited to that which is unavoidable to accomplish the scientific goal.

England led the way, with its 1868 Animals Act, in placing some government restrictions on how animals are used. Since then, other countries and jurisdictions have enacted laws. Along with these laws and regulations, scientists and veterinarians over the years have developed standards for self-regulation of animal use.

In the United States, the first national law was the Laboratory Animal Welfare Act of 1966. In 1966, Congress sought to regulate some peripheral aspects of laboratory animal welfare without actually interfering with how scientific experiments were performed. The law dictates how animals, especially dogs and cats, may be obtained for research and how a dog vendor or a laboratory must document that they are not trafficking in stolen animals. The law specifies how animals should be housed in a laboratory and created a team of inspectors in the United States Department of Agriculture (USDA) to visit laboratories and verify these matters. The law also required that adequate veterinary care be provided for laboratory animals. But the law stopped its coverage as soon as the animal left the animal housing area and went down the hall into the laboratory.

The Laboratory Animal Welfare Act regulated animal care but not animal use, with some curious results. Although inspectors scrupulously enforced any departure from strict hygiene that might result in animal infections, no welfare rules covered intentionally infecting animals as part of an experiment. Though the law required veterinary care of animals, scientists had no oversight in conducting experiments that might intentionally make an animal sick.

This exclusion of laboratory practices from laboratory animal welfare laws was not a stable arrangement and it did not stand. The U.S. Congress has amended the Laboratory Animal Welfare Act (now called simply the Animal Welfare Act) several times. They expanded the requirement for adequate veterinary care, adding in the use of painkillers and anesthetics for many experiments, with a veterinarian, not the scientist, prescribing the pain medications. Similarly, they expanded the regulations about housing animals, to include providing exercise for caged dogs and psychological well-being programs for caged monkeys and apes.

The most important innovation in the regulation of laboratory animal welfare has been the requirement that most institutions that conduct experiments on animals have some sort of animal care and a committee that reviews every planned use of animals. These Institutional Animal Care and Use Committees (IACUC) have been required in most American laboratories since 1986, and many countries require similar committees. A scientist who wishes to use animals must apply to the committee for approval. She or he must describe why animals are necessary, must consult with a veterinarian on pain management and anesthesia, must describe the qualifications of anyone who will work with the animals and, in general, must assure that everything is being done to minimize animal pain and distress to that which is unavoidable. She or he must document a search for alternatives to the painful use of animals. The IACUC also must have a system in place that allows concerned individuals and "whistle-blowers" to anonymously report their concerns about animal care and use.

Animal pain and distress are the overriding focus of animal welfare policies. One framework for reducing pain and distress is to think in terms of the "Three Rs" of alternatives: replace, reduce, and refine. Replacement alternatives are conceptually the most straightforward: find ways to generate research data without using sentient animals at all. Candidates for consideration include studying cells in tissue culture (*in vitro* techniques), developing computer simulations, making better use of human epidemiological data and human volunteers, or using inanimate models in teaching. Reduction is just as it sounds—efforts to lower the numbers of animals used. This often means rethinking statistical tests, using just the number necessary for statistically valid results. Refinement alternatives are the most varied because they comprise all the myriad ways to rethink animal care and use to reduce the potential for pain or distress. Refinements can include more aggressive use of animal pain-killers, using noninvasive techniques, such as X-rays, instead of invasive dissections or surgeries to see inside the animal's body, or housing animals in compatible groups instead of all alone in steel cages.

Scientists are not barred from causing pain and disease in animals. There are some studies where this is unavoidable. Many studies of cancer, for example, call for inducing cancer in the animals. Developing a new painkiller for human use often involves causing pain to animals to see if the new medication is effective. The scientist, veterinarian, and committee's jobs are to limit the pain and illness. If the project is studying cancer prevention or biological processes that happen early in cancer, then there may be no reason to allow animals to progress to advanced disease. Thus, the scientist and committee refine their experimental endpoints in favor of those that happen early on, either treating the cancer at its first appearance or humanely euthanizing the animals. In the study of pain and the development of painkillers, the scientist may mostly use pain stimuli that are mild and that the animal can opt to end. For example, a scientist may time how long a rat that has received a particular painkiller will tolerate having her foot on a hot plate before she withdraws it on her own.

Critics of the current degree of animal welfare regulation raise several issues. For one, scientists are still allowed to hurt and kill animals, even though they should try to minimize any suffering. Second, in the American system, some animals are not covered by the regulations. The Animal Welfare Act only covers mammals, and at that, excludes mice and rats, overwhelmingly the most numerous mammals in laboratories. Another law (the Health Research Extension Act of 1985) covers all vertebrate animals if they are on projects and on campuses that receive federal research grants. This leaves the potential that animals at private companies and small schools that receive no federal grants may not have government oversight at all. Invertebrate animals, even sensitive species such as octopuses, are not covered by American laws at all.

Another criticism of the current system is that IACUC is a form of self-regulation, and that has the potential for abuse. Scientists on the committee assess the work of their peers and coworkers and department-mates. To limit the potential for abuse, the laws require that a public or unaffiliated member (or members) be appointed to the committee. USDA inspectors review the work of the IACUC during their inspections, and institutions and their IACUC report annually to the USDA and to the National Institutes of Health's Office of Laboratory Animal Welfare (which enforces the Health Research Extension Act). Additionally, many institutions voluntarily seek to have their animal facilities and their IACUC program accredited by the Association for the Assessment and Accreditation of Laboratory Animal Care, International, with its teams of scientists and veterinarians who conduct site visits. Still, self-regulation, with its strengths and weaknesses, remains the core of welfare oversight for the majority of laboratory animals.

Working in the animals' favor is the realization that to a great extent good science and good animal care are intertwined. Though animals may get ill or may suffer during the course of an experiment, the vast majority of experiments require that animals enter the study in uniformly good health and that pain and distress are minimized throughout. If animals are carrying various infections as they start an experiment, the scientist may never know whether she or he is seeing the results of the experiment or simply the results of the illness. If animals are stressed during an experiment, their biology is affected, and again, interpretation of data is muddied. Although it is best that scientists

While legislation has been passed concerning the treatment of many laboratory animals, the Animal Welfare Act covers only mammals and, at that, excludes mice and rats. Courtesy of Larry Carbone.

feel a moral responsibility to treat their animals well, there is also self-interest in keeping their animals free of disease and distress. To this end, the Institute of Laboratory Animal Resources published its *Guide for the Care and Use of Laboratory Animals*, a combination of ethical standards and expert guidance on ways to minimize pain and distress.

Ultimately, no law and no committee can see everything everywhere at all times, and so the personal, ethical responsibility of the scientists, veterinarians, and students working with animals is the main determinant of animal welfare.

Further Resources

Carbone, L. (2004). *What animals want: Expertise and advocacy in laboratory animal welfare policy*. New York: Oxford University Press.

Institute of Laboratory Animal Resources. (1996). *Guide for the care and use of laboratory animals*. Washington, DC: National Academy Press.

Orlans, F. B. (1993). *In the Name of science: Issues in responsible animal experimentation*. New York: Oxford University Press.

Rowan, A. N. (1984). *Of mice, models, and men: A critical evaluation of animal research*. Albany: State University of New York Press.

Russell, W. M. S., & Burch, R.L. (1959). *The principles of humane experimental technique*. London: Methuen & Co., Ltd.

Stevens, C. (1990). Laboratory animal welfare. *Animals and their legal rights* (pp. 66–105). Washington, DC: Animal Welfare Institute.

Larry Carbone

Research
Laboratory Human-Animal Bonds

Many established animal researchers will recall times during their training when they were discouraged from getting "too close" to the animals they worked with. Playing with the animals, naming them, or even referring to them as "he" or "she" rather than "it" was widely frowned upon. Concerns about the experiences and premature deaths of animals due to research were sometimes treated hostilely, as if they were criticisms of animal experimentation as a whole.

Some facilities took a different view, that relationships between animals and their human caretakers are beneficial to animals, staff, and research quality. Since the early 1990s this perspective has become increasingly widespread—in association with other changes such as increasing concern for animal welfare, stronger roles for technical staff, and changing demographics in the field of animal-based research (for example, greater participation of females and people from urban backgrounds).

The key advantages of meaningful relationships between humans and animals in the laboratory are thought to be the following.

Animal Welfare

Animals that share a relationship with a human caregiver can deal more calmly with experimental procedures. This reduction of stress can be developed further by the use of rewards and training, and replacing coercive procedures with ones where the animal actively cooperates. Human caregivers who are familiar with their animals will also be more adept at noticing when they are unwell or suffering from poor welfare and developing ways to improve animal welfare, such as refined experimental procedures and enriched environments.

Increasing Human Job Satisfaction

It is almost inevitable that the people who work closely with animals become attached to them. These staff members feel dissatisfied when time spent with animals is cut back or impaired, when their feelings for the animals are disregarded, and when animals are treated callously by other workers. However, if the caregiving staff is encouraged to understand and advocate for their animals as an integral part of the research effort, their jobs become more meaningful and satisfying. This has an effect on staff development, retention, and research success.

Meaningful Research

Researchers' attachments to animals, either directly or via caregiving staff, reminds them of the costs of the work they do and acts as a constant source of motivation to ensure, as much as possible, that the experiments are well designed and pursue the most promising lines of investigation for the most worthwhile goals. Attentive caregiving of animals ensures the psychological and physical normality of these animals, maximizing the validity of the animal research model. It is imperative that work that causes suffering or death to animals has a sound justification that is clearly discussed with and supported by all participating staff members.

There are a number of concerns that need to be addressed once relationships between humans and animals in the laboratory are acknowledged.

Human Stress and Grief

There is evidence that experimenters who work with animals inevitably experience stress and discomfort when their work leads to animal suffering or death. This underrecognized distress is described by the sociologist Arnold Arluke in a prominent article entitled "Trapped in a Guilt Cage." His study of biomedical scientists in the late eighties showed that most had been left alone to struggle with their feelings about the use of animals in research. This commonly lead to feelings of discomfort and in some cases more extreme "depression or anxiety, such as nightmares, sleep loss, and increased alcohol consumption."

This response can be better accommodated when it is brought out into the open and workers are allowed to participate in making the research as effective, efficient, and as free from suffering as possible. Allowance should be made for caregivers to take responsibility for procedures done to their animals, including killing them when this is required—or for these duties to be carried out by a less attached staff member if they become too stressful. Some people benefit from opportunities to express their feelings to sympathetic colleagues, or to be given "alone time" to feel grief for the animals they care for.

Memorials

The community at a center of research may benefit from making a formal acknowledgement of the contribution made by nonhuman animals. These may range from informal records of animals (photographs in the break room) to full ceremonies, where those who participate in the complete research process describe and celebrate the benefits of the research and acknowledge the contributions of animals. Memorials of this type have a long tradition in some nations, such as Japan and Korea, where animals are acknowledged in regular services at abattoirs, markets, and research institutes.

Relationships between humans and animals are almost inevitable in any settings, including the research or testing laboratory. It must be recognized that these bonds, whether encouraged or discouraged, will impact experimental results. Animals are very sensitive to the expectations of their caregivers and this may make them perform better in experimental tasks, reducing data error. It may also act as a confounding factor, for example, by causing animals like rats to stay in the part of an apparatus that is nearest to a familiar handler and so impairing the ability of the equipment to accurately measure qualities such as fearfulness or cognitive abilities. These biases can be avoided, for example, by having the handler stand outside the testing room and record results through closed-circuit cameras.

It is now clear that the promotion of positive human-animal relationships is seen as the ideal situation in laboratories, although it may not yet be the norm. Most academic journals require that animals be referred to by gendered pronouns, and the participation of animal caretakers in ethical review and approval of experiments is now commonplace. Misleading euphemisms (e.g., "sacrifice" instead of "kill") are dropping out of use and the role of research technicians is developing to encompass their natural role as informed advocates for animals.

However, changes are coming far more slowly in facilities that use large numbers of short-lived and traditionally disdained animals, such as rodents, perhaps because bonds with these animals are less likely to form or are less strong than those with traditional pet or agricultural species or primates. Underdeveloped, small animals are still often treated largely as disposable research materials rather than as sentient animals with whom we share deep, implicit bonds and associated duties of care and gratitude.

See also

Research—*Memorial Services for Research Animals*

Further Resources

Arluke, A. (1992). Trapped in a Guilt Cage. *New Scientist, 134*.

Davis, H., & Balfour, D. (Eds.). (1992). *The inevitable bond*. Cambridge, MA: Cambridge University Press.

———. (2002). Implications of human-animal interactions and bonds in the laboratory. *ILAR Journal, 43*(1).

Emily Patterson-Kane

■ Research
Memorial Services for Research Animals

Ceremonies to acknowledge and commemorate the role of animals in research are not uncommon in the Far East. However, such rituals are not typically part of North American institutional culture. On April 7, 1993, a landmark event occurred at the University of Guelph in Ontario, Canada. For the first time, a North American university held a campuswide memorial service for the animals it used in teaching and research during the past year. Initiated by Hank Davis and Allison Taylor, this ceremony brought together faculty, technical staff, and students for a brief yet dignified ritual. Approximately a month after this ceremony, a stone monument was set in place, prominently located along the path to the University Center. A bronze plaque on the stone bore the words, "In recognition of the animals used by the University of Guelph community in support of excellence in teaching and research."

This simple ceremony drew wide attention and in subsequent years has given rise to similar rituals in other North American research institutions, including Merck Pharmaceuticals and the University of Washington Medical School. Temple Grandin, who designs and evaluates animal handling and slaughter facilities, has argued that simple rituals of acknowledgment, such as a ceremony, prevent the development of undesirably mechanical attitudes toward one's work with animals. Philosopher Bernard Rollin has described the process of compartmentalization, which often occurs in animal-based scientific research. Like the mechanical attitudes described by Grandin, compartmentalization works to distance the individual from unpleasant tasks he or she must perform. Rituals of acknowledgment, such as an Animal Memorial Service, can reduce this inner conflict as well as promote or maintain respect for animals.

Although the impetus for the University of Guelph Memorial Service came from elaborate Buddhist-based rituals held at Japanese research facilities, the group at the university believed that a more secular approach was better suited to its and other North American communities. The university has continued to offer these ceremonies on a yearly basis—always in the early spring—and, although the spoken words vary somewhat from year to year, the fundamental message remains the same. The purpose of the gathering is not to offer thanks, nor to plead forgiveness. The ceremony is simply there to raise awareness of the important role played by animals in teaching and research. The ceremony also offers an opportunity to acknowledge the often conflicting emotions experienced by primary animal care workers in the course of their daily routines. Such individuals are often drawn to the field because of their attachment to animals, yet they may be required to perform procedures that cause pain or distress to the animals. The gathering was intended to recognize and validate such potentially conflicting emotions and to support members of the university community in the evolution of their attitude toward animals.

It is worth quoting the words spoken at the opening of the first Memorial Service in 1993. The leaders began by acknowledging, "You are probably all a bit apprehensive about what we are going to do here today. Let us tell you what we are not going to do: we're not going to invoke religious dogma; we're not going to take a pro-research or anti-research stance. We are going to share some simple thoughts on what we view as a serious and overdue occasion." The organizers noted that they had set aside their original plan to use music to make this a richer experience. They recognized that music would set an emotional tone for the gathering, but they were unsure which emotions were appropriate: "The music we had earlier considered ran the gamut from funereal to joyous. We realized that our quandary reflects the range of emotions that were likely to be experienced by participants." The leaders decided to avoid the use of music because they wanted neither to discount nor to prompt the occurrence of any particular emotion in our audience.

The leaders of the ceremony noted that "the University of Guelph has a highly active animal research community, as well as a scrupulous animal care policy. Some of its animal subjects are species many people care deeply about, such as dogs and cats. The university also uses animals hardly anyone cares about, like fish and snakes." They then pointed out, "Very few of the animals used in the past year are still alive." They reminded participants that the university and its animal care staff had been singled out for unprecedented national awards for their work and also noted that the university is home of the multidisciplinary Center for the Study of Animal Welfare. However, they concluded, "For some of us, all of this is still not enough. There is still some extra distance, perhaps only a symbolic distance, we would like to go in our animal care work. It is our hope that this gathering will help to satisfy that need."

There are some harsh realities associated with the use of animals in teaching and research institutions, no matter how compassionate and well trained their personnel may be. To quote again from the ceremony,

> By any reckoning, we are working in an unnatural system. We are causing animals to be born, causing them to live through a variety of unusual experiences, and causing them to die. This is a form of power that cannot be taken lightly. Today is an opportunity to acknowledge the animals' role in what we do. To acknowledge that, without them, our research and teaching would be fundamentally altered. . . . To thank the animals seems logically inappropriate because their contribution was taken, not given. Yet we are grateful for, and even dependent upon, their role. Such gratitude does not preclude the use or killing of animals, but it does suggest that such acts should not be taken for granted.

After these words were spoken, the group proceeded from the small auditorium to an outdoor green space where the memorial plaque was located. At this point each participant was given a flower that he or she lay at the base of the memorial stone. The ceremony was concluded with the following words: "Our community permits us the use of animals in teaching and research. At the same time, it encourages us to temper this power with sensitivity. We believe that such sensitivity on all our parts will not dilute the effects of what we do. Rather it will result in more efficient animal use, a heightened sensitivity to the animals' well-being, and better animal care." Participants were encouraged to visit this memorial occasionally and to spend a few moments reflecting on the things talked about at the ceremony.

The memorial organizers continue to hear from participants in previous gatherings who recall the simple power of this ceremony in their lives. Often, these people go on to work in other institutions where they initiate their own version of a Memorial Service. Although not everyone within the University of Guelph community is comfortable with the idea of an Animal Memorial Service, the overall reception has remained positive and there has never been less than full support from the administration of the institution. A wide range of people attends these gatherings; there have been students, technicians, principal investigators, as well as secretaries who type manuscripts and grant applications. Obviously, each of these persons—regardless of their role—feels invested in the process. It is the hope of those who developed the Animal Memorial Service that it will provide the kind of benefit and support the participants need most.

Further Resources

Asquith, P. (1983). The monkey memorial service of Japanese primatologists. *Royal Anthropological Institute News*, *54*, 3–4.

Grandin, T. (1988). Behavior of slaughter plant and auction employees toward the animals. *Anthrozoos*, *1*, 205–13.

Strauss, S. (1991). Mind and matter: Dead animals merit a prayer and a wake from researchers. *Toronto Globe and Mail,* March 30.

Hank Davis

Research
Mice Experimentation and Laboratory Use

Mice have been used in the laboratory by humans for hundreds of years. During that time, they have helped us make profound discoveries in subjects such as disease, psychology, genetics, and behavior. Many of these discoveries would have been impossible without the laboratory mouse.

History

The modern laboratory mouse originates from human desires for unusual breeds. In 1900, a retired schoolteacher, Abbie Lathrop, started breeding for the late Victorian craze of "fancy" mice. These are pet mice whose roots go back to seventeenth-century Asia, where breeders began to select and breed unusual-looking mutant mice—such as the albino, dwarf, and waltzing mouse (so named because an inherited inner-ear defect makes the mouse appear to dance). In 1902, Lathrop received an order from a zoologist named William Castle who was curious whether the genetic laws that Mendel had developed on plants were true for more complex organisms such as mammals. The variability in mice of their coat color, size of ears, type of hair, and unusual behaviors made mice ideal for scientists to visualize the results of their genetic experiments.

One of Castle's undergraduate students, Clarence Cook Little, solidified the mouse's scientific fate. His innovation was the "inbred strain." By mating brother to sister over and over, he created mice that were genetically alike. After 20 generations the mice were nearly 99 percent identical. In 1909 he created the first inbred strain, dba, which is still used in research. In 1929, Little helped start an independent research facility, the Jackson Laboratory, and mouse research flourished. Before long, scientists worldwide were making and studying mice that developed cancer, alcoholism, obesity, and so on. Once the ability to manipulate DNA was developed in the 1970s, they developed diabetic mice and mice with glaucoma and dozens of other conditions to gain insight into human diseases.

General Biology

Mice have an extremely high metabolic rate. They utilize large amounts of oxygen for their size (22 times more oxygen per gram of body weight than an elephant) and have a rapid respiratory rate, a short tracheal-bronchus distance, a high blood carrying capacity for oxygen, and a high blood sugar concentration. This means that sufficient food and water need to be consistently available as they have a smaller range for error than larger animals. Mice are omnivorous. They have incisors and molars only; their incisors grow continuously and they must be checked for malocclusion. Heart rates and blood pressures vary widely from strain to strain; a heart rate can range from 310–840 beats per minute between different strains. Mice void only one or two drops of urine at a time. This is very concentrated and contains a large amount of protein used for their territorial and social marking systems. Sexual maturity varies between strains and is sensitive to the environment; for instance, noise, light, diet, and population density can all affect the hormonal system and reproductive rate. Females are often group-housed to synchronize their estrous cycles before being paired with males. Males can be bred between 49–70 days and the females between 45–65 days. Gestation takes 19–21 days and the average litter size ranges from 1 to 12 pups depending on the strain. Although mice can live up to two years and some strains can reproduce for that long, most female breeders are retired after one year and most inbred strains are only active breeders for six months. The females nurse their young for three weeks; their milk production peaks at 12 days postpartum and slowly lessens until normal weaning at three weeks

Behavioral Biology

Laboratory mice can be timid but social animals. Contact with conspecifics (others of their species) is important and a mouse housed alone may become more aggressive. Although wild mice are generally nocturnal, laboratory mice have active periods during both the day and night. Categories of common behaviors of mice include the following: (1) maintenance behaviors (grooming, eating, drinking, nesting); (2) investigative/exploratory behaviors (climbing, digging, chewing, sniffing); and (3) social

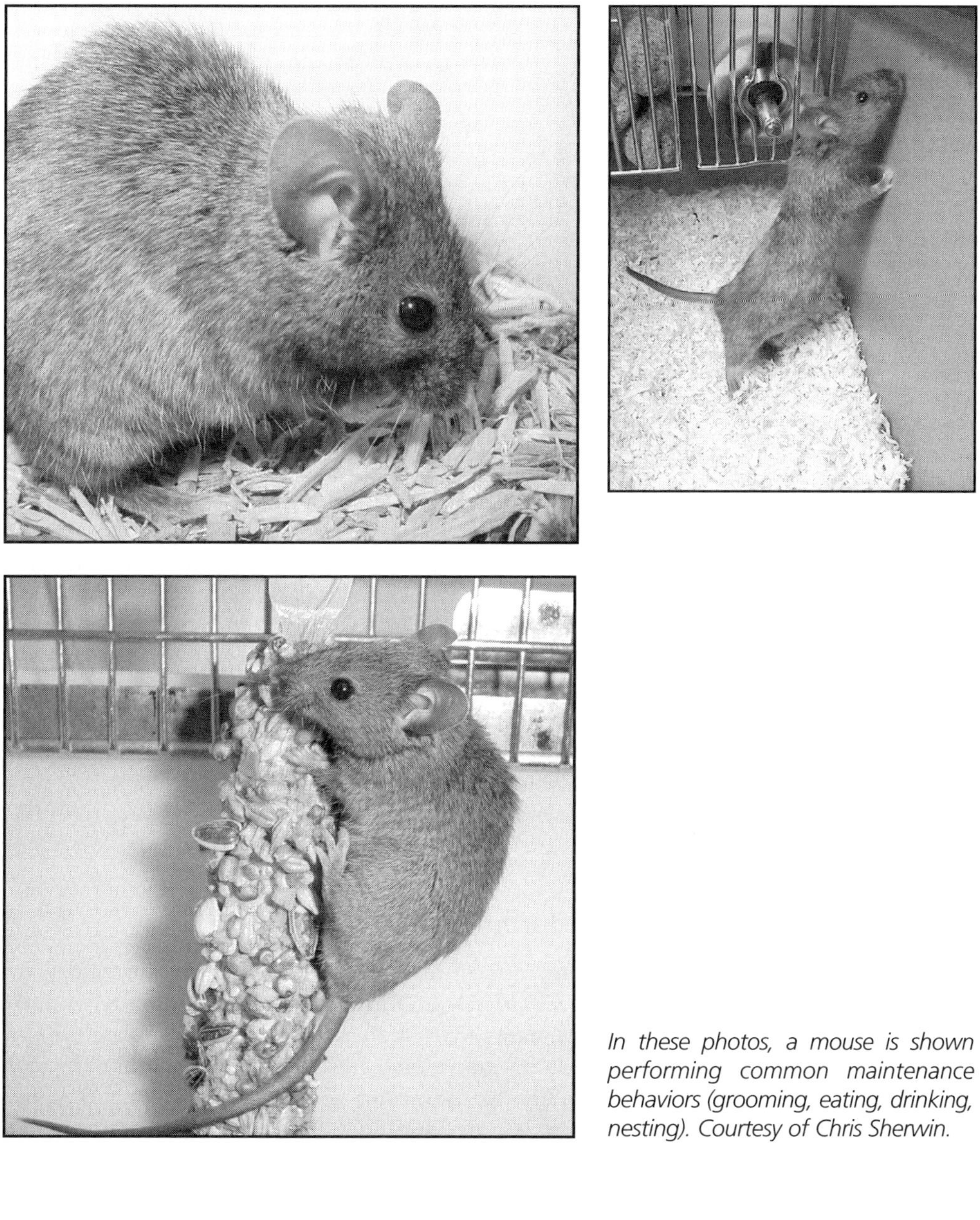

In these photos, a mouse is shown performing common maintenance behaviors (grooming, eating, drinking, nesting). Courtesy of Chris Sherwin.

interactions (huddling together, grooming one another, scent/territorial marking, aggression, defense, sexual behavior). Mice spend a great deal of time manipulating their bedding material, and if the material allows they will build tunnels and underground nests.

The mouse's world is dominated by smell. Odors are used to detect and assess food and predators, recognize individuals, evaluate sexual and social status, and demarcate territory. Their taste sense appears broadly similar to humans, although they do not respond to some compounds that taste sweet to us and ingest substances that we find disgustingly bitter. Mice are very sensitive to touch. Their whiskers (vibrissae) send tactile information to specialized "whisker barrels" in the neocortex, allowing mice to feel textures and avoid obstacles even when they are unable to see. The body hairs are used to sense overhead cover and vertical surfaces. This is important to mice, which generally attempt to retain contact with solid objects (thigmotaxis), especially when frightened. Mouse vision is reasonably well developed, although acuity is poor compared to humans. Mice are very sensitive to movement and changes in light intensity and use visual cues to demarcate territorial boundaries, navigate, or move to cover. Their retinas are composed mainly of rods, giving them sensitive vision in dim light but little color perception. Furthermore, their cones' peak spectral sensitivities differ from those of humans. They lack a long-wave photopigment potentially causing insensitivity to red wavelengths, but they are sensitive to ultraviolet wavelengths. Mice are thus likely to perceive hue differently than humans. Finally, mice have well-developed hearing. They can detect frequencies from 80 Hz up to 100 kHz (ultrasound) but are most sensitive in the 15–20 kHz range and around 50 kHz. Audible vocalizations can often be heard during aggressive encounters, whereas ultrasound is used in sexual communication and also by pups when they have fallen out of the nest. In rats, there is some evidence that ultrasonic calls are used in echolocation and judging the depth of drops in darkness. Such behavior has yet to be confirmed in mice but might help explain why despite their limited visual abilities their depth perception is good, allowing them to make long and accurate jumps (Olsson et al., 2003; Latham and Mason, 2004).

While a mouse's vision is relatively good, the body hairs are used to sense overhead cover and vertical surfaces. This is important to mice, who generally attempt to retain contact with solid objects. Courtesy of Chris Sherwin.

The Laboratory Mouse in Modern Research

Mice are by far the most predominant animal species used in the laboratory by humans. In 2005, 68 percent of all licensed research in the United Kingdom used mice (Home Office, UK), although other estimates are as high as 90 percent for research in the United States. There are approximately 30 million mice in laboratories worldwide, and their use is increasing. Mice are the predominant research species for a variety of reasons. They are mammals and therefore often appropriate models of human disease or other aspects of human biology; they are a highly adaptable animal; they are small, so many of them can be kept in a reduced space for a lower cost; they are not dangerous; they are easily handled; they have a high breeding rate and short gestation period (one million descendants after 425 days!); and they are widely regarded as a pest species, which makes experimentation upon them more easily justified to some people.

Human-Laboratory Mouse Relationship

People working with mice in the laboratory generally do not become as emotionally attached to this species as they might with dogs, cats, or primates. This is partly because mice are usually kept in much greater numbers, mice appear very similar or identical so are rarely perceived as individuals, and mice do not behave in ways that humans can easily interpret. The fact that mice are generally regarded as a pest species also means that the human relationship with this research species is often different than with others.

Types of Research Using Laboratory Mice

The types of research that mice are used for range as wide as the subject of research itself. There are few aspects of human life that have not been studied using the mouse as the model species.

In the United Kingdom in 2005, the total number of mice used in licensed research was 1,961,049. Broken down according to body systems these were as follows: respiratory, 46,599 (2%); cardiovascular, 52,843 (3%); nervous, 217,453 (11%); senses, 21,283 (1%); alimentary, 27,971 (1%); skin, 32,697 (1%); musculoskeletal, 27,788 (1%); reproductive, 140,645 (7%); immune, 416,173 (21%); other, 38,782 (2%); multiple systems, 380,152 (20%); system not relevant, 558,663 (28%).

Genetics Research

In recent years, the development of different strains and the use of genetically altered animals have allowed profound developments in our understanding of genetics and disease. Again, the mouse has been the predominant species in this research, partly because rodents have higher mutation rates than other orders (Latham and Mason, 2004), and they have rapid and prolific breeding rates. Genetics research is now the largest contributor to the use of mice in research and has led to an increasing number of mice being used during recent years. Of the licensed research projects in the United Kingdom in 2005, approximately 814,000 mice were genetically normal, 235,000 were considered to have a harmful genetic defect, and 900,000 were genetically modified mice. Strains are being developed at an astonishing rate. The Jackson Laboratory in the United States advertises that it develops 100 strains a year, which equates to approximately one new strain every 3–4 days from just this one laboratory alone!

Outbred mice are a closed population, for at least four generations, of genetically variable animals that are bred to maintain maximum heterozygosity. The goal is to limit inbreeding to less than 1 percent of the genome per generation. The standardized nomenclature for outbred stocks consists of a laboratory designation, a colon, a stock designation, and a dash and mutation designation (if present), for example, Hsd:SD or Crl:ZU-fa.

Inbred mice are a closed population of genetically uniform animals that result from 20 or more consecutive generations of brother and sister (or parent and offspring) matings. Inbreeding reduces genetic variability by increasing the probability that animals homozygous at a particular locus will be mated with each other. Approximately 98 percent of gene loci are homozygous after 20 generations (F20). Inbred animals are less vigorous than noninbred animals because of chance fixation of deleterious recessive genes in the homozygous condition, which can make them bad models for human disease. If a subpopulation of a strain branches off between F20 and F40 or is maintained separately for more than 100 generations, it is designated as a substrain. The standardized nomenclature for inbred strains consists of a strain designation, a diagonal line, and then a substrain designation, which usually represents the laboratory that maintains the substrain, for example, C57BL/6J. One- to three-letter strain abbreviations can also be utilized, for example, B6. One inbred strain is the nude mouse, which bears mutations that result in a lack of hair and an impaired immune system, particularly the lack of lymphocyte populations. Nude mice can be used in cancer studies because they do not reject cells and tissue from other mice or even other species.

Knockout mice are an inbred strain that differs from the parent inbred strain at only one gene locus. The mutation is specifically targeted to a gene of interest using current molecular technologies, that is, the mutation did not arise spontaneously but was induced by genetic manipulation. The nomenclature consists of the inbred strain designation, a dash, the alleles at the mutant gene locus, and a laboratory designation added as a superscript, for example, BALB/c- Mbp^{m1Dn}/Mbp^{m1Dn}. Knockout mice have aided the study of many conditions, including heart disease, diabetes, cancer, obesity, arthritis, and Parkinson's disease.

Transgenic mice have a foreign segment of DNA in every cell of their bodies. These are produced by injection of the foreign DNA into the pronucleus of a one-cell embryo. The embryo is transplanted into a pseudopregnant female animal, and the animal that develops from that embryo is transgenic. Currently, even though the transgene is present in all cells of the transgenic animal, transgene expression can sometimes be manipulated so that it occurs only in certain cell populations or can be turned on and off. Nomenclature for a transgenic strain consists of the rodent strain/stock designation, a dash, Tg, the transgene designation in parentheses, and the laboratory designation, for example, C57BL/6J-Tg(CD8Ge)23Jwg.

Mice as Models of Human Mental Suffering

Humans experience emotions that are sometimes so extreme they become debilitating and require action to prevent or mitigate the effects. Often this requires drugs to treat negative mental states such as depression, stress or anxiety. Mice are often used to develop these drugs by exposing the mice to an adverse environment or treatment and observing the effects of the drug. Since 1990, over 1,300 studies have been published on the responses of mice to the elevated plus maze—just one of the types of apparatus used to test the effects of anxiety-reducing drugs, and over 120 studies have been published where mice were used as models of depression. It seems rather contradictory to use these animals to test for drugs that influence these negative mental states but dismiss the possibility the animals experience these mental states themselves.

Welfare of the Laboratory Mouse

Society generally adopts a utilitarian approach and accepts that some research using animals is necessary. But attitudes differ markedly on what is acceptable to do to animals and what is not. Laboratory animal welfare has become an increasing concern during recent years as we develop greater knowledge about the sentience of the animals that we experiment upon. The welfare issues of laboratory mice vary from experiment to experiment, depending on what research the mouse is being used for; however, there is one issue that is particularly relevant for almost every laboratory mouse—its housing. This issue is particularly important because it influences almost every laboratory mouse and can have its impact throughout the life of the mouse, not just during the experiment.

Laboratory Mouse Housing and Welfare

In science, the prevailing conditions of a study must be controlled, or taken into account, by the investigator. The easiest way to achieve this is to make the conditions as minimalistic as possible. This means that laboratory animals are usually housed in small, barren cages, they receive relatively little interaction with humans or animals other than any cage mates, and environmental conditions (e.g. light schedule, food, noise, temperature, humidity) are controlled to vary hardly at all. It is now believed that such highly minimalistic conditions can cause suffering.

In research units, mice have seemingly thrived; however, they often perform abnormal behaviors indicative of reduced welfare. One of these is stereotypies, that is, highly repeated, relatively invariant behaviors with no apparent function (the public see these most frequently in zoo animals, e.g., bears pacing around their enclosure repeatedly along the same track). In mice, stereotypies can include somersaulting against the walls and lid of the cage, following the same path about the cage, or jumping at the walls of the cage. Mice also perform another abnormal behavior in which one individual trims the whiskers or facial hair of another. This is called barbering or whisker-plucking. These abnormal behaviors can become highly prevalent in some mice and they raise concerns about animal welfare, which are heightened by the poor breeding performance and high sensitivity to environmental change recorded in some strains. Such effects lead us to suspect that aspects of the housing and husbandry have adverse effects on the mice.

In order to maintain control in a laboratory setting, the animals are usually housed in unenriched settings. Courtesy of Chris Sherwin.

Additional space Mice are highly motivated for access to space additional to that provided by standard laboratory cages. However, they do not appear to differentiate between the amounts of additional space offered, suggesting it is not simply the quantity of space that is important to the mice, but also the quality, that is, what is in the space.

Nesting material When suitable materials are available, mice build nests to protect their young, or in nonbreeding animals, to regulate temperature and light levels and to hide and retreat from cage mates or other threatening experiences. Providing nesting material is easily and inexpensively achieved, and it is one of the best and most versatile improvements in cages for laboratory mice.

Tunnel-building When given damped peat with rocks, laboratory mice will build complex tunnel systems, sometimes within a few hours, despite the fact that they and their many previous generations never had the opportunity to build tunnels.

Flooring Laboratory cages often have wire mesh floors for collection of feces or urine. Such floors stop us providing floor substrate, which thwarts several behaviors that mice are motivated to perform, and can also result in health problems such as pressure sores and urological problems. Mice prefer a solid resting site and will generally spend more time on a solid surface rather than a grid floor. Sometimes a section of the cage floor can be covered, or a receptacle of substrate provided for resting. The mice usually avoid soiling this substrate, so it stays relatively clean.

Lighting The relatively high light intensities of laboratories can lead to eye abnormalities, including retinal atrophy or retinal detachment. This is a particular problem for albino strains lacking protective visual pigment and for mice in top-row cages. To protect mice from high light intensities, cages—especially transparent cages—should be provisioned with nesting material and a light baffle (sheet of wood or plastic) placed over the top row. Making the environment of young mice more complex improves vision. Most conventional laboratory lighting emits little or no ultraviolet (UV) light. Humans with normal eyes cannot see UV light, so this is not a problem for us, but it could have consequences for mice that are visually sensitive to UV light.

Sound Mice find sound pressure levels aversive at 20 dB less than humans find aversive. Juvenile mice can become sensitized to loud sounds, including ultrasound. In some strains, this can increase the incidence of audiogenic convulsions or seizures, decreased activity, reduced fertility, and changes in blood glucose and corticosteroid levels, that is, indicators of chronic stress. Common laboratory equipment such as pressure hoses, running taps, computer monitors, or oscilloscopes can emit ultrasound at very high sound pressures. This is silent to humans but potentially could have considerable effects on the welfare of mice. Commercial "bat detectors" register ultrasonic frequencies and could be used to detect whether equipment is generating ultrasound or when mice are vocalizing in response to distressful procedures (e.g., injections).

Weaning Mice are often weaned earlier in the laboratory than they might be under more natural conditions, and post-weaning young mice might remain exposed to auditory and olfactory cues from their mothers but are unable to make physical contact.

Social Organization Mice form highly complex organizations and each animal plays a role in this. Upsetting this organization by addition or removal of mice, perhaps only one individual, can have considerable consequences that might ultimately affect the welfare of all mice within the group. There is generally no problem in group-housing young mice and nonbreeding females, but housing males together is more of a problem, especially in smaller groups of two or three, which can put excessive amounts of stress on the subordinate animals. Aggression levels are dependent on many factors, such as age, group size, cage size, previous experience of the animals, and the situation.

Effects of Laboratory Housing on the Quality of Science

A second reason that we need to be concerned about laboratory housing has recently emerged. It has been argued that minimalistic laboratory housing can adversely affect the normal development and biological functioning of animals, thereby compromising the quality of science (Wurbel, 2002; Sherwin, 2002, 2004; Olsson et al., 2003). Stereotypy has been linked to dysfunction of the brain regions controlling the initiation and inhibition of behavior—the animal seems "unable" to stop certain behaviors. Similarly, barbering may be linked with obsessive-compulsive disorder, and the recipients of barbering are likely to be abnormal as whisker-trimming alters the function and anatomy of the barrel cortex. Physiological and anatomical measures of brain structure and function show the potential impact of housing laboratory mice in barren, nonstimulating environments. Studies have shown that increasing environmental complexity and/or providing opportunities to move under cover can increase brain weight, alter the relative weights of different brain structures, increase neural connectivity and neurogenesis, affect neurochemical changes, delay the onset of degenerative diseases, improve visual acuity, and alter performance in behavioral tasks, such as open field activity and food-seeking behaviors. Overall, we can see that the great differences between complex and standard minimalistic laboratory housing potentially have a major impact on the normalcy of brain and behavioral functioning (see Würbel, 2001, for further discussion). This means these animals may be fundamentally flawed in terms of representing a normal population, which is required for many experiments.

Further Resources

Bateson, P. (1986). When to experiment on animals. *New Scientist, 109* (1496), 30–32.

Home Office, UK. *Statistics of animals used in research.* http://www.homeoffice.gov.uk/rds/pdfs06/spanimals05.pdf

The Jackson Laboratory, http://www.jax.org/

Latham, N., & Mason, G. (2004). From house mouse to mouse house: The behavioural biology of free-living, *Mus musculus*, and its implications in the laboratory. *Applied Animal Behaviour Science, 86* (3–4), 261–89.

Olsson, I. A. S., Nevison, C. M., Patterson-Kane, E., Sherwin, C. M., van de Weerd, H. A., & Würbel, H. (2003). Understanding behaviour: The relevance of ethological approaches in laboratory animal science. *Applied Animal Behaviour Science, 81,* 245–64.

Sherwin, C. M. (2002). Comfortable quarters for mice. In V. Reinhardt & K. Reinhardt (Eds.) *Comfortable Quarters for Animals* (pp. 6–17). Washington, DC: Animal Welfare Institute. http://www.awionline.org/pubs/cq02/cqindex.html

———. (2004). The influences of standard laboratory cages on rodents and the validity of research data. *Animal Welfare, 13* (supplement), S9–15

Wurbel, H. (2002). Behavioral phenotyping enhanced—beyond (environmental) standardization. *Genes, Brain and Behavior, 1* (1), 3–8.

Chris M. Sherwin

Research
Toxicity Testing and Animals

There is a movement to refine, replace, and reduce the number of animals used in toxicity experiments in scientific research. The term "the 3 Rs" was generated by Russell and Birch in their 1959 book *The Principles of Humane Experimental Technique*. The 3 Rs refer to reduction, replacement, and refinement of whole animal use in scientific research. The concept of alternatives does not necessarily refer to a complete eradication of animals from the research arena but an attempt to decrease suffering of laboratory animals by reduction, replacement, and refinement.

A *reduction alternative* substantially decreases the number of whole animals necessary to perform a test. A number of *in vitro* assays are now being used as screening tests for the Draize test (a test for ocular irritancy), reducing the number of animals required to fully evaluate the potential irritancy of a chemical. A reduction in the numbers of animals could be possible if testing techniques are refined and made more sensitive in screening processes. A *replacement alternative* is one that entirely eliminates the need for whole-animal testing. For example, a replacement could be the use of an invertebrate instead of a vertebrate animal. *Refinement alternatives* are those that improve the design and/or efficiency of the test, therefore lessening the distress or discomfort experienced by laboratory animals. An example of a refinement to the Draize test is that the test is no longer performed using substances that are known to be severely irritating to the eye.

History of Movement in the United States and Europe to Refine, Reduce, and Replace

By the eighteenth and nineteenth centuries, animal research had become commonplace. According to Andrew Rowan, author of the book *Of Mice, Models and Men: A Critical Evaluation of Animal Research*, several medical advances influenced public perception concerning the benefits of animal research, including the development of ester anesthesia (1846), antiseptic surgical practices (1860s), and the identification of many disease-causing bacteria. Not everyone was in favor of using animals in experimentation, and the formation of organizations that opposed animal cruelty also started to appear at this time, particularly in Europe. The surge in animal protection was influenced by Darwin's theory of evolution, Jeremy Bentham's utilitarian argument against using animals ("The question is not can they reason, nor can they talk, but can they suffer"), and the prevailing Victorian sentiment of the time (that preventing cruelty to animals was seen as an extension to prevent cruelty to human beings).

The National Anti-Vivisection Society (NAVS) was the first organization formed to oppose animal experiments. Formed in 1875, with the help of Miss Frances Power Cobbe, the society helped get England's Parliament to pass the first national antivivisection law, the Cruelty to Animals Act, in 1876. The law required all experimenters to have permits, and it established guidelines for researchers. However, the Cruelty to Animals Act did not ban animal research and was therefore opposed by some antivivisection societies.

The first American anti-vivisection organization was formed in 1883, followed by the formation of the New England Anti-Vivisection (NEAVS) in 1895. The results obtained by American anti-vivisection, however, were far less impressive than those in England. The U.S. scientific community resisted most attempts to regulate the use of animals in research. Although U.S. anti-vivisection bills were frequently introduced in Congress beginning in the 1890s, none passed.

The anti-vivisection movement lost momentum after WWI, when the focus for animal humane societies shifted to establishing humane education programs and enforcing animal cruelty laws. During the 1950s, many humane societies established programs concerned with the humane care of laboratory animals, but such organizations were not publicly opposed to animal experimentation, and many humane societies compromised with medical establishments. For example, in 1952, the Metcalf-Hatch bill was passed in New York, which mandated pound seizure. Pound seizure required shelters to sell their cats and dogs to institutions that performed animal research. Andrew Rowan attributes the marginalization of the anti-vivisection movement to the success of well-organized, powerful lobbying efforts of medical researchers in opposing anti-vivisection efforts, the lack of anti-vivisection resources, and lacking credibility of anti-vivisection societies, who supported unorthodox medical theories such as repudiation of germ theory and vaccinations.

In the 1960s, the first efforts to raise funds for the development of alternative tests were successful and groups formed with the specific aim of incorporating alternatives in accordance with the 3Rs philosophy. In 1962, the first European trust for moneys dedicated for the search of alternatives to animal testing appeared in the name of the Lawson Tait Trust. This British group formed the trust with the goal of working with medical researchers. Now known as the Human Research Trust, the fund continues to play an important role in funding the development of alternatives. The U.S. group United Action for Animals, formed in 1967 and campaigned specifically for replacement alternatives. In 1969 the UK group, Fund to Replace Animals in Medical Research (FRAME), raised moneys and launched a quarterly publication called Alternatives to Laboratories Animals (ATLA) to disseminate pertinent information concerning the search for alternatives to scientists. In 1973, the Lord Dowding Fund, established by the National Anti-vivisection Society, began dispensing research grants to individuals *not* holding licenses under the UK Cruelty to Animals Act for research projects *not* involving the use of live animals for experimental purposes for projects likely to lead to the alleviation of human or animal suffering.

Private companies also donated to the search for alternatives to animal testing. A report that the Draize eye irritancy test seemed amenable to alternative options spurred animal activist Henry Spira to begin his campaign against the cosmetic industry to deter use of the test. The Draize test was a good test to challenge because the suffering rabbits endured from the test could be made visible to the public. Spira pursued a very public campaign by exposing people to graphic images of suffering animals and asking society "if another shampoo was worth blinding rabbits." Cosmetics companies were vulnerable because they promoted beauty, which contrasted starkly with appalling images of rabbits undergoing a Draize test. Cosmetic corporations are also reliant upon the public's financial support, in the form of purchasing products, for their longevity. Spira did not insist that the cosmetic industry end all animal testing immediately. Instead he asked cosmetic companies, such as Revlon, to donate money (one hundredth of one percent of Revlon's net profit = $170,000) to search for alternatives and in the meantime reduce the numbers of animals being used in Draize testing. Other companies followed suit. Avon and Bristol-Myers Squibb allocated one million dollars to Johns Hopkins University to establish the Center for Alternatives to Animal Testing (CAAT) in 1981, and in 1982 Colgate-Palmolive provided $300,000 for the investigation of the chorio-allantonic membrane system.

Legislation and the 3Rs

European legislative initiatives to aid in the search for alternatives to animal testing appeared before U.S. attempts. In 1971, Council of Europe Resolution 621 suggested that an alternatives database be established. The first grant to be given to a group to aid in the search for alternatives to animals in testing was given to FRAME in 1984.

In the United States, by 1981 there were seven bills on alternatives and/or regulation of animal experimentation pending in the Subcommittee on Science, Research, and Technology of the House Committee on Science and Technology. In a subcommittee hearing, a draft of the bill that incorporated aspects of the seven prior bills was generated and referred to the House Committee on Energy and Commerce. Eventually, in 1985, the provisions of this bill were incorporated into the Health Research Extension Act, requiring those awarded research monies by the National Institutes of Health to consider the use of alternatives.

Validation of Alternative Tests

The major obstacle in reduction, refinement, and replacement of animals in toxicity testing is validation of alternative tests by appropriate regulatory agencies. Validation of *in vitro* tests required the establishment of new agencies to coordinate the processes of development, acceptance, and dissemination of information between scientists, regulatory agencies, and the public. Directive 86/609/EEC regulates the use of animals for experimental and other scientific purposes in the European Union. A Communication from the Commission to the Council and the Parliament in October 1991, pointing to a requirement in Directive 86/609/EEC on the protection of animals used for experimental and other scientific purposes, led to the establishment of the European Centre for the Validation of Alternative Methods (ECVAM). The U.S. National Institutes of Health Revitalization Act of 1993 established criteria for the validation and regulatory acceptance of alternative testing and recommended the creation of a process to scientifically validate alternative methods so they can be accepted for regulatory use. This Act prompted the creation of the Interagency Coordinating Committee on the Validation of Alternative Methods (ICCVAM) and its support center, The National Toxicology Program Interagency Center for the Evaluation of Alternative Toxicological Methods (NICEATM). ICCVAM uses information from toxicological test methods to support human health or environmental risk assessments and represents 14 different U.S. regulatory agencies. The recommendations regarding the usefulness of test methods provided by ICCVAM allows regulatory agencies to assess risks of various test methods and make regulatory decisions.

Validation of alternative tests has proved to be an obstacle in the search for alternatives. Animal testing has long been the standard method companies utilize to test the safety of their products, and regulatory agencies have accepted animal tests as valid. Regulatory agencies have to be convinced to accept the validity of new, alternative methods. There are many obstacles to convincing regulatory agencies such as the Consumer Product Safety Commission (CPSC), the Environmental Protection Agency (EPA), Occupational Health and Safety Association (OHSA), and the U. S. Department of Agriculture (USDA), to accept new methods of testing. Some obstacles include tradition, prior regulations, lack of validated *in vitro* methods, lack of a process to determine validity, and resistance from the biomedical community. Understanding the mechanisms by which *in vitro* tests work takes effort and training by those evaluating them. There is a certain comfort level in familiar tests that have always satisfied regulations.

Table 1. Two Examples of U.S.-Validated Alternative Tests

The Local Lymph Node Assay

The Lymph Node Assay was the first alternative test accepted as valid by U.S. regulatory agencies such as EPA, FDA, and OSHA in 1998. This *in vivo* test (a test that uses a whole animal) measures skin sensitivity by measuring the severity of the lymphocyte response post application of a testing substance to the ear of mice. This test is not a replacement test but rather a refinement test. By virtue of its methodology, this test decreases animal distress.

Corrositex

Corrositex is an *in vitro* test (a test performed in a test tube using animal cell systems but not the whole animal) used to determine the corrosivity of a chemical. The test is performed in a glass tube filled with a chemical detection fluid. The time it takes for a substance to pass through a bio-barrier membrane in the tube is recorded and compared to a classification chart. The Corrositex test is accepted as valid by the following EU and U.S. groups: CPSC, ECVAM, the EPA, FDA, International Air Transportation Association, National Institute of Environmental Health Sciences, and OSHA.

Table 2. Alternative Tests with European Regulatory Validation

EpiSkin^{TM} skin corrosivity test
3T3 NRU phototoxicity test
EpiDerm^{TM} skin corrosivity test
Rat TER skin corrosivity test
In vitro tests for percutaneous absorption
Deletion of the acute oral toxicity test, Lethal Dose (LD50)
Local Lymph Node Assay for skin sensitization (LLNA)
ELISA test for batch potency testing of erysipelas vaccines
ELISA test for batch potency testing of tetanus vaccines for human use
Toxin Binding Inhibition (ToBI) test for batch potency testing of tetanus vaccines for human use

There are a few alternative tests that are validated by the relatively newly formed ICCVAM and therefore are accepted by regulatory agencies as qualified substitutions for traditional testing. Two tests are the Local Lymph Node Assay and Corrositex (Table 1). The process of validation by ICCVAM is seen as a major success for the alternatives movement because validating alternatives has been a complicated process. Validation of tests for toxicity will aid in the European drive to ban animal testing for cosmetics. A ban currently exists on finished cosmetic products tested on animals in the European Union. A future aim is to ban animal testing of cosmetic product ingredients in September 2009.

Validation of alternative methods will need to extend globally as the United States develops, imports, and exports more products. ICCVAM has a firm relationship with ECVAM, and both groups will be instrumental in the validation of the alternative processes (see validated European Alternative tests in Table 2). In the last few weeks of 2000, the ICCVAM Authorization Act was passed, which firmly established the organization's role in validating alternative methods in the future. Another success for the alternatives movement was the acceptance of an animal-friendly approach, Test Smart, toward the numerous studies that will be conducted in the future by various agencies to determine the hazardous potential of 2,200 U.S.-produced chemicals, namely, the High Production Volume Chemical Challenge. A future endeavor of ICCVAM will be to pursue alternatives to animal tests used to assess the toxins contained in popular anti-wrinkle treatments such as Botox.

Replacement, refinement, and reduction will continue in the United States and Europe, decreasing pain and distress for laboratory animals. Total replacement of animal testing will not take place in the near future. Some animal testing seems necessary at this point in time in order for regulatory agencies to fulfill their responsibility to the public to provide safe consumer products.

Further Resources

Altweb, the Alternatives to Animal Testing Web site. http://altweb.jhsph.edu/about.htm

Frazier, J. M. (1992). *In vitro toxicity testing: Applications to safety testing*. New York: Marcel Dekker.

Johns Hopkins University Center for Alternatives to Animal Testing Web site. http://caat.jhsph.edu/

Rowan, A. N. (1984). *Of mice, models and men: A critical evaluation of animal research*. Albany, NY: State University of New York Press.

Rowan, A. N., & Loew, F. M., with Weer, J. (1995). *The animal research controversy: Protest, process and public policy. An analysis of strategic issues.* N. Grafton, MA: Tufts Center for Animals and Public Policy, School of Veterinary Medicine.

Rudacille, D. (2000). *The scalpel and the butterfly: The war between animal research and animal protection.* New York: Farrar, Straus & Giroux.

Singer, P. (1998). *Ethics into action: Henry Spira and the animal rights movement.* New York: Bowman and Littlefield.

Nicole Cottam

Sentience and Cognition
Animal Consciousness

Defining Animal Consciousness

Consciousness, in a strict medical sense, is the property of being awake rather than asleep or in a coma. When we ask whether another animal is conscious, we are usually not referring to whether that animal is awake. Clearly animals can be awake or asleep, awake or in a coma, or conscious or unconscious. When we ask whether an animal is conscious, what we are inevitably getting at is whether other animals are aware of their own thoughts and can think about themselves. This question amounts to the question of whether another animal is sentient or *self-aware*. Consciousness, *sensu stricto*, is a necessary condition for awareness, but self-awareness is the gist of the issue.

The scientist most identified with animal consciousness is Donald Griffin, who galvanized the field of animal behavior by suggesting that animals might have the capacity to reason and, therefore, are sentient. His seminal work in this area, the now-famous book *Animal Minds: Beyond Cognition to Consciousness*, was originally published in 1992, and the second edition in 2001. Griffin viewed the minds of other animals as different from ours but similar in the fundamental sense that animals are reasoning sentient beings. In the second edition of his book in 2001, Griffin offered the following assessment of animal consciousness: "The principal difference between human and animal consciousness is probably in their content" (p. 15). Griffin's major contribution was to establish the field of animal sentience as an important domain of inquiry.

The idea that other species might be sentient or self-aware stands in direct opposition to the view of animals set forth by Rene Descartes in the seventeenth century. In Descartes' view, other animals are complex organic machines or "automata" devoid of thoughts, rationality, and a mind. He based his supposition primarily on the observation that other animals do not possess human language. Descartes' view is not supported in any strong sense by most philosophers and scientists today, but it continues to have an insidious influence on some of the ways other animals are thought of. Certainly one's acceptance of the validity and importance of the question of whether other animals are self-aware presupposes a rejection of Descartes' view in favor of one that appreciates the continuity across species despite differences.

Self-awareness has been identified with a variety of related terms that are fundamentally very similar in concept. These terms include phenomenal consciousness, self consciousness, metacognition, and autonoetic consciousness. All of these designations ultimately converge on the broader concept of self-awareness, that is, awareness of one's own identity, one's own thoughts, and the consequences of one's own actions through time.

Phenomenal consciousness refers to the subjective, experiential, or phenomenological aspects of conscious experience, sometimes identified with qualia. To consider animal consciousness in this sense is to consider the possibility that, as expressed by Nagel in 1974, there might be "something it is like" to be a member of another species. Phenomenal consciousness might be considered the basic minimum for more complex forms of self-awareness.

Self consciousness refers to an organism's capacity for second-order representation of the organism's own mental states. Because of its second-order character (thought about thought) the capacity for self consciousness is closely related to "theory of mind" in nonhuman animals—whether any animals are capable of attributing mental states to others. A synonymous term for self-consciousness is *metacognition* (cognition about cognition), the ability to introspect on one's own thoughts and feelings.

Another expression for self-consciousness that some might feel extends self-consciousness or metacognition is *autonoetic consciousness*. Autonoetic consciousness is the capacity to recursively introspect on one's own subjective experience through time, that is, to perceive the continuity in one's identity from the past to the present and on into the future. Autonoetic consciousness has been likened to the concept of "stream of consciousness" by William James.

Thus, when we contemplate the question of animal self-awareness we are asking whether other animals have a concept of self and a concept that they have an ongoing life. The question of self-awareness in other animals is a matter of active and often exuberant scientific controversy. Most of the attention in this area has been focused on chimpanzees and to a more limited extent on the other great apes and other large-brained mammals, such as monkeys, dolphins, whales, elephants, and highly encephalized birds such as crows and parrots. Other mammals, such as dogs, are not exempt from this line of inquiry. There is a tendency, however, to neglect others kinds of vertebrates, such as reptiles and fish, and invertebrates when it comes to this question. Although, since we have yet to come to a comprehensive understanding of the dimensions of self-awareness in other animals at this point in time we cannot make assured statements about the phylogenetic distribution of self-awareness in the animal kingdom.

Evidence for Self-Awareness in Other Species

For the major part of human history the question of self-awareness in other species remained a philosophical one. Potentially relevant observations could not be interpreted with any scientific rigor until research methods were developed that could provide strong tests of hypotheses. Thus, the domain of inquiry into animal self-awareness was typically considered beyond the reach of science and forever limited to "thought experiments" and anecdotes. However, in the 1970s this view was dealt a serious blow with the publication of evidence for mirror self-recognition in chimpanzees in the well-respected journal *Science*. Since then the study of animal self-awareness has become a dynamic subfield of animal behavior science.

Self-Recognition

The first experimental test of self-awareness in another species was conducted by Gordon Gallup in 1970 when he presented evidence that chimpanzees recognize themselves in mirrors. Gallup and other proponents of this test argue that mirror self-recognition is an indicator of self-awareness. That is, if an animal recognizes him/herself in a mirror then, at the very least, that animal has a sense of self, that is, self-identity, on a physical level. There has been protracted debate about whether mirror self-recognition is related to more abstract levels of self-awareness, for example, metacognition, or not, but the resolution of this debate awaits further evidence.

Gallup adopted an approach to this question that was similar to studies with young children. The basic paradigm involves exposing mirror-naive chimpanzees to a mirror. The chimpanzees in Gallup's study showed what has turned out to be a very typical pattern of behavior for chimpanzees in this situation. Chimpanzees initially react to their mirror image as though it is a social stimulus but they quickly (sometimes over a matter of minutes) learn that the mirror image is not another chimp. When social responses wane, chimpanzees begin to use the mirror to test the contingencies between the mirror image and their own body (e.g., rocking the body in front of the mirror) and investigate parts of the body only visible in the mirror (e.g., sticking out the tongue). The transition from social to self-directed responding at the mirror is compelling evidence for self-recognition. But Gallup pushed the question into the experimental realm by following these observations with a hypothesis-driven test. Once the chimpanzees reliably showed self-directed behavior at the mirror they were anesthetized and a nontactile, nonolfactory red dye was applied to parts of their face that were not visible without a mirror. Gallup argued that when his subjects awoke from the anesthesia and saw their altered image they, if so motivated, would use the mirror to touch and investigate the marks. Gallup showed that chimpanzees engage in vigorous mark-directed behavior at the mirror, providing conclusive evidence that they understand the mirror image is themselves.

Since this initial study a substantial literature on mirror self-recognition has accumulated on the phylogenetic distribution of self-recognition among primates. This literature converges on the finding that most chimpanzees, orangutans, and some gorillas show convincing evidence of mirror self-recognition, but lesser apes and monkeys, despite understanding the contingencies of mirrors, do not use mirrors to investigate their bodies. Only one other nonprimate species—the bottlenose dolphin—has been shown to possess mirror self-recognition. In 2001 Reiss and Marino reported conclusive evidence of mirror self-recognition in two captive bottlenose dolphins. In a series of tests that amounted to controlled variations of the procedures used with primates, both dolphins in the study consistently used a mirror to investigate marked parts of their bodies. This finding is all the more intriguing because beyond sharing a high level of encephalization, primates and dolphins have not shared a common ancestor for close to 95 million years and, moreover, possess brains with very different cortical architectures.

Other mammals, such as dogs and cats, initially react socially to their mirror image but later ignore it entirely. The findings on birds, such as crows and parrots, remain equivocal. Some authors argue that the mirror test may not be a valid test of self-awareness in many species because passing the test depends specifically on the ability to match motor to visual information, a skill that may not have evolved in a majority of species. Therefore, there is still considerable debate about the interpretation that should be given to results of the mirror self-recognition test. Yet, it is clear that, for whatever reason, mirror self-recognition is a rare capacity in the animal kingdom.

Metacognition

Metacognition (cognition about cognition) straightforwardly embodies the notion of self-awareness. One way to ask whether another animal is metacognitive is to experimentally assess whether that animal can indicate its subjective sense of certainty about information the animal needs in order to perform a task. This kind of question was experimentally posed by David Smith and his colleagues a few years ago with startling results. Smith placed human adults, bottlenose dolphins, and rhesus monkeys in the same auditory discrimination task. All participants could optimize rewards by sometimes choosing a bail-out option, called an "uncertain response," on each trial that presented very difficult material. The human subjects reported verbally, and the dolphin and monkey subjects reported by hitting buttons and paddles respectively. What Smith and his colleagues found is that the overall pattern of response across the three species was essentially identical. Humans were able to respond optimally because they were able to introspect on their certainty or confidence about any given trial and opt out of those trials that were deemed too difficult to complete successfully. It turns out that dolphins and monkeys also responded in the same manner. In other words, dolphins and monkeys *know* when they do not know something. This is compelling evidence that dolphins and rhesus monkeys possess metacognitive abilities. Moreover, these findings are even more interesting in light of the fact that rhesus monkeys do not show evidence of mirror self-recognition, hinting at the heterogeneous nature of self-awareness.

Perspective Taking and Theory of Mind

Some authors have argued that if one is self-aware then one is in a position to use one's experience with one's own mental states to infer and model mental states in others. This is called *theory of mind* and is perhaps the most controversial area of animal self-awareness research. Theory of mind in other animals is an enormously complex notion. The literature on theory of mind in chimpanzees and other primates has been equivocal. It appears that in some circumstances chimpanzees are able to take the visual perspective of another individual and use that information to formulate behavioral strategies in competitive situations. At other times it appears that chimpanzees are not attentive to seemingly simple cues about perspective and knowledge in others. There has been relatively little work done on perspective taking and theory of mind in other primates and mammals. One exception is a body of experimentation in dogs that shows that dogs can take the visual perspective of others into account. It is not known to what extent they model the mental states of others. Furthermore, it has been argued that evidence for the ability to attribute mental states in a wide range of species might be better sought in natural activities, such as social play, rather than in laboratory settings. The role of ecological validity in theory of mind studies continues to be an important point of discussion.

Implications of Self-Awareness in Other Species

Philosophy often begins with questions about the place of humans in nature. Our own self-awareness demands that we contemplate the question of self-awareness in other animals. This line of questioning is fundamental to our philosophy but also to our scientific understanding of the natural history and evolution of cognition, sentience, and mind.

Others would argue that the question of sentience in other animals is relevant to the ethics of how we treat other animals. It is not uncommon for the argument to be made that if another species is not sentient then it should not be given moral consideration. Certainly our knowledge of the minds of other animals should shape how we treat and interact with them. However, it is a false dichotomy to argue that other animals are either automata or sentient. The emerging scientific literature reveals that sentience, that is, self-awareness, is not monolithic but rather an extremely complex characteristic that exists at different levels and in different forms in different species. It may be the case that we will never know—on a subjective level—what it is like to be a bat. However, the emerging evidence says that it is like something.

See also

Human Perceptions of Animals—*Humanness and What It Means to Be a Human Animal*
Sentience and Cognition—*Animal Pain*
Sentience and Cognition—*Selfhood in Animals*

Further Resources

Bekoff, M. (2006). *Animal passions and beastly virtues.* Philadelphia: Temple University Press.

Griffin, D. R. (1992). *Animal minds.* Chicago: University of Chicago Press.

Parker, S. T., Mitchell, R. W., & Boccia, M. L. (1994). *Self-awareness in animals and humans.* Cambridge, MA: Cambridge University Press.

Lori Marino

Sentience and Cognition
Animal Pain

Which nonhuman animals experience conscious pain? Common sense suggests that all mammals and birds obviously do. But people's intuitions begin to waver when it comes to reptiles, amphibians, fish, or invertebrates. Do lobsters feel pain when boiled alive? A recent study by the Norwegian government said that they do not. But Norway has a significant lobster fishing industry to protect, so some have regarded the study with skepticism.

Is there any hope that science will provide answers where common sense falters? This question is very important when thinking about animal welfare. All technologically advanced countries have laws designed to promote animal welfare. But many people think these laws do not go far enough. The general trend is toward making the laws have broader scope, reflecting changing relationships between animals and humans over the past century. Thus, the British Animals (Scientific Procedures) Act was amended in 1993 to extend protection to all mammals, birds, reptiles, fish, amphibians, and the common octopus. This list was intended to cover those animals judged capable of pain and suffering. The Canadian parliament has considered a different approach. Instead of attempting to list all the species capable of feeling pain, the Canadians have introduced bills that would expand the scope of protection to all animals capable of feeling pain. But whichever way the law is written, it is still necessary to know which animals actually do feel pain.

The United States' approach is similar to the British approach in that it depends on explicitly listing the protected species. Although the long-term trend is toward more inclusive coverage, recent legislation has recently gone in the other direction. In 1999 antivivisectionists brought a lawsuit against the U.S. Department of Agriculture (USDA) challenging the USDA's policy of exempting rats, mice, and birds (the majority of animals used in research) from inspections required under the Animal Welfare Act (AWA).

Initially, the USDA agreed to settle the lawsuit by including these animals in their inspections. But in 2002 the U.S. Congress responded to lobbying from the drug industry by amending the AWA to explicitly exclude these animals from the AWA requirements. The motives for excluding rats, mice, and birds were clearly political because there is certainly not any scientific basis for discriminating between the pain-feeling capacities of rats and rabbits.

All of these laws require an answer to the question of which animals feel pain. But even if one agrees that some animals feel pain consciously, it does not necessarily follow that it is impermissible to use them in research, agriculture, and so forth. Nevertheless, if it can be established which animals feel pain, this is relevant to the ethical issues because causing pain would require special justification for such procedures to be allowed at all.

What Science Tells Us about Animal Pain

What, then, does science tell us about animal pain? An important distinction is between nociception—the capacity to sense noxious stimuli—and pain. Nociception is one of the most primitive sensory capacities. Neurons that are specialized for nociception occur in many invertebrates and have been studied in species including leeches and sea slugs. But these organisms have very tiny brains, and they have a relatively limited range of responses to nociception. Nevertheless, they share the basic neural biochemistry of nociception. Pain is defined by the International Association for the Study of Pain as an unpleasant sensory and emotional experience. Because we cannot directly ask them, a big problem with judging the pain felt by invertebrates and other animals is determining to what extent emotions and unpleasantness are involved. One behavioral approach involves seeing how hard animals will work to avoid noxious stimuli. Another approach looks at the effects of analgesics and anesthetics; the effects on mammals and birds are similar to the effects on humans. These drugs appear to be less effective for reptiles, amphibians, fish, and invertebrates, but it is difficult to say whether this is because there is no unpleasant experience for them to relieve, or whether the drugs we use just happen to be designed to work better on animals more like us.

It also seems that the vertebrate spinal cord itself (even when severed from the brain) can react very precisely to noxious stimuli and even learn about relationships among painful stimuli. No brain is required for these capacities, so if we accept the phrase "no brain, no pain," then the kinds of reactions and learning shown by many invertebrates, which are comparable to those of the spinal cord in vertebrates, do not give very strong evidence of conscious pain experiences. It is important to note, though, that not all invertebrates should be considered equivalent—many cephalopods (not just the common octopus protected by British law) seem to have a much more sophisticated range of cognitive capacities than the basic forms of learning found in sea slugs or the spinal cords of rats. Much more research would be needed to make more definitive claims, but one might worry about whether this research is ethical.

In vertebrates, nociceptive neurons go through complex neural gateways in the spinal cord that control the strength of the signal sent to the brain, and the brain also exerts a top-down influence on how much of the signal gets through. (The brains of sea slugs also exert some top-down influence.) The "classical" view of human pain holds that there are at least two pathways involved in the experience of pain in humans. One pathway is responsible for features of pain sensations such as pain's intensity and location (the sensory pathway). The other is responsible for how much one "minds" the pain or how unpleasant the pain is (the affective pathway). This classical two-systems view has not actually been rigorously examined in nonhuman animals—in fact, it is very difficult to do so because it is not clear how to "dissociate" the sensory and affective pathways in an experimentally rigorous way.

The Way Forward in Studying Animal Pain

So far, this essay has briefly described some analogies and disanalogies between the human pain system and what is found in a variety of different animals. For some people, the existence of these analogies is sufficient to establish that other animals experience pain consciously. Sometimes, the analogy is bolstered by statements about how closely related humans are to other animals, but of course, this addition carries less weight as we get further away from the great apes and other primates. For others, the disanalogies weigh more heavily. For every similarity between the behavior or neurology of humans and other nonhuman animals, there is a dissimilarity that can be used to deny the inference to conscious pain in nonhumans. Without any theoretical reason for saying what the relevant analogical properties are, the result is something of an impasse.

One way forward would be to give a theory of consciousness and explain how the anatomical, physiological, neurological, and behavioral evidence relate to the theory. Some philosophers think that consciousness requires high-level cognitive abilities, such as being able to think about your own mental states, and they think that this kind of self-reflective, conceptual understanding of mental states is beyond most if not all nonhuman animals. According to this view, the various kinds of available analogical evidence are only relevant if they can be shown to relate to the self-reflective nature of consciousness. For this reason, the fact that many chimpanzees, some other great apes, and perhaps some dolphins appear capable of recognizing their own mirror images is also taken to support the idea that they are capable of consciously experiencing pain. But this highly cognitive theory of consciousness is not scientific consensus, so we cannot say that science gives straightforward support to the view that (at most) only a few other animals experience pain (or anything else) consciously.

Still, the radical denial of consciousness in the vast majority of animals gets one thing right: anyone who wants to go beyond straightforward arguments by analogy, which already are biased in favor of species more closely related to humans, will need to explain more precisely *why* the available evidence supports attributions of conscious pain.

What kind of approaches are there to answering these questions? It is especially important to say why conscious pain is functionally useful to animals so that we can look for the relevant functionality in a wide variety of species. It might seem obvious that pain is functional. Doesn't feeling the pain of a pin prick cause you to withdraw your hand, which is good for protecting you against injury? But this is not so obvious once we realize that the withdrawal reflex starts before we consciously experience any pain and that the pain-withdrawal reflex can be managed entirely through a spinal-cord circuit (although it can also come under top-down control). What about learning from painful stimuli? Here we need to be careful because there are different kinds of learning, some of them unconscious. So not all learning is going to provide equally strong evidence of conscious pain.

Consciousness seems, however, to play a central role in some cases where there is learning about the consequences of actions (in what psychologists call "operant conditioning") and where there is learning about two stimuli with a time gap between them (called "trace conditioning"). Although a scientific approach still does not yet provide clear answers here, the fact that learning sometimes depends on *noticing* the relationship between two temporally separated stimuli, or between a behavior and its consequences, seems to suggest that there is a role for something like consciousness. Using a variety of analgesic drugs such as morphine, it appears to be possible to make some noxious stimuli detectable in a sensory way, as measured by withdrawal reflexes, while diminishing the affective component to the point where the animal does not change its overall behavior. From here it would be possible to study the effects on learning and to possibly find different roles for the different components of the sensory experience.

Of course, a determined skeptic might continue to insist that no amount of anatomical, physiological, and behavioral evidence can tell us anything about the conscious nature of animal experiences. But this view would equally rule out the possibility of studying human consciousness. A less radical but equally determined skeptic points to the limited cognitive abilities of animals to use language, or to engage in higher conceptual thinking about mental states. But such skeptics have not provided any scientific methods for testing their claims that consciousness serves only these functions. The fact that we know that consciousness is involved in our own language use and self-consciousness does not imply that it is not involved in other cognitive abilities.

The conscious experience of pain is not just an "alarm bell" telling us when and how to act so as to minimize tissue damage. It seems to be intrinsically involved in helping us learn quickly about new kinds of threats. But there remains much we do not know about how this all works, in humans and in other animals. Nociception-based learning and central (top-down) modification of nociception are both found in the sea slug, but its range of learning abilities is much less sophisticated than mammals and other vertebrates. The learning capacities of invertebrates with more sophisticated nervous systems, like the cephalopods, have not been thoroughly studied. In fact, studies have only been done for a very limited range of vertebrates.

If science is to help answer the question with which we started, much more work in this area is needed. Although the unfolding scientific story about the functions of pain across the animal kingdom is more complicated than we have yet imagined, there is nothing to indicate that it is beyond our ability to understand it. But there are, of course, questions about the ethical propriety of doing more of this kind of work, precisely because it might cause morally objectionable pain. It may seem obvious to common sense that we do not need to do this work on such animals as dogs, but there are many other cases where common sense fails us, and we must make an ethical decision about the price of knowledge.

Further Resources

Allen, C. (2004). Animal pain. *Noûs, 38*, 617–43.

Allen, C., Fuchs, P. N., Shriver, A., & Wilson, H. (2005). Deciphering animal pain. In M. Aydede (Ed.), *Pain: New essays on the nature of pain and the methodology of its study* (pp. 352–66). Cambridge, MA: MIT Press.

Grau, J. W. (2002). Learning and memory without a brain. In M. Bekoff, C. Allen, & G. M. Burghardt (Eds.), *The cognitive animal: Empirical and theoretical perspectives on animal cognition* (pp. 77–88). Cambridge, MA: MIT Press.

Perry of Southwark and the Nuffield Council on Bioethics. (2005). The capacity of animals to experience pain, distress and suffering. In *The ethics of research involving animals*. Report of the Working Party on the Ethics of Research Involving Animals. Retrieved June 15, 2006, from http://www.nuffieldbioethics.org/go/print/ourwork/animalresearch/publication_178.html

Robinson, W. S. (1997). Some nonhuman animals can have pains in a morally relevant sense. *Biology and Philosophy, 12*, 51–71.

Colin Allen

Sentience and Cognition
Descartes, René

The French philosopher René Descartes (1596–1650) exerted a strong influence on human-animal relationships by explaining humans and animals as radically different beings. Descartes, who is called the father of modern philosophy, defended a dualistic position. In his view, reality consists of two components that are separate: the material (such as objects and bodies) and the mental (consciousness or souls). Nonhuman animals have only the first component. Descartes thought of them as mindless machines, devoid of any true thoughts or feelings. Humans possess both components. Besides having a material body, humans distinguish themselves from nonhuman animals through possession of a thinking soul.

Descartes argued that through the practice of "methodical doubt," people need to wonder what ideas are really reliable. We may cast doubt on what we perceive around us because who can say that all this is not merely a dream? For Descartes, at least one truth could not be denied: the fact that he doubted things and that therefore he existed. This resulted in his famous words "I think, therefore I am" (*Cogito ergo sum*). Humans are thinking beings (*res cogitans*), and we can think because we have a rational, immaterial, and immortal soul. Our innate ideas, which are already present while we are developing in our mother's womb, allow us to understand the world around us. In Descartes' view, all space has to be understood in material terms (*res extensa*)—there is no empty space. This holds not only for the earth and plants, but also for nonhuman animals.

Descartes held a mechanistic view of the body. His ideas were inspired by the hydraulic automata in the French Royal Gardens of Saint-Germain-en-Laye. Visitors stepped on concealed panels that sent water through a network of pipes and thus caused statues of Greek Gods to move. In the *Traité de l'Homme* (1664), Descartes compares the human and animal body with such automata. The nerves and animal spirits are like the pipes and water of the automata. The heart is the source of the water, and the cavities of the brain are like storage tanks. But whereas nonhuman animals are merely automata, the human body is linked with the soul through the pineal gland.

In the *Discours de la Méthode* (1637), Descartes mentions two tests to tell the difference between nonhuman animals and humans. First, the language test requires that one be able to use language in a creative way. According to Descartes, deaf-mutes use signs in a meaningful way, but nonhuman animals such as parrots merely utter words as imitations. Their words are not expressions of thought. Second, the action test refers to being able to act appropriately in a variety of areas. Machines may do some things better than humans, but will fail at many others. Nonhuman animals act mechanically—from the disposition of their organs—but not by reason. For Descartes, failure of these two tests "shows not merely that the beasts have less reason than men, but that they have no reason at all."

There exists some ambiguity in Descartes' view of animals. John Cottingham has argued that Descartes' explanation of nonhuman animals as natural automata does not mean that he held them incapable of feelings or sensations. He points out that Descartes wrote about anger, fear, hunger, and joy in nonhuman animals. Tom Regan and Daisie and Michael Radner agree that nonhuman animals may have sensations, but they reply that Descartes distinguished several grades of sensations. The first grade refers to merely mechanical processes, wherein sensory organs are affected by external objects. The second grade comprises immediate mental results, as a result of the soul being united with the body. Examples are the perception of pain, pleasure, hunger, thirst, and cold. The third grade includes judgments about external objects and involves reasoning. Regan and the Radners argue that Descartes attributed only sensations of the first grade to nonhuman animals. Indeed, Descartes seemed to confirm this in a particular, clear way in a 1640 letter to his friend the priest Marin Mersenne: "I do not explain the feeling of pain without reference to the soul. For in my view pain exists only in the understanding. What I do explain is all the external movements which accompany this feeling in us; in animals it is these movements alone which occur, and not pain in the strict sense." In short, for Descartes, the cries of animals apparently are not different from those of machines—they are all imitations. Having a thinking soul is not only a condition to have thoughts; it is also a requirement for the having of a conscious mental life at all.

The Cartesian position that nonhuman animals are devoid of souls has two major advantages. First, it excludes the possibility that nonhuman animals might attain an immortal afterlife in heaven. Descartes rejected the ideas of doubting the existence of God and of believing that "after this present life we have nothing to fear or to hope for, any more than flies and ants." Second, Descartes offered an important justification for using nonhuman animals by claiming that they cannot feel pain. He commented that his view is "not so much cruel to animals as indulgent to human beings . . . since it absolves them from the suspicion of crime when they eat or kill animals." Descartes experimented on animals in order to understand their anatomy and physiology. In *La Description du Corps Humain* (1664), he suggests, for example, slicing off the pointed end of the heart of a live dog, so that one can insert a finger and feel the pulsation of the dog's heart. These experiments were done without the application of anesthesia, which was only introduced during the nineteenth century. Cartesian followers kicked pregnant dogs or nailed dogs on boards to vivisect them. Contemporaries protested against such animal abuse, including the philosopher Voltaire, who noted, "You discover in it all the same organs of feeling that are in yourself. Answer me, machinist, has nature arranged all the means of feeling in this animal, so that it may not feel?" The Cartesian position that nonhuman animals cannot suffer continues to influence current thinking of scientists and others. Few defend it in an explicit way, but the idea that nonhuman animals and humans strongly differ in terms of sentience remains prevalent in discussions on the use of nonhuman animals.

Further Resources

Bekoff, M. (Ed.). (1998). *Encyclopedia of animal rights and animal welfare.* Westport, CT: Greenwood Press.

Cottingham, J. (1978). "A brute to the brutes"?: Descartes' treatment of animals. *Philosophy, 53,* 551–59.

Cottingham, J., Stoothoff, R., & Murdoch, D. (Trans.). (1985). *The philosophical writings of Descartes* (3 vols.). Cambridge, MA: Cambridge University Press.

Guerrini, A. (2003). *Experimenting with humans and animals: From Galen to animal rights.* Baltimore: Johns Hopkins University Press.

Radner, D., & Radner, M. (1996). *Animal consciousness.* Amherst, MA: Prometheus Books.

Regan, T. (1983). *The case for animal rights.* Berkeley: University of California Press.

Regan, T., & Singer, P. (Eds.). (1989). *Animal rights and human obligations* (2nd ed.). Englewood Cliffs, NJ: Prentice-Hall.

Koen Margodt

Sentience and Cognition
Morality in Humans and Animals

Do animals exhibit moral behavior? Might they feel empathy, have a sense of fairness, and respect a set of rules about right and wrong behavior? More and more biologists, neuroscientists, philosophers, and ethologists are convinced that the answers to these questions are probably yes. If morality has a biological basis—if our own patterns of moral behavior represent millions of years of evolution—then it seems to follow that our evolutionary relatives should share many of these traits. Exploring morality in nonhuman animals (hereafter simply "animals") might help us understand ourselves better. At the same time, we may come to find that we have once again underestimated how nuanced and complex are the inner lives and social relationships of other animals.

What Do We Mean by "Morality"?

Morality covers a wide range of behaviors, and boundaries and definitions shift over time to accommodate new ideas and research. For now, let us define morality, in its most skeletal form, as prosocial behavior, or behavior aimed at promoting (or at least not diminishing) the welfare of others. Morality is an essentially *social* phenomenon: it arises in the interactions between and among individuals. Fleshing this out, we might say that moral behavior includes (but may not be limited to) cooperation, reciprocity, empathy, helping, and an internalized set of rules for social behavior within a community. In addition, morality is enforced through a number of regulating mechanisms: anger, indignation, guilt, conscience, shame, reputation, ostracism, and retribution.

Evolution of Moral Behavior

The idea that morality may have evolved over millions of years is not new, nor is the notion that animals share many of these behaviors. Charles Darwin tentatively proposed that human moral sentiments were a product of the evolutionary process and speculated about moral sentiments in animals. But it was not until recently that scientists gave these questions serious and sustained attention. What is emerging now is a fascinating tapestry of research into the biology of morality. We are beginning to recognize the role of morality in lives of other species and to piece together the neurophysiological roots of moral emotion and cognition—roots that we share with other species that evolved from our common ancestor.

Let us briefly canvas some examples of moral behavior in animals. Cooperation and reciprocity have been particularly well studied, and intraspecies and even interspecies cooperation have been found to be widespread. Animals hunt together. Wolves and coyotes, for example, hunt in packs and then distribute food. Animals form alliances. Female chimpanzees will form groups to protect themselves from an aggressive male. Female rats sometimes nest and nurse young communally, even sharing milk. Food sharing is common in primates and social carnivores. Animals will combine forces to guard against predation: meerkats, for example, take turns watching for predators while the others eat. Primates groom each other. There are cheaters and rule breakers, but not enough that the system of trust breaks down.

When we view behavior through the lens of social morality, even behaviors such as aggression take on a new face. Frans de Waal, who has conducted extensive research on moral behavior in primates, argues that aggressive behavior is one of the key tools animals use to shape relationships in a cooperative, mutually beneficial direction. When individual interests diverge (e.g., in a struggle for dominant status), aggression is one means of resolving the conflict. Perhaps counterintuitively, aggression is a highly *prosocial* behavior: it is an effective way to maintain social order and reestablish balance (de Waal, 1996). Subordination is also a prosocial behavior: once the battle for dominance is won, the loser generally finds a satisfactory place in society. There is a panoply of behaviors for expressing subordination.

Animals employ other means of maintaining social order, including direct negotiation, third-party mediation, and reconciliation, all of them manifestations of what de Waal calls community concern ("the stake each individual has in promoting those characteristics of the community or group that increase the benefits derived from living in it by that individual or its kin," 1996, p. 207). Community concern begins to look suspiciously like morality: those behaviors that tear the social fabric are "wrong," and those that create the kind of community in which individuals thrive are "right."

Empathy—the ability to "feel with" another—is also a widespread moral trait. Rats, for example, will help other distressed rats and will avoid delivering an electric shock to them even at the cost of not eating. The same is true for rhesus monkeys.

Recent research into the neurobiology of moral behaviors, including empathy, trust, love, anger, and revenge, reveals the deep evolutionary underpinnings of morality. Humans share morality-related neurological structures and chemicals with many other animals. Emotions such as empathy are located in the amygdala and hypothalamus of the brain and are mediated by neurotransmitters such as dopamine, serotonin, and oxytocin. These shared physical structures and chemical actions suggest that the behaviors they control are also shared.

One of the most interesting areas of neurological research related to empathy has been work on "mirror neurons," which were first studied in monkeys and subsequently in humans. These neurons allow us to "read the mind" of others; they cause us to respond to a gesture made by someone else as if we were performing the same gesture—we "mirror" another's state of mind, feeling what he or she feels. Mirror neurons may be an evolved mechanism for empathizing.

Even a sense of fairness has neurological roots: researchers at Princeton have demonstrated that unfair treatment triggers a specific set of neural circuits in a region of the brain called the anterior insula (Sanfey et al., 2003). Research with capuchin monkeys has produced a similar result: they have "inequality aversion"—they do not like to be treated unfairly.

There are several complementary explanations for how moral behaviors might have evolved. One mechanism is kin selection: if a moral behavior (say, for example, altruism) promotes the survival of offspring or brothers and sisters, the altruist's genes will be passed along, even though the altruist has sacrificed his or her own welfare. Another mechanism is reciprocal altruism: if you scratch my back, I will scratch yours, and we will both be better off than the bloke who lives in the next tree and refuses to scratch backs. Finally, members of a group probably survive better through mutual cooperation, reciprocity, empathy, or fairness than members of another, less "moral" group.

Morality is both "instinctual"— hardwired in brains and genes—and open to behavioral flexibility, guided not only by interactions with others and with the environment, including other organisms, but also (in a few species at least) by reflective thought. And it may be that some aspects of morality are more " hardwired" than others. It is also likely that varying "degrees" of morality depend on cognitive capacity: simple forms of empathy such as mimicry may require less cognitive sophistication than more complex empathic responses such as perspective taking.

It is likely that morality has evolved in conjunction with certain cognitive capacities. The social intelligence hypothesis, which states that intelligence evolved in animals living in social groups, may very well apply to morality as well. Morality probably evolved under the same pressures, so we might expect species with highly developed social and cognitive capacities to also display the most well-developed moral behaviors.

Distinguishing ultimate from proximate explanations for moral behavior helps take the edge off "selfish gene" arguments (arguments that so-called morality is really just selfishness in disguise). The ultimate explanation for the evolution of morality is, indeed, about the survival of genes. But the proximate causes of moral behavior are "pure" in the vernacular sense. We really do feel emotions of love, compassion, and empathy, and we really do care about fairness. As Frans de Waal says, "Evolution depends on the success of a trait over millions of years; motives spring from the here and now. . . . Motivations lead a life of their own, which is why we describe them in terms of preferences, desires, and intentions rather than survival value" (de Waal, 2005, p. 171).

The Role of Play Behavior

Some researchers—most notably Marc Bekoff—have argued that play behavior may be a rudimentary form of morality, or a mechanism for learning moral behavior. During social play, animals test out and fine-tune ground rules of social interaction. Because play typically involves action patterns that are used in other contexts—predatory behaviors such as biting or mating behaviors such as mounting—keeping play playful requires ongoing communication as well as a base level of trust. There are "rules of engagement" for playful encounters, including that play will be fair and symmetrical (dominant animals will let subordinates be equals during play). Play has been studied most extensively in primates and social carnivores, but may be an important behavioral trait for many other mammals and perhaps other species.

The Darker Side

If we ascribe morality to animals, must we not also ascribe to them immorality? We do, indeed, understand moral behavior within the context of a range of possible behaviors, many of which are harmful or cruel or antisocial. It makes sense to label behaviors that tear the social fabric as wrong or immoral. It seems reasonable to understand animal morality in the same way.

There are behaviors among animals that parallel what is typically understood as immoral behavior in humans, and we can see that groups of social animals seem to have systems in place for dealing with violations of the moral code. Animals seem to understand not only fairness, but also its opposite. In species such as chimpanzees, in which reciprocity and fairness figure large, there are punishments for those who break the rules. Those who fail to share appropriately are treated with less generosity by others; they may be ostracized.

Are animals cruel? Empathy is the capacity to understand others, in particular their suffering, and that capacity makes cruelty possible. We know how to cause pain and distress. Both rely on the ability to imagine how one's own behavior affects others. In animals with the capacity for cognitive empathy, it seems reasonable to conclude that this capacity might be put to use in antisocial as well as prosocial ways.

Here is a question to ponder. Even after witnessing brutality and genocide among chimpanzees in Gombe, Jane Goodall maintains that only humans have the capacity for evil. Keeping in mind that evil and immorality may not be equivalent, do you agree?

Taxonomic Distribution of Moral Behaviors

There is evidence of moral behavior or "proto-morality" in primates, social carnivores (most well-studied are wolves, coyotes, and hyenas), some cetaceans (dolphins and whales), and at least some other species, such as rats. At this point, it would be premature to pronounce other species lacking—much more careful consideration and research are needed to flesh out similarities and differences across taxonomic lines. Using clues such as play behavior, sociality, and cognitive capacities, we may discover that morality is even more widespread than we have thought.

Counterarguments

Many people are uncomfortable with the idea of ascribing morality to animals. Marc Hauser, for example, argues in his book *Wild Minds* that notions of duty and responsibility are central to morality, and animals lack the cognitive capacity to understand these concepts. Terrence Deacon, in *The Symbolic Species*, argues that although there is undoubtedly an unbroken continuity between human and nonhuman minds, there is also a singular discontinuity: humans use symbolic language to communicate. The use of words has changed our brain over time. If our brains are significantly different, and morality is essentially a product of our brain, then wouldn't we possibly be unique in this respect?

An evolutionary view of morality is also at odds with many of the central tenets of Western philosophy and theology, both of which tend to view humans as different in kind, and not just degree, from other animals. For example, many Christian theologians are uncomfortable with removing the sharp line between humans (who are made in the image of God) and the rest of creation (who are not). Morality is understood as a living-out of God's will among his people.

Our Moral Relationship to Animals

Understanding the rich inner lives of animals, and seeing how animals exist in complex societies, will undoubtedly influence how we view ourselves in relationship to them. Ascribing moral behavior to animals does not necessarily lead to the conclusion that we must therefore treat them with more compassion. Yet each step we take toward recognizing the continuity between our own species and our evolutionary kin raises questions about our moral obligations toward nonhuman life. The more we see that we are like them and they like us—particularly when we recognize that they experience emotions such as empathy, trust, anger, and grief—the more we may engage our own empathetic sense to guide our interactions with animals.

See also

Ethics and Animal Protection
Play

Further Resources

Bekoff, M. (2004). Wild justice and fair play: Cooperation, forgiveness, and morality in animals. *Biology & Philosophy, 19,* 489–520.

Brosnan, S. F., Schiff, H., & de Waal, F. B. M. (2005). Tolerance for inequity increases with social closeness in chimpanzees. *Proceedings of the Royal Society B* 272: 253–258. Available at http://www.emory.edu/LIVING_LINKS/pdf_attachments/Brosnan_Tolerance05.pdf

Deacon, T. W. (1997). *The symbolic species: The co-evolution of language and brain.* New York: Norton.

Gazzaniga, M. S. (2005). *The ethical brain.* New York: Dana Press.

Hauser, M. (2000). *Wild minds.* New York: Holt.

Sanfey, A. G., Rilling, J. K., Aronson, J. A., Nystrom, L. E., & Cohen, J. D. (2003, June 13). The neural basis of economic decision-making in the Ultimatum Game. *Science, 300,* 1755–58.

de Waal, F. B. M. (1996). *Good natured: The origins of right and wrong in humans and other animals.* Cambridge, MA: Harvard University Press.

Jessica Pierce

Sentience and Cognition
Selfhood in Animals

The question of whether nonhuman animals possess or experience a sense of self is a controversial one, mainly because it threatens the privileged position of humans above animals. Along with culture, rationality, and language, the self is one of the experiences that many people would consider uniquely human. However, the capacities deemed necessary for the self have been applied arbitrarily, from an anthropocentric (or human-centered) position. The more we learn about animals' capacity for thought, emotion, communication, and other abilities once reserved for human beings, the greater the likelihood of selfhood among animals appears.

Some difficulty arises in defining the "self." Here, the term indicates an awareness of oneself and one's environment. The term incorporates consciousness, which refers to an individual's awareness that experiences (such as hunger or pain) are happening to him or her. This usage of consciousness is distinct from the popular use, in which "conscious" refers to the state of being awake, as opposed to "unconscious" or asleep. The term "consciousness" is often used interchangeably with "self-consciousness."

Scholars, theologians, and others throughout history have devoted considerable effort to demonstrating that animals are not conscious. The arguments against consciousness among animals supported anthropocentrism, or the belief that humans occupy a privileged status over all other creation. If animals could not feel or understand what was happening to them, then human beings could use them in any way they chose. One obstacle to demonstrating the existence of consciousness in animals is the problem of "other minds." This refers to the difficulty in understanding the experiences of any being other than oneself. The problem arises with animals because we cannot use language to learn about their subjective experience. During the seventeenth century, the French philosopher René Descartes dismissed the possibility of consciousness among animals. He determined that any cries of pain that animals expressed during vivisection were insignificant because animals lacked awareness that the pain was happening to them. Their cries were merely responses to physical stimulus, much as a twig makes a "crack" upon breaking. According to Descartes, animals could not demonstrate consciousness through language, which consequently became a requirement for being. The Cartesian view justified vivisection without anesthetics and other forms of cruelty on the basis that the suffering of animals did not deserve moral consideration. Although the view that animals lack consciousness had widespread support, Descartes' opponents included Voltaire and John

Locke. Some contemporary thinkers, such as Peter Carruthers, continue to deny the possibility of consciousness among animals.

During the nineteenth century, Charles Darwin and George Romanes argued for evolutionary continuity between human and nonhuman animals. This continuity included not only anatomical characteristics, but also mental and emotional capacities. Animals' ability to feel pain and suffering, regardless of their ability to talk about it, emphasized by English philosopher Jeremy Bentham, fueled the first legislation against cruelty. The rise of behaviorism hindered serious scientific investigation of animal consciousness during much of the twentieth century. Behaviorists argue that the mind cannot be observed and therefore cannot be studied. However, interest in and concern for the subjective experiences of animals increased during the 1970s. The field of cognitive ethology, which acknowledges that animals can think rather than simply respond to stimulus, opened the way for research into animal consciousness. A 1974 essay by Thomas Nagel—titled "What Is It Like to Be a Bat?"—sparked curiosity about how animals see their worlds. Donald Griffin, known for discovering that bats use echolocation, or radar, to navigate in the dark, argued that such sophisticated behavior involved conscious thought rather than merely instinct. These pioneers, along with others such as Marc Bekoff, Frans de Waal, Jane Goodall, Marian Stamp Dawkins, Dian Fossey, Roger Fouts, Dorothy Cheney, and Robert Seyfarth, have documented consciousness among various species of animals.

Research has debunked the idea that language is a uniquely human capacity. Numerous species of animals have learned to communicate using symbols, computers, and American Sign Language (or ASL). The first chimpanzee to learn ASL was Washoe, raised by Beatrix and Alex Gardner. Washoe knew 140 ASL gestures and could use twice as many two-sign combinations. Koko, the lowland gorilla raised by psychologist Penny Patterson, could use over 600 signs. Critics say that animals may be able to learn the names for things, but they do not necessarily understand the meaning of language, and they cannot innovate on their own with it outside of the context of the basic drills in experiments. However, Koko and other primates have shown that they understand and use sign language even outside the experimental setting. Species other than chimps can also use language. Irene Pepperberg's research with Alex, an African Grey parrot, revealed that birds could use language. Alex's abilities surpass simply naming objects, which he regularly did in the drills in Pepperberg's research. Alex occasionally violated the rules of the experiments, which indicated that he not only knew the rules, but also understood the abstract and complex idea of breaking them.

Less language-centered attempts to study consciousness (or self-awareness) have involved mirror self-recognition experiments in primates. Gordon Gallup and his colleagues placed mirrors in rooms in which individual chimpanzees lived. At first, the chimps acted as if the reflections were other chimpanzees. After a few days, however, the chimps began to recognize that the reflections were of themselves. They began to make faces in the mirrors and use the mirrors to engage in grooming behaviors, such as inspecting the insides of their mouths and other parts of their bodies that they could not ordinarily see. This was evidence that the chimps understood that they were the source of what they saw in the mirror. To examine the possibility of self-recognition further, Gallup anesthetized the chimps and placed nontoxic red marks on their brows and above the ears. Without looking in the mirror, the chimps did not know the marks were there. However, when they looked in the mirror, the chimps touched the marks repeatedly. Some examined and even smelled their fingers afterward. When Gallup conducted this study with several species of monkeys, his team found that the capacity for self-recognition appeared only among chimpanzees. They concluded that self-recognition might be limited to most of the great apes, such as orangutans and bonobos (but not gorillas), which are the primates most closely related to human beings. However, other species, such as pigeons and bottlenose dolphins, have also demonstrated mirror self-recognition abilities.

Using a sociological approach, researchers have found evidence of consciousness in animals' relationships with others, particularly humans. From a sociological perspective, consciousness implies the capacity for self, which refers to a larger process that takes into account self-awareness and awareness of others. A self develops as an individual adapts his or her actions, thoughts, and emotions in response to the perceived reactions of others. The emphasis on others highlights the extent to which sociological theories of the self assume that it develops socially, through interaction. Consequently, this research has focused mainly on dogs and cats because they have the most frequent contact with humans. Clinton Sanders studied how people attribute a sense of self to their dogs. Sanders observed everyday interaction between dogs and people and paid special attention to the ways that people incorporate dogs into social routines in the human household. Through consistent interaction, dogs take on a specific role within the human-dog relationship. Doing so indicates the dogs' ability to "take the role of the other," in sociological terminology. The ability to see oneself in the context of other beings, such as members of the family, indicates the capacity to distinguish self from other. Sanders also outlined how people come to understand their dogs' distinct personalities and mental and emotional capacities. Because dogs cannot talk, guardians must give voice to what they think their dogs are experiencing. At the vet or in a training class, people engaged in what Sanders calls "speaking for" dogs. This involves saying what the dog would say if he or she could speak, and it makes use of intimate knowledge of a dog's preferences and disposition. Sanders pointed out that the practice of hiding, which many animals use in hunting, also indicates self-awareness. The need to hide implies the ability to see oneself as an object visible to others. Janet and Steven Alger conducted extensive research in a shelter for domestic cats. In their book *Cat Culture*, they explain how the cats engaged in complex behavior that indicated self-awareness. The cats exhibited strong preferences for food, toys, and human and feline companions. They demonstrated a range of emotions and communicated their emotions to others through vocalizations. Other sociological research builds on models of subjective experience among infants to suggest similarities with the experience of animals. Animals express intentions and share emotions and thoughts with their human caregivers. The ability of animals to interact in such ways suggests that they manifest many of the characteristics that constitute selfhood.

Emotions, role taking, communication, and other behaviors in animals indicate their capacity to adapt and innovate, rather than simply respond through instinct. These indicate the likelihood of selfhood. To acknowledge the possibility that animals have selves is not necessarily to equate them with humans. Although humans and animals share many capacities, they are different in many respects. Whereas humans and at least some nonhuman animals may share the capacity for behaviors such as recognizing others of the same species and sensing the emotional state of an other, animals probably do not experience the autobiographical sense of self so characteristic of humans. The evolution of human beings requires us to recall many details of our lives and to put together stories of who we are. Animals' lives do not require this of them. However, this difference is one of degree rather than kind. Even though animals cannot compose their autobiographies, they nevertheless manifest evidence of self-awareness, with degrees of complexity that vary across species. The higher-level cognitive capacities of animals also have implications for their moral standing in the human community. More specifically, the possibility of selfhood raises questions about our treatment of animals. If animals are self-aware and are not

Cartesian machines, then they have an interest in not suffering. We humans, as other self-aware creatures, must not cause them harm. We must also think seriously about what "harm" means. In short, the likelihood of animal selfhood conveys profound obligations on individuals and on society.

See also

Human Perceptions of Animals—*Humanness and What It Means to Be a Human Animal*
Sentience and Cognition—*Animal Consciousness*
Sentience and Cognition—*Descartes, René*

Further Resources

Allen, C., & Bekoff, M. (1997). *Species of mind: The philosophy and biology of cognitive ethology*. Cambridge, MA: MIT Press.

Dawkins, M. S. (1993). *Through our eyes only: The search for animal consciousness*. San Francisco: Freeman.

Irvine, L. (2004). *If you tame me: Understanding our connection with animals*. Philadelphia: Temple University Press.

Leslie Irvine

Sports
Animals as Sports Mascots

As humans, our interactions with animals penetrate almost every area of our lives. As children we hugged our teddy bears and laughed at a famous mouse, and as adults we use animals as the symbols of the businesses and companies we build. Our affinity for animals even spills over into the realm of another great human love: sports. The use of animals as sports mascots is the norm for most sports and sports teams. Because we oftentimes associate animals with human values or characteristics, specific animal mascots are chosen to portray desired characteristics that they are seen as stereotypically possessing.

There are approximately 326 Division I teams in the NCAA as of 2006. Of those teams, 57.6 percent use animals as their mascots. These animals range from obvious choices such as snarling tigers and bucking broncos to the not so obvious choices, such as peahens or turtles (see Table 1). Animals are commonly used as mascots within the professional sports realm as well. Of 136 professional sports teams, 32.4 percent have an animal as a mascot, with a wide variety of animals chosen. For example, there are the usual suspects, such as bears, cats, and buffalo (or bison). However, there are also several types of birds and even an aquatic mammal, the dolphin.

From a taxonomic standpoint, professional sports team mascots represent a wider number of classes than NCAA mascots, but the NCAA is more diverse in the orders represented by their mascots (Table 1). The largest order represented in both sports realms is the order Carnivora (carnivorous mammals). Within this order, the family Felidae (cats) is the most popular. Within class Aves (birds), order Falconiformes (birds of prey) is the top choice by far among NCAA teams, but this order trails Passeriformes (perching birds)

Table 1. Taxonomic Distribution of Animal Mascots among Professional and NCAA Division I Teams

	Professional	College
Class Actinopterygii		
Perciformes	1	0
Class Amphibia		
Anura	0	1
Class Aves		
Anseriformes	1	1
Cuculiformes	0	1
Falconiformes	5	30
Galliformes	0	4
Passeriformes	6	8
Spenisciformes	1	1
Strigiformes	0	3
Class Chondrichthyes		
Subclass Elasmobranchii	1	0
Rajiformes	1	0
Class Insecta		
Araneae	1	0
Hymenoptera	2	4
Lepidoptera	1	0
Class Mammalia		
Artiodactyla	5	15
Carnivora		
Canidae	4 (1)*	35 (29)*
Felidae	8	54
Mustelidae	0	2
Ursidae	3	10
Cetacea	2	1
Diprotodontia	0	3
Perissodactyla	2	8
Rodentia	0	2
Xenarthra	0	1
Class Reptilia		
Crocodilia	0	1
Squamata	1	1
Testudines	0	1

*The number in parentheses represents the number of domesticated canids (dogs) represented in the total number of canids.

Examples of stereotypical sports mascots, including a cat, a buffalo, a cardinal, and a lumberjack, gather before the Tampa Bay Buccaneers' 17 to 9 victory over the Houston Texans, 2004. ©Cut and Deal Ltd/Alamy.

by only two teams in professional sports. Generally, animals with claws (or talons), sharp teeth, or both are dominant among mascots (50 percent in professional teams and 70 percent in NCAA teams with animal mascots).

Although the types of animals chosen to represent sports teams are highly variable, each is chosen to represent a certain aspect of human behavior. Mascots are seen as the representation of their sports team as a whole. Therefore, the main purpose of a mascot is to portray something that the whole team can identify with, that a whole stadium of fans can rally behind, and that can also negatively affect the morale of the opposing team. For example, irrespective of whether it is biologically true or not, cats (Felidae) are stereotypically seen as being cunning, quick, and fierce. Perhaps this is the reason that this family of mammals is chosen so often to represent a sports team. Similarly, no sound-minded person would want to confront a ferocious bear. This persona of fear is exactly why such a mascot is chosen.

To this end, live mascots are sometimes brought to games and paraded in front of fans and opposing players. At Baylor University, the athletic program keeps a live bear mascot, which is brought to all home football games. Similarly, the University of Colorado often leads its mascot, an American bison (buffalo), in a "stampede" around the football field during home games. Although many other teams have similar live mascots, mascots are more often represented by caricatures of the animal, which are brought to life by costumed humans.

Not all animals that are chosen as sports mascots are stereotypically seen as possessing characteristics that would make it easier to win a game, such as strength or ferocity. These animal mascots are just as hallowed as their growling counterparts, so why are they chosen? The Banana Slugs of the University of California–Santa Cruz (NCAA Division III) are a perfect example. This animal offers no sense of strength, competition, or fear. In fact, it seems to offer nothing at all. Yet the slugs are still a cherished icon of the school. According to the school's Web site, the mascot was chosen to portray still another valued human characteristic: "that the joy of participating is more important than winning" (http://www.ucsc.edu/about/campus_mascot.asp). Another team with a nonconformist mascot is the Terrapins of the University of Maryland. This mascot was chosen to reflect a region rather than a trait because the state reptile of Maryland is the diamond-backed terrapin, a species once common in the estuaries of this region. In the professional sports realm, dolphins are an odd choice of a mascot because they conjure up a feeling of friendliness and playfulness, not ferocity. However, this mascot makes sense for a team based in Miami, where dolphins can easily be observed. It would appear that anomalies to the basic pattern of animal mascots are chosen on the basis of alternative valued traits, or perhaps to reflect the school's or team's specific geographic location.

However, recently, the trend for schools with alternative mascots has been to revamp their mascot's image, suggesting an underlying desire to portray strength and opposition. In order to capture the "fighting spirit" of their team, Temple University recently toughened up its sports icon, the owl, by placing the symbol in attack mode. Similarly, UC–Santa Cruz has also tried a new angle with their mascot. Now, banana slug fans proudly wear t-shirts that proclaim "Banana Slugs—No Known Predators."

As is true of many human endeavors, animals permeate our lives and therefore find themselves very much at home as our sports team mascots. Clearly, the choice of a mascot represents many different things to different organizations. It seems, however, that teams favor mascots that are stereotypically seen as ferocious, dangerous, and strong, which thus infuse the team with the qualities needed to lead them to victory.

Further Resources

White, R. B. (2002, May 13). No more Mister Nice Mascot. *Time,* 18–22.
http://www.time.com/time/magazine/article/0,9171,1002439,00.html

Susan Garnett and Howard Whiteman

Sports
Blood Sports and Animals

Definition

Blood sports are organized activities in which animals are placed at great risk of injury or death for entertainment. Current common blood sports include bullfighting; dogfighting; cockfighting; and nonsubsistence hunting, fishing, and falconry. Bullfighting is an example of animal baiting, in which an animal is goaded into aggression through pain, taunting, cornering, and so on. Dogfighting and cockfighting are typically not considered baiting because the animals are usually not goaded to fight at the time of the event, but rather are trained and bred to fight beforehand. Hunting and coursing are not addressed in this entry.

The animals subjected to blood sports can suffer terribly. Especially in fighting and baiting, the wounds they suffer are intentionally gory and painful. The animals are chosen for the damage they can do; they are trained and bred to be relentlessly savage.

History

The first documentation of cricket fighting comes from China's Song Dynasty (1213–1275 CE). Probably originally used to warn armies of danger (when the crickets stop singing), crickets were caught and bred for fighting. There was much money and prestige to be gained from the fights, and coffins for champion crickets are quite beautiful. Cricket fighting in China became much less popular after the Communist revolution because of its association with the bourgeoisie. It is illegal in Hong Kong and the Macao Province, but its popularity is unfortunately increasing in other parts of China, as well as in other countries.

Fights involving dogs were popular in Europe at least by the time of Roman occupation. Bearbaiting was popular in Tudor England; Henry VII constructed a large "bear garden" at Whitehall. Elizabeth I was especially fond of bearbaiting; she was said to giggle like a schoolgirl at the plight of the animals, and her interest in baiting helped increase its popularity. The fighting pits of her reign also began to stage the brutal deaths of a wider range of animals. Bulls, boars, rats, badgers, and even more exotic animals all found themselves set upon in the pits. To turn the bears raised for baiting into the nasty beasts needed for an entertaining spectacle, the animals were subject to all sorts of abuse and cruelty, such as whipping, beating, stoning, starving, and being forced to sleep on beds of thorns. Before a fight, bulls might have their noses stuffed full with cayenne pepper. The treatment of the dogs to be set upon these animals was no better.

Dogfighting was also practiced in Japan by the Kamakura period (1185–1333 CE). It was promoted among the samurai themselves, many of whom regarded dogfighting as a way to keeping their own combat acumen sharp during times of peace. Infamously, the daimyo of the Tosa province (present-day Kochi) and Akita prefecture were strong proponents of dogfighting; the fighting dogs bred in these areas are now well known.

It is believed that cockfighting was first practiced in Southeast Asia thousands of years ago. It spread westward via Persia, Greece, and the Roman Empire. It also may have begun on its own elsewhere. Typically, roosters fight until one of them is too severely mauled to continue fighting; the loser often dies. Fighting roosters may have their wattles docked to prevent them from ripping and bleeding during fights. Sometimes, the birds' spurs are covered with longer spikes or blades to make the fight all the bloodier and quicker. "Naked heel" fights conducted without spurs can last for hours—too long for the attention span of most of those who watch this sort of event.

The Puritans attempted to outlaw baiting, but it was not until the social revolutions of the Victorian era that efforts to ban animal cruelty—and many blood sports—were successful. An especially grand milestone in European law for blood sports was the Humane Act of 1835 in England, which amended a previous act (the 1822 Act to Prevent Cruel and Improper Treatment of Cattle) illegalizing cruelty—including fighting and baiting—to bulls, bears, dogs, and sheep. The ban spread to England's possession around the world. Coursing, however, was legal until the first part of the twentieth century.

In 1836, Massachusetts was the first state to ban cockfighting; it is still legal in New Mexico and Louisiana. Oklahoma is the most recent state to illegalize cockfighting. The American Society of the Prevention of Cruelty to Animals (ASPCA) advanced the protection of animals (including from blood sports) with the passage of an anticruelty law in 1866, and the Animal Welfare Act—which was adopted in 1966—prohibited interstate transportation or exportation of fighting roosters. (England had passed a ban in

1849.) Unfortunately, cockfighting is still legal and popular in many other parts of the world.

Current Situation

After the Humane Act of 1835, English owners of bullbaiting dogs—bulldogs—focused more on fights between dogs than on fights with bulls. Bulldogs were originally bred to help farmers herd and manage bulls—not kill them. The heavy build and strength that was useful against bulls was not such an asset against other dogs, so it is believed that the bulldogs' owners began crossing them with the swift and equally tenacious terriers, creating bull terriers. Staffordshire bull terriers, pit bull terriers, and American Staffordshire terriers all trace their lineages to these putative bulldog-terrier mixes.

In addition to hunting, dogfighting and cockfighting are arguably the predominant blood sports today. Cockfighting is popular in parts of the United States, Latin America, Africa, Southeast Asia, the Philippines, Indonesia, and the Near East. Although illegal in a larger number of countries, dogfighting is probably more commonly practiced than cockfighting. The adoption of "game-bred" dogs by the American pop culture has surely exacerbated its spread.

When the culture and authorities allow, fighting events in many places take on the appearance of a fair, with whole families—young children included—watching. At these events, traditional and professional dogfights and cockfights follow strict rules (which do not protect the animals, but simply ensure fairness of combat). Matches are regulated, and animals are highly trained. There are variations to the ways fights are managed. According to Cajun rules, dogfights are held in pits that are fifteen to twenty feet square with two- to three-foot walls. Diagonal "scratch" lines are made in opposite corners twelve feet apart. Before a match, the dogs are weighed and washed. Washing prevents owners from covering their dogs with poison or something that makes it harder for the other dog to maintain a hold. At the start of a match, the dogs are placed facing each other behind the scratch lines. Then the referee commands the "players" to release their dogs. The matches are hauntingly quiet, as the dogs grab and relentlessly tear at each other's mouths, faces, throats, and legs. If a dog moves so that his head and shoulders are not facing his opponent, a "turn," is called and the dogs are separated and repositioned behind the scratch lines. The dog that turned is held by his owner. The other dog is released and allowed to attack the held dog. If the released dog attacks the held dog, the held dog is released and the match continues. If the released dog does not attack the held dog, the match is over. The match is also over any time a dog stops fighting, dies, jumps out of the ring, or is pulled out by the owner. Winning dogs are treated well; losing dogs certainly are not.

In contrast to the regulated dogfights are the casual fights that occur in streets, parks, and neighborhoods. Whereas traditional matches were organized in advance, fights now can happen between strangers with a simple "Want to fight your dog?" These dogs are usually not well trained. They may simply be forced to be more aggressive—toward other dogs, other animals, and people. Being less structured, the fights are more chaotic and dangerous to bystanders.

Gambling has long been strongly associated with many blood sports, and dog and cockfighting are no exceptions. In addition, when raids and seizures are made of dog or cockfighting rings, authorities very often find illegal weapons as well as drugs.

Fighting animals are more than a source of money for their owners. The animals can lend prestige and a sense of power to their owners; the owners very often feel that their animal's power and aggressiveness reflects on them. The word *sabong*, for example, is

Balinese for both "rooster" and "penis," and there is little attempt to hide the allusions brought about by fighting cocks.

Not only are the owners associated with a terrible animal, but they are also able to control it. It comes as no surprise that people for whom all other avenues of empowerment have been cut off may turn to building their image with a powerful dog who loyally obeys its owner to the brutal end.

Breeding

Like the wolves from which they evolved, dogs do not naturally fight each other to the death. Normally, dogs will simply posture and feint, but not resort to actually fighting. When fights do occur, they are swift and very rarely lethal. Once one dog demonstrates that it submits, the other dog relents, and the hierarchy is established. Game-bred dogs have had this tendency to break off an attack when they see submission cues bred out of them. In addition, these dogs have been bred not to relent no matter what injury they suffer. In short, game-bred dogs are bred to attack other dogs regardless of the circumstances. Throughout history, different dogs have been bred to fight; one era's fighting dog is another era's loving companion. In addition, fighting dogs are bred not only for gameness: As any owner of a pit bull will attest, these dogs are very loyal.

Lineage is as important to a professional dogfighter as it is to any breeder at a dog show. As much money as owners can make gambling, they can make more by breeding their dogs.

Training and Conditioning

Breeding is important to prepare a dog to fight, but it is not enough. In order to fight, dogs must be trained to do so. A fighting dog's training usually starts at a very young age. Every opportunity is taken to enhance the aggressiveness and tenacity of the dogs. To build their endurance, dogs are made to run on treadmills or chase a small animal (e.g., small dog, cat, squirrel) that is kept just out of their reach. After a training session, the small animal is usually given to the dog as a reward and as a way to develop the dog's taste for blood. So-called trainers increase a dog's strength by having him wear heavy chains or weights for long periods. The dogs are also made to jump up and hang from ropes to develop their lunge and bite. Throughout all of the training, the dog's tolerance for pain is pushed to the limit, for it is not so much the stronger dog who wins, but the one who can withstand more pain.

Roosters are trained a lot like dogs are. They run on treadmills to develop their stamina. They may wear gloves on their feet or have their spurs covered to let them practice fighting without undue injury. They are also set to taunt other roosters to increase their aggressiveness.

The Future

Laws banning blood sports can help save countless animals from horrendous deaths—when they are enforced. Much progress has been made to prevent these horrific events, but the problem is still very large. The Humane Society of the United States estimates that there are at least 40,000 professional dogfighters in the United States—a country in which dogfighting is illegal. Law enforcement officers and governments do not always see the importance of these crimes or their association with other crimes. Grassroots advocacy to enforce these laws and pass new ones can only help.

Many of those who turn to animal fighting seem to do so because they have few other ways to create an impressive self-image. In addition to economic and educational assistance, communities are finding nonviolent ways for dogs to strut their stuff. Owners can gain satisfaction and pride when their dog's strength wins at a weight pull instead of a deadly fight.

Further Resources

Fleig, D. (1996). *History of fighting dogs.* (W. Charlton, Trans.). Neptune, NJ: T. F. H. Publications.

Geertz, C. (2000). Deep play: Notes on the Balinese cockfight. In *The interpretation of cultures.* New York: Basic Books.

Homan, M. (2000). *A complete history of fighting dogs.* New York: Howell Books House.

Shirlyn, H., & Lyons, T. (1999). Field crickets. *Insecta Inspecta World.* Retrieved March 12, 2006, from http://www.insecta-inspecta.com/crickets/field/index.html

William Ellery Samuels, Lieve Meers, and Debbie Coultis

Sports
Sport and Animals

Throughout history, animals have fulfilled a variety of important functions in humans' lives, spanning a continuum from disposable food sources to cherished companions. Interspersed in this tapestry of occasionally contrasting relationships is another sometimes-overlooked thread: the involvement of animals in human sports. This essay attempts to illuminate some of the various ways in which animals have participated, unwittingly or not, in humans' recreational pursuits. Starting with definitions of sport, we move to ancient origins of animals in sport, followed by a discussion of the sociology of sport and how animals have contributed (and still contribute) to humans' leisure enjoyment. The essay concludes with some current issues concerning animals and sport and how cultural trends influence attitudes toward these interactions.

Before animals are introduced into the picture, it is important to understand not only what constitutes sport, but also why people participate in sports. What is the motivation? One definition is given by Norbert Elias and Eric Dunning (1986):

> Every sport—whatever else it may be—is an organized group activity centered on a contest between at least two parties. It requires physical exertion of some kind. It is fought out according to known rules, including, if physical force can be used at all, rules which define the permitted limits of violence.

Elias and Dunning go on to describe the motivation for sport as a "quest for excitement":

> That is, voluntary sport appears to be largely about *obtaining satisfaction* from engaging in physical movements, from the social contacts that are made in sports, and from the *arousal of* affects which bear a playful and pleasurable resemblance to the *emotions* which are generated in seriously critical situations [emphasis added].

Thus, sport is about entertainment and excitement, whether experienced personally or vicariously as a spectator. Sport is about competition, tension, and resolution, as well as an outlet for socially acceptable forms of violence. Greatest satisfaction is achieved when one side wins and the other loses.

How do animals figure into this explanation? The incorporation of animals and sport can take any of three different forms: animals competing against other animals (for the entertainment of humans), humans competing against animals, and humans competing *with* animals (against some other arbitrary measure, such as time). In some cases, more than one of these may apply; for example, sport hunting with dogs involves dogs cooperating with humans against other animals. The arousal and enthusiasm that sport inspires need not be confined to humans either. Dogs specifically bred to perform a task derive great excitement from participating in that activity, as anyone present at the start of the Iditarod sled dog race in Alaska or any hunting dog trial can attest. Additionally, animal sports can be considered "consumptive" if a participant dies, thereby removing it from the gene pool or ecosystem (hunting, bullfighting, pit sports), or nonconsumptive if everyone usually lives to compete again (racing, catch-and-release fishing, rodeo, many dog sports). The pursuit of excitement that plays such a large part in sport applies in especially large measure to those events considered "blood sports," where the object of the game is the death of a participant. These activities surface in humans' earliest writings and feature animals on sometimes grand scales.

Hunting, as one of the earliest blood sports, did not originate as a sport at all, but instead as a means of procuring necessary food. Hunting wild animals for entertainment appeared in ancient art and literature after the advent of agriculture and described the beginnings of a perceived gap between man and the natural world. Ancient Greek writings portrayed hunting as a confrontation between culture and nature, a war by humanity against the wilderness. Hunting was seen as cultivating manly virtues necessary in combat, and because the lives of prey animals had no intrinsic worth, no thought was given to the suffering of the beasts involved. The kill was the end goal, and the anticipation and effort required to arrive at this result were merely added benefits.

Hunting inspired great excitement and satisfaction, not only for participants, but also for spectators. The public delighted in the bloody staged hunts (*venationes*) conducted by ancient Romans for the entertainment of the assembled masses. Gladiatorial battles fought on colossal scales featured scores of animals pitted against human soldiers, slaves, or other animals. Often marking the return of victorious generals and emperors after foreign campaigns, exotic animals transported from far-flung lands were paraded through the streets before being herded into the amphitheater to be slaughtered. The carnage was truly incredible. Titus had five thousand wild animals killed on the opening day of the Colosseum in 80 CE. Twenty years later, Trajan dispatched eleven thousand beasts to celebrate his Dacian victory. Even as some classical writers lamented the gruesome spectacles as "the source of man's inhumanity to man," wealthy rulers continued to keep, exhibit, and hunt exotic animals for pleasure (Cartmill, 1993).

Medieval England saw the establishment of its own royal hunting traditions. Vast game parks were created for the exclusive use of the king and his courtiers, with social class stratification ensuring that poachers (usually peasants) were mercilessly persecuted, tortured, and even put to death. As a principle target, red deer (*Cervus* sp.) were often hunted with packs of dogs, the hunters following on horseback. Dogs were specifically bred for their prowess in pursuing certain types of game, as well as their ferocity, tenacity, size, and speed. Hunters often derived much pleasure in watching their dogs work and commented on the apparent gusto with which the dogs undertook their responsibilities. Because firearms at this point were primitive and unwieldy, the kill itself was carried out using swords, daggers, bows and arrows, dogs, or some combination thereof. For small game and birds, falcons or hawks might provide the *coup de grace*. Recreational hunting became the sole province of the elite ruling class, with development of its own lexicon and ceremony to tout the genteel manners of the participants.

As the medieval period gave way to the Middle Ages, a "civilizing process" changed social perceptions regarding behavior and the appropriate balance between pleasure and restraint (Elias & Dunning, 1986). With regard to sport, the pleasure manifest in the excitement of the hunt's kill became tempered with restraint in the form of increasingly complex rules. Putting stipulations and codes of behavior on sport hunting was designed to prolong the action, increasing anticipation and pleasurable tension before the kill. In the case of fox hunting, a sport originally justified through the need for vermin extermination, the kill itself became of secondary importance to the chase and ceremony associated with an organized hunt. As the fox-hunting nobility sought to distance itself from what became considered more crass expressions of pleasure, the kill was relegated to the dog pack, and shooting foxes during the hunt became forbidden. During this time, too, quiet murmurs of discontent were occasionally heard as dismay over cruel treatment of animals portended an emerging welfare attitude. Cruelty, however, would not go away quickly, as people found new and increasingly grisly ways to amuse themselves using animals.

If fox hunting was the domain of the landed gentry, pit sports found favor with all social classes. As the civilizing process deemed it increasingly inappropriate to settle disputes using physical violence against people, pit sports provided an acceptable outlet for daily frustrations, as well as spirited entertainment for visiting royalty, foreign ambassadors, or the unwashed masses. Bullbaiting, bearbaiting, cockfighting, and dogfighting pitted animals against other animals in mortal combat—all occurred with regularity across England and Europe, and later North America. "Baiting" involved tethering an animal to a stake and then allowing one or several dogs to attack the restrained creature. All manner of beasts were baited, including bears, bulls, badgers, apes, mules, and occasionally horses. For some time it was believed that bullbaiting was necessary to ensure flavorful, tender meat and was compulsory before a bull could be butchered (Thomas, 1983). Baiting sports became illegal in England in 1835.

As opposed to animals used for baiting, pit fighting contestants were often highly valued and vigorously prepared for battle. Roosters used for cockfighting were brought up on special diets and exercised to increase their stamina. Wattles and combs were cut off to reduce targets for opponents, and artificial spurs were strapped to their feet to increase the lethality of attacks. Spirited wagering accompanied matches, and flaring emotions occasionally spurred spectator riots. Gambling also accompanied organized dogfights. Breeds such as the Staffordshire bull terrier (and later, the American pit bull terrier), their aggressive tendencies rerouted from the baiting arena to the dogfighting pit, were trained by sacrificing smaller, docile dogs for practice and pampered lavishly by their sometimes poverty-stricken owners. Although these fights are largely outlawed today, organized underground networks continue to practice cockfighting and dogfighting, and large sums of money are often recovered from police raids, along with dead, injured, and mutilated animals.

The ritualized Spanish sport of bullfighting developed out of Roman gladiatorial battles, combined with the rites of Mithraism, an early religion of the Roman Empire. In mythology, the god Mithra's slaying of the bull-god brought forth great miracles, and Mithraism represented the secret of regeneration, assuring its devotees of immortality. When the spread of Christianity threatened Mithraism, Spain was able to successfully fuse the two religions, and the bull came to represent the devil. Some consider the pageant of bullfighting an art form. It remains a popular spectator sport in Spain and Mexico, invariably ending with the death of the bull. Crowds consider the matador's bravery, style, skill in controlling the bull, and ability to kill the bull efficiently—successful and popular matadors are treated like royalty and enjoy rock-star status. Gorings are not uncommon, and are occasionally deadly.

Other forms of animal-related sport are speed contests, where bloody violence is downplayed. Horse racing is an originally aristocratic pastime that became known as the "sport of kings." Steeplechasing events (horse racing over fences and water obstacles) provide spectator excitement in the form of dramatic spills over jumps and unceremoniously dumped jockeys. Pigeon racing is a relatively demure sport practiced in urban settings from rooftop coops. Dog racing evolved from the coursing of live (often fenced) hares by greyhounds and lurchers (greyhound crosses) and has become a sport unto itself, with live game replaced by artificial lures. In colder climes, sled dog racing grew out of the practical need to keep teams of hardy dogs for transportation across frozen expanses. Many of these sports exist today with only modest changes differentiating them from activities practiced in centuries past.

The Romantic period's changing ethic and outcry against cruelty, including the use of animals in some sports, might have been lauded as a sign of an enlightened public concern for animal pain and suffering. However, early changes in doctrine regarding proper treatment of animals arrived not out of concern for the animals themselves, but out of concern that mistreatment of animals would lead to depravity against men. This anthropocentric view was combined with various interpretations of the Old Testament, which ensured human dominion over all animals, but cautioned against unnecessary suffering. The resulting combination of religious piety and bourgeois sensibility led to the banning and social stigmatization of many previously popular animal sports. Hunting, however, remained largely outside these restrictions, with the separation between legitimate meat acquisition, predator or vermin eradication, and pleasurable entertainment used as justification.

The American West had its own evolution of thought regarding animal sports. Early settlers were amazed at the number and diversity of game animals, and greed brought on by the fur trade and apparent inexhaustibility of animal resources led to some mind-boggling excesses. The demise of the passenger pigeon and great buffalo herds are two of the most impressive examples of human myopia, much of it carried out in the name of sport. Theodore Roosevelt was an enthusiastic sportsman, killing thousands of animals in hunting trips across North America and Africa. He believed that shooting game was necessary "to cultivate that vigorous manliness" that comes from close contact with nature (Mighetto, 1991). At the same time, he was concerned that continued exploitation of resources could lead to wildlife shortages, a sentiment shared with a small but influential group of men of his time. He is credited in 1888 with cofounding the Boone and Crockett Club, one of the first conservation organizations. As such, the club was concerned not with animal welfare so much as worried that overhunting would leave future generations without adequate stocks of game species. Land for habitat was set aside in establishment of the first wildlife preserves to help ensure future sport-hunting opportunities.

During this time, too, the sport of rodeo emerged as a series of competitive activities associated with the cattle drives of the American South and Midwest. Cowboys bored by endless days in the saddle amused themselves by holding impromptu contests of skill and bravery, including bull and bronc riding, calf roping, and steer wrestling, among others. When the great cattle drives ended, rodeo continued on as an organized sport and still enjoys a wide audience across the United States and Canada.

Today, current moral concerns related to animals in sport lie with the welfare of animals themselves, a shift from the anthropocentric and largely utilitarian mindset. This change in climate around some controversial aspects of sport (e.g., rodeo calf roping, open field coursing, "canned hunts," "rattlesnake roundups") has lent encouragement to nonconsumptive (racing, catch-and-release fishing, flyball) and cooperative sports (dog agility, rally obedience, freestyle). Sport hunting is increasingly polarized, with a huge popular base of support, countered by a vocal opposition. People will always enjoy the competition, excitement, and culminating resolution of sport. It remains to be seen how the changing mores of society will ultimately influence humans' inclusion of animals as part of sporting entertainment.

Further Resources

Atyeo, D. (1979). *Blood and guts: Violence in sports.* New York: Paddington Press.

Cartmill, M. (1993). *A view to a death in the morning: Hunting and nature through history.* Cambridge, MA: Harvard University Press.

Elias, N., & Dunning, E. (1986). *Quest for excitement: Sport and leisure in the civilizing process.* Oxford, UK: Basil Blackwell.

Franklin, A. (1999). *Animals and modern cultures: A sociology of human-animal relations in modernity.* London: Sage.

Fulton, J. (1971). *Bullfighting.* New York: Dial Press.

Hummel, R. (1994). *Hunting and fishing for sport: Commerce, controversy, popular culture.* Bowling Green, OH: Bowling Green State University Popular Press.

Mighetto, L. (1991). *Wild animals and American environmental ethics.* Tucson: University of Arizona Press.

Thomas, K. (1983). *Man and the natural world: Changing attitudes in England 1500–1800.* London: Allen Lane.

Toynbee, J. M. C. (1973). *Animals in Roman life and art.* Baltimore: Johns Hopkins University Press.

For more information on organized dog sports, please visit:

http://www.akc.org/events [The American Kennel Club sponsors many dog-related sporting events]

http://www.iditarod.com [for information on the Iditarod sled dog race]

http://www.nadac.com [for information on dog agility competition, sponsored by the North American Dog Agility Council]

Cynthia J. McFadden

Trapping
See Hunting, Fishing, and Trapping

TV
See Media and Film

Urban Animals
Animals and Urbanism

Cities have been a major feature of the global landscape since the beginning of recorded history. Projections by urban studies specialists suggest that cities will continue to play a critical role in the future—as cultural hearths, as economic centers, and as crucibles of modernization and rapid social change. For many human beings, urban development heralds an increased array of educational and professional opportunities. However, the downsides are also significant, indeed even alarming, especially when considering urbanization's impact on the natural landscape and on many animal species. As long as industrialization remains, as it has been, the driving force behind the creation and expansion of modern cities, urbanization will continue to pose major challenges (both short- and long-term) to the sustainability of the physical environment and to the survival of many living beings—both human and animal alike.

Arenas of Compassion, Cruelty, and Contradictions

At the outset, a few points about cities should be noted. Cities are human creations—human constructions—that are connected intricately with the development of civilizations. Although the benefits of urbanization are many, cities' effects on animals and human-animal relationships can be of a decidedly mixed nature. The major part of this essay focuses on a specific category of city, that is, the modern industrial cities of the past 200 years or so—the cities of today. Such cities include, among others, the relatively wealthy, so-called First World cities, such as New York, Chicago, London, and Tokyo (these cities are increasingly called global cities because their communications and financial networks link them dynamically to broader systems around the world). In addition to First World cities, a number of other cities, sometimes termed developing or Third World cities, are also of prime importance. Cities such as Indonesia's Jakarta, India's Mumbai (formerly called Bombay), and Nigeria's Lagos are representative of the fast-growing, densely populated mega-cities that will typify urbanism of the twenty-first century.

At the core of the discussion is the following theme. Industrializing cities encapsulate a wealth of contradictions, particularly with respect to the treatment of animals. On the one hand, cities such as London and New York—among the first to industrialize in the early 1800s—gave birth to animal protection groups and to the humane movement in the nineteenth century. To this day, the premier cities of the world, particularly those in Western Europe, Canada, and the United States, are generally supportive of policies that safeguard the welfare of dogs, cats, and other individual domestic animals. Dog parks, well-stocked "pet" stores, and high-tech veterinary facilities are common features of contemporary urban landscapes, and many city-dwellers regard their companion animals as valued members of the family.

Yet, at the same time, the processes of industrialization are extremely problematic, as they have ushered in a whirlwind of practices that are damaging to the lives of countless animals. Urban growth is predicated to a large extent on the initial uprooting of ecosystems, along with the dislocation of numerous animals. Historically, the building of cities has meant that natural habitats are destroyed or seriously polluted. Over the past two centuries, some animal species have become extinct as a result of industrializing activities. Moreover, industrialism has produced a nightmarish scenario for the billions of animals raised in factory farms and killed en masse for their skins and feathers, as well as for the many who are held captive in modern scientific laboratories. Although the industrial facilities may be located geographically outside city limits, as they generally are these days, the facilities generate goods aimed in part for urban consumers and commercial markets. More troubling, the facilities are products of an industrializing philosophy—one that supports vast systems of production and exploits the most vulnerable living beings for the purposes of maximizing monetary profit. Large-scale industrializing activities remain of paramount concern for individuals who care about animals.

Preindustrial Cities—A Note on History

Although industrial cities embody the spirit of the modern era of the past two centuries or so, cities have long been a vital part of world civilizations. Some of the earliest cities, like those in the Mesopotamian valley of the Tigris and Euphrates rivers, date back to the ancient era, to more than 5,000 years ago. Other great historical cities originating in ancient times include Athens, Rome, Beijing, and Jerusalem. Defining attributes of ancient cities (and their civilizations) included systems of trade and organized economic activities; development of political and legal structures; and the use of written language to record monetary transactions, political events, and stories from religious and cultural traditions.

Etymologically, the English words "city" and "civilization" share the same Latin root. "*Civis*," or citizen, connotes membership in a society that is organized, developed, and complex. Key are the themes of complexity and organization. Conceptually, life in cities (urbanism) is often contrasted with life in the countryside (ruralism, or pastoralism), which is characterized by simplicity and proximity to nature. Although such a categorization is overly simplistic, it reveals a general understanding of cities—and civilizations—as places of sophistication, human ingenuity, and mastery over natural forces. Even though animals have lived with and alongside humans in most cities throughout time, a sense of separation between humans and animals may also seem a trait of urbanism. In historical terms, cities are generally thought to epitomize humankind's gradual transition from an earlier existence as hunters and gatherers within a state of nature to a human life defined increasingly by settlement in fixed communities amid complex human-designed systems and structures.

Some works of ancient literature are expressive of such a view. In the Mesopotamian *Epic of Gilgamesh* (c. 2000 BCE), one of ancient civilization's most important sources, one suggestive leitmotif is a sense of loss experienced by ancient humans as they moved from a condition of innocence within nature to the harsher confines of existence in the human-made world. For Enkidu, a leading character, the early stage of his life was characterized by a peaceful and protective relationship with the animals of the forest. Later, when Enkidu loses his innocence, he must leave his bucolic sanctuary to enter the human world, symbolized by the cities of Mesopotamia and defined, at times, by conquest and competition. Although the story's theme of "nature as paradise" is no doubt idealized, it does appear to allow a meaningful glimpse into the experience of ancient humans as they began to move into cities thousands of years ago.

When examining historical cities, it should be noted that records for the ancient era are much scarcer than they are for the modern centuries. Many artifacts and written documents have either been destroyed or been lost to the ravages of time. What remains (and has been found) is only a fraction of what existed initially. The evidence that does survive, however, suggests that the treatment of animals then, as now, varies to some extent—from culture to culture, from era to era, and even from individual to individual. Sources from ancient Greece and Rome, for instance, show that some people kept doves, small dogs, and other animals as pets. To what extent these animals were valued as companions, it is difficult to gauge. Evidence shows also that abuse of animals in Greece and Rome was, at times, absolutely heinous. Animals housed in urban markets for purposes of slaughter may have fared particularly badly. Writers as diverse as Pythagoras (c. 580 BCE–c. 500 BCE), Ovid (43 BCE–17 CE), and Plutarch (c. 46 CE–c. 120 CE) all complained of barbaric practices against these animals, and they urged their peers to consider vegetarianism.

Cruel practices were probably commonplace in rural areas as well. However, the limited conditions of city space, in combination with marketplace demands, may have intensified whatever callous tendencies already existed. One obvious difference between locales is that abuses to animals may have been more obvious and undeniable in dense urban areas than they had been in isolated rural pockets. Most disturbing, no doubt, was the practice of animal abuse as a genre of amusement. Coliseums, amphitheaters, and other large entertainment facilities were established in many towns and cities throughout the Roman Empire. Coliseum entertainment typically included hours of animals being forced to fight one another; humans fighting animals; and humans fighting one another. In a document from the first century CE, the Emperor Caesar Augustus boasts of how he sponsored gladiatorial games, as well as "beast hunts" involving the mass killing of thousands of wild animals. Although the practice of pitting animals against another for entertainment was not unique to Roman cities, violent gladiatorial games were for several centuries a distinguishing feature of Roman life.

When we survey cities throughout history, patterns similar to Rome immediately become apparent. Towns and cities, by definition, are hubs of human activity of all types, commerce being one of the most vital. Cities tend to attract large numbers of people, many searching for livelihoods and other opportunities. Although human behaviors in cities are not necessarily harsher or crueler to animals than those anywhere else, questions of scale are a factor. In a city with a substantial population, the number of affected animals will be much higher, particularly if the society is based on a meat-eating culture or uses and exploits animals in significant ways. In addition, the conditions of urban existence may render animal abuse more visible. Cruelties practiced in open markets, amphitheaters, and other highly trafficked areas will be harder to ignore (or to downplay) than those glimpsed in remote rural outposts. Although constant exposure to public forms of violence and neglect may desensitize some, if not most, individuals, the historical record shows also that some people will be affected, perhaps even traumatized, and some individuals may even protest. Writings from various ancient, medieval, and modern cities attest to the phenomenon whereby exposure to animal cruelty spurs some individuals to action. The genesis of the modern humane movement, to be discussed as this essay continues, is the most recent and momentous example.

An intensified nostalgia for the company of animals and the comforts of nature may also result from urbanism. Manifestations of this trend span the centuries, from the pastoral frescoes and country villas of wealthy Roman urbanites to the fondness for companion animals (and country houses) displayed today by cosmopolitan types. For the Middle Ages—the period between the ancient and modern eras—an emblem of this pattern is the Italian figure St. Francis of Assisi (c. 1181 CE–1226 CE). Francis, one of the most popular saints of the Middle Ages, was renowned for his respectful and kind attitude toward animals. Significantly, he and his immediate admirers belonged to an era of urbanization. The twelfth and thirteenth centuries in western Europe saw the rise of major cities such as London and Paris, as well as the proliferation of walled towns in many areas across the European continent. Stories of Saint Francis preaching to birds and fish may have evoked for medieval listeners and readers a sense of nostalgia for simpler, gentler times. His fans also would have found appealing the story of Francis shaking hands (and paws) with a wolf that was menacing the townspeople of Gubbio. Perhaps most telling is that Francis was the author of a poem titled "Brother Sun, Sister Moon," an enchanting mystical work in which the humble friar expressed his delight with the sun, skies, stars, wind, and flowers, as well as with all the living creatures of the planet.

Modern Industrial Cities

By the standards of the twenty-first century, the cities of the Middle Ages may seem relatively quaint. Industrial cities, as experienced by modern folks, are much larger, more dramatic, faster-paced venues—highly populated, visually spectacular, and invigorated continually by a whirlwind of social and technological changes. The first major cities to undergo industrialization included, among others, London and Paris in Europe and New York and Chicago in the young United States of the early 1800s. Countless smaller cities were also members of the early industrializing set.

Although all cities, past and present, share certain commonalities, the advent of industrialization has intensified key aspects of the urban experience. For instance, many cities have become more densely populated and congested than ever before. They have also become "taller," evolving skylines of soaring heights. Nineteenth-century innovations, which included electricity, elevators, and the cheap manufacture of steel, were effectively combined to produce high-rise buildings, wherein a single building can house hundreds, if not thousands, of individuals in aerial space, high above the ground.

When we envision the first industrial cities of the 1800s, Dickensian-inspired images of gritty factories and soot-filled skies may immediately come to mind. At its core, the Industrial Revolution was a revolution, or change, in how people worked. To this day, factories are not simply buildings packed with machines and workers. More fundamentally, they represent organized systems of production. Their purpose is to generate as many products as quickly, cheaply, and easily as possible with the end goal of maximizing monetary gain. Yet it is important to remember also that the buildings themselves may be less significant than the philosophy that underlies them. Profit is pivotal. Consideration for human beings, particularly workers, may be valued less than the goal of making money.

Animals tend to fare even worse. For literally billions of animals, industrial systems and philosophies have proved catastrophic, particularly with respect to agriculture. The gigantic, bloody slaughterhouses found in such cities as early twentieth-century Chicago and described in Upton Sinclair's bestseller *The Jungle* (1906) are emblematic of industrialism's darker side. Problematic also are generalized attitudes that commodify trees, plants, water, and virtually anything found in nature while reducing animals, who are clearly individualized sentient beings, to the status of mere physical property—to units of production, to resources that are exploitable.

Although the broader picture of the past two centuries is one largely detrimental to animals, there have been several intriguing developments to counter industrialism's crueler and more exploitative tendencies. Industrial cities of the nineteenth century also provided the setting, somewhat paradoxically, for the birth of the humane movement. It was in the bustling cities of London and New York that animal welfare organizations got their start. Among the first were England's Society for the Prevention of Cruelty to Animals, the SPCA, founded in 1824; and the American Society for the Prevention of Cruelty to

Animals, founded in New York in 1866. (In 1840 London's society gained the backing of Queen Victoria and added the prefix Royal to its title. Hence, to this day, it is known as the RSPCA.) In the decades following, humane societies opened throughout the United States, Canada, and western Europe. Some of the earliest included the Massachusetts Society for the Prevention of Cruelty to Animals (1868) based in Boston; the San Diego Humane Society (1880); and Canada's Toronto Humane Society (1887).

Underpinning the creation of those societies was a viewpoint—inspired in part by various Enlightenment thinkers—that hailed human compassion as a cardinal virtue. Children's literature and parenting manuals from the mid-1800s urged families to consider the needs of all living creatures—from bugs and butterflies to cats and dogs—and to treat them all with kindness. The ideas of English thinker John Locke (1632–1704) may have played a role in this new approach. Although best-known for his political treatises, Locke's many other writings also circulated broadly. In *Thoughts Concerning Education* (1692), Locke encouraged parents to use milder child-rearing methods and foster in children an abhorrence of cruelty. Echoes of Locke's message are strewn throughout the stories of *Youth's Penny Gazette*, a popular children's magazine, as well as in the parenting guidebooks of Lydia Maria Child and Lydia Sigourney and other U.S. and European writers.

It seems that the everyday realities of cities—increasingly crowded, increasingly in a hurry—gave renewed impetus to the humane message. In cities jam-packed with people and animals, scenes of cruelty were a fixture of daily life. Some people beat horses and donkeys to make them move faster. Vendors often mistreated cows, chickens, turtles, birds, and other forms of live merchandise. By all accounts, dogfighting and cockfighting were common amusements. In nineteenth-century London, New York, and other municipalities, abbatoirs, or slaughterhouses, were often located within cities' perimeters. The smells, sights, and sounds of those factories could be overwhelming, particularly on hot summer days. It appears that acts of cruelty in close quarters on a regular basis proved to be a source of dismay for the cities' more sensitive residents and propelled some to decisive action.

The case of New York illustrates this point. In the mid-1800s, New York was a rapidly growing city, teeming with masses of people and animals. Life was tough for many inhabitants, human and animal alike. Newspaper accounts and illustrations reveal that dogs, cats, chickens, and other animals roamed the streets. It was common practice at the time to harness dogs, as if they were mini-horses, to small wooden carts and wagons. The city's poorer folk—ragpickers, street vendors, the homeless—relied on canine labor, not voluntary on the dogs' part, to transport personal goods and trading wares. As of yet, there were no spay-and-neuter procedures to limit reproduction, and so animals not only multiplied exponentially, they were in seemingly endless supply to anyone who wished to exploit them for personal use. One municipal method of animal control, used in New York until 1894, was to gather dogs in large cages that were then plunged into the cold depths of the East River.

In 1866 a man named Henry Bergh founded the American Society for the Prevention of Cruelty to Animals (ASPCA) in Manhattan. Not only was the ASPCA the first animal protection organization in the United States but, as noted previously, its founding sparked the creation of similar groups across the country. A number of prominent urbanites, including newspaperman Horace Greeley and John Jacob Astor Jr., joined Bergh in his pioneering efforts. For Bergh, the cruelties of the street were simply unbearable. Determined to protect New York's animals from heinous abuses, he opened his organization, using the earlier English model, the RSPCA, as part of his inspiration.

Of immediate concern to Bergh were the city's horses. In the decades before the invention of the automobile, horses were used, as they had been for centuries, as a key transportation source. Thousands trod through the city's largely unpaved thoroughfares, pulling carriages, railroad cars, and cargo vehicles. Amid the hustle and bustle of the hyperactive commercial landscape, horses' missions had become even more difficult, as drivers expected them to move heavier loads at increasingly faster rates. Many exhausted horses worked in all types of weather, often without access to adequate food or fresh water. To make matters worse, many drivers beat their horses, often mercilessly, sometimes to the point of the horses' collapse or even death. Newspaper accounts from the time tell of hideous scenes of people overcrowding streetcars during rush hours and of horses struggling to pull them along.

Bergh soon became famous as the man who intervened to stop such horrific scenes of cruelty. Dressed in a dark suit and a top hat, a style fashionable for the time, the six-foot "gentle soul" strolled along the city's streets and admonished those who abused horses, dogs, cattle, livestock, and other animals. Bergh garnered the nickname the Great Meddler and attracted quite a bit of hoopla in his daily endeavors. Many New Yorkers, including many in the middle and upper classes, supported his efforts, and their backing helped to guarantee the ASPCA's success in its early years. Other New Yorkers, however, resented and ridiculed Bergh. His enemies included dogfight promoters such as the notorious Kit Burns. Bergh sparred regularly with P. T. Barnum, the flashy circusman, over Barnum's irresponsible use of animals. Businessmen involved in meat, dairy, and other animal-based industries also begrudged Bergh.

However, Bergh and his colleagues worked tirelessly in the city to advocate for policies to protect animals. They insisted on a humane ethic, encouraging New Yorkers to treat animals with respect and compassion. The initial successes of the ASPCA included the passage of humane legislation as well as humane education campaigns to encourage sensitivity to animals. One noteworthy law, passed in 1867, banned the practice of dogs pulling vendor carts unless the individuals involved had licenses. Another signature achievement was the introduction of large animal ambulances to assist collapsed horses, along with the construction of outdoor water fountains that accommodated horses, dogs, and other four-footed urban critters.

As the decades progressed and as the Industrial Revolution forged further ahead, motorized cars and trucks eventually replaced the horse-drawn vehicles of the earlier era. The horrible treatment of horses, which had resulted in a showdown on the streets between the forces of cruelty and those of compassion, had ceased to be as critical an issue. In its stead, other problems grew more pressing, and new challenges emerged, namely those involving the exploitative practices of the food, drug, and cosmetic industries. By the early twentieth century, innovations in electricity, housing, transportation, and medicine had ushered in a generally safer, more sanitized, and comfortable way of life for many humans. For city-dwellers, especially those in the upper and middle classes, the material benefits of industrialization had translated into significantly longer life spans with relatively easy access to hospitals, medical technologies, and an array of life-enhancing resources.

Some companion animals, primarily some dogs and some cats, have been beneficiaries as well. As the twentieth century proceeded, the ASPCA and other humane societies focused a portion of their efforts on upgrading the status and treatment of companion animals, lobbying successfully for stronger laws, for instance, to safeguard domestic animals from individual abusers. Improvements in veterinary care contributed also to a positive picture, as did the mass production of canned and boxed foods, along with other animal care items. More humane attitudes toward companion animals are found in many areas today, whether rural, urban, suburban, or exurban. Yet it is also clear that urbanism has played a leading role to foster these profound sociocultural changes with respect to animals and human-animal relationships. First-rate veterinary facilities, dog parks, animal day care centers, and fully stocked pet stores are common features of modern urban landscapes.

Yet the essential irony is that contradictions continue to abound. Some individuals may spend thousands of dollars for products and services for their own pets, but they may also eat meat, wear leather, and purchase other animal-based wares. Moreover, life in modern cities is predicated to some extent on extensive use of natural resources and the emission of pollution and gases destructive to the atmosphere.

This is the crux of the matter. Since the beginnings of recorded history, human beings have organized systems of living designed for the enrichment of human life. Cities have long been a dynamic part of civilizations—a manifestation of human empowerment and a magnet for individual ingenuity. However, the implications for animals and ecosystems have been of a decidedly mixed nature. Large-scale exploitation of animals and their habitats has generally accompanied the urban impulse.

With the advent of industrialization over two centuries ago, the stakes became significantly higher. Industrialization has intensified and accelerated urbanizing processes. Over about the last fifty years the world's population doubled from about 3 billion to 6 billion people—and it will most likely increase to 9 billion or more in the next fifty. The implications of these developments are enormous. (If even a fraction of those additional 3 billion are carnivorous, animals will be significantly impacted.) For all intents and purposes, industrialization has proved troublesome for animals, as well as for the world's more vulnerable human beings. The reality is that industrialism devalues some living beings at the expense of powerful, profit-seeking individuals and corporations. As long as industrialization remains the driving force of urbanization, and undoubtedly, it will, countless numbers of animals—indeed, whole species—are at risk, as are large swaths of natural land.

Demographic specialists project that large numbers of people in the twenty-first century will reside in the world's mega-cities. According to the Mega-Cities Project, cities such as Indonesia's Jakarta, Pakistan's Karachi, and Bangladesh's Dhaka will continue to grow larger and more congested. Already these cities, and many others, are seriously overcrowded and polluted, and many of their human inhabitants struggle with asthma and other breathing problems. Although there may be some hope for individual companion animals, particularly if humane movements gain a stronger footing in these areas, the broader picture is one that includes destruction of habitats, global warming, and increased exploitation of animals in factory farms and other industrial facilities. The implications are largely problematic—for humans and animals alike.

See also

Geography—*Animal Geographies*
Living with Animals

Further Resources

Adkins, L., & Adkins, R. A. (2004). *Handbook to life in ancient Rome*. New York: Facts on File.

Caves, R. W. (Ed.). (2005). *Encyclopedia of the city*. New York: Routledge.

Dracker, P. (2006, Spring). Regarding Henry. *ASPCA Animal Watch*. Retrieved March 30, 2006, from the Web site of the American Society for the Prevention of Cruelty to Animals, http://www.aspca.org/site/PageServer?pagename=about_history

Epic of Gilgamesh. (1972). (N. K. Sandars, Trans.). New York: Penguin Classics.

Grier, K. C. (1999). Childhood socialization and companion animals, United States, 1820–1870. *Society & Animals*, 7(2). Retrieved April 20, 2007, from http://www.psyeta.org/sa/sa7.2/sa7-2.html

Motavalli, J., et al. (2005). Cities of the future. *E, The Environmental Magazine, 16* (5), 26–36. Article related to the Mega-Cities Project. Retrieved March 30, 2006, from http://findarticles.com/p/articles/mi_m1594/is_5_16/ai_n15674915

Ness, I. (1999). *Encyclopedia of world cities*. Chicago and London: Fitzroy Dearborn.

Pace, M. (1995). *Friends of the animals: The story of Henry Bergh*. Ashland, KY: Jesse Stuart Foundation.

Christina Stern

Urban Animals
Red Foxes in Urban Areas

During the twentieth century, red foxes colonized cities in Australia, Europe, and North America. However, foxes are most abundant in British cities, where they have developed a unique relationship with urban residents. For many city dwellers, the sight of a fox sunning itself on their patio chair or waiting outside the back door to be fed is a very personal and highly valued interaction with an elusive carnivore that is rarely seen outside built-up areas because, although common, it is widely persecuted in the surrounding countryside.

Red foxes started to colonize British cities in the 1930s, when financial changes led to a boom in private housing. Much of this was a new style of accommodation—semi-detached houses, with a typical density of thirty to thirty-five houses per hectare. By British standards this was a low housing density, roughly a quarter of that seen hitherto. This change to low-density housing meant that during the 1930s British cities grew in size dramatically, often up to four-fold, and in the process created large areas of enclosed residential gardens. As these matured they provided both cover and food for foxes, which quickly learned to feed, den, and rear their cubs in this new habitat. By the 1940s foxes were common in the outer suburbs of many British cities and by the 1960s were being seen in the very center of large conurbations such as London. When house building resumed after World War II, rising land prices meant that houses were built with progressively smaller and smaller gardens. Since these are not as attractive to foxes, the suburbs built in the 1930s still hold the highest fox densities.

When they first appeared in British cities, foxes were considered a pest, and from the 1940s the government organized shoots in the London suburbs, killing large numbers of foxes each year. From 1970, the responsibility for urban fox control was passed to local authorities, but many of these ceased fox control in the 1970s and 1980s, largely in response to public pressure. Surveys showed that most urban residents by then were opposed to killing foxes, and anyway this had had no demonstrable impact on fox numbers. In the 1970s and 1980s urban foxes were also occasionally killed to supply trims for the international fur trade. Nowadays, very few foxes are deliberately killed in British cities, although many die on the roads.

Urban fox densities can be quite staggering. In northwest Bristol in the 1990s, spring fox densities rose to thirty-seven adults per square kilometer, producing twenty-one cubs per year; this was the highest fox density recorded anywhere in the world. One of the reasons fox densities were so high was the abundance of food, with one in ten households feeding the foxes regularly. This level of provisioning led to very large social groups, with an average of just over six adult foxes per group; one had at least ten adults. Such large fox groups had not previously been observed anywhere in the world and reflected the abundance of resources and lack of persecution.

When densities were high, the foxes were also very tolerant of humans and would often be seen out during the day, even trotting unconcernedly between people on busy pavements. The presence of very tame foxes also stimulated local residents to provide even more food, largely because they were enthralled to have such confiding animals approaching them to be fed. This in turn led to even higher fox densities, such that the complex social systems seen in the Bristol fox population were in no small part due to the interactions between the foxes and their human neighbors.

However, the whole relationship between the foxes and Bristol residents changed dramatically in 1994 following the arrival of sarcoptic mange, a progressive infection caused by a mite that leads to a loss of fur, physical deterioration, and ultimately death. This disease killed over 95 percent of Bristol's foxes in just two years, despite the efforts of many local people who tried to contain the disease by feeding their local foxes food laced with ivermectin, a drug used to kill a wide range of parasites.

Population recovery following this epizooty has been slow; a decade later fox numbers were still only 20 percent of those seen in the early 1990s. Coupled with the change in density was a very marked, and unexpected, change in behavior. The foxes became less dependent on people for food, even though the amount of food put out by local residents per fox actually increased (although the total amount decreased) because there were fewer foxes left to eat what was put out. The foxes now also breed less often in residential gardens, preferring patches of waste land and woodland, and are generally much more wary of people. Why these behavioral changes occurred is unclear.

Urban fox—countryside comes to town. Courtesy of Shutterstock.

Even when densities were very high, Bristol's foxes only caused a few, relatively minor, problems, most notably fouling gardens adjacent to breeding or lie-up sites. The maximum rate of predation on domestic animals (mainly rabbits, guinea pigs, and chickens) was just 0.2 pets per fox per year, and even this low level of loss could easily have been avoided with better housing. There is no evidence that urban foxes pose a significant disease risk to humans in Britain, and unlike domestic dogs, there has been no serious attack on a child by a wild fox.

It is hardly surprising, therefore, that most city dwellers welcome urban foxes. In a recent survey, householders across Britain were asked to score their attitudes to all the wild mammals found in their gardens on a scale of 1 to 10. Of the 3,409 people who expressed a view on foxes, 8.5 percent disliked them (score 1–3) and 25.8 percent had no strong views either way (score 4–7), but the overwhelming majority (65.7 percent) liked the foxes in their gardens (score 8–10).

However, even though foxhunting was an entirely rural activity, urban foxes featured prominently in the debate leading up to the ban on hunting foxes with dogs in England and Wales, which came into effect in February 2005 (foxhunting was banned slightly earlier in Scotland). Before the ban, and subsequently, there has been an extensive press campaign by the prohunting lobby portraying the fox as a major pest that has to be controlled. As part of this, there have been numerous claims that urban foxes hunt in packs, terrorize people and their dogs, spread disease, and pose a threat to unattended babies and small children. None of these claims are supported by the facts and, fortunately, so far this anti-fox campaign has done little to assuage the overwhelmingly positive attitudes to urban foxes.

Further Resources

Baker, P., Funk, S., Harris, S., Newman, T., Saunders, G., & White, P. (2004). The impact of human attitudes on the social and spatial organisation of urban foxes (*Vulpes vulpes*) before and after an outbreak of sarcoptic mange. In W. W. Shaw, L. K. Harris, & L. Vandruff (Eds.), *Proceedings of the 4th international symposium on urban wildlife conservation* (pp. 153–63). Tucson, AZ: University of Arizona Press.

Baker, P., Funk, S. M., Harris, S., & White, P. C. L. (2000). Flexible spatial organization of urban foxes, *Vulpes vulpes,* before and during an outbreak of sarcoptic mange. *Animal Behaviour, 59,* 127–46.

Baker, P., Newman, T., & Harris, S. (2001). Bristol's foxes—40 years of change. *British Wildlife, 12,* 411–17.

Baker, P., Robertson, C. P. J., Funk, S. M., & Harris, S. (1998). Potential fitness benefits of group living in the red fox (*Vulpes vulpes*). *Animal Behaviour, 56,* 1411–24.

Harris, S. (1981). An estimation of the number of foxes (*Vulpes vulpes*) in the city of Bristol, and some possible factors affecting their distribution. *Journal of Applied Ecology, 18,* 455–65.

Harris, S., & Baker, P. (2001). *Urban foxes.* Stowmarket, Suffolk: Whittet Books.

Harris, S., & Rayner, J. M. V. (1986). Urban fox (*Vulpes vulpes*) population estimates and habitat requirements in several British cities. *Journal of Animal Ecology, 55,* 575–91.

Smith, G. C., & Harris, S. (1991). Rabies in urban foxes (*Vulpes vulpes*) in Britain: the use of a spatial stochastic simulation model to examine the pattern of spread and evaluate the efficacy of different control régimes. *Philosophical Transactions of the Royal Society of London Series B, 334,* 459–79.

Stephen Harris and Philip Baker

Urban Animals
Wildlife in Urban Areas: A Personal Essay

Stories told at my childhood dinner table often were stories of our dogs and pet mice, of our cockatiels and my grandfather's racehorses. It was clear, as I listened to these stories, that our animals were sentient creatures that thought about their circumstances and set out to accomplish whatever it was they might have been thinking about. Beyond the dinner table and the house, outside the picture windows, in the woods edging the suburbs, along the stretch of forest at the end of the street and hiding near the creek, lived the wild animals: crow, squirrel, turtle, snake, opossum, raccoon, fox. These creatures, like our companion animals, also had intentions and desires—to eat, to fly, to raise babies, to run, to slither, to rest alone in deep grass. It seemed a simple and undeniable fact of human existence that when a dog—or a squirrel or a crow or a turtle—"spoke," people were to listen. The most direct way of answering an animal involved asking several short questions: *What might the dog want? What is the bird trying to say? Does the squirrel need this now?* This was how, in the way that time passes quietly and solidly, I came to the understanding that though animals did not need exactly the same things as did I, or that animals did not think about the same things as did I, there was nevertheless a continuity between us, a place where, with imagination and empathy on my part, we could meet. Which was, and is, to say, really, that a relationship between a person and a nonhuman animal is not terribly different from a relationship between two people: No one person ever truly feels and thinks and experiences life in the exact same way as another person. We must imagine and empathize our way into and through the complications and the joys of a relationship.

The years ticked on, and by the time I walked into that first college-level zoology class my belief that animals have emotions and thoughts was as firmly a part of me as my own skin. I always have been puzzled by the indisputable fact that though as humans we spend our childhoods in a world dripping with the lessons of nature as evidenced by the lives of animals—animals in picture books, animals wild, animals stuffed and decorative, companion animals, literary animals who become our first literature and philosophy professors and who introduce to us the ideas of ethics and morality and friendship—once we venture out into the larger world we are told it's all been a bunch of rubbish. Lies. A sham. *Animal feelings!?* exclaims society. . . . *They don't feel attached or lonely or sad or happy*. Put away your childish thoughts. Grow up, already.

I am parked, with my three-year-old daughter, alongside a golf course that is behind our local Bed, Bath, and Beyond. The golf course, surrounded by thin strips of wooded areas, was a part of the landscape long before the strip malls and highways, and now the course is a green magnet for the urban animals that survive—sometimes thrive—amidst the bustle and hustle of suburban Washington, DC. It is January in the mid-Atlantic, and every early evening on this golf course, between the cool fall and winter months of October through March, thousands upon thousands of crows are drawn to these wide swaths of grass and trees behind Bed, Bath, and Beyond to eat and socialize till dusk, when they fly away to retire for the night in their winter roost in brittle and bare trees along the six-lane highway. Theirs is a roost not far from apartments and restaurants, Trader Joes, the bakery, and every other imaginable type of store.

But for the next twenty or so minutes before the crows depart, I sit my little girl, Lucienne, in my lap and open the window for her to hear the voices of crows. Not that she hasn't heard them all before, all the lesser-heard throaty grunts and rattles, as well as the predictable "caw, cawww, cawwing." In fact, the word "crow" was—when my daughter was still crawling—her first word. Forget "mama"—*crow*! It should not have surprised me, having strolled my infant around the neighborhood as the crows flew and hopped along beside us each morning that spring, summer, and fall of her first year on earth. The birds—wild birds accustomed to my feeding them as we walked—were big and black and easy for Lucienne's developing eyes to see. Loud and busy and urgent and whimsical in their calling, crows made Lucienne smile.

Now in the car with me, she grabs the steering wheel and pretends to drive. This holds her attention for a few minutes and gives me a chance to focus on the few dozen crows seemingly content playing in the puffs of winter snow left melting on the golf course. This is when, quite simultaneously, a great horned owl—one of crow's biggest predators—drops from a tree and soars toward the crows in the snow, while two red foxes bound like little red fires from the woods. "An owl . . . foxes . . . look!" I yell to Lucienne, who is keen to see a fox. She has heard stories about foxes from her ten-year-old sister, Madeleine, who, lucky girl, has spotted several in the Washington, DC, suburbs.

Lucienne and I watch crows leap from snow into sky. Instantly the air thickens with thousands of screaming crows, crows mad, crows circling and darting and diving. Several dozen crows chase the owl to a lone tree in the middle of the golf course, where the owl, encircled by families of vexed crows, huddles on a wide branch to fend for itself. My daughter can see better the foxes, who use the uproar to their advantage and smuggle themselves closer in to chase those crows who, still lollygagging in the snow, obviously have decided that chasing away the owl just wasn't their job today. One fox coming around a hill; the other fox holding still, then speeding out across these plains of the suburbs. But their prey is fast; and soon the trees are beaded with crows. The foxes give up, find each other, and retreat, side by side, into the woods. All of this happens in a matter of mere minutes behind the Bed, Bath, and Beyond, which gives new meaning to the word "beyond."

Lucienne, beside herself with having seen her first fox, demands to see them again and again. How could they leave, she wants to know, when she desires them to stay. We are left with the sounds of traffic, the slamming of car doors, the voices of people heading in and out of stores, people in the city who've no idea of the wild magic just stirred up behind Bed, Bath, and Beyond. When my daughter is older it is likely we will be shopping in this area. Though I will remind her of what she has just witnessed, I have a sense her body will not have forgotten these earliest years of her life, a life that so far has been filled with the language, playfulness, and lives of crows and foxes and owls in the city.

The news: A press release about cities and urbanization, from the United Nations Population Division, released March 24, 2004, reports: "Forty-eight percent of the world's population lived in urban areas in 2003. It is projected to exceed the 50 percent mark by 2007, thus marking the first time in history that the world will have more urban residents than rural residents. The proportion of the world population that is urban is expected to rise to 61 percent by 2030."

A "Fund for Animals" press release reports: "Every day people and animals are forced into closer contact. A farm is turned into a housing development. A few acres of woods become an industrial park. Wildlife habitat gives way to urban sprawl. But to our surprise, many of the former residents don't run away. They adapt with great resourcefulness to their new circumstances. The result is a rising number of conflicts between people and wildlife."

A local suburban Maryland newspaper, the Bethesda Gazette, reports: "Several coyote sightings throughout the Olney Oaks community have left many residents fearful. . . . At the annual homeowner's association meeting . . . the topic of coyotes came up and a lot of people raised their hands with sightings or concerns. . . ."

One day a woman in my neighborhood sights a bird flying above her. She is walking along my street, which is set on a ridge above the Potomac River, in a dense urban area outside of Washington, D.C. The woman stops in front of my cottage and asks me, "What kind of bird is that flying over us?"

"It's a vulture," I tell her.

"Not an eagle, are you sure it's not an eagle?"

I take a second, longer look. "No, it's a vulture."

"How do you know?"

"The shape of its wings, the way it flies."

"*Not an eagle, then?*"

"No, a vulture."

"*Well, I don't care about that.*"

On a quiet weekday afternoon, I head into the woods by a creek where Madeleine saw one of her foxes. It is winter in our old neighborhood along the Potomac River, and without all the dense underbrush and vines it can seem, peering through the forest, that the trees are like people standing alone in the cold, carrying the sky and the clouds on their wide-shouldered branches. When I stand still I hear what I call the breathing of trees, which is the sound of trees when wind blows through them. When I move, there is the clamor of fallen leaves that break beneath my footsteps—noise that undoubtedly the fox, sleeping away the lazy afternoon in its den, likely hears, however faintly. Suddenly the breathing forest is punctuated with . . . could it be the call of a blue jay or a red-tailed hawk? I squint into the canopy of the forest bathed in bold winter sun. At the last second, as the bird is flying out of the forest and toward the river, I see it is a red-tailed. During my walk, I venture out of the woods toward the yard of neighbors who every year have a Christmas Party. I go to this yard because during this year's party Madeleine and many others stepped into the night for a glimpse of a wild Eastern screech owl that was living in a tree there. This little owl, at Christmas time: the best present my daughter received.

Not surprisingly, I do not spot the owl, or the fox, and so head over the pedestrian bridge that crosses a high-speed parkway in order to get to the banks of the Potomac River, where, in the coming spring, painted turtles resting on fallen trees will sun themselves as cars speed into and out of Washington, D.C. In these woods—along the city's river—live the coyotes, the raccoons, the deer, the opossums, mice, rats, bats, woodpeckers, crows, vultures, eagles, foxes, and multitudes of others. These are the urban residents who've not run away. Still, their presence does not guarantee a glimpse of them, even in the stark and bare winter forest.

It is the great fallacy about urban wildlife: that the land is barren of creatures because humans see little but ourselves in our developed environments. Our relationship with, and our protection of, urban wildlife must be nurtured by the wild imaginations and spirited empathy we felt as children for the animals living so close to us. Do not be fooled by your eyes; listen to your heart. For what we actually see—in the forest, in a vacant lot, in a backyard—is, as in most situations in life, only a small fraction of reality.

At the end of the day, it might make sense, for clarity's sake, to know if the bird flying over your neighborhood was indeed a vulture or an eagle. But must the fact of mere identity figure into how much we feel, or care? Isn't it more that above you a bird soared on its six-foot wingspan and crossed into the mystery of your questions and thoughts? Isn't it more that—at that moment, no matter how old or young you are, and when the sky was just a certain way in your eyes—a bird became a part of you?

Lisa Couturier

■ Veterinarians.

See Applied Anthrozoology and Veterinary Practice

Zoos and Aquariums
Amphibians and Zookeepers

A growing amount of evidence (mostly anecdotal) indicates that many low-vertebrates may be able to recognize their human caretakers and may respond differently to different persons. Although the scientific literature on similar topics is rapidly increasing (especially concerning reptile/human relationships), most of the scientists are still skeptical. Any behavioral changes in low-vertebrates species due to interaction with their keepers are difficult to explain with uncritical anthropomorphism. Low-vertebrate/human interaction as well as human and low-vertebrate reciprocal responses represent a complex and rich issue deserving further study.

When dealing with human/low-vertebrate interactions, the first question in anthropozoological terms is whether an animal subject (in this case an amphibian) is able to recognize a given human person. In fact, only after having recognized with a good degree of certainty that the compound stimulus set represented by a human figure is distinguishable by the animal partner in its environment can we speculate about an "affective bond" possibly established between the amphibian and the human subjects.

Amphibian social behaviors are difficult to interpret by ethologists and professionals of animal behavior. In fact, it is hard for humans to recognize "affectionate" or affiliative behaviors expressed by amphibians in the course of intra- and/or interspecific social interactions. However, the richness and complexity of their social behavior are somehow predictive of their capability to establish some kind of bond with those humans regularly spending time with them.

Although among some amphibian species many conspecifics may be cohabitant in the same natural site, these animals are reportedly "lonely" and "asocial" outside the reproductive period. Starting from the 1980s, a proliferating number of ethological studies on amphibian reproduction (especially performed on anurans) indicated that, among conspecifics, relationships may be complex and such relationships include at least sex and species recognition. Among frogs, vocalizations are an important element of the social behavioral pattern. During the reproductive season, male frogs aggregate in chorusing behavior to attract females. Social facilitation stimulates calling activity, one or more males calling inducing other individuals to call, leading to a self-perpetuating chorus. Chorusing behavior enhances females' attraction to males, which likely use the calling of other individuals as a cue to determine when to exhibit. Some anuran species display a complex vocal repertoire during social interactions. For example, in the course of aggressive interactions, male pickerel frogs (*Rana palustris*) vocalize at least three call types: an advertisement call and two additional calls ("snicker" and "growl"). Analogously, when a male green climbing mantella (*Mantella laevigata*) sees a female approaching, he changes his vocalizations from the louder (two-note) advertisement call to the softer (single-note) courtship call.

Among amphibians, sex recognition is presumably performed by means of visual and behavioral cues as well as of chemical (pheromonal) cues. Laboratory studies on the genera *Triturus* and *Cynops* indicate that the abdominal gland in the newts' cloaca is the source of a pheromone that attracts females by activation of their olfactory mucosa.

Most amphibian species do not provide parental care. However, these animals are the only group of vertebrates (with the exception of the teleost fishes) that exhibits all four forms of parental care, namely no care, female care, male care, and biparental care. In those amphibians that take care of their offspring, parental contributions are extremely diverse, and may include "affectionate" behaviors (egg guarding; transport of tadpoles orally, in the stomach, or on adults' bodies; or live bearing, namely providing nutrition to the developing embryos by the "uterine milk"). For example, poison dart frogs, *Dendrobates pumilio,* avoid laying their eggs in ponds and streams. Instead, the eggs develop on land until the tadpoles are ready to hatch. Then the mother carries the tadpoles on her back to water-filled bromeliads (epiphytic plants) in the trees. The tadpoles complete their development in these tiny, predator-free pools, and the mother feeds them with unfertilized eggs. Female red-backed salamanders (*Plethodon cinereus*) provide protection for juveniles by defending territories from cannibalistic intruders or by feeding on large invertebrates that are predators of their offspring. In captivity these mothers show kin discrimination, being able to discriminate their offspring from unrelated neonates. However, as for reptiles and other low-vertebrates, a variety of elements of the complex social behavioral patterns typically displayed by many mammalian species and interpreted by humans as expression of affection seem largely absent. From the human's point of view, low-vertebrates' social behavioral repertoire is apparently poor and less complex than that exhibited by mammals. In the amphibian/human interaction (and more in general in low-vertebrate/human relationship), any behavioral response due to individual recognition and bond is likely to be extremely subtle and not easily recognizable by their caretakers, and seemingly these mainly include species-specific components of antipredator and avoidance responses. Amphibians perceive the surrounding environment mainly by detecting vibration and chemical cues, sensory abilities reportedly reduced in humans. Moreover, acoustic signals as well as postures displayed by amphibians in the course of intra and/or interspecific social interactions rarely overlap with familiar mammalian behaviors (e.g., those expressed by dogs and cats, the most common pet animals) and are generally difficult to interpret. Probably responses such as avoidance and flight reaction might represent useful measures to assess their responses to a familiar or unfamiliar caretaker.

See also

Zoos and Aquariums—*Reptiles and Zookeepers*

Further Resources

Alleva, E., & Scattoni, M. L. (2004). Introductory keynote. The state of the art in animal experimentation. *Annali Istituto Superiore di Sanità, 40,* 151–55. [Website Istituto Superiore di Sanità: http://www.iss.it/engl/index.html]

Davis, H., & Balfour, D. (Eds.). (1992). *The inevitable bond: Examining scientist-animal interactions.* Cambridge, UK: Cambridge University Press.

Frost, D. (2002). Reptiles. In N. Eldredge (Ed.), *Life on Earth: An encyclopedia of biodiversity, ecology, and evolution.* Santa Barbara, CA: ABC-CLIO.

Visalberghi, E., & Alleva, E. (1993). Book review of: *The inevitable bond: Examining scientist-animal interactions. The Quarterly Journal of Experimental Psychology, 46B,* 222–24.

Enrico Alleva and Nadia Francia

Zoos and Aquariums
Animal Welfare, Animal Rights, and Conservation at Zoos

The keeping of animals in zoos has spurred ethical debate at least since the birth of public zoos in the nineteenth century. As a result, zoos have tried to redefine themselves, in particular over the last decades. The pictures on stamps of wild-caught animals had to be replaced by ones of conservation centers that keep ambassadors of their species in naturalistic enclosures. However, the ethical controversy surrounding zoos has not disappeared—it has even intensified in some ways, and the key words in this discussion are animal welfare, animal rights, and species conservation. In terms of human-animal relationships, zoo advocates state that zoos raise respect for the animals shown and their relatives in the wild. Critics of zoos object that the philosophy of zoos is based upon the idea that humans may exploit nonhuman animals against their own interests.

Animal Welfare inside Zoo Enclosures

The major reason for zoos being ethically controversial is related to concern for the welfare of animals living in zoos. Until a few decades ago breeding was very limited in zoos, and most animals were chased and captured in the wild to start or replenish exotic collections. Parental bonds were often broken and parents even killed in order to get hold of their young ones, who were considered easier to handle and transport over long distances and presumed to live longer in captivity. If they arrived alive in zoos, the animals had to adapt to their new captive environment in order to survive. Through trial and error, zoos have built up experience over many decades in terms of diets, climatological requirements, prevention and treatment of diseases, social needs, breeding, and raising young ones, allowing natural behavior and offering mental stimulation. Since the 1970s and 1980s international wildlife regulations have severely limited the wildlife trade, and thus zoos were forced to rely more and more on captive breeding for their existence. Zoos saw themselves confronted with the difficulties of managing relatively small captive populations. Breeding programs were developed in order to avoid inbreeding and to maintain maximal genetic variation by exchanging animals among zoos.

During the last decades zoos have given increased attention to the psychological welfare needs of animals living in their care. The traditional welfare view of animals merely needing clean enclosures and daily rates of prepared food turned out to be too simplistic. The boredom caused by lack of mental stimulation in monotonous enclosures, the stress due to inescapable elements (such as noisy visitors or aggressive animals of the same species), and the frustration caused by the lack of essential aspects (e.g., substrate for digging or building nests) may lead to various abnormal behaviors. Well known are the stereotypical behaviors of big cats pacing to and fro in their enclosure, elephants weaving from one forepaw onto the other, and bears bobbing their heads up and down or swimming fixed rounds (polar bears). It has been suggested that such stereotypies (frequent mechanical repetition) may increase the release of opiates in the brain and thus have an analgesic effect, but this remains subject to debate. Stereotypies nevertheless are associated with trying to cope with poor welfare conditions that are otherwise beyond the animal's control. Other abnormal behaviors that have been found in zoos include repeatedly regurgitating and reingesting food, hyperaggression, and automutilation. In some cases this has resulted in very harmful consequences—primates have been seen to gnaw entire body parts away, and captive dolphins have bumped their heads against the edge of the pool until they died. However, reactions to poor welfare conditions do not need to be that extreme and may for example result in less affiliative behavior or increased passivity. The apathy of some zoo animals may be explained as a state of learned helplessness due to their captive surroundings being inescapable.

Behavioral research indicates that a rich and stimulating environment is of fundamental importance for the psychological welfare of at least many animals. Experiments demonstrate that animals prefer to work for their food instead of having it served by a caregiver. Animals need a feeling of control, of living their own lives, in order to flourish. Therefore, several zoo enclosures have become more spacious and complex, larger social groups have been formed, and behavioral enrichment schedules have been introduced. There is no doubt that enrichment efforts have resulted in considerable improvement for many animals. There is a huge difference between the welfare of a lonely chimpanzee living in a small, dark, monotonous cage with merely a shelf for sleeping and that of a social group of twenty chimpanzees that share a grassy island enclosure with trees for climbing; branches with fresh leaves for feeding; hills for running, playing, and hiding; ropes for swinging; an artificial termite mound for fishing sticky foods with twigs; and the opportunity to forage for nuts, seeds, and fruits that have been scattered throughout the enclosure.

However, though enrichment can enhance the welfare of animals living in zoos, the major question remains whether this really results in a positive welfare situation, in the leading of a satisfying life. Some zoos evaluate whether enrichment has a positive impact, but where is the evaluation of the animal's overall welfare situation? Is this impossible, or are zoos not interested in an overall analysis because they do not want to put the keeping of particular species—and ultimately their own existence—into question?

Apart from this fundamental question, zoos have been criticized for not going far enough in their welfare efforts. Zoos might, for example, allow for a larger degree of autonomy by offering animals the choice to retreat from visitors and thus to have some privacy. But in many zoos animals may not even choose whether they want to stay outdoors or indoors, unless when the indoor area can be viewed by visitors as well. Furthermore, many zoos only want to allow enrichment as far as everything looks very naturalistic, even when they know most animals in their care will never be brought to the wild. For example, captive great apes may like glancing through magazines, watching television, or playing computer games. Though it has been said that these enrichment devices might be more helpful to stimulate their minds and relieve boredom than merely living on grassy areas, most zoos withhold such experiences from the animals in their care because otherwise their captive condition would look too unnatural.

It may also be observed that welfare improvements are compromised because of zoos still wanting to show too many species and in particular too many large animals. Have modern zoos become enriched stamp collections? The number of species shown may have decreased, but is it necessary to show a large variety of, for example, big cats (such as tigers, lions, leopards, and jaguars), great apes (like chimpanzees, gorillas, and orangutans), and birds of prey (e.g., owls, falcons, vultures, buzzards, condors, and eagles) in a single zoo? Some researchers believe that an animal's welfare may benefit from showing a smaller selection of species.

Besides this, it could be noted that zoos should be selective in the sense of not keeping animals that are clearly not faring well in captivity. Research by zoologists Ross Club and Georgia Mason (Oxford University) has demonstrated that in particular animals that roam over large areas in the wild—like polar bears—are prone to welfare problems in captivity, including high infant mortality and an increased frequency of stereotypic behavior. It appears that the prevention of natural behavior results in stress and frustration. We take it for granted that blue whales cannot be kept in zoos, but should a similar question be asked about animals like killer whales, dolphins, polar bears, and elephants? Interestingly, the Universities Federation for Animal Welfare (UFAW) has suggested that an enclosure may be made more suitable by keeping smaller animals. For example, it may be wise to rearrange an enclosure for polar bears—whose typical enclosure size is about one-millionth of its minimum home-range size—into one with many climbing opportunities for a small primate species, such as a social group of lion tamarins.

Animal Welfare beyond Zoo Enclosures

Welfare concerns are not limited to the impact of zoo enclosure design. Zoos exchange animals for breeding purposes and to maintain genetic variation. But what is the welfare impact of transferring an animal (repeatedly) to a new physical and social environment in another zoo? What are the consequences for the group that remains behind? What about animals that develop strong and enduring social bonds, such as elephants and great apes? In the wild, animals may also move to another group, but animals in zoos have no choice about whether and when to leave and about their destination.

Concern has also been expressed about so-called surplus animals in zoos. What happens to animals that are considered no longer useful for the zoo (e.g., because they have delivered a sufficient number of young ones according to the captive breeding program)? Zoos provide very little information about these situations, but they have been criticized for putting surplus animals in small, dark, and monotonous behind-the-scenes enclosures or sending them to substandard places, like roadside zoos, circuses, and hunting ranches.

Many zoo administrators favor the idea of killing healthy "surplus" animals (see entry, *The Great Ape Project*). It has been argued that this may benefit captive breeding programs for endangered species by freeing up space and financial resources. It is also said that animals should be able to show as wide a range of natural behavior as possible and that this includes the regular having of young, which should be killed when reaching weaning age. Zoos have been reproached for being hypocritical by organizing on the one hand baby animal parties and contests to find original names for newborns and on the other hand pleading against so-called sentimentality and defending the killing of healthy animals that are considered surplus. Such a "breed-and-kill" policy may be ethically questionable, but it may be economically highly interesting because many visitors are strongly attracted by the presence of baby animals. Those who disagree with such killings refer to the welfare interests of the animals that are killed. They state that zoos have a "cradle-to-the-grave" responsibility for all animals in their care—that zoos should not breed animals if they cannot offer all of them at the least reasonably enriched welfare conditions and a natural lifespan.

Animal Rights

Some ethical positions state that it does not suffice to strive for humane and enriched welfare conditions for animals living in zoos. The level of animal welfare that may be offered in zoos and the keeping of wild animals in captivity themselves are questioned. Animal rights views hold that the interests of animals need to be protected by the granting of basic rights. It is said that these include not only a right to be free of pain and a right to live a natural lifespan, but also a right to freedom or liberty. Though zoos seek to create naturalistic enclosures and wild habitats have been called "mega-zoos," there nevertheless remains a huge difference between the best zoo enclosures and animal habitats in the wild. Animals in the wild have far more space and live in much more complex environments, which allow them more opportunities for living their own lives. No zoo can recreate the complexity and richness of the wild and offer similar rich experiences to, for example, captive dolphins, tigers, orangutans, elephants, eagles, and otters as what is possible for their relatives in the wild in terms of swimming, diving, wandering, leaping, flying, climbing, feeding, and chasing. Moreover, wild animals live in habitats to which they have adapted over millions of years.

However, animal rights advocates see themselves also confronted with a number of challenging ethical questions. Life in the wild may at times be very hard in terms of, for example, food shortages, diseases, and predation. Zoos say that animals in zoos are well fed, receive medial attention, and are not attacked by predators. Animal rights proponents counter that the animals face other challenges, such as stress due to inescapable factors like visitors. And how far does it help animals in the wild to put a limited number of animals in zoos? Would it be preferable to spend resources that are currently going to animals living in zoos on their wild relatives? For instance, would it be desirable to intervene on behalf of animals, with the inclusion of providing food and medical support when necessary and protecting animals preyed upon against predators?

Destruction by humans is imposing enormous stress upon animals, and many species face the risk of vanishing entirely in the wild. Some animal advocates have stated that it would be better for some animals to end their lives freely in the wild—and thus for their species to disappear—rather than being kept as captives in zoos. But is this indeed what serves the animal's interests in the best way? Is not a captive life in an enriched zoo enclosure to be preferred above extermination in the wild? Or is this a black-and-white picture—does the creation of well-protected areas in the wild offer an alternative solution?

Also, if the keeping of animals in captivity is *fundamentally* wrong, should we not stop the keeping of companion animals as well? Or is there a difference between zoos and the keeping of companion animals in terms of, for example, many dogs and cats having more autonomy in captivity and leading happier lives than they would in the wild, a poor option because of the domestication process? Would we become upset by the keeping of dogs and cats in zoo enclosures? But should we redirect the billions of dollars currently spent for companion animals into wildlife conservation?

Conservation

According to zoologist Edward Wilson, millions of species risk disappearing from the wild. The people who run zoos often acknowledge that conservation in the wild (or *in situ* conservation) is to be preferred above zoo conservation (or *ex situ* conservation), but add that they may offer a last resort to many species that otherwise would indefinitely disappear. Zoo professionals bring up numbers that range around a potential of 1,000 to 2,000 species that might be saved by them. Species mentioned by zoos as having profited from captive breeding include the Arabian oryx, the California condor, golden lion tamarins, and black-footed ferrets. However, zoo conservation faces several inherent disadvantages. Animals in zoos have far less experience and knowledge as compared with their wild relatives. This results in their (re-)introduction in the wild being a very complicated and risky process, which may result in high mortality figures. Very few reintroduction programs are successful. Benjamin Beck of the AZA's (Association of Zoos and Aquariums, formerly the American Zoo and Aquarium Association) Reintroduction Advisory Group wrote in 1995 that only 11 percent of 145 reintroduction projects were successful. Another major disadvantage is the high cost of operating zoos. Modern zoos put millions of dollars in the construction of enclosures, and also caring for and reintroducing animals is extremely expensive. For these reasons, it is more desirable to conserve species in the wild. Where necessary, animals might be translocated to a safer habitat. Translocations turn out to be more successful (around 75 percent) and cheaper than reintroduction programs. However, this requires that at least sufficient habitat remains that can be effectively protected and that the population is still a viable one.

Questions may be raised about the species zoos select for keeping. Ulysses Seal (Conservation Breeding Specialist Group) wrote in 1991 that only 5–10 percent of the space available in zoos participating in the ISIS (International Species Information System) is allocated to endangered species. One might expect zoos to try to keep as many endangered species as possible—for example by focusing on smaller, endangered species. However, zoos tend to keep in particular mammals and among these especially large, charismatic animals, such as hugely popular animals including elephants, western lowland gorillas, and bottle-nosed dolphins. It is questionable that these animals are most in need of captive breeding programs—bottle-nosed dolphins are not considered endangered, and there are still several tens of thousands of elephants and gorillas, which is much more than many other species. Furthermore, one may wonder whether it is even necessary or desirable to set up captive breeding programs for (critically) endangered species, which count only very limited numbers in the wild (say, fewer than 2,000 individuals). For example, zoologist George Schaller (Wildlife Conservation Society) has expressed criticism about keeping giant pandas in captivity and argues instead that conservation efforts should focus on protecting giant pandas in the wild. And there seems to exist no support for setting up a breeding program for the critically endangered mountain gorillas in zoos, even though these great apes count only a few hundred individuals in the wild.

Zoos point out that they are visited by more than 600 million people each year. They state that they raise conservation awareness among visitors and that they are important fundraisers for supporting conservation projects in the wild. An excellent example of conservation efforts by a zoo is the Bronx Zoo, whose Wildlife Conservation Society has more than 270 conservation projects around the world. Zoo critics ask where the research is that shows the educational impact of zoos and also add that the billions of dollars going to zoos should instead be used entirely for conservation in the wild. However, the question remains how important zoos are in order to raise conservation funds—how much money would current zoo visitors be prepared to spend on wildlife conservation if no zoos existed?

Zoos versus Sanctuaries?

Most zoos take it for granted that species have far more value than individuals and that the latter are subsidiary to the former. But this view has been disputed. The philosopher Dale Jamieson at New York University, for example, indicates that not species, but only individuals, are organisms: "Individual creatures often have welfares, but species never do. The notion of a species is an abstraction. . . . While there is something that it is like to be an animal there is nothing that it is like to be a species." One might remark that one does not need to make a choice between conserving species and protecting individual animals. Both may be combined—species conservation may go together with or even be based upon respect for the individual animals that make up species. In practice, zoos could limit their breeding programs to those species that really need captive breeding to survive and in cases that would be in the best interests of the animals themselves. Zoos could support individual animals by offering them a new home. They could play an important role as sanctuaries for animals currently living in awful conditions in, for example, circuses, substandard zoos, biomedical laboratories, and private places. A sanctuary role by zoos may raise questions in connection with limiting breeding opportunities and visitor access in the animals' interests. However, such a role remains a largely unexplored area for zoos that may provide an opportunity for finding common ground among zoo supporters, conservationists, and animal advocates.

The relationship between zoos and sanctuaries is currently rather tense—in particular in connection with the keeping of elephants. Zoos may feel threatened by elephant sanctuaries because of some animal advocates stating that elephants are better off in spacious sanctuaries and should no longer be kept in the captivity of a zoo. A proposal to offer elephants in Chicago enclosures of at least ten acres was described on the AZA Web site as being the work of animal rights extremists, whereas "caring professionals at AZA-accredited zoos are the elephant experts." However, the picture appears to be a bit more complicated. Several AZA zoos announced their intention to send their remaining elephants to the PAWS Ark 2000 Sanctuary (San Andreas, California) or The Elephant Sanctuary (Hohenwald, Tennessee), where they would have hundreds of acres of varied space to explore instead of one or a few acres in zoos. Some zoo professionals, such as David Hancocks and Les Schobert, have expressed their support for such a move by stating that zoo enclosures are too cramped for elephants. Problems mentioned for elephants living in zoos include chronic foot infections, arthritis at an early age, reproductive problems, and neurotic behaviors such as swaying and rocking. However, according to Hancocks, "The American Zoo [and Aquarium] Association has threatened member zoos with expulsion for sending elephants to a sanctuary."

How will zoos evolve? Will they continue to display and breed a large variety of animals? Will they specialize and keep only one or very few species in much larger areas? Will they end or limit their breeding programs and become sanctuaries for animals desperately in need of a new home? Or will zoos disappear? We do not know the future course of zoos, but it will depend upon the outcome of the ongoing discussion about animal welfare, animal rights, and conservation.

See also

Conservation and Environment—*Elephant Conservation and Welfare at the Amboseli Elephant Research Project*

Ethics and Animal Protection

Further Resources

American Zoo and Aquarium Association. AZA elephant care and conservation speak louder than extremist hype. Accessed April 20, 2007. http://www.aza.org/Newsroom/PR_IDA_Eleph.

Bekoff, M. (Ed.). (1998). *Encyclopedia of animal rights and animal welfare.* Westport, CT: Greenwood Press.

Bostock, S. C. (1993). *Zoos & animal rights: The ethics of keeping animals.* New York: Routledge.

Clubb, R., & Mason, G. (2003). Captivity effects on wide-ranging carnivores: Animals that roam over a large territory in the wild do not take kindly to being confined. *Nature, 425,* 473–74.

Croke, V. (1997). *The modern ark: The story of zoos: past, present and future.* New York: Scribner.

Hancocks, D. (2001). *A different nature: The paradoxical world of zoos and their uncertain future.* Berkeley: University of California Press.

———. (2005, September 9). Bamboo should be sent to a place where she can heal. *The Seattle Times.* Available at http://seattletimes.nwsource.com/html/opinion/2002481819_hancocks09.html

Hanson, E. (2002). *Animal attractions: Nature on display in American zoos.* Princeton, NJ: Princeton University Press.

IUDZG—The World Zoo Organization and the Captive Breeding Specialist Group of IUCN/SSC. (1993). *The world zoo conservation strategy: The role of the zoos and aquaria of the world in global conservation.* Brookfield, IL: The Chicago Zoological Society. Available at http://www.waza.org/conservation/wczs.php

Jamieson, D. (1995). Zoos revisited. In B. G. Norton, M. Hutchins, E. F. Stevens, & T. L. Maple (Eds.), *Ethics on the ark: Zoos, animal welfare and wildlife conservation* (pp. 52–66). Washington, DC: Smithsonian Institution Press.

Johnson, W. (1990). *The rose-tinted menagerie.* London: Heretic Books.

Malamud, R. (1998). *Reading zoos: Representations of animals and captivity.* London: MacMillan Press.

Margodt, K. (2000). *The welfare ark: Suggestions for a renewed policy in zoos.* Brussels: VUB University Press.

Noelker, F. (2004). *Captive beauty: Zoo portraits by Frank Noelker.* Urbana, IL: University of Illinois Press.

Poole, T., & Law, G. (1996). *Inexpensive ways of improving zoo enclosures for mammals.* Universities Federation for Animal Welfare (UFAW)/International Academy of Animal Welfare Sciences (IAAWS).

Schobert, L. (2005, September 28). L.A. Zoo needs to give its elephants a break. *Daily News.* Available at http://pets.groups.yahoo.com/group/EthologicalEthics/message/1167

Seal, U. S. (1991). Life after extinction. In J. H. W. Gipps (Ed.), *Beyond captive breeding: Reintroducing endangered mammals to the wild: The proceedings of a symposium held at the Zoological Society of London on the 24th and 25th November 1989* (pp. 39–55). Oxford, UK: Clarendon Press.

Schaller, G. B. (1993). *The last panda.* Chicago: University of Chicago Press.

Shepherdson, D. J., Mellen, J. D., & Hutchins, M. (Eds.). (1998). *Second nature: Environmental enrichment for captive animals.* Washington, DC: Smithsonian Institution Press.

Wilson, E. O. *The diversity of life.* Harmondsworth, UK: Penguin Books.

Koen Margodt

Zoos and Aquariums
Enrichment and Well-Being for Zoo Animals

Traditionally, zoos have been the primary connectors of people to exotic wildlife. A few decades ago, however, zoos were little more than menageries of animals for public entertainment, sometimes at the animals' expense. Today's leading zoos are much more responsible and go to great lengths to maintain their animals in good, healthy environments. Many also participate in conservation efforts and take pride in their outreach programs to educate the public about animals and their conservation needs. To meet these goals, exhibits of zoo animals must show the animal in a respectful way that emphasizes the animal's natural environment and behavior. Only then will the zoo provide the optimal animal-human connection that promotes conservation-mindedness among zoo visitors.

In recent years, the general public has begun to become familiar with the term *enrichment.* Environmental enrichment may be defined as the actions taken to enhance the well-being of captive animals by identifying and providing key environmental stimuli. *Well-being* is a notoriously slippery concept that is difficult to define and measure, but good well-being generally includes good health and biological functioning, the ability to maintain physiological homeostasis, and—the most difficult to measure—good psychological health.

Early in the twentieth century zoo professionals were the first to express concern about what today would be called *psychological well-being*, noting that animal behavior in zoos often seemed abnormal compared with that observed in the wild. A few decades later zoos led a concerted effort to improve their facilities to better meet the needs of their animal charges. The practice of enrichment later spread to more intensively managed captive settings, such as farming and animal laboratories. Largely due to public concern for animal welfare in all these settings, governments began to legislate minimum standards for animals held in captivity, many of which involve enrichment. Captive environments only rarely approximate the variety of stimuli and environmental contingencies present in nature. In comparison with the wild, these environments are unchanging (lacking novelty), are spatially limited, are stimulus-poor (lacking complexity), and generally provide the inhabitant with little control over its environment. The result is animals with a great deal of time with nothing to do. Without opportunities to engage in species-typical natural behaviors, many animals show signs of poor well-being, such as stereotypies—highly repetitive behaviors, invariant in form, with no obvious function. Pacing is the stereotypy form most frequently seen in many mammal species.

Types of Enrichment

Visitors to zoos are likely to see enrichment in action when, for example, they witness cheetahs sprinting after mechanical rabbits, monkeys sifting through piles of straw for food tidbits, or a bear endeavoring to extract peanut butter from crevices in a log. Other forms of enrichment do not necessarily involve food rewards, relying instead on the animal's natural curiosity to explore novel and interesting changes in their environment. Something as simple as a burlap bag stuffed with straw can keep a giant panda entertained for hours. But successful enrichment strategies involve much more than tossing a random mix of interesting items into an animal's enclosure.

The types of enrichment have taken many different forms in the literature. In one prevalent schematic, enrichment may be divided into five categories: (1) Occupational enrichments are those efforts that try to keep the animal busy, for example, encouraging the animal to work for food or providing some sort of exercise equipment; (2) Another strategy—physical enrichment—attempts to improve the quality of the enclosure through permanent changes or temporary introduction of novel objects. The enclosure may be enlarged or made more complex, and climbing structures, water pools, soft substrate, or vegetation may be added. In one of the most highly visible types of enrichment, animals are given novel "toys" that encourage exploration and play, which in addition to providing psychological benefits to the animal are sure to entertain the zoo-going public; (3) Sensory enrichment can be similar to novel object enrichment, but the aim is to activate the senses with visual, auditory, olfactory, or other stimuli; (4) In nutritional enrichment, animal caretakers attempt to introduce more natural variation in diet and feeding schedules. Rather than plopping down a bowl of processed, quickly consumed food once a day, they scatter the feeding times at various times throughout the day and present the food in ways that encourage the animal to use its natural foraging behavior, for example, hiding it in the crevices of logs and rocks. They may also provide a more varied diet and include food items that are more challenging to consume. Giraffes may be given browse (tree branches) instead of hay, and lions may be given bones or whole carcasses instead of ground meat; and (5) Finally, social enrichment can provide endless opportunities for challenge and change and can meet species needs for social interaction. Overlap among these types of enrichment is inevitable, but these distinctions are useful when devising a well-rounded, holistic enrichment program.

Why Use Enrichment?

What difference can enrichment make? Consider the following scenario. A polar bear in a zoo enclosure moves rapidly to and fro in the back corner of its exhibit. Upon closer inspection it can be seen that with each step the foot falls at the exact same location where the bear stepped in the previous circuit, tracing the exact same route in an almost robotic fashion. In the wild, the bear might traverse 100 miles in a single day, yet in its enclosure it is using only a small fraction of the space available to it. After a half-hour of such pacing the bear hears the activities of its keeper arriving for the morning feed, moves to the keeper door and begins to sway back and forth, peering into the food preparation area. It continues this highly repetitive movement for another half-hour until the keeper delivers a pile of ground meat, which the bear consumes in a few short minutes. Complacent for the moment, the bear looks out at its surroundings—a concrete enclosure about 20 meters across, an old tree trunk, a small pool with steep gunnite walls holding it in. Moments later, the bear returns to the back corner and resumes its routine, pacing again, its footfall pattern just as before.

Many miles away in another zoo, a polar bear wakes as the sun rises. It ambles around its enclosure, exploring. It stops to sniff some fresh cedar branches, finds the faint scent of cloves placed by keepers on a log some days ago, then flops down in a pile of pine bark mulch, rolls around vigorously and rubs the bark chips on it head, shoulders, and neck. Afterward, it moves down to a large pool and gazes at the fish darting about, swats at the water and pounces at the fish but fails to catch one. It swims out to the deep end where it finds a large floating barrel, which it grabs and wrestles, tossing it across the pool and draping its body over it, forcing it deep underwater before letting its buoyancy pull it back to the surface. After an hour of vigorous water play, the bear hears its keeper's whistle and comes running to the keeper door and is let inside. In its bedroom it finds a large cardboard box it must demolish to find a few choice tidbits of food. When allowed to go back outside, the bear finds a large bone tied to a stump and a number of new changes in the environment.

These two scenarios portray the potential pitfalls of maintaining wild animals in captivity and the best solutions available for countering what amounts to poor welfare. The bear at the first zoo lives a life all too different from that of its wild counterparts. Its environment is relatively barren with few stimuli to evoke natural behavior. In the wild it would be faced with constant change and challenge and be forced to adapt its behavior, but in this particular zoo its environment is static and it has no control over what happens to it. This bear's food simply arrives at a predetermined interval, and it must do nothing to procure it. In the absence of any control over its environment and lack of behavioral opportunity, this bear develops stereotypies. The bear in the second zoo, by contrast, is actively engaged in its environment, which is stimulus-rich and ever-changing, approximating the diversity and challenge characterizing the life of a wild polar bear. Its environment affords it many opportunities to engage in its natural motivation to explore and even play, and access to food is contingent upon its own behavioral actions. We would say that its enclosure is "enriched" and that its keepers provide it with opportunities for "behavioral enrichment."

Why is enrichment necessary and when is it used? Most often, unfortunately, enrichment is used—or improved—when animals in our care show signs of poor well-being. Sometimes poor reproduction or health or physiological signs of stress alert zoo animal caretakers to the possibility of poor well-being, but most often it is the readily observable abnormal behaviors such as stereotypies that key us into a developing problem. Stereotypies can take several forms. Reviews of the literature on zoo animals suggest that pacing is the most common, followed by oral stereotypies (such as tongue-flicking), and other repetitive movements (e.g., head bobbing). We interpret these behaviors with a degree of anthropomorphism, likening them to the effects of a prison cell on its prisoner. Although we may never fully understand the subjective experience of another species, the scientific evidence is clear that stereotypies are more often than not associated with poor well-being. Sometimes stereotypies can continue as a "scar" from past poor environments even after improvements have been made, so stereotypic behavior is not a sure-proof measure of an animal's current psychological state or the quality of its environment. Thus, it is recommended that stereotypies alone should not be used to infer psychological well-being, though in actuality they often are. One interpretation of stereotypies—with some supporting evidence—is that they are used to cope with suboptimal environments. Thus, the goal of management should not be to prevent the stereotypy itself, but to re-create the environment to meet the animal's needs and obviate its reliance on stereotypy as a coping mechanism.

Documented Benefits of Enrichment

But does enrichment really work or does it just make us humans feel better about keeping animals in captivity? In fact, a great deal of science has shown clearly that animals do benefit from enrichment. Much of this research has taken place outside the arena of zoos because zoo researchers often cannot achieve the level of experimental control necessary to test the effects of enrichment rigorously and because they typically avoid research methods that are invasive and potentially harmful to the animals.

Several studies have demonstrated a variety of positive developmental effects on brain function. Animals reared in more enriched environments have heavier brains with more synaptic connections between neurons and enhanced levels of neurotransmitters—all indications of a more effective and efficient brain. These animals are better learners, adapt to change more readily, and show less hormonal evidence of stress. The benefits of stress reduction are significant because stress can suppress immune system function and reproduction. Thus, enriched animals are less prone to disease and reproduce better. Enriched environments also promote a greater diversity of species-typical behaviors and fewer abnormal behaviors. Literature surveys of published zoo enrichment studies indicate that the typical enrichment program reduces stereotypies by more than half. However, the ultimate goal of completely eliminating stereotypies with enrichment has not yet been fulfilled.

The weight of evidence from these and other studies also suggests a clear role for enrichment in maintaining animals in captivity for conservation purposes, one of today's zoos' major goals. In addition to creating a better atmosphere for conservation education, enrichment promises to increase successful mating and rearing of offspring and promote the development of more behaviorally competent candidates for reintroduction to the wild. In fact, enrichment is playing an increasing role in specifically preparing captive-bred endangered species for release back to the wild.

Theories of Enrichment and Well-Being

It would be a disservice to conclude a discussion of enrichment here, with little mention of the contributions of motivational theory to our understanding of welfare problems and enrichment efficacy. Zoo-goers understand that these enrichments provide stimulation for animals and keep them from getting "bored," promoting good psychological health. Although true in essence, the motivational theories underpinning the use of enrichment can be quite complex, and researchers are not altogether clear why some enrichments work and some do not. Zoo enrichment practitioners have shown great creativity and energy in their efforts to enrich zoo animals, but much more work needs to be done to create a science of enrichment to better guide these efforts. The ultimate—and not fully realizable—goal of enrichment science should be to predict when well-being problems such as stereotypies are most likely to develop and to determine the precise forms of enrichment that are needed to reduce and abolish these problems across species and a variety of captive environments. To do this, researchers have devised a number of motivational theories that may explain why animals suffer from poor well-being and what kinds of enrichment should best address deficits in well-being. These theories have already significantly improved the implementation of enrichment programs—and improved the lives of countless animals—but they also need to be articulated more clearly and tested more rigorously if we are to make further improvements.

The list of theories that have been advanced to explain these aspects of animal well-being is long and many of them share conceptual overlap. Each of these theories needs to be further refined so that clear—and mutually exclusive—predictions can be made and tested. Some are just vague ideas, whereas others are formal motivational models yielding testable predictions. In the future, welfare scientists will need to set up experiments that test competing predictions made by these various theories. A partial list of some of the theories most prevalent in the zoo literature follows.

1. *Mimic nature.* This is the grandfather of all enrichment theories, but it is more of a philosophical stance than a theory. The basic idea is that when enriching the lives of captive animals one must look to nature for guidance and re-create as much of the natural environment of the species as possible. The problem is that the captive environment can never faithfully copy nature because there is not enough room (not to mention money) to do so. The theory provides little guidance as to which aspects of nature are most important to emulate, relegating enrichment to a somewhat blind approach guided by knowledge of the natural environment of the species and the animal caretaker's intuition. Indeed this approach spawned a controversy when, in the 1970s and 1980s, new approaches involving less natural enrichments were developed, such as pulling a lever to acquire food. The practitioners of this approach, called behavioral engineering, argued that naturalness per se was not the key issue. What these scientists considered important is that enrichment re-established a connection between the animal's behavior and its environment—that action is rewarded with the opportunity to meet some need, such as access to food and water. Certainly, animals in nature must perform such work to acquire resources, so this re-establishes a natural connection to the environment even if the devices used are not natural themselves. The debate has subsided, and today most recognize that looking to nature is a useful tool to guide enrichment, but what matters most is whether animals use the enrichment and whether it has beneficial effects—an empirical not philosophical question.

2. *Ethological needs and information primacy.* In 1988 behavioral scientists Hughes and Duncan were among the first to develop a more structured and testable model that provided a synthesis of the mimic nature and behavioral engineering approaches. In their ethological needs model of motivation they proposed that animals have evolved needs to *perform* certain species-typical behaviors that are used to acquire resources (called "appetitive" behaviors). Thus, animals need not only the actual resource, such as food and shelter, but they also need to use these behaviors to access the resource. If they do not have the opportunity to perform these highly motivated behaviors, then well-being will suffer, resulting in, among other things, stereotypy performance. Enrichment strategies, then, should be devised to allow performance of these behaviors, which may include searching, digging, extracting, and so forth. In one of the best-documented examples, mink show signs of elevated stress if they are not given the opportunity to swim and will work to gain access to water for swimming. Like behavioral engineering, enrichment based on ethological needs allows the animal to reconnect its behavior to the environment. If the behavioral connector need not be a precise evolved motor pattern, then the ethological needs model also predicts appetitive behaviors that are "less natural" functional analogues to more natural ones will also suffice. A second theory—information primacy—provides a subtle alternative to the ethological needs model. Supporters of this model argue that it is not the performance of the behavior *per se* that matters, but the active pursuit of information. Under this hypothesis animals are motivated to explore their environment, even when food is readily available, in order to learn about the availability and distribution of food and other resources for future use when resources are more limited. European starlings, for instance, will leave behind a dish full of meal worms in order to go search for worms hidden under artificial leaves. Of course, it is difficult (though not impossible) to determine whether such behavior is motivated by the need to acquire information or to perform highly motivated behavior.
3. *Control.* The concept of control was first introduced to enrichment during the pioneering behavioral engineering approach. In its simplest version, giving an animal control means making an animal's access to some resource contingent upon its own behavioral action. Other terms, such as *behavioral contingency*, *choice*, *challenge*, and *empowerment*, are also used to refer to similar motivational processes involved in well-being and enrichment. According to this theory, the emphasis is not on the naturalness of the behavior or that a certain behavior must be performed, but on the simple fact that the animal's behavior needs to have consequences. If the animal approaches another animal, it may have to deal with threats and the potential for conflict. If the animal digs in the dirt, it can create a shelter. If the animal pulls a lever, it gains access to food or water. If it explores its environment, it may find useful resources. If the animal moves into the shade, it reduces heat stress. The goal of enrichment, then, is to give the animal as many options to employ its behavior to useful ends as possible.
4. *Boredom and lack of sensory stimulation.* The concept of boredom offers a more general model that hypothesizes that animals must have *something* to do, but it does not provide precise guidelines as to what kinds of activities will allay boredom. It is based on the notion that animals will strive to reach an optimum level of arousal and, therefore, animals should be given options to self-regulate their arousal level. If a diverse and complex environment is not available, then the animal becomes bored in the sense that it cannot engage in stimulating behavioral opportunities. A sister hypothesis postulates that low stimulus diversity leads to sensory deprivation and that animals should be given more opportunities to explore with their five senses.

5. *Stress and coping.* Stress is frequently advanced to explain poor well-being and stereotypy performance. Although stress is clearly associated with poor well-being, it is better viewed as one mechanism by which other factors exert their effects on the animal. For example, failure to meet an animal's ethological needs may lead to stress, stereotypy performance, and other measures of poor well-being. To ascribe poor well-being to stress is probably a circular argument. Enrichment may indeed reduce stress, but this begs the question *why*? Coping is another concept that is used frequently to describe how animals deal with suboptimal environments, often emphasizing how coping mechanisms act to reduce stress. There is growing evidence that stereotypies may allow animals to cope with aversive captive environments. Enrichment is designed to reduce aversiveness to the environment or provide an alternative coping mechanism, reducing the animal's reliance on stereotypic behavior.

These and other theories need to be disentangled and tested so that more optimal enrichment strategies can be devised and implemented. Perhaps then we will be able to prevent stereotypies from developing in the first place or eradicate those already existing, moving us one step closer to optimal well-being for captive animals.

Studying Enrichment and Well-Being

The science of enrichment involves more than just the theories that are tested. How we go about doing science can facilitate or compromise our objective of discovering the secrets of optimal well-being. The answers we get are only as good as the science we use to address the questions. The zoo environment provides exceptional challenges to carrying out good science, but with greater effort zoo research can approximate that found in the more controlled settings of the laboratory. Zoo environments often offer little experimental control. Researchers need to work more closely with animal care personnel to reduce the number of confounding variables that may affect the results. Where possible, husbandry practices should be held constant during the course of an enrichment study. Sample size—essential for legitimate statistical analysis and interpretation of results—is another problem plaguing zoo research. When a zoo has only a few members of a species, researchers may need to collaborate with other zoos to obtain a sufficient sample size.

One frequent failing of zoo enrichment research is the tendency to use the "everything-but-the-kitchen-sink" approach. Here enrichment practitioners make so many changes to the environment at the same time—with the reasonable hope that at least something will help their animals—that it is impossible to determine which changes had beneficial effects. In these cases, we learn little about the underlying motivation that led to improved well-being and we are ill equipped to provide guidance to others that need to know what enrichments work best. For scientific purposes, one thing at a time needs to be changed so that we can draw a conclusion about its effects. However, this does not mean that animals should be kept in barren environments and given one measly enrichment item at a time. Enrichment programs should always be holistic, but scientific studies need to measure the effects of simple changes to the program that may or may not provide incremental improvements to well-being.

Another important point to consider when testing enrichment strategies is that the goal should be to understand the motivational factors underlying poor and good well-being. By understanding motivation we are better able to predict when poor well-being will arise elsewhere and will be better able to address it with appropriate enrichment. This has consequences for the experimental design used to test enrichment efficacy. For example, an enrichment study may find a significant reduction in stereotypic behavior, but this may result from the simple fact that the animals used the enrichment and therefore had less time leftover to perform stereotypies. If, after the animal tires of the enrichment, it returns to stereotyping at the same rate, have we really affected its motivation or done anything to enhance its well-being? The goal of enrichment is to reduce the *need* to perform stereotypic behavior by making the environment less aversive. A careful experimental design, such as measuring the rate of stereotypy in the aftermath of an interaction with enrichment, can help us determine whether the motivation to perform stereotypies has been reduced.

The importance of detailed descriptions of the forms of stereotypies, enrichment, and the behavioral response to enrichment cannot be overemphasized. Too often researchers omit these details from their publications, leaving the reader guessing. These details are important for a variety of reasons. Significantly, the form of the stereotypy can provide insight into its motivational cause; for example, oral stereotypies may be related to thwarted motivation to forage, whereas pacing may be related to the need to express natural ranging behavior. It is also important to describe precisely the enrichments used and even attempt to quantify the properties of enrichment because it is the properties that determine how animals will use enrichment. For example, with novel object enrichment it is important to know if it is moveable, manipulable, destructible, or stimulates the senses. Is the object complex, does it respond unpredictably, and does it allow the animal to exercise control? These factors and more will determine whether and how the animal uses the enrichment. Moreover, each enrichment item may evoke a unique suite of behaviors that map on to its properties, underscoring the importance of also recording the behavioral details of how the animal interacts with the enrichment. These information needs are not just for academic purposes but are essential to understand why some enrichments work better than others and how enrichment can be designed to more effectively target the animal's needs. If properly understood, the right combination of enrichments may act together to meet all an animal's psychological needs.

Conclusions

Although enrichment researchers should continue to pursue the holy grail of finding the most important general motivational theories that explain poor well-being and enrichment effectiveness, it goes without saying that a one-size-fits-all approach will not work. It may take more than one theory to explain the multiple types of stereotypies displayed by even a single individual. The effectiveness of an enrichment strategy may vary among species and between animals of different sex and age. However, we should not let this natural variation prevent us from searching for general principles and global strategies that are more likely to work more of the time than alternatives, and then revising them for individual idiosyncrasies as necessary.

There are ways to tackle welfare problems other than enrichment. Low-stereotyping animals may be bred to produce a population free of stereotypy, but does this address the underlying problem (poor well-being), or does it eliminate one of the animal's most important mechanisms for coping with an aversive environment? Similarly, drugs can be used to eliminate stereotypic behavior, obstacles can be placed to prevent the behavior, or animals can be trained not to rely on stereotypy. The advantage that enrichment has over all these alternative methods is that it addresses the root cause of the observable behavioral problem (well-being) not the symptom (stereotypy and other measures). In fact, many enrichment advocates argue that enrichment is *the* key concept for maintenance of captive animals, on par with food, water, and shelter.

See also

Enrichment for Animals

Further Resources

Carlstead, K. (1996). Effects of captivity on the behavior of wild mammals. In D. G. Kleiman, M. E. Allen, K. V. Thompson, & S. Lumpkin (Eds.), *Wild mammals in captivity* (pp. 317–33). Chicago: University of Chicago Press.

Hughes, B. O. & Duncan, I. J. H. (1988). The notion of ethological "need," models of motivation and animal welfare. *Animal Behaviour, 36,* 1696–1707.

Mason, G. J., Cooper, J. & Clarebrough, C. (2001). Frustrations of fur-farmed mink. *Nature, 410,* 35–36.

Mason, G. J., & Rushen, J. (Eds.). (2007). *Stereotypic animal behaviour: Fundamentals and applications to welfare* (2nd ed.). Wallingford, UK: CAB International.

Moberg, G. P. & Mench, J. A. (2000). The biology of animal stress: Basic principles and implications for animal welfare. Wallingford, UK: CAB International.

Sambrook, T. D., & Buchanan-Smith, H. M. (1997). Control and complexity in novel object enrichment. *Animal Welfare, 6,* 207–16.

Shepherdson, D. J., Mellen, J. D., & Hutchins, M. (1998). *Second nature: Environmental enrichment for captive animals.* Washington, DC: Smithsonian Institution Press.

Swaisgood, R. R. (In press). Current status and future directions of applied behavioral research for animal welfare and conservation. In R. R. Swaisgood (Ed.), *Special Issue: Animal Behaviour, Conservation and Enrichment. Applied Animal Behaviour Science.*

Swaisgood, R. R., & Shepherdson, D. J. (2005). Scientific approaches to enrichment and stereotypies in zoo animals: What's been done and where should we go next? *Zoo Biology, 24,* 499–518.

Ronald R. Swaisgood

■ Zoos and Aquariums
Marine Mammals and Aquariums

The maintenance of marine mammals for public display in aquariums is among the most controversial of human-animal relationships in the world today. Depending on the views and values that people attach to aquariums and the marine mammals they hold, people might think of aquariums as amusement parks, public education centers, scientific research sites, conservation centers, or simply as prisons. Essentially, these various ways of thinking about marine mammals and aquariums fuel the different arguments that either justify or condemn the practice of keeping marine mammals in human care.

The history of keeping marine mammals in captivity spans hundreds of years. People have placed many different kinds of marine mammals on display for public viewing, including live polar bears, walruses, seals, otters, porpoises, manatees, whales, and a variety of dolphin species. But aquariums as we know them today—marine parks that often feature acrobatic dolphins that regularly perform "shows" for audiences of people—only first appeared in 1938 with the opening of Marine Studios (later renamed Marineland) near St. Augustine, Florida. The star attractions at Marine Studios were several bottlenose dolphins that had been caught from nearby waters. During feeding times, the dolphins are said to have fallen into a routine of jumping up to catch their fish, thereby creating a spontaneous spectacle that delighted visitors. Those were the beginnings of the typical dolphin show repertoire seen today. Over the next several decades, especially after the 1960s, public display of marine mammals proliferated around the globe. Today, more people visit aquariums every year than zoos, despite the average admission fee at aquariums being more than twice that of the average zoo. Indeed, the commercial success of aquariums in the Unites States is astounding; for example, in 2003 more than 50 million people patronized aquariums with marine mammals, where they spent more than one billion dollars.

The standards of care and maintenance for marine mammals kept in aquariums in the United States are enforced by the Animal and Plant Health Inspection Service (APHIS), as set out by the 1994 amendments to the Marine Mammal Protection Act. The standards of care require aquariums with marine mammals to meet *reasonable* conditions for their animals (a particular enclosure size, for example)—not necessarily *optimal* conditions. Some aquariums have the interest and financial wherewithal to far exceed APHIS standards, whereas others simply meet the minimum standards required by law. To be sure, standards for keeping marine mammals in captivity vary a great deal around the world. Thus, the quality of the conditions among aquariums varies a great deal. As a result, the quality of life for marine mammals in different aquariums varies considerably as well.

Captive Marine Mammals

Of all the marine mammals, captive cetaceans (whales, porpoises, and dolphins) have prompted the most heated debates surrounding captivity. Cetaceans seem to have a special place in public affections. Because of their intelligence, sociability, and beauty, many people seem interested in cetaceans for more than scientific or economic reasons—people care about the welfare of cetaceans because of the way they *feel* about them. Yet, some researchers suggest distorted scientific evidence and popular conceptions about cetaceans has led the public to hold inaccurate images of whales and dolphins as superior beings with only positive and amiable traits. Whatever the reasons, interest in cetaceans (especially killer whales and dolphins) is the primary force that drives millions through the admission gates of aquariums worldwide, as well as what fuels the furor over captive cetaceans and the argument against their public display.

Those in favor of keeping cetaceans and other marine mammals in aquariums argue that they are ambassadors for their species. By allowing a large number of people to see them alive and up close, they educate and raise awareness and concern about the animal species and their natural environment. Several studies commissioned by the Alliance of Marine Mammal Parks and Aquariums found that most people believed that aquariums performed valuable educational functions and contributed to conservation. Indeed, most institutions that keep marine mammals offer various types of educational programs and support a range of activities intended to promote conservation. Still, there is no clear evidence regarding the quality of what is being presented at different aquariums and whether the educational messages conveyed actually make a positive difference for the public or wild marine mammal populations.

Opponents of captive display facilities argue that any educational and/or conservation benefits obtained cannot offset the harm caused by the loss of freedom and integrity experienced by individual animals at aquariums. Critics of captivity contend that the same educational benefits could be provided by many other, less invasive forms of presentation, such as books, documentaries, field trips to natural habitats, or classroom instruction. Furthermore, those against captivity suggest that public displays of marine mammals are providing distorted educational messages. For example, dolphin performances often convey anthropomorphic images or provide false or misleading information. Audiences at such dolphin shows also witness close interactions between dolphins and their trainers. In this way, aquariums may inadvertently lead people to believe, by example, that feeding and swimming with dolphins in the wild are safe and acceptable activities.

Those in favor of aquariums also argue that keeping marine mammals in human care provides a valuable opportunity to study the animals' biology, physiology, and behavior. Opponents do not argue that such research is unimportant; but they do suggest that we have learned all that we need to learn from captive populations of marine mammals and that further research would not be meaningful enough to justify the costs to individual animal welfare. Contrary to captive display advocates' argument that marine mammals are actually better off in human care—where they are provided with excellent care and a life free from the dangers of the wild—critics argue that none of these benefits ought to outweigh individual animals' freedom to live without human-imposed restrictions and in a way that honors the particular animals' needs and interests. To be sure, different animals (species and individuals) respond differently to captivity; although some adapt quite readily, others do not do well in human care and exhibit signs of significant stress and poor health in captivity. Ultimately, many of these arguments depend on the demands that any particular animal faces in its natural habitat and on the qualities of care provided in a particular aquarium.

See also

Conservation and Environment—*Whale and Dolphin Culture and Human Interactions*
Culture, Religion, and Belief Systems—*Dolphin "Mythology"*
Culture, Religion, and Belief Systems—*Japan's Dolphins and the Human-Animal Relationship*
Living with Animals—*Dolphins and Humans: From the Sea to the Swimming Pool*

Further Resources

Alliance of Marine Mammal Parks and Aquariums. (2005, November 26). http://www.ammpa.org

Bekoff, M. (2002). Ethics and marine mammals. In W. Perrin, B. Würsig, & J. Thewissen (Eds.), *Encyclopedia of marine mammals* (pp. 398–404). San Diego, CA: Academic Press.

Davis, S. (1997). *Spectacular nature: Corporate culture and the Sea World experience.* Los Angeles: University of California Press.

Kestin, S. (2004, May 16). Marine attractions: Below the surface. *Sun-Sentinel.* Accessed January 18, 2006 at http://www.sun-sentinel.com/news/sfl-marinestorygallery,0,2119297.storygallery?coll=sfla-home-dots-utility

The Marine Mammal Protection Act of 1972. 16 U.S.C. Sec. 1361 et seq.

Reeves, R. R., & Mead, J. G. (1999). Marine mammals in captivity. In J. R. Twiss & R. R. Reeves (Eds.), *Conservation of marine mammals* (pp. 412–36). Washington, DC: Smithsonian Institutional Press.

Reynolds, J. E. I., Wells, R. S., & Eide, S. D. (2000). *The bottlenose dolphin: Biology and conservation.* Gainesville: University Press of Florida.

Kristin L. Stewart

Zoos and Aquariums
Reptiles and Zookeepers

The first problem encountered when dealing with human being/lower vertebrates interactions is, in anthropozoological terms, the possibility (or reality) that, for example, a reptilian subject is able to recognize a given human person. In fact, only after having recognized with a good degree of certainty that the compound stimulus set represented by a human is distinguishable by the animal subject in its environment can we speculate about an "affective bond" possibly established between the reptile and the human subjects.

Reptilian social behaviors are difficult to interpret by humans. In fact, it is hard for humans to recognize "affectionate" or affiliative behaviors expressed by reptiles in the course of intra- and/or inter-specific social interactions.

In the past, many reptilian species (especially most snakes) were considered as "asocial" outside the reproductive and breeding periods. However, an increasing number of ethological studies indicate that, among snake conspecifics, relationships may be more complex than previously thought and that such relationships include individual as well as sex and species recognition. Many snake species show gregarious behaviors during the neonatal phase, and may aggregate also at adulthood, developing truly social-dominance hierarchies. Observations in captivity conditions showed that neonate plains garter snakes (*Thamnophis radix*), displaying high levels of competition for food, tended to develop dominant behavioral patterns. Moreover, outside the feeding context, competitive subjects showed a marked preference to aggregate with noncompetitive conspecifics.

Among reptiles, many species of lizards and crocodilians are highly social and gregarious. Crocodilians and some snake species take care of their offspring, also showing "affectionate" behaviors (e.g., the mother moves neonates keeping them in her mouth and without wounding or swallowing them, a behavioral pattern very similar to mammalian retrieving). However, a variety of elements of the complex social behavioral patterns typically displayed by many mammalian species and interpreted by humans as expressions of affection seem largely absent in reptiles. From the human's point of view, reptilian social behavioral repertoire is apparently poor and less complex than that exhibited by mammals. In the reptile-human interaction, any behavioral response due to individual recognition and bond is likely to be extremely subtle, slow, and seemingly mainly including specie-specific components of antipredator and avoidance responses.

Reptiles perceive the surrounding environment mainly by detecting chemical cues, a sensory ability reportedly reduced in humans. Moreover, visual and acoustic signals displayed by social species of reptiles rarely overlap with familiar mammalian signals and are generally difficult to interpret. In general, responses such as visual orientation and rate of tongue flicking (especially in snakes) may represent useful measures to assess their responses in both intra- and inter-specific interactions.

A growing amount of evidence indicates that reptiles may be able to recognize their human caretakers and may respond differently to different persons. Although the scientific literature on this topic is rapidly increasing, some animal behavior experts are still cautious on this latter point.

The human/reptile bond and reptilian ability to recognize their caretakers was examined and discussed by Bowers and Burghardt (1992) in their interesting overview. The authors describe the case of a particular tortoise that was observed to approach following the call of only certain people. This tortoise apparently expressed "affection" by tapping its beak on the caretakers' feet. Some have speculated that the tortoise may have been gathering olfactory information or eliciting feeding, whereas others have interpreted the tortoise behavior as a reliable index of affection. They also reported that giant Aldabran and Galapagos tortoises (*Geochelone* spp.) at the Philadelphia Zoo rose up on their legs and solicited neck scratching by their caretaker, allowing the underside of their shell to be inspected. However, if the keeper was present and ignored the tortoises' approaches, tortoises approached and solicited other people. One tortoise in particular nipped the keeper's leg if its solicitations were ignored. Other tortoises learned through observation to solicit neck scratching by their caretaker and other familiar keepers. These observations indicated that attention and scratching were reinforcing aspects for the tortoises to interact with human caretakers. Tortoise behavior has been biologically explained by the fact that wild birds perch on tortoises and remove parasites.

Some people consider as affectionate those snakes that cling to their keeper's arms, constricting and coiling about them, whereas others explain this behavior by the notion that snakes are ectotherms and often rest quiet in warm places for a long time, and warm people could serve this function as well.

To disentangle this issue between Scylla of those vividly negating any "personality" to lower vertebrates (for birds, see the elegant collection of papers in Carere, *Behaviour,* in press) and the Cariddi of those providing any vertebrate species (including Cyclostomi) of human-like behavioral traits, we have illustrated the reality of reptile/human quality of social-type interactions considering the experiences reported by zookeepers during their long-lasting relationships with reptilian species.

When interviewed, zoo curators regularly assert that reptiles are unable to recognize and respond to individual human caretakers. However, daily routine care procedures (especially those related to feeding) may modify a reptile's behavior in a way that from the human's point of view could be easily interpreted as the manifestation of a greeting behavior, or affection. In captivity, feeding procedures are reinforcing, especially for phytophagous species (e.g., those of the Sauria Suborder and testudines), which, because of their diet, need to be fed daily by caretakers. These reptilian species seem to learn the time of eating, moving toward the door box and approaching their curator when he or she enters the box. Stefano and Diego (the two zookeepers of the Rome "Bioparco" we interviewed) describe a similar behavior for crocodilians. Fulvio Fraticelli (general curator at the Rome "Bioparco") and his collaborators state that an animal's approach behavioral pattern does not change when an unknown (but skilled) caretaker performs the same feeding procedure. So, it is likely that these reptiles do not recognize or respond to a specific caretaker. Probably they learn to recognize chemical, visual, and noise cues associated with the feeding procedure, displaying a pattern of ritualized behaviors.

Handling may also modify reptiles' behavior, reducing aggressive responses. For example, wild snakes strike violently and hiss when picked up. This defensive behavior has been observed also in most captive species. However, many species, such as the common pet ball python (*Phython regius*), tend to become less defensive after repeated and prolonged handling. Reduction in the python's defensive behavior is not due to recognition of its handler because, as Fraticelli affirms, the python strikes and bites when its regular handler introduces a hand in the casket invading its territory.

In conclusion, any behavioral changes in reptiles due to interaction with their keepers are difficult to explain with uncritical anthropomorphism. Reptile/human interaction, as well as human and reptile reciprocal responses, represents a complex and rich issue deserving further study.

See also

Zoos and Aquariums—*Amphibians and Zookeepers*

Further Resources

Alleva, E., & Scattoni, M. L. (2004). *Introductory keynote. The state of the art in animal experimentation. Annali Istituto Superiore di Sanità, 40,* 151–55. Website Istituto Superiore di Sanità: http://www.iss.it/engl/index.html

Davis, H., & Balfour, D. (Eds.). (1992). *The inevitable bond: Examining scientist-animal interactions.* Cambridge, UK: Cambridge University Press.

Frost, D. (2002). Reptiles. In N. Eldredge (Ed.), *Life on Earth: An encyclopedia of biodiversity, ecology, and evolution.* Santa Barbara, CA: ABC-CLIO.

Visalberghi, E. & Alleva, E. 1993. Book review of: *The inevitable bond: Examining scientist-animal interactions. The Quarterly Journal of Experimental Psychology, 46B,* 222–24.

Enrico Alleva and Nadia Francia

Zoos and Aquariums
Southeast Asia's Zoos

Southeast Asia is known for its unique diversity of fauna and flora. Yet the region harbors one of the highest densities of humans in the world. Several species of plants and animals are fast disappearing in Southeast Asia due to human population growth, habitat destruction, unsustainable land use patterns, poaching, trade in endangered species, and other environmental calamities. Also, the illegal trade in wildlife totals billions of dollars per year globally, and conservationists say the problem is more acute in Southeast Asia. Despite national and international laws to crack down on the trade, live animals and animal parts from endangered species are often sold in markets throughout the region. Strong demand, porous borders, and the lure of big money make it a lucrative business. Therefore, public awareness campaigns and conservation of endangered species in captivity are essential for the fight against species extinction. Zoos thus play an important role in Southeast Asia to bring awareness among people to safeguard the dwindling forest habitats and wildlife.

Most zoos and recreational parks are affiliated with the Southeast Asian Zoos Association, which is a major zoological union in the region. The zoo association was officially formed in 1990 with the objectives to strengthen conservation, increase captive breeding, improve standards of animal welfare, provide better recreational experiences for zoo visitors, and educate the public about wildlife conservation. Since 1993, the association comprises twelve countries and territories including Brunei, Cambodia, Hong Kong, Indonesia, Laos, Malaysia, Myanmar, Philippines, Singapore, Taiwan, Thailand, and Vietnam.

Although recognized zoos in Southeast Asian countries work hard to improve standards of welfare and ethics, animal rights activists criticize that animals are sometimes abused in zoos. Also troubling are reports that resorts, recreational theme parks, and even restaurants are increasingly displaying wildlife with less legal, ethical, and professional scrutiny. As a consequence, stringent ethical and welfare regulations and systematic evaluations of zoos become crucial to maintain high professional standards among member zoos.

The Ethics and Welfare Committee of the Southeast Asia Zoo Association has conducted evaluations to assess welfare and ethical problems in zoos since 1998. The objective of the evaluation is not to measure animal welfare scientifically but to identify, rectify, and prevent ethical- and welfare-related problems in zoos. The most serious problems that the zoos face are overcrowding of animals in small cages, poor hygiene associated with overcrowding, lack of enrichment, old/unsuitable indoor animal enclosures, use/abuse of animals in shows and photography, lack of enrichment for animals in exhibits and holding areas, and need of policies to take responsibility of animals that are traded or exchanged to other zoos. These problems are seen even in well-managed zoos and in big zoos as well as small zoos.

Zoos in Southeast Asia are blessed with fast-growing lush green vegetation because the region is located in the tropics, and most outdoor exhibits habitually have naturalistic surroundings. But animal enclosures regularly lack behavioral and environmental enrichment devices to stimulate natural behavior among animals, which could be easily improved by adding ropes, artificial vines, branches, and other necessary "furniture" to stimulate activities for the animals. During zoo evaluations by the Ethics and Welfare Committee, most zoo employees have taken the criticisms constructively—showing immediate progress by solving some problem—a good indication that zoo managers are concerned about problems related to animal welfare and eager to demonstrate their ethical/professional obligations to provide humane care for animals.

Zoos in Southeast Asian countries continue to rescue various species of animals, both common and endangered, which trigger overcrowding and other welfare-related problems instantaneously due to the lack of space and manpower. Instead of waiting for funds to rebuild cages and to increase manpower, zoos should embark on projects to relocate rescued animals to more specialized centers and also could release healthy animals back into the wild by strictly following national and international guidelines.

Recently, animal rights and conservation activists have criticized zoos in Thailand, Indonesia, Malaysia, and Singapore, highlighting various welfare and ethical concerns. The Malaysian zoo's gorilla controversy is perhaps known globally. The crackdown on zoos in Thailand by law enforcing officials was unprecedented—armed policemen raided various zoos, including the Safari World in Bangkok, which harbors over one hundred orangutans, many illegally. In Singapore, local activists asked the zoo and night safari to ban all animal shows, citing cases of animal attacks on visitors.

Animal rights and conservation groups sometimes condemn zoos without doing much in practical efforts to alleviate animal suffering. A relatively few animal welfare organizations have been willing to conduct constructive dialogue with zoos in Southeast Asia and to work closely to improve welfare conditions.

The Ethics and Welfare Committee of the Southeast Asian Zoos Association does not discriminate against poor zoos nor favor rich zoos, and opinions from zoo managers, conservationists, and animal rights activists are held in equal regard. Although it is customary that these independent stakeholders of the global wildlife wealth seldom compromise or work closely together, and may in fact have disagreements, there is evidence that agreement can be reached. A synergized approach to accomplishing the shared, yet seemingly conflicting, objectives of the various groups is essential, which could do much more toward improving the welfare standards of zoos in the region.

Conducting zoo evaluations in the culturally diverse Southeast Asian countries is a complex task, and presenting evidence of animal suffering in a constructive manner without being openly unpleasant is even harder. However, there is evidence that the zoo community is open to constructive criticism. Several of the zoos operate with insufficient funds and thus face the dual challenge of maintaining welfare standards and keeping the economic bottom line. Yet the zoo managers in Southeast Asian zoos seem willing, overall, to commit their efforts to upgrade welfare and ethical standards in their zoos.

Further Resources

Agoramoorthy, G. (2002). Animal welfare and ethics evaluations in Southeast Asian zoos: Procedures and prospects. *Animal Welfare, 11,* 295–99.

———. (2004). Ethics and welfare in Southeast Asian zoos. *Journal of Applied Animal Welfare Science, 7,* 189–95.

Agoramoorthy, G., & Hsu, M. J. (2001). South East Asian Zoos association. In C. Bell (Ed.), *Encyclopedia of the world's zoos* (pp. 1164–65). Chicago: Fitzroy Dearborn.

Govindasamy Agoramoorthy

Appendix: Chronology of Historical Events in Animal Protection

Following is a brief chronology of some historical events in the United States, unless otherwise indicated, related to the use of animals and to animal rights and animal welfare. "UK" stands for the United Kingdom.

For more information see the *Encyclopedia of Animal Rights and Animal Welfare* (M. Bekoff, editor, Greenwood Publishing Group, 1998). Also see these Web sites:

- Michigan State University College of Law: Animal Legal & Historical Web Center. http://www.animallaw.info/
- Animal Law Review: http://www.lclark.edu/org/animalaw
- National Center for Animal Law: http://www.lclark.edu/org/ncal
- Society for Animal Protective Legislation: http://www.saplonline.org/
- A Chronology of Key Events in the Scientific Use of Chimpanzees in the United States: http://www.releasechimps.org/pdfs/chronology-of-key-events.pdf
- The National Association for Biomedical Research: Animal Law Section. http://www.nabr.org/AnimalLaw/contactUs.htm
- A global summary of animal protection legislation: http://worldanimal.net/const-leaflet.htm
- A summary of species used in research: http://www.hsus.org/animals_in_research/species_used_in_research/
- A timeline of progress for farm animals: http://www.americanhumane.org/site/PageServer?pagename=pa_farm_animals_timeline
- Details about the federal Animal Welfare Act: http://www.nal.usda.gov/awic/legislat/usdaleg1.htm

Doing a general search on an Internet search engine for "history animal protection" will lead to numerous Web sites for legislation in specific countries and for specific species.

The Animal Welfare Information Center (AWIC) newsletter updates information in its "Congress in Action" section (see also http://awic.nal.usda.gov/nal_display/index.php?info_center=3&tax_level=1).

Chronology

1822	Ill-Treatment of Cattle Act
1822	Martin's Anticruelty Act (UK)
1824	Society for the Prevention of Cruelty to Animals (SPCA) (UK) founded

1826	Bill to Prevent the Cruel and Improper Treatment of Dogs
1832	Warburton Anatomy Act (UK)
1840	SPCA becomes the Royal Society for the Prevention of Cruelty to Animals (RSPCA) with patronage of Queen Victoria (UK)
1866	American Society for the Prevention of Cruelty of Animals (ASPCA) founded
1868	Massachusetts Society for the Prevention of Cruelty to Animals (MSPCA) founded
1875	Victoria Street Society for the Protection of Animals from Vivisection (UK) founded
1876	Cruelty to Animals Act (UK)
1877	American Humane Association founded
1883	American Anti-Vivisection Society founded
1889	American Humane Education Society (AHES) founded
1891	The Humanitarian League founded
1895	New England Anti-Vivisection Society founded
1898	British Union for the Abolition of Vivisection (UK) founded
1906	Animal Defence and Anti-Vivisection Society (UK) founded
1911	Protection of Animals Act (England, UK)
1912	Protection of Animals Act (Scotland, UK)
1925	The Performing Animals (Regulations) Act (UK)
1926	University of London Animal Welfare Society founded (name changed to Universities Federation for Animal Welfare [UFAW] in 1938) (UK)
1929	National Anti-Vivisection Society (UK) founded (formerly Victoria Street Society for the Protection of Animals from Vivisection)
1946	National Society for Medical Research founded
1948	Morris Animal Foundation founded
1949	The Docking and Nicking of Animals Act
1950	Animal Protection Law (covers farm animals and bans battery cages) (Denmark)
1951	Animal Welfare Institute founded
1952	Institute for Animal Laboratory Resources founded
1954	Humane Society for the United States (HSUS) founded
1954	The Protection of Animals (Anaesthetics) Act (UK)
1955	Society for Animal Protective Legislation founded
1957	Friends of Animals founded

1958	Humane Slaughter Act
1959	Beauty without Cruelty (UK) founded
1959	Wild Horses Act
1959	Catholic Society for Animal Welfare (now International Society for Animal Rights) founded
1960	The Abandonment of Animals Act (UK)
1961	Lawson-Tait Trust (UK) founded
1962	Bald and Golden Eagle Protection Act
1962	The Animals (Cruel Poisons) Act (UK)
1963	British Hunt Saboteurs Association (UK) Act
1965	Brambell Report on Farm Animal Welfare (UK)
1965	Littlewood Report (UK; a discussion of alternatives to the use of animals in testing and research)
1965	American Association for Accreditation of Laboratory Animal care founded
1966	Laboratory Animal Welfare Act
1967	Fund for Animals (UK) founded
1967	Farm Animal Welfare Advisory Committee (UK) founded
1968	Animal Protection Institute founded
1969	Council of Europe Convention on Animals in Transport
1969	International Fund for Animal Welfare (IFAW) founded
1969	Endangered Species Act
1969	Fund for the Replacement of Animals in Medical Experiments (FRAME) (UK) founded
1969	International Association against Painful Experiments on Animals (UK) founded
1970	Laboratory Animal Welfare Act broadened and renamed Animal Welfare Act; legislation extended to include all warm-blooded animals (including pet and exhibition trades)
1970	Dr. Hadwen Trust for Humane Research (UK) founded
1971	Greenpeace (now International) founded
1971	Wild Free-Roaming Horse and Burro Act
1971	Law requiring approval of new buildings for animal protection (Sweden)
1972	American Zoo and Aquarium Association accreditation standards and code of professional ethics
1972	Marine Mammal Protection Act
1972	Animal Protection Act (Germany)

1973	International Primate Protection League founded
1973	National Antivivisection Society founded
1973	Endangered Species Act
1973	Convention on International Trade in Endangered Species (CITES) of wild fauna and flora (international) is signed by 167 countries
1976	Animal Rights International (Henry Spira) founded
1976	Animal Welfare Act broadened to cover, among other things, transportation and prohibitions against dog fighting and cockfighting
1976	Horse Protection Act
1976	Fur Seal Act
1976	Protest at American Museum of Natural History (Henry Spira)
1976	The Dangerous Wild Animals Act (UK)
1977	First International Conference on the Rights of Animals, Trinity College, Cambridge, England (organized by Andrew Linzey and Richard Ryder)
1978	Humane Slaughter Act broadened
1978	Animal Legal Defense Fund founded
1978	Swiss Animal Welfare Act
1979	Association for Biomedical Research (founded as Research Animal Alliance) founded
1979	Coalition to Abolish the Draize Test (Henry Spira) founded
1979	First European Conference on Farm Animal Welfare, the Netherlands
1979	Packwood-Magnuson Amendment to the International Fishery Conservation Act
1980	People for the Ethical Treatment of Animals (PETA) founded
1980	Psychologists for the Ethical Treatment of Animals (PsyETA) founded
1981	Association of Veterinarians for Animal Rights (AVAR) founded
1981	Johns Hopkins Center for Alternatives to Animal Testing founded
1981	Silver Spring monkeys case, which led to the 1985 revision of the federal Laboratory Animal Welfare Act
1981	The Zoo Licensing Act (UK)
1981	Foundation for Biomedical Research founded
1982	Marine Mammal Protection Act reauthorized
1982	World Women for Animal Rights/Empowerment Vegetarian Activist Collective founded
1983	In Defense of Animals founded
1984	Humane Farming Association founded

1984	Performing Animal Welfare Society founded
1984	Break-in, Head Injury Clinical Research Laboratory, University of Pennsylvania
1985	Improved Standards for Laboratory Animals Act (an amendment of the Animal Welfare Act) to include requirements for psychological enrichment for nonhuman primates. It mandates minimal cage size (for chimpanzees 5 x 5 x 7 feet)
1985	Head Injury Clinical Research Laboratory closed
1985	National Association for Biomedical Research (merger of National Society for Medical Research, Association for Biomedical Research and Foundation for Biomedical Research) founded
1985	Jews for Animal Rights founded
1986	Farm Animal Reform Movement (FARM) founded
1986	Animal Welfare Information Center founded
1986	European Directive Regarding the Protection of Vertebrate Animals Used for Experimental and Other Scientific Purposes (Council of Europe)
1988	Swedish Animal Welfare Act
1989	Veal Calf Protection Bill hearings (U.S. Congress)
1990	Veal Crate Ban (UK)
1990	Pet Theft Act, amendment to the Animal Welfare Act
1990	Rutgers Animal Rights Law Center founded
1991	The Ark Trust, Incorporated, founded
1991	Americans for Medical Progress founded
1991	European Union Regulation against Leghold Traps
1992	Czechoslovakian Law against Cruelty on Animals (first welfare legislation in former Communist countries)
1992	Wild Bird Conservation Act
1992	International Dolphin Conservation Act
1992	Driftnet Fishery Conservation Act
1992	Protection of Animal Facilities Act
1992	Animal Enterprise Protection Act
1993	National Health Revitalization Act
1993	First World Congress on Alternatives and Animals in the Life Sciences, Baltimore, Maryland
1993	European Centre for the Validation of Alternative Methods (ECVAM)
1995	Second World Congress on Alternatives and Animals in the Life Sciences, Utrecht, the Netherlands

1996	House of Representatives holds a hearing on the Society Animal Protection Legislation (SAPL) supported Pet Safety and Protection Act
1996	The Pet Protection Act is considered
1997	Dolphin Protection Consumer Information Act makes it a violation of the Federal Trade Commission Act for any producer, importer, exporter, distributor, or seller of any tuna product that is exported from or offered for sale in the United States to include on the label of that product that the term "dolphin safe" or any other term or symbol that falsely claims or suggests that the tuna contained in the product were harvested using a method of fishing that is not harmful to dolphins if the product contains tuna harvesting.
1998	Multinational Species Conservation Fund as created to carry out the African Elephant Conservation Act, the Asian Elephant Conservation Act, and the Rhinoceros and Tiger Conservation Act
1999	New Legislation bans the creation, sale, and possession with intent to sell, of animal crushing or stomping films
1999	Depiction of Animal Cruelty makes it a crime knowingly to create, sell, or possess any visual or audio depiction of animal cruelty with the intention of placing that depiction in interstate or foreign commerce for commercial gain. It provides an exception for "any depiction that has serious religious, political, scientific, educational, journalistic, historical, or artistic value."
2000	The New Zealand Animal Welfare Act becomes law. Great apes are banned from use in research, testing, or teaching.
2000	The U.S. passes the Chimpanzee Health Improvement, Maintenance, and Protection (CHIMP) Act. The CHIMP Act provides for the retirement and lifetime care of chimpanzees not in active protocols, prohibits euthanasia and breeding, but allows for them to be recalled back into research.
2000	The Great Ape Conservation Act established a $5 million conservation fund to assist in global projects to conserve great ape populations
2000	New legislation requires the immediate termination of the Department of Defense practice of euthanizing military working dogs at the end of their useful working life, and facilitates the adoption of retired military working dogs
2000	Dog and Cat Protection Act of 2000 makes it unlawful to import into or export from the United States any dog or cat fur product; or to engage commerce of any dog or cat fur product
2000	ICCVAM Authorization Act of 2000 provides that the Interagency Coordinating Committee on the Validation of Alternative Methods (ICCVAM) shall among other things review and evaluate new or revised or alternative test methods. The ICCVAM was established by the Director of the National Institute of Environmental Health Sciences.
2002	Senate passes the Bear Protection Act eliminates the incentive to kill bears for their gallbladders by making it illegal to sell, import, or export the internal organs of a bear, as well as products containing bear parts

2002	Farm Bill includes a Resolution dictating the Humane Methods of Slaughter Act of 1958 should be fully enforced, preventing the needless suffering of animals; requires the Secretary of Agriculture to track violations of the Act and report results to Congress
2002	Rhinoceros and Tiger Conservation Act, African Elephant Conservation Act, and Asian Elephant Conservation act all reauthorized
2002	In 37 states, cruelty to animals now a felony, and four new laws enacted
2002	Sweden bans the use of great apes in biomedical research, including a ban on the lesser apes, gibbons, and siamangs
2003	The Captive Wildlife Safety Act prohibits the interstate transport of exotic big cats for private ownership as pets
2004	Marine Turtle Conservation Act states that its purpose is to assist in the conservation of marine turtles and the nesting habits of marine turtles in foreign countries by supporting and providing financial resources for projects to converse the nesting habitats, conserve marine turtles in those habitats, and addresses other threats to the survival of marine turtles
2005	The House of Representatives passes an amendment to stop the use of taxpayers' dollars to fund horse slaughterhouse inspection, effectively banning horse slaughter for one fiscal year
2006	The Supreme Court of India bans breeding animals in zoos
2006	Germany bans imported seal products from the country
2006	Arizona and Michigan pass animal protection laws in their respective states. Arizona prohibits confining calves in veal crates and confining breeding pigs in gestation crates. Michigan rejects a proposal that would have permitted a target-shooting season on the mourning dove (the state's official bird of peace), a protected species there since 1905.
2007	New federal legislation requiring stronger punishments for those who promote or encourage the brutal practice of blood sports such as dog fighting and cockfighting was approved in the United States.
Ongoing	The Society for Animal Protective Legislation (SAPL) continues to work on a range of issues, including legislation to ban the use of steel jaw leghold traps, the slaughter of horses for human consumption, and the sale of dogs and cats by random source dealers

Selected Resources

Books, Journals, Magazines, Organizations, Videos, and Websites

The following list contains general resources for the vast array of topics considered in this wide-ranging encyclopedia. Each resource and each entry in the encyclopedia also contains valuable resources, and interested readers are encouraged to seek them out for more detailed information. This is a wonderful source for class projects. Because the number of available resources is staggering, general Web sites for specific topics are included. These contain information for numerous topics and cultures worldwide, for example:

- *http://www.vetmed.ucdavis.edu/CCAB/hailit,1.htm;*
- *http://worldanimalnet.org/new.asp;*
- *http://www.deltasociety.org/TextOnly/AnimalsHealthChildrenReferences.htm.*

Adams, C. J. (1994). *Neither man nor beast: Feminism and the defense of animals.* New York: Continuum Publishing Company.

Adams, R. (2005). *Watership down.* New York: Scribner.

Africa Network for Animal Welfare. http://www.anaw.org/

Aftandilian, D. (Ed.). (2006). *What are the animals to us? Approaches from science, folklore, literature, and art.* Knoxville, TN: University of Tennessee Press.

Aisenberg, N. (Ed.). (1989). *We animals: Poems of our world.* San Francisco: Sierra Club Books.

Alger, J., & Alger, S. F. (2003). *Cat culture: The social world of a cat shelter.* Philadelphia, PA: Temple University Press.

Alpers, A. (1961). *Dolphins: The myth and the mammal.* Boston: Houghton-Mifflin.

American Anti-Vivisection Society. http://www.aavs.org/home.html

American Society for the Prevention of Cruelty to Animals. http://www.aspca.org/site/PageServer

American Sociological Association [section on animals and society]. http://www.asanet.org/sectionanimals

Anderson, D. (2004). David Anderson's literature of human-animal studies. http://www.vetmed.ucdavis.edu/CCAB/haibooks.htm

Anderson, D. (2006). *The guide to pet loss resources* (3rd ed.). Lincoln, CA: RockyDell Resources. http://rockydellresources.homestead.com/petloss.html

Anderson, V. D. (2004). *Creatures of empire: How domestic animals transformed early America.* New York: Oxford University Press.

Animalisti Italiana. http://www.animalisti.it/

Animal Law and Animal Rights: An Introductory Guide to Selected Resources.http://www.lib.uchicago.edu/e/law/news/AnimalLaw.pdf#search=%22animal%20law%20international%22

Animal Legal Defense Fund. http://www.aldf.org/

Animal Metaphors. http://artsedge.kennedy-center.org/content/2379/2379_nahuales_metaphor.pdf#search=%22animal%20metaphors%22

Animal Movies: The top 50. http://happyandhealthypets.com/nov22-03-animals-movies.html

Animal Protection Institute. http://www.api4animals.org/

Animal Rights India. http://animalrightsindia.blogspot.com/

Animal Rights Law Project, Rutgers University. http://www.animal-law.org/
Animals and Society Institute. www.animalsandsociety.org/
Animals Asia Foundation. http://www.animalsasia.org/
Animals, Culture, and Society. [book series published by Temple University Press].
Animals in art. http://www.decordova.org/decordova/exhibit/2006/animals/animals.html
Animals in movies. http://www.funtrivia.com/en/Movies/Animals-in-Movies-7694.html
Animals in the Bible. http://www.christiananswers.net/dictionary/animals.html
Animal Welfare [journal published by the Universities Federation for Animal Welfare]. http://www.ufaw.org.uk/
Animal Welfare Institute. http://www.awionline.org/
Anthrozoös. [A multidisciplinary journal of the interactions of people and animals; published by the International Society for Anthrozoology.] http://www.vetmed.ucdavis.edu/CCAB/isaz.htm
Applied Animal Behaviour Science. [An international journal reporting on the application of ethology to animals managed by humans.] http://www.elsevier.com/wps/find/journaldescription.cws_home/503301/description#description
Arluke, A. (2004). *Brute force: Animal police and the challenge of cruelty*. West Lafayette, IN: Purdue University Press.
Arluke, A. (2006). *Just a dog: Understanding animal cruelty and ourselves*. Philadelphia, PA: Temple University Press.
Arluke, A., & Sanders, C. R. (1996). *Regarding animals*. Philadelphia, PA: Temple University Press.
Assistance Dog Institute. http://www.assistancedog.org/
Baker, S. (1993). *Picturing the beast: Animals, identity and representation*. Manchester: Manchester University Press.
Balcombe, J. P. (2000). *The use of animals in education: Problems, alternatives, and recommendations*. Washington, DC: Humane Society of the United States.
Balcombe J. P. (2006). *Pleasurable kingdom: Animals and the nature of feeling good*. London: Macmillan.
Baldick, J. (2000). Animal and shaman: Ancient religions of central Asia. New York: New York University Press.
Barash, D., & Barash, N. R. (2005). *Madame Bovary's ovaries: A Darwinian look at literature*. New York: Delacourte.
Beck, A. M., & Katcher, A. H. (1996). *Between pets and People: The importance of animal companionship* (Rev. Ed.). West Lafayette, IN: Purdue University Press.
Becker, M. (2002). *The healing power of pets*. Hyperion, New York.
Bekoff, M. (Ed.). (1998). *Encyclopedia of animal rights and animal welfare*. Westport, CT: Greenwood Publishing Group.
Bekoff, M. (2002). *Minding animals: Awareness, emotions, and heart*. New York: Oxford University Press.
Bekoff, M. (2006). *Animal passions and beastly virtues: Reflections on redecorating nature*. Philadelphia, PA: Temple University Press.
Bekoff, M. (2007). *The emotional lives of animals: A leading scientist explores animal joy, sorrow, and empathy and why they matter.* Novato, CA: New World Library.
Bekoff, M., & Jamieson, D. (1996). Ethics and the study of carnivores: Doing science while respecting animals. In J. L. Gittleman (Ed.), *Carnivore behavior, ecology, and evolution*, vol. 2 (pp. 15–45). Ithaca, NY: Cornell University Press.
Bekoff, M., & Nystrom, J. (2004). The other side of silence: Rachel Carson's views of animals. *Zygon, 39*, 861–83.
Belk, R. (1996). Metaphoric relationships with pets. *Society and Animals, 4*, 121–46.
Belozerskaya, M. (2006). *The Medici giraffe*. New York: Little Brown.
Bennett, D. H. (1983). Some aspects of Aboriginal and non-Aboriginal notions of responsibility to non-human animals. *Australian Aboriginal Studies, 2*, 19–24.

Benyruys, J. M. (2002). *Biomimicry: Innovation inspired by nature*. New York: Perennial.

Berenbaum, M. R. (1995). *Bugs in the system: Insects and their impact on human affairs*. Cambridge, MA: Perseus Books.

Borowski, O. (1998). *Every living thing: Daily use of animals in ancient Israel*. Walnut Creek CA: AltaMira.

Bouse, D. (2000). *Wildlife films*. Philadelphia, PA: University of Pennsylvania Press.

Burkert, W. (1998). *The creation of the sacred: Tracks of biology in early religions*. Cambridge, MA: Harvard University Press.

Burt, J. (2002). *Animals in film*. London: Reacktion Books.

Candland, D. K. (1993). *Feral children and clever animals: Reflections on human nature*. Oxford: Oxford University Press.

Caras, R. (2002). *A perfect harmony: The intertwining lives of animals and humans throughout history*. New York: Simon & Schuster.

Carbone, L. (2004). *What animals want: Expertise and advocacy in laboratory animal welfare policy*. New York: Oxford University Press.

Carmack, B. J. (2003). *Grieving the death of a pet*. Minneapolis, MN Augsburg Books.

Carson, R. (1962). *Silent spring*. Boston: Houghton Mifflin.

Caruso, L. L. (2006). *Blessing the animals*. Woodstock, VT: Skylights Path.

Caspari, E. (2003). *Animal life in nature, myth and dreams*. Wilmette, IL: Chiron Publications.

Cavalieri, P., & Singer, P. (Eds.). (1993). *The great ape project: Equality beyond humanity*. London: Fourth Estate.

Center for Respect of Life and Environment. http://www.crle.org/prog_courses_anthro.asp

Center for the Interaction of Animals and Society. http://www2.vet.upenn.edu/research/centers/cias/

Center for the Study of World Religions. http://www.hds.harvard.edu/cswr/

Clark, K. (1977). *Animals and men: Their relationship as reflected in Western art from prehistory to the present day*. New York: William Morrow.

Clutton-Brock, J. (1999). *A natural history of domesticated mammals* (2nd Ed.). New York: Cambridge University Press/The Natural History Museum.

Coleman, J. T. (2006). *Vicious: Wolves and men in America*. New Haven, CT: Yale University Press

Collard, A. (with J. Contrucci). (1989). *Rape of the wild: Man's violence against animals and the earth*. Bloomington, IN: Indiana University Press.

Concern for Helping Animals in Israel. http://www.greenpeople.org/searchResults.cfm?memid=313

Conservation Biology [journal published by the Society for Conservation Biology]. http://www.conbio.org/

Cooper, J. (1983). *Animals in war*. London: Heinemann.

Cosselett, T. (2006). *Talking animals in British children's fiction, 1786–1914*. Burlington, VT: Ashgate.

Couturier, L. (2005). *The hopes of snakes: And other tales from the urban landscape*. Boston: Beacon Press.

Crist, E. (1999). *Images of animals: Anthropomorphism and animal mind*. Philadelphia, PA: Temple University Press.

Cronin, W. (Ed.). (1996). *Uncommon ground: Rethinking the human place in nature*. New York: W. W. Norton.

Datson, L., & Mitman, G. (2005). *Thinking with animals: New perspectives on anthropomorphism*. New York: Oxford University Press.

Davis, K. (1996). *Poisoned chickens poisoned eggs: An inside look at the modern poultry industry*. Summertown, TN: Book Publishing Company.

Davis, K. (2001). *More than a meal: The turkey in history, myth, ritual, and reality*. New York: Lantern Books.

Davis, S. E., DeMello, M. (2003). *Stories rabbits tell: A natural and cultural history of a misunderstood creature*. New York: Lantern Books.

Davis, S. G. (1997). *Spectacular nature: Corporate culture and the Sea World experience.* Berkeley, CA: University of California Press.
Dawkins, M. S. (1992). *Through our eyes only?* New York: Oxford University Press.
Deacon, T. W. (1997). *The symbolic species: The co-evolution of language and brain.* New York: W. W. Norton.
De Jonge, F., & van den Bos, R. (Eds.) (2005). *The human-animal relationship.* Assen, the Netherlands: Royal van gorcum.
Derr, M. (1997). *Dog's best friend: Annals of the dog-human relationship.* New York: Henry Holt.
Derr, M. (2004). *A dog's history of America: How our best friend explored, conquered, and settled a continent.* New York: North Point Press.
Egypt, Animals, and Belief. http://www.prm.ox.ac.uk/AnimalMummification.html
Ehrenfeld, D. (1981). *The arrogance of humanism.* New York: Oxford University Press.
Eisner, G. A. (1997). *Slaughterhouse.* New York: Prometheus.
Eisner, T. (2003). *For love of insects.* Cambridge, MA: Harvard University Press.
Environmental Ethics [An interdisciplinary journal dedicated to the philosophical aspects if environmental problems]. http://www.cep.unt.edu/enethics.html
Environmental Values. http://www.cep.unt.edu/values.html
Ethologists for the Ethical Treatment of Animals: Citizens for Responsible Animal Behavior Studies. http://www.ethologicalethics.org/
Fascione, N., Delach, A., & Smith, M. E. (Eds.). (2004). *People and predators: From conflict to coexistence.* Washington, DC: Island Press.
Fauna Foundation. http://www.faunafoundation.org/ff/
Fictional animals in theatre, literature, television, comics and puppetry, film, songs, video games, and other media. http://www.answers.com/topic/list-of-fictional-animals
Fine, A. (Ed.) (2006). *Handbook on animal-assisted therapy.* San Diego: Elsevier.
Foltz, R. C. (2005). *Animals in Islamic tradition and Muslim cultures.* Oxford: Oneworld.
Foreman, D. (2004). *Rewilding North America: A vision for conservation in the 21st century.* Washington, DC: Island Press.
Foreman, R., et al. (2003). *Road ecology: Science and solutions.* Washington, DC: Island Press.
Fox, C. H., & Papouchis, C. M. (Eds.). (2004). *Cull of the wild: A contemporary analysis of wildlife trapping in the United States.* Sacramento, CA: Animal Protection Institute.
Fox, M. W. (1981). *Returning to Eden: Animal rights and human responsibility.* New York: Viking Press.
Fox, M. W. (2001). Bringing life to ethics. Global bioethics for a humane society. Albany, NY: State University Press.
Fundación Altarriba. http://www.altarriba.org/
Gandhi, M., Husain, O., & Panjwani, R. (2001). *Animal laws of India.* Delhi: Universal Law Publishing Company Pvt. Ltd.
Gentry, C. (1983). *When dogs run wild: The sociology of feral dogs and wildlife.* Jefferson, NC: McFarland & Company.
Goodall, J., & Bekoff, M. (2002). *The ten trusts: What we must do to care for the animals we love.* San Francisco: HarperCollins.
Gottschall, J., & Wilson, D. S. (Eds.). (2005). *The literary animal: Evolution and the nature of narrative.* Evanston, IL: Northwestern University Press.
Greek, C. R., & Greek, J. W. (2000). *Sacred cows and golden geese: The human costs of experiments on animals.* New York: Continuum.
Grier, K. C. (2006). *Pets in America: A history.* Chapel Hill, NC: University of North Carolina Press.
Guerrero, D. L. (2007). *Blessing of the animals. A guide to prayers and ceremonies celebrating pets and other creatures.* New York: Sterling Publishing.
Halliday, W. R. (1922). Animal pets in ancient Greece. *Discovery, 3,* 151–54.
H-Nilas [Nature in Legend and Story]. http://www.h-net.org/~nilas/about.html

Hargrove, E. C. (Ed.). (1992). *The animal rights/environmental ethics debate: The environmental perspective*. Albany, New York: SUNY Press.

Hart, D., & Sussman, R. W. (2005). *Man the hunted: Primates, predators, and human evolution*. Cambridge Center, MA: Westview Press.

Harvey, G. (2005). *Animism: Respecting the living world*. London: C. Hurst & Co. / New York: Columbia University Press / Adelaide: Wakefield Press.

Hays, H. R. (1973). *Birds, beasts, and men*. Baltimore, MD: Penguin Books.

Heinrich, B. (1999). *Mind of the raven: Investigations and adventures with wolf-birds*. New York: HarperCollins.

Hobgood-Oster, L. (2007). *Holy dogs and asses: Animals in Christianity*. Urbana: University of Illinois Press.

Hogan, L., Metzger, D., & Peterson, B. (Eds.). (1998). *Intimate nature: The bond between women and animals*. New York: The Ballantine Publishing Group.

Hoogland, J. L. (1995). *The black-tailed prairie dog: Social life of a burrowing mammal*. Chicago: University of Chicago Press.

Horowitz, A. C., & Bekoff, M. (2007). Naturalizing anthropomorphism: Behavioral prompts to our humanizing of animals. *Anthrozöos, 20*, 23–35.

House, A. (2000). *Francis of Assisi: A revolutionary life*. Mahwah, NJ: Hidden Spring.

Huffman, M. A. (2002). Animal origins of herbal medicine. In Fleurentin, J., Pelt, J-M., & Mazars, G. (Eds.), *From the sources of knowledge to the medicines of the future* (pp. 31–42). Paris: IRD Editions 2002.

Human-animal interactions and companion animal welfare. http://www.vetmed.ucdavis.edu/CCAB/compan~1.htm

Human-animal interactions books. http://books.google.com/books?q=human+animal+interactions&ots=kcl7vmRMZn&sa=X&oi=print&ct=title

Human-animal interactions literature. http://www.vetmed.ucdavis.edu/CCAB/hailit~1.htm

Human Ecology Review [journal published by the Society for Human Ecology] http://www.societyforhumanecology.org/)

Humane Society of the United States. http://www.hsus.org/

In Defense of Animals. http://www.idausa.org/

International Association of Human-Animal Interaction Organizations. http://www.iahaio.org/

International Fund for Animal Welfare. http://www.ifaw.org/ifaw/general/default.aspx

International Institute for Animal Law. http://www.animallaw.com/

International Society for Anthrozoology. http://www.vetmed.ucdavis.edu/CCAB/isaz.htm

Irvine, L. (2004). *If you tame me: Understanding our connection with animals*. Philadelphia, PA: Temple University Press.

James, W. (2004). *The ceremonial animal: A new portrait anthropology*. New York: Oxford University Press.

Jamieson, D. (2003). *Morality's progress*. New York: Oxford University Press.

Jordan, W. (2003). *A cat named Darwin: Embracing the bond between man and pet*. Boston: Mariner Books.

Journal for the Study of Religion, Nature, and Culture. http://www.religionandnature.com/journal/board.htm

Journal of Applied Animal Welfare Science. http://www.psyeta.org/jaaws/

Journal of Contemporary Ethnography. http://jce.sagepub.com/

Kahn, P. H. Jr. (2001). *The human relationship with nature: Development and culture*. Cambridge, MA: MIT Press.

Kalof, L. (2006). *Looking at animals in human history*. London: Continuum.

Kalof, L., and Fitzgerald, A. (Eds.) (2007). *The animals reader: The essential classic and contemporary writings*. New York: Berg.

Kellert, S. R. (1996). *The value of life: Biological diversity and human society*. Washington, DC: Island Press.

Kellert, S. R., & Farhham, T. (Eds.) (2002). *The good in nature and humanity: Connecting science, religion, and spirituality with natural world*. Washington, DC: Island Press.

Kellert. S. R., & Wilson, E. O. (1993). *The biophilia hypothesis*. Washington, DC: Island Press.

Key References on Human-Animal Interactions for Children. http://www.deltasociety.org/TextOnly/AnimalsHealthChildrenReferences.htm

Kidd, A. H., & Kidd, R. M. (1980). Personality characteristics and preferences in pet ownership. *Psychological Reports, 46*, 939–49.

Knight, J. (2006). *Waiting for wolves: An anthropological study of people-wildlife relations*. Honolulu, HI: University of Hawaii Press.

Knight, R. L., & Gutzwiller, K. J. (Eds.). (1995). *Wildlife and recreation: coexistence through management and research*. Washington, DC: Island Press.

Kowalski, G. (1997). *Goodbye, friend: Healing wisdom for anyone who has ever lost a pet*. Walpole, NH: Stillpoint Publishing.

Kruger, K. A., Trachtenberg, S. W., & Serpell, J. A. (2004). Can animals help humans heal? Animal-assisted interventions in adolescent mental health. Center for the Interaction of Animals and Society, University of Pennsylvania School of Veterinary Medicine. http://www2.vet.upenn.edu/research/centers/cias/pdf/CIAS_AAI_white_paper.pdf

Laboratory Primate Advocacy Groups. http://www.lpag.org/

Latham Foundation. http://www.latham.org/Magazine/magazine.asp

Lauck, J. E. (2002). *The voice of the infinite in the small: Re-visioning the insect-human connection*. Boston: Shambhala Publications.

Lawrence, E. A. (1982). *Rodeo: An anthropologist looks at the wild and the tame*. Knoxville, TN: University of Tennessee Press.

Lawrence, E. A. (1985). *Hoofbeats and society: Studies of human-horse interactions*. Bloomington, IN: Indiana University Press.

Lawrence, E. A. (1990). The tamed wild: Symbolic bears in American culture. In Browne, R., Fishwick, M., & Browne, K. (Eds.), *Dominant symbols in popular culture* (pp. 140–53). Bowling Green, OH: Bowling Green State University Popular Press.

Laytner, A., & Bridge. D. (2005). *The animals' lawsuit against humanity*. Louisville, KY: Fons Vitae.

Lear, L. (2007). *Beatrix Potter: A life in nature*. New York: St. Martin's Press.

Le Chêne, E. (1997). *Silent heroes: The bravery and devotion of animals in war*. London, UK: Souvenir Press.

Le Guin, U. K. (1987). *Buffalo gals and other animal presences*. Santa Barbara, CA: Capra Press.

Levinson, B. (1969). *Pet-oriented child psychotherapy*. Springfield, IL: Charles C. Thomas.

Levinson, B. (1972). *Pets and human development*. Springfield, IL: Charles C. Thomas.

Linzey, A. (1995). *Animal theology*. Chicago: University of Illinois Press.

Lippincott, L., & Blühm, A. (Eds.). (2005). *Fierce friends: Artists ad animals, 1750–1900*. New York: Merrell.

Lippit, A. K. (2000). *Electric animal: Toward a rhetoric of wildlife*. Minneapolis, MN: University of Minnesota Press.

Lopez, B. (1977/1990). *Giving birth to thunder, sleeping with his daughter: Coyote builds North America*. New York: Avon Books.

Louv, R. (2005). *Last child in the woods: Saving our children from nature deficit disorder.* Chapel Hill, NC: Algonquin Books.

Lynge, F. (1992). *Arctic wars, animal rights, endangered peoples*. Hanover, NH: University Press of New England.

Mack, A. (Ed.). (1999). *Humans and other animals*. Columbus, OH: Ohio State University Press.

Majupuria, T. (1991). *Sacred animals of Nepal and India.* Gwalior, India: M. Devi.

Malson, L. (1972). *Wolf children and the problem of human nature.* New York: Monthly Review Press.

Manning, A., & Serpell, J. (Eds.). (1994). *Animals and human society changing perspectives.* New York: Routledge.

Marcus, E. (2005). *Meat market: Animals, ethics, and money.* Newfield, NY: Brio Press.

McDaniel, J. B. (1989). *Of God and pelicans: A theology of reverence for life.* Louisville, KY: Westminster/John Knox Press.

McDonnell, P. (2003). *Mutts: The comic art of Patrick McDonnell.* New York: Harry N. Abrams.

McElroy, S. C. (1995). *Animals as teachers and healers.* Troutdale, OR: NewSage Press.

McNeill, W. H. (1976) *Plagues and peoples.* Garden City, NJ: Anchor Press.

Melson, G. F. (2001). *Why the wild things are: Animals in the lives of children.* Cambridge, MA: Harvard University Press.

Metaphor and Symbol. http://www.leaonline.com/loi/ms?cookieSet=1

Micah Publications [books on Judaism and animals, vegetarianism, and the environment]. http://www.micahbooks.com/

Midgley, M. (1983). *Animals and why they matter.* Athens, GA: University of Georgia Press.

Midgley, M. (1995). *Beast and man: The roots of human nature.* New York: Routledge.

Millman, S. T., Duncan, I. J. H., Stauffacher, M., & Stookey, J. M. (2004). The impact of applied ethologists and the International Society for Applied Ethology in improving animal welfare. *Applied Animal Behaviour Science, 86,* 299–311.

Mitman, G. (1999). *Reel nature: America's romance with wildlife on film.* Cambridge, MA: Harvard University press.

Morris Animal Foundation. http://www.morrisanimalfoundation.org/home.asp

Myers, G. (1998). *Children and animals: Social development and our connections to other species.* Boulder, CO: Westview Press.

Myers, G. (2006). *The significance of children and animals.* West Lafayette, IN: Purdue University Press.

National Center for Animal Law. http://www.lclark.edu/org/ncal

Nelson, B. (2000) *The wild and the domestic: Animal representation, ecocriticism, and Western American literature.* Reno, NV: University of Nevada Press.

Newkirk, I. (2005). *Making kind choices: Everyday ways to enhance your life through Earth- and animal-friendly living.* New York: St Martin's Griffin.

Norris, K., & Pain, D. J. (2002). *Conserving bird biodiversity: General principles and their application.* New York: Cambridge University Press.

Odendaal, J. S. J. (2002). *Pets and our mental health: The why, the what and the how.* New York: Vantage Press.

Ogorzaly, M. A. (2006). *When bulls cry: The case against bullfighting.* Bloomington, IN: AuthorHouse.

Olson, E. (1997). *The human animal: Personal identity without psychology.* Oxford: Oxford University Press.

Overby, C. Animal slang and the nature of words. http://www.mdc.mo.gov/kids/out-in/1998/1/2.html

Pacheco, J. E. (1993). *An ark for the next millennium* (M. Sayers Peden, Trans.). Austin, TX: University of Texas Press.

Palmatier, R. A. (1995). *Speaking of animals: A dictionary of animal metaphors.* Westport, CT: Greenwood Press.

Patton, K., & Waldau, P. (Eds.). (2006). *A communion of subjects: Animals in religion, science, and ethics.* New York: Columbia University Press.

People for the Ethical Treatment of Animals. http://www.peta.org/

Peterson, A. L. (2001). *Being human: Ethics, environment, and our place in the world.* Berkeley and Los Angeles: University of California Press.

Phelps, N. (2004). *The great compassion: Buddhism and animal rights.* New York: Lantern Books.
Philo, C., & Wilbert, C. (2000). *Animal spaces, beastly places.* London: Routledge.
Plumwood, V. (1993). *Feminism and the mastery of nature.* New York: Routledge.
Qualitative Sociology. http://www.springerlink.com/content/1573–7837
Quinn, D. (1992). *Ishmael.* New York: Bantam.
Radford, M. (2001). *Animal welfare law in Britain: Regulation and responsibility.* New York: Cambridge University Press.
Rational Animal. http://www.rational-animal.org/
Regan, T. (1984) *The case for animal rights.* New York: Routledge.
Regenstein, L. G. (1991). *Replenish the earth: A history of organized religion's treatment of animals and nature—including the Bible's message of conservation and kindness toward animals.* New York: Crossroad.
Religion and animals. http://members.iinet.com.au/~rabbit/churchan.htm
Religion, ethics, and animals. http://www.bbc.co.uk/religion/ethics/animals/index.shtml
Richards, G. (1982). *The philosophy of Gandhi.* London: Curzon Press.
Ritvo, H. (1987). *The animal estate: The English and other creatures in the Victorian age.* Cambridge, MA: Harvard University Press.
Ritvo, H. (1997). *The platypus and mermaid and other figments of the classifying imagination.* Cambridge, MA: Harvard University Press.
Rivera, M. (2001). *Hospice hounds.* New York: Lantern Books.
Robinson, M. J. (2005). *Predatory bureaucracy: The extermination of wolves and the transformation of the west.* Boulder, CO: University Press of Colorado.
Robson, M. (1997). *St. Francis of Assisi.* London: SCM Press.
Rollin, B. E. (1989). *The unheeded cry: Animal consciousness, animal pain and science.* New York: Oxford University Press (reprinted 1998, Iowa State University Press).
Roots & Shoots. http://www.rootsandshoots.org
Rothenberg, D. (2005). *Why birds sing: A journey through the mystery of birdsong.* New York: Basic Books.
Ryder, R. D. (1989). *Animal revolution: Changing attitudes towards speciesism.* Cambridge, MA: Basil Blackwell.
Salotto, P. (2001). *Pet assisted therapy: A loving intervention and an emerging profession: Leading to a friendlier, healthier, and more peaceful world.* Norton, MA: D.J. Publications.
Sanders, C.R. (1993). Understanding dogs: Caretakers' attributions of mindedness in canine-human relationships. *Journal of Contemporary Ethnography, 22*(2), 205–26.
Sanders, C. R. (1999). *Understanding dogs.* Philadelphia, PA: Temple University Press.
Sax, B. (2001). *The mythical zoo: An encyclopedia of animals in world myth, legend and literature.* Santa Barbara, CA: ABC-CLIO.
Schneider, S. H., & Roots, T. L. (Eds.). (2002). *Wildlife responses to climate change: North American case studies.* Washington, DC: Island Press.
Scholtmeijer, M. (1993). *Animal victims in modern fiction: From sanctity to sacrifice.* Toronto: University of Toronto Press.
Schubert, L. (2006). *Ballet of the elephants.* (R. A. Parker, Illus.). Brookfield, CT: Roaring Brook Press.
Schwabe, C. W. (1994). Animals in the ancient world. In A. Manning & J. Serpell (Eds.), *Animals and human society: Changing perspectives* (pp. 36–58). London: Routledge.
Schwartz, R. H. (2001). *Judaism and vegetarianism.* New York: Lantern Books.
Scully, M. (2002). *Dominion: The power of man, the suffering of animals.* New York: St. Martin's Press.
Serpell, J. (1986). *In the company of animals.* New York: Basil Blackwell.
Serpell, J. (1996). *In the company of animals: A study of human–animal relationships.* Cambridge: Cambridge University Press.
Sheldrake, R. (1999). *Dogs that know when their owners are coming home, and other unexplained powers of animals.* New York: Crown.

Shepard, P. (1996). *The others: How animals made us human.* Washington, DC: Island Press.
Sideris, L. (2003). *Environmental ethics, ecological theology and natural selection.* New York: Columbia University Press.
Singer, P. (1991). *Animal liberation* (2nd ed.). London: Thorsons.
Slifkin, N. (2001). *Nature's song: An elucidation of Perek Shirah, the ancient text that lists the philosophical and ethical lessons of the natural world (Torah universe).* Nanuet, NY: Feldheim.
Smith, D. W., Peterson, R. O., & Houston, D. B. (2003). Yellowstone after wolves. *Bioscience, 53,* 330–40.
Society and Animals Forum. http://www.psyeta.org/sa
Solisti, K., & Tobias, M. (Eds.). (2006). *Kinship with animals.* Tulsa, OK: Council Oaks Books.
Sponberg, A. (1997). Green Buddhism and the hierarchy of compassion. In M. E. Tucker & D. R. Williams (Eds.), *Buddhism and ecology* (pp. 351–76). Cambridge, MA: Harvard University Press.
Steiger, B. (1999). *The werewolf book: The encyclopedia of shape-shifting beings.* Detroit and London: Visible Ink Press.
Sterckx, R. (2002). *The animal and the daemon in early China.* Albany, NY: State University of New York Press.
Symbolic Interaction. http://www.ucpress.edu/journals/si
Taylor, B. (Ed.). (2005). *The encyclopedia of religion and nature.* New York: Thoemmes Continuum.
The Bible and Animals. http://www.thebibleandanimals.org/
Thorpe, W. H. (1974). *Animal nature and human nature.* Garden City, NY: Anchor Press/Doubleday.
Tobias, M. (2000). *Kids and animals: A healing partnership.* [Award-winning video.]
Tobias, M. (2000). *Life force: The world of Jainism.* Fremont, CA: Jain Publishing Company.
Toynbee, J. M. C. (1973). *Animals in Roman life and art.* Ithaca, NY: Cornell University Press.
Turner, J., & D'Silva, J. (Eds.). (2006). *Animals, ethics, and trade.* London: Earthscan Publishing.
Tye, L. C. (2005). *The animal in me is plain to see.* Portland, OR: WestWinds Press. http://www.gacpc.com/imprints/ww/index.htm
Universities Federation for Animal Welfare. http://www.ufaw.org.uk/
Walker, B. L. (2005). *The lost wolves of Japan.* Seattle, WA: University of Washington Press.
Weil, Z. (2003). *Above all, be kind: Raising a humane child in challenging times.* Gabriola Island, BC, Canada: New Society Publishers.
Weston, R., & Ross, C. (2004). *Kids & dogs.* Crows Nest, Australia: Allen & Unwin.
Wildlife Conservation Society. http://www.wcs.org/
Wilson, E. O. (1984). *Biophilia.* Cambridge, MA: Harvard University Press.
Wise, S. M. (2000). *Rattling the cage: Toward legal rights for animals.* Cambridge, MA: Perseus Books.
Wolch, J., & Emel, J. (Eds.). 1998. *Animal geographies: Place, politics, and identity in the nature-culture borderlands.* London: Verso.
Woodroffe, R., Thirgood, S., & Rabinowitz, A. (Eds.). (2005). *People and wildlife, conflict or coexistence?* New York: Cambridge University Press.
World Animal Net Directory. [The world's largest database of animal protection societies, with more than 17,000 listings and 10,000 links.] http://worldanimalnet.org/new.asp
World Society for the Protection of Animals http://www.wspa-usa.org/
Wrangham, R., & Conklin-Brittain, N. (2003). Cooking as a biological trait. *Comparative Biochemistry and Physiology, Part A, 136,* 35–46
Zeuner, F. E. (1963). *A history of domesticated animals.* New York: Harper and Row.
Zimmerman, M. E., Callicott, J. B., Sessions, G., Warren, K. J., & Clark, J. (Eds.). (1993). *Environmental philosophy: From animal rights to radical ecology.* New York: Prentice-Hall.
Zinsser, H. (1935). *Rats, lice and history.* Boston: Little, Brown.
Zygon [Journal of Religion and Science]. http://www.blackwellpublishing.com/journal.asp?ref=0591-2385

About the Editor and Contributors

About the Editor

Marc Bekoff is Professor Emeritus of Biology at the University of Colorado, Boulder, and cofounder, with Jane Goodall, of Ethologists for the Ethical Treatment of Animals. He has won many awards for his scientific research, including a Guggenheim Fellowship, and he is a prolific writer with more than 200 articles as well as two encyclopedias to his credit. The author or editor of numerous books, including the *Encyclopedia of Animal Rights and Animal Welfare; The Ten Trusts: What We Must Do to Care for the Animals We Love* (with Jane Goodall); and the *Encyclopedia of Animal Behavior*, his most recent books include *The Smile of a Dolphin*, *Minding Animals*, *Animal Passions and Beastly Virtues: Reflections on Redecorating Nature, The Emotional Lives of Animals*, and *Animals Matter*. In 2005 Bekoff was presented with The Bank One Faculty Community Service Award for the work he has done with children, senior citizens, and prisoners. His Web site is http://literati.net/Bekoff.

About the Contributors

Elisa Aaltola
Research Fellow in Philosophy, University of Turku, Turku, Finland
Ethics and Animal Protection—*Interest Conflicts between Animals and Humans*
Media and Film—*Animal Monsters in Film*

Evelyn Lawino Abe
Wildlife Consultant, London, UK
Living with Animals—*Elephants and Humans* (with Gay A. Bradshaw)

Charles I. Abramson
Professor of Psychology, Oklahoma State University, Stillwater, Oklahoma
Conservation and Environment—*Earthworms: The "Intestines of the Earth"*
Conservation and Environment—*Pesticides' Effects on Honeybees* (with Janko Bozic)
Culture, Religion, and Belief Systems—*Animal Symbolism in Native American Cultures* (with Wilma Bold Warrior)
Culture, Religion, and Belief Systems—*Snakes as Cultural and Religious Symbols* (with Aaron J. Place)
Health—*Chagas Disease and Insect Behavior* (with Elis Aldana)
Health—*Insect Pests in Human Economy and Health* (with Janko Bozic)
Health—*Rabies* (with Harrington Wells)
Living with Animals—*Pesticide Effects on Honeybees* (with Janko Bozic)
Research—*A Honeybee Model of Alcohol-Induced Behavior* (with Janko Bozic and Harrington Wells)

Celia Ackerman
Independent Scholar, New York, New York
Bonding—*Discrimination between Humans by Gentoo Penguins* (Pygosceli papua papua/ellsworthii) (with Hank Davis and Anne E. Silver)

Rick A. Adams
Associate Professor of Biology, University of Northern Colorado, Greeley, Colorado
Living with Animals—*Bats and People*

Dave Aftandilian
Preceptor and Program Coordinator, Environmental Studies Program, University of Chicago, Chicago, Illinois
Archaeology—*Archaeology and Animals*
Culture, Religion, and Belief Systems—*Shapeshifting* (with Marion W. Copeland)

Govindasamy Agoramoorthy
Professor of Pharmacy, Tajen University, Taiwan
Conservation and Environment—*Conservation and Wildlife Trade in India*
Conservation and Environment—*Conservation Conflicts with Hunting Wild Animals in Asia*
Conservation and Environment—*The Great Apes of Asian Forests, "The People of the Forest"*
Conservation and Environment—*India's Bats and Human Attitudes*
Culture, Religion, and Belief Systems—*India's Sacred Animals* [sidebar: *Animal Protection in India's Bishnoi Community*]
Culture, Religion, and Belief Systems—*Monkeys and Humans in India* [sidebar: *The Monkey God Hanuman*]
Literature—*Caste Discrimination in Animals* [sidebar to *Metaphors about Animals*]
Zoos and Aquariums—*Southeast Asia's Zoos*

Candace S. Alcorta
Research Scientist in Anthropology, University of Connecticut, Storrs, Connecticut
Culture, Religion, and Belief Systems—*Rituals of Humans and Animals* (with Richard Sosis)

Elis Aldana
Professor of Animal Parasite Vectors, Universidad de Los Andes, Merida, Venezuela
Health—*Chagas Disease and Insect Behavior* (with Charles I. Abramson)

Colin Allen
Professor of History and Philosophy of Science and Cognitive Science, Indiana University, Bloomington, Indiana
Sentience and Cognition—*Animal Pain*

Enrico Alleva
Director, Section of Behavioural Neurosciences, Department of Cell Biology and Neurosciences, Istituto Superiore di Sanità, Rome, Italy
Hunting, Fishing, and Trapping—*Falcons, Hawks, and Nocturnal Birds of Prey* (with Nadia Francia)

Zoos and Aquariums—*Amphibians and Zookeepers* (with Nadia Francia)
Zoos and Aquariums—*Reptiles and Zookeepers* (with Nadia Francia)

Stephen Alter
Author, Mussoorie, India
Culture, Religion, and Belief Systems—*India and the Elephant*

Roland C. Anderson
Biologist, The Seattle Aquarium, Seattle, Washington
Conservation and Environment—*Mollusk Extinction*
Living with Animals—*Giant Octopuses and Squid*

Virginia DeJohn Anderson
Professor of History, University of Colorado, Boulder, Colorado
History—*Colonial America and Domestic Animals*

Arnold Arluke
Professor of Sociology, Northeastern University, Boston, Massachusetts
Children—*The Appeal of Animals to Children*
Cruelty to Animals—*Harming Animals and Its Impact on People*
Cruelty to Animals—*Law Enforcement of Anticruelty Legislation*
Ethics and Animal Protection—*Hoarding Animals* (with Gary Patronek)
Human Perceptions of Animals—*Social Construction of Animals* (with Clinton R. Sanders)

Kellar Autumn
Associate Professor of Biology, Lewis and Clark College, Portland, Oregon
Biomimicry—*How Gecko Toes Stick*

Melissa Bain
DVM, Diplomate of American College of Veterinary Behaviorists, School of Veterinary Medicine, Companion Animal Behavior Program, University of California, Davis, California
Bonding—*Behavior of Pets and the Human-Animal Bond*

Philip Baker
School of Biological Sciences, University of Bristol, Bristol, UK
Urban Animals—*Red Foxes in Urban Areas* (with Stephen Harris)

Jonathan Balcombe
Research Scientist and Author, Physicians Committee for Responsible Medicine, Washington, DC
Music, Dance, and Theater—*Music and Animals*

Alan M. Beck
Dorothy N. McAllister Professor of Animal Ecology, School of Veterinary Medicine, Purdue University, West Lafayette, Indiana
Health—*Benefits of Animal Contact*
Health—*Dog Bites and Attack*

Piers Beirne
Professor of Sociology and Legal Studies, University of Southern Maine, Portland, Maine
Bestiality—*Bestiality* [sidebar: *Sexual Assault of Animals*]

Janine M. Benyus
Author, Biomimicry Guild, Helena, Montana
Biomimicry—*Biomimicry: Innovation Inspired by Nature*

Penny L. Bernstein
Associate Professor of Biological Sciences, Kent State University Stark, North Canton, Ohio
Living with Animals—*Cat and Human Relationships*

Holley Bishop
Independent Scholar, New York, New York
Living with Animals—*Honeybee and Human Collaboration*

Stephan Blatti
Visiting Assistant Professor of Philosophy, Duke University, Durham, North Carolina
Culture, Religion, and Belief Systems—*Animalism and Personal Identity*

David E. Blockstein
Executive Secretary, Council of Environmental Deans and Directors, Senior Scientist, National Council for Science and the Environment, Washington, DC
Conservation and Environment—*The Passenger Pigeon*

John Bock
Professor of Anthropology, California State University, Fullerton, California
Bonding—*Chimpanzee and Human Relationships* (with Cristy Watkins)

Wilma Bold Warrior
Independent Scholar, Ponca Nation, Ponca, Oklahoma
Culture, Religion, and Belief Systems—*Animal Symbolism in Native American Cultures* (with Charles I. Abramson)

Oded Borowski
Professor of Biblical Archaeology and Hebrew, Emory University, Atlanta, Georgia
Culture, Religion, and Belief Systems—*Animals in the Hebrew Bible*

Brian Boyd
Professor of English, University of Auckland, Auckland, New Zealand
Play—*Humans, Animals, and Laughter*

Janko Bozic
Assistant Professor of Ethology, University of Ljubljana, Ljubljana, Slovenia
Conservation and Environment—*Pesticides' Effects on Honeybees* (with Charles I. Abramson)
Health—*Insect Pests in Human Economy and Health* (with Charles I. Abramson)

Living with Animals—*Pesticide Effects on Honeybees* (with Charles I. Abramson)
Research—*A Honeybee Model of Alcohol-Induced Behavior* (with Charles I. Abramson and Harrington Wells)

Gay A. Bradshaw
Environmental Sciences Graduate Program, Oregon State University, Corvallis, Oregon, and Pacifica Graduate Institute, Santa Barbara, California
Living with Animals—*Elephants and Humans* (with Evelyn Lawino Abe)

Keri Brandt
Assistant Professor of Sociology and Gender/Women's Studies, Fort Lewis College, Durango, Colorado
Bonding—*Horse Whispering, or Natural Horsemanship*
Communication and Language—*Human-Horse Communication*

Dorothee Brantz
Research Fellow, German Historical Institute, Washington, DC
Health—*Epizootics: Diseases that Affect Animals*

Susan Bratton
Professor, Department of Environmental Studies, Baylor University, Waco, Texas
Living with Animals—*Horses and Humans: From Prey to Partner* (with Heidi Marcum)

Andrea Brooks
Director of Education and Client Advocacy, Pets Are Wonderful Support, San Francisco, California
Ethics and Animal Protection—*Human-Animal Support Services*

John Buckeridge
Head of School of Civil, Environmental and Chemical Engineering; RMIT University; Victoria, Australia
Living with Animals—*Kiwis and Humans*

Roger Burrows
Lecturer (retired), University of Exeter, Exeter, UK
Conservation and Environment—*African Wild Dogs and Humans*

Jonathan Burt
Independent Scholar, Waterbeach, UK
Media and Film—*Animals in Film*

Philip Cafaro
Associate Professor of Philosophy, Colorado State University, Fort Collins, Colorado
Literature—*Thoreau and the Human-Animal Relationship*

Christine Caldwell
Naropa University, Boulder, Colorado
Health—*Human Emotional Trauma and Animal Models*

Jennifer Calkins
Research Scientist, University of Washington, Seattle, Washington
Evolution—*Nineteenth-Century Naturalists and the Theory of Evolution*
Literature—*Animals in Literature*

Larry Carbone
Laboratory Animal Veterinarian, University of California, San Francisco, California
Euthanasia—*Animal Euthanasia*
Research—*Animal Models and Animal Welfare*
Research—*Animal Use by Humans in Research and Experimentation*
Research—*Laboratory Animal Welfare*

Peggy Cattan
Grenada Society for the Prevention of Cruelty to Animals, St George's, Grenada
Culture, Religion, and Belief Systems—*The Pothounds and Pompeks of Grenada* (with Calum Macpherson)

Arnold S. Chamove
Senior Lecturer Psychology, Massey University, Palmerston North, New Zealand
Enrichment for Animals—*Sanctuary Construction* (with Carol J. Chamove)

Carol J. Chamove
Palmerston North, New Zealand
Enrichment for Animals—*Sanctuary Construction* (with Arnold S. Chamove)

Juanita Choo
PhD Candidate, The University of Texas at Austin, Austin, Texas
Animals as Food—*Entomophagy (Eating Insects)*

Douglas Clark
PhD Candidate, Wilfrid Laurier University, Waterloo, Ontario, Canada
Conservation and Environment—*Bears and Humans*

Ethan D. Clotfelter
Assistant Professor of Biology, Amherst College, Amherst, Massachusetts
Culture, Religion, and Belief Systems—*Fish Fighting in Southeast Asia* (with Maureen G. Manning)

Richard M. Clugston
Executive Director, Center for Respect of Life and Environment, Washington DC
Conservation and Environment—*The Earth Charter* [sidebar: *The Main Principles of the Earth Charter*]
Conservation and Environment—*Humane Sustainable Development*

Juliet Clutton-Brock
South Barn, Fen Ditton, Cambridgeshire, UK
Domestication—*The Domestication Process: The Wild and the Tame*

Priscilla N. Cohn
Professor Emerita of Philosophy, Abington College, Pennsylvania State University, Abington, Pennsylvania
Ethics and Animal Protection—*Political Action Committees (PACs) for Animal Issues*
Hunting, Fishing, and Trapping—*Hunting Beliefs*

Scott L. Coleman
Postdoctoral Research Fellow, University of North Texas Health Science Center, Ft. Worth, Texas
Enrichment for Animals—*Emotional Enrichment of Captive Big Cats* (with Louis Dorfman) [sidebar: *Do Big Cats Purr?*]

Lisa M. Collins
Independent Scholar, Toronto, Canada
Ethics and Animal Protection—*Compassionate Shopping*

Lisa Collis
Department of Psychology, University of Guelph, Ontario, Canada
Bonding—*Discrimination between Humans by Honeybees* (with Hank Davis and Gard W. Otis)

Marion W. Copeland
Lecturer and Tutor, Center for Animals and Public Policy, Tufts University, Pelham, Massachusetts
Archaeology—*Archeology and Animals*
Culture, Religion, and Belief Systems—*Shapeshifting* (with Dave Aftandilian)

J. Michael Cornwell
DVM, Faculty, St. Petersburg College, School of Veterinary Technology, St. Petersburg, Florida
Health—*Animal Bite Prevention*

Nicole Cottam
Behavior Service Coordinator, Cummings School of Veterinary Medicine, Tufts University, North Grafton, Massachusetts
Research—*Toxicity Testing and Animals*

Debbie Coultis
President and CEO, People, Animals, Nature, Naperville, Illinois
Animal Assistance to Humans—*Animal-Assisted Interventions* (with Lieve Meers and William Ellery Samuels)
Biosynergy—*Biophilia* (with William Ellery Samuels and Lieve Meers)

Lisa Couturier
Author, Dickerson, Maryland
Urban Animals—*Wildlife in Urban Areas: A Personal Essay*

David Crawford
Executive Director, Rocky Mountain Animal Defense, Boulder, Colorado
Ethics and Animal Protection—*Humans, Animals, and Activism: Rocky Mountain Animal Defense* [sidebar to *Practical Ethics and Human-Animal Relations*]

Davide Csermely
Associate Professor, University of Parma, Parma, Italy
Bonding—*Infant Signals and Adopting Behavior*
Ethics and Animal Protection—*Raptor Rehabilitation and Behavior after Release*

Andrew Cuk
Theatre Instructor, Cégep John Abbott College, Ste-Anne-Bellevue, Québec, Canada
Music, Dance, and Theater—*Animals in Dance*
Music, Dance, and Theater—*Animals in Theater*

Thomas J. Daniels
Vector Ecology Lab, Louis Calder Center, Fordham University, Armonk, New York
Living with Animals—*Feral Dogs and Humans*

Hank Davis
Professor of Psychology, University of Guelph, Ontario, Canada
Bonding—*Discrimination between Humans by Cockroaches* (with Emily Heslop)
Bonding—*Discrimination between Humans by Emus and Rheas*
Bonding—*Discrimination between Humans by Gentoo Penguins* (Pygosceli papua papua/ellsworthii) (with Celia Ackerman and Anne E. Silver)
Bonding—*Discrimination between Humans by Honeybees* (with Lisa Collis and Gard W. Otis)
Bonding—*Rats and Humans*
Research—*Memorial Services for Research Animals*

Karen Davis
President, United Poultry Concerns, Machipongo, Virginia
History—*The Turkey in History*

Susan Davis
Independent Writer and Editor, Alameda, California
Literature—*Children's Literature: Rabbits*
Literature—*Rabbits' Roles in* Watership Down

B. Witkind Davis
Research Associate, International Fund for Animal Welfare, Yarmouth Port, Massachusetts and Center for Animals and Public Policy, Cummings School of Veterinary Medicine, Tufts University, North Grafton, Massachusetts
Animal Assistance to Humans—*Assistance and Therapy Animals*

Margo DeMello
Lecturer, Dept. of Communities, Humanities and Social Sciences, Central New Mexico Community College, Albuquerque, New Mexico
Living with Animals—*Rabbits in Human Society*

Mark Derr
Author, Miami Beach, Florida
Animal Assistance to Humans—*Assistance Dogs*
Domestication—*Dog Breeds*

Ben Dirlikov
Department of Psychology, University of Michigan, Ann Arbor, Michigan
Culture, Religion, and Belief Systems—*The Zodiac and Animals* (with Geoffrey E. Gerstner)
Health—*Parasites and Humans* (with Geoffrey E. Gerstner)

Louis Dorfman
Animal Behaviorist, International Exotic Feline Sanctuary, Boyd, Texas
Enrichment for Animals—*Emotional Enrichment of Captive Big Cats* (with Louis Dorfman)

Joyce D'Silva
Ambassador, Compassion in World Farming, Petersfield, UK
Ethics and Animal Protection—*Compassion in World Farming*

Lee Alan Dugatkin
Professor, Department of Biology, University of Louisville, Louisville, Kentucky
Evolution—*Charles Darwin and the Theory of Evolution*

Jamie Dutcher
Film Producer, Founder of Living with Wolves, Sun Valley, Idaho
Living with Animals—*Wolf Emotions Observed* (with Jim Dutcher)

Jim Dutcher
Film Producer, Founder of Living with Wolves, Sun Valley, Idaho
Living with Animals—*Wolf Emotions Observed* (with Jamie Dutcher)

Diane Dutton
Senior Lecturer in Psychology, Liverpool Hope University, Liverpool, UK
Bonding—*Animal Personality and the Human-Animal Bond*
Human Perceptions of Animals—*Animal Minds and Human Perspectives*
Literature—*Metaphors in Constructing Human-Animal Relationships*

Marion L. East
Research Scientist, Leibniz Institute for Zoo and Wildlife Research, Berlin, Germany
Living with Animals—*Hyenas and Humans* (with Heribert Hofer)

Sarah Ellis
Lecturer in Animal Management, Askahm Bryan College, York, UK
Enrichment for Animals—*Pets and Environmental Enrichment*

Ritu Esbjörn
Social Worker, True to Life Children's Services, Sebastopol, California
Media and Film—*Advertising and Animals*

Joan Esnayra
President, Psychiatric Service Dog Society, Arlington, Virginia
Animal Assistance to Humans—*Psychiatric Service Dogs*

Margaret Fidler
University of Southampton (retired), Lymington, Hants, UK
Animals at Work—*Animals in the London Blitz, 1939–1945*
Culture, Religion, and Belief Systems—*Animal Immortality*

William Fielding
Director of Planning, and Lecturer in Research Methods, The College of The Bahamas, Oakes Field, Nassau, The Bahamas
Culture, Religion, and Belief Systems—*Potcake Mongrels in the Bahamas*

Amy J. Fitzgerald
Assistant Professor of Criminology, University of Windsor, Windsor, Ontario, Canada
Conservation and Environment—*Environmental Sociology and Animal Studies*
Human Perceptions of Animals—*Sociology and Human-Animal Relationships*
Hunting, Fishing, and Trapping—*Hunting Recruitment Initiatives*

Richard C. Foltz
Associate Professor of Religion, Concordia University, Montreal, Canada
Culture, Religion, and Belief Systems—*The* Book of Animals
Culture, Religion, and Belief Systems—*Islam and Animals*
Culture, Religion, and Belief Systems—*Islam's Animal Fables:* Kalila and Dimna
Culture, Religion, and Belief Systems—The Parrot Book
Culture, Religion, and Belief Systems—*The Pure Brethren of Basra*

Dave Foreman
Executive Director, The Rewilding Institute, Albuquerque, New Mexico
Conservation and Environment—*Rewilding*

Camilla H. Fox
Wildlife Advocate and Author, Larkspur, California
Conservation and Environment—*Coyotes, Humans, and Coexistence*
Hunting, Fishing, and Trapping—*Trapping Animals*

Michael W. Fox
Veterinarian and Syndicated Columnist, Minneapolis, Minnesota
Culture, Religion, and Belief Systems—*India's Holy Cows and India's Food: Issues and Possibilities*

Nadia Francia
PhD student, Section of Behavioural Neurosciences, Department of Cell Biology and Neurosciences, Istituto Superiore di Sanità, Rome, Italy
Hunting, Fishing, and Trapping—*Falcons, Hawks, and Nocturnal Birds of Prey* (with Enrico Alleva)
Zoos and Aquariums—*Amphibians and Zookeepers* (with Enrico Alleva)
Zoos and Aquariums—*Reptiles and Zookeepers* (with Enrico Alleva)

Susan Frey
Director of Education, Walden Woods Project, Lincoln, Massachusetts
Conservation and Environment—*Animal Conservationists* (with William Ellery Samuels)

Toni Frohoff
Director of Wildlife Research, TerraMar Research, Bainbridge Island, Washington
Living with Animals—*Dolphins and Humans: From the Sea to the Swimming Pool*

Eiji Fujiwara
President, Elsa Nature Conservancy, Tsukuba, Japan
Culture, Religion, and Belief Systems—*Human-Animal Relationships in Japan*

Greta Gaard
Associate Professor of English, University of Wisconsin, River Falls, Wisconsin
Ecofeminism—*Ecofeminism and Animals*

Susan Garnett
Graduate Student, Murray State University, Murray, Kentucky
Sports—*Animals as Sports Mascots* (with Howard Whiteman)

Geoffrey E. Gerstner
Associate Professor, Department of Biologic and Materials Sciences, Department of Psychology, University of Michigan, Ann Arbor, Michigan
Culture, Religion, and Belief Systems—*The Zodiac and Animals* (with Ben Dirlikov)
Health—*Parasites and Humans* (with Ben Dirlikov)
Research—*Animal Models in Health Research*

Cathy B. Glenn
Speech and Communication Studies, San Francisco State University, San Francisco, California
Ethics and Animal Protection—*Factory Farm Industry Discourse*

Sylvia Glover
Senior Counsel, Assistant Attorney General, Washington State Office of the Attorney General, Washington State University Division, Pullman, Washington
Law—*The Legal Status of Companion Animals* (with François Martin)

Jane Goodall
DBE, Founder, The Jane Goodall Institute (www.janegoodall.org) and UN Messenger of Peace
Bonding—*Animal Beings I Have Known: A Personal Essay*

James L. Gould
Professor of Ecology and Evolutionary Biology, Princeton University, Princeton, New Jersey
History—*Harvesting from Honeybees* [sidebar: *Honeyguides: The Birds that Lead to Beehives*]

Ray Greek
President, Americans For Medical Advancement, Los Angeles, California
Research—*Animal Use in Science*

Fabrizio Grieco
Independent Scholar, Wageningen, The Netherlands
Anthropomorphism—*Human Observations of Animals, Subjective vs. Objective*

Stewart Elliott Guthrie
Professor Emeritus of Anthropology, Fordham University, New York, New York
Culture, Religion, and Belief Systems—*Religion's Origins and Animals*

Donna J. Haraway
Professor, History of Consciousness Department, University of California at Santa Cruz, California
Bonding—*Agility Training*

Stephen Harris
Professor of Environmental Sciences, University of Bristol, Bristol, UK
Urban Animals—*Red Foxes in Urban Areas* (with Philip Baker)

Donna Hart
Department of Anthropology, University of Missouri—St. Louis, St. Louis, Missouri
Hunting, Fishing, and Trapping—*Humans as the Hunted* (with Robert W. Sussman)

Lynette Hart
Professor of Human-Animal Interactions and Behavior, School of Veterinary Medicine, University of California, Davis, California
Culture, Religion, and Belief Systems—*Indian and Nepali Mahouts and their Relationships with Elephants* (with Piers Locke)
Health—*Epidemiology and Human-Animal Interactions* (with Locksley L. McV. Messam)

Graham Harvey
Lecturer in Religious Studies, The Open University, UK
Culture, Religion, and Belief Systems—*Animism*
Culture, Religion, and Belief Systems—*Chief Seattle's Speech*
Culture, Religion, and Belief Systems—*Shamanism*

Eva Hayward
Professor of Media Arts, University of New Mexico, Albuquerque, New Mexico
Living with Animals—*Corals and Humans*

Bernd Heinrich
Professor Emeritus of Biology, University of Vermont, Burlington, Vermont
Living with Animals—*Ravens and Humans*

Keith Heller
Department of Biology, University of Michigan, Ann Arbor, Michigan
Research—*Animal Models in Health Research*

Sakae Hemmi
Director, Institute for Environmental Science and Culture, Inc., Tsukuba, Japan
Culture, Religion, and Belief Systems—*Japan's Dolphins and the Human-Animal Relationship*

Harold Herzog
Professor of Psychology, Western Carolina University, Cullowhee, North Carolina
Ethics and Animal Protection—*Attitudes toward the Treatment of Animals*
Human Perceptions of Animals—*Gender Differences in Human-Animal Interactions*

Emily Heslop
Independent Scholar, Guelph, Ontario, Canada
Bonding—*Discrimination between Humans by Cockroaches* (with Hank Davis)

Suzanne Hetts
Certified Applied Animal Behaviorist, Animal Behavior Associates, Inc., Littleton, Colorado
Applied Anthrozoology and Veterinary Practice—*Applied Animal Behaviorists*

Laura Hobgood-Oster
Paden Chair in Religion, Southwestern University, Georgetown, Texas
Culture, Religion, and Belief Systems—*Blessing of the Animals Rituals*
Culture, Religion, and Belief Systems—*Christian Art and Animals*
Culture, Religion, and Belief Systems—*Christian Saints and Animals*
Culture, Religion, and Belief Systems—*Noah's Ark*

Heribert Hofer
Director, Leibniz Institute for Zoo and Wildlife Research, Berlin, Germany, and Professor of Interdisciplinary Wildlife Research, Freie University, Berlin, Germany
Living with Animals—*Hyenas and Humans* (with Marion L. East)

Linda Hogan
Author, Scholar in Residence, Professor Emeritus, University of Colorado, Boulder, Colorado
Culture, Religion, and Belief Systems—*Mustang: A Personal Essay*

Alexandra C. Horowitz
Adjunct Professor of Psychology, Barnard College, New York, New York
Anthropomorphism—*Anthropomorphism*

Minna J. Hsu
Associate Professor of Biological Sciences, National Sun Yat-Sen University, Kaohsiung, Taiwan
Conservation and Environment—*Extinction of Animals in Taiwan*
Culture, Religion, and Belief Systems—*Taiwan and Companion Animals*
Law—*Taiwan: Animal Welfare Law*

Michael A. Huffman
Associate Professor and Head, Section of Ecology, Director, Field Research Center, Primate Research Institute, Kyoto University, Kyoto, Japan
Culture, Religion, and Belief Systems—*Animals as Sources of Medicinal Wisdom in Traditional Societies*

Leslie Irvine
Associate Professor of Sociology, University of Colorado, Boulder, Colorado
Ethics and Animal Protection—*Animals in Disasters*
Sentience and Cognition—*Selfhood in Animals*

Lucas F. Johnston
PhD Candidate in Religion and Nature, University of Florida, Gainesville, Florida
Conservation and Environment—*Animal Reintroduction and Ecological Restoration*
Human Perceptions of Animals—*Humanness and What It Means to Be a Human Animal* (with Anna L. Peterson)

Susan D. Jones
Associate Professor of History of Science, University of Minnesota, St. Paul, Minnesota
Health—*Diseases between Animals and Humans (Zoonotic Disease)*

Nick Jukes
Coordinator, InterNICHE, Leicester, UK
Education—*Alternatives to Animals in Life Science Education*

Juha Jurvelius
Fisheries Biologist, Finnish Game and Fisheries Research Institute, Enonkoski, Finland
Conservation and Environment—*Advertising and the Endangered Saimaa Ringed Seal in Finland*
Conservation and Environment—*Arctic Char, Zander Fish, and Global Warming*
Conservation and Environment—*Finland and Fishery Conservation Issues*

Richard Kahn
Teaching Fellow, University of California, Los Angeles, California
Bestiality—*Zoophilia and Bestiality*

Linda Kalof
Professor of Sociology, Michigan State University, East Lansing, Michigan
Art—*Animals in Art*

Morgan G. Keay
Executive Director, The Itgel Foundation, Boulder, Colorado
Culture, Religion, and Belief Systems—*Mongolia's Tsaatan Reindeer Herders*

Mark G. E. Kelly
PhD Student, Department of Philosophy, University of Sydney, Sydney, New South Wales, Australia
Ethics and Animal Protection—*Political Rights of Animals*

Lisa Kemmerer
Assistant Professor of Philosophy, Montana State University, Billings, Montana
Culture, Religion, and Belief Systems—*Pantheism*
Ethics and Animal Protection—*Regan, Tom, and Singer, Peter*
Ethics and Animal Protection—*Tolstoy, Leo*

Barrett Anthony Klein
PhD Candidate, The Department of Ecology, Evolution and Behavior, University of Texas at Austin, Austin, Texas
Art—*Insects in Art*

Karen Kraft
Service Dog Trainer and Writer, Westminster, Maryland
Animal Assistance to Humans—*Service Dogs: A Personal Essay*

S. Chinny Krishna
Chairman, Blue Cross of India, Chennai, India
Animal Assistance to Humans—*India and Animal Therapy*
Health—*India and Rabies Control*
Research—*Animal Experimentation in India*

Renee Kuriyan
PhD Candidate, University of California, Berkeley, California
Conservation and Environment—*Elephants and Humans in Kenya* (with George Wittemyer)

Michael LaFlamme
Socioecological Systems Scientist, CSIRO, Alice Springs, Australia
Conservation and Environment—*Behavioral Ecology and Conservation*

David C. Lahti
NIH Postdoctoral Fellow, University of Massachusetts, Amherst, Massachusetts
Communication and Language—*Birdsong and Human Speech*
Communication and Language—*Similarities in Vocal Learning between Animals and Humans*
Culture, Religion, and Belief Systems—*Birds as Symbols in Human Culture*
Living with Animals—*Birds and Problems from Humans*

Beverly Lambert
Director, Prosser Library, Bloomfield, Connecticut
Literature—*Children's Literature: Dogs*

Heidi Leader
Lecturer in Animal Care, Hartpury College, Gloucestershire, UK
Bonding—*Homelessness and Dogs* (with Pauline Williams)

Linda Lear
Research Professor of Environmental History, George Washington University, Washington, D.C., and Senior Research Scholar, University of Maryland, Baltimore County, Maryland
Conservation and Environment—*Carson, Rachel*
Literature—*Children's Literature: Beatrix Potter*

Leah Lemieux
Author and Independent Scholar, Roots and Shoots: The Jane Goodall Institute, Guelph, Canada
Ecotourism—*Whales, Dolphins, and Ecotourism*

Berel Dov Lerner
Western Galilee College, Akko, Israel
Culture, Religion, and Belief Systems—*Judaism and Animals* [sidebar: *Balaam's Ass*]

Peter Li
Assistant Professor of Political Science at the University of Houston–Downtown, Houston, Texas
Culture, Religion, and Belief Systems—*Chinese Youth Attitudes toward Animals*

Andrew Linzey
Faculty of Theology, University of Oxford, and Director of the Oxford Centre for Animal Ethics, Oxford, UK
Culture, Religion, and Belief Systems—*Religion and Human-Animal Bonds*

Piers Locke
Department of Anthropology, University of Kent, Canterbury, UK
Culture, Religion, and Belief Systems—*Indian and Nepali Mahouts and their Relationships with Elephants* (with Lynnette Hart)

Celia M. Lombardi
Investigator, Museo Argentino de Ciencias Naturales, Buenos Aires, Argentina
Research—*Experimental Psychology*

Ralph H. Lutts
Goddard College, Plainfield, Vermont
Literature—*Nature Fakers*

William S. Lynn
Assistant Professor, Center for Animals and Public Policy, Tufts University, North Grafton, Massachusetts
Education—*Human-Animal Studies*
Ethics and Animal Protection—*Practical Ethics and Human-Animal Relations*
Ethics and Animal Protection—*Wolf Recovery*

Calum Macpherson
Dean of Graduate Studies, St. George's University, Grenada
Culture, Religion, and Belief Systems—*The Pothounds and Pompeks of Grenada* (with Peggy Cattan)

Maureen G. Manning
Technician, Department of Biology, Amherst College, Amherst, Massachusetts
Culture, Religion, and Belief Systems—*Fish Fighting in Southeast Asia* (with Ethan D. Clotfelter)

Heidi Marcum
Senior Lecturer, Department of Environmental Studies, Baylor University, Waco, Texas
Conservation and Environment—*Birds and Recreationists*
Living with Animals—*Horses and Humans: From Prey to Partner* (with Susan Bratton)
Living with Animals—*Snakes and Humans*

Koen Margodt
Independent Scholar in Moral Philosophy, Boutersem, Belgium
Communication and Language—*Great Apes and Language Research* [sidebar: *Nim Chimpsky*]
Ethics and Animal Protection—*The Great Ape Project*
Sentience and Cognition—*Descartes, René*
Zoos and Aquariums—*Animal Welfare, Animal Rights, and Conservation at Zoos*

Lori Marino
Senior Lecturer in Neuroscience and Behavioral Biology, Emory University, Atlanta, Georgia
Classification—*The Scala Naturae*
Culture, Religion, and Belief Systems—*Dolphin Mythology*
Sentience and Cognition—*Animal Consciousness*

Josephine Martell
Campaigns Officer, International Fund for Animal Welfare, South Yarmouth, Massachusetts
Ethics and Animal Protection—*Fashion and Animal-Friendly Trends*

François Martin
Associate Director of the Center for the Study of Animal Well-Being and Head of People-Pet Partnership, Washington State University, Pullman, Washington
Applied Anthrozoology and Veterinary Practice—*Bustad, Leo Kenneth (1920–1998): Pioneer in Human-Animal Interactions*
Law—*The Legal Status of Companion Animals* (with Sylvia Glover)

Jennifer A. Mather
Professor of Psychology, University of Lethbridge, Lethbridge, Alberta, Canada
Education—*Teaching Human-Animal Interactions*

Elly Maynard
President and Founder, Sirius Global Animal Charitable Trust, Tauranga, New Zealand
Animals as Food—*Dogs in China May Be Food or Friend* (with Paul S. C. Taçon)

Donald McCaig
Author, Williamsville, Virginia
Animals at Work—*Stock Dogs and Livestock*

Patrick McDonnell
Author and Cartoonist, Middlesex County, New Jersey
Media and Film—*Cartoonists, Comic Strips, and Animals*

Cynthia J. McFadden
Department of Wildlife and Fisheries Sciences, Texas A&M University. College Station, Texas
Sports—*Sport and Animals*

Paul McGreevy
Senior Lecturer in Veterinary Science, University of Sydney, Sydney, Australia
Applied Anthrozoology and Veterinary Practice—*Stresses at the Vet's Office* [sidebar to *Veterinarian Training and the Human-Animal Connection*]
Health—*The Benefits of Petting Dogs* [sidebar to *Benefits of Animal Contact*]

Susan McHugh
Assistant Professor of English, University of New England, Biddeford, Maine
Literature—*Animal Stories across Cultures*

Carron Meaney
Research Associate, Denver Museum of Nature and Science, Denver, Colorado, and Curator Adjoint, University of Colorado Museum, Boulder, Colorado
Conservation and Environment—*Preble's Meadow Mouse and the Endangered Species Act* [sidebar to *Endangered Species Act*]

Eraldo Medeiros Costa Neto
Professor of Ethnobiology, Feira de Santana State University, Feira de Santana, Bahia, Brazil
Living with Animals—*Insect-Human Connections*

Michael P. Meehan
PhD Candidate, Lecturer at School of Veterinary Science, University of Queensland, Brisbane, Australia
Bonding—*Attachment between Humans and Animals*

Lieve Meers
Research Fellow, Laboratory for Ethology, Ghent University, Ghent, Belgium
Animal Assistance to Humans—*Animal-Assisted Interventions* (with Debbie Coultis and William Ellery Samuels)
Biosynergy—*Biophilia* (with William Ellery Samuels and Debbie Coultis)
Sports—*Blood Sports and Animals* (with William Ellery Samuels and Debbie Coultis)

Gail F. Melson
Professor Emerita, Purdue University, West Lafayette, Indiana
Children—*Children and Animals*

Locksley L. McV. Messam
Center for Animal Alternatives, University of California, Davis, California
Health—*Epidemiology and Human-Animal Interactions* (with Lynette Hart)

Myrna Milani
Independent Scholar, Charlestown, New Hampshire
Human Influences on Animal Reproduction—*Canine Surgical Sterilization and the Human-Animal Bond*

Tema Milstein
Assistant Professor of Communication and Journalism, University of New Mexico, Albuquerque, New Mexico.
Literature—*Human Communication's Effects on Relationships with Animals*

Russell A. Mittermeier
President, Conservation International, Washington, D.C.
Animals as Food—*Global Diversity and Bushmeat* (with Anthony L. Rose)

Sy Montgomery
Author, Hancock, New Hampshire
Hunting, Fishing, and Trapping—*Man-Eating Tigers*

Heather Moore
Senior Writer, People for the Ethical Treatment of Animals
Animals as Food—*Veganism*
Ethics and Animal Protection—*People for the Ethical Treatment of Animals*

Aimee Morgana
Independent Researcher, New York, New York
Communication and Language—*Interspecies Communication—N'kisi the Parrot: A Personal Essay*

Patricia Morris
Graduate Student, Northeastern University, Boston, Massachusetts
Applied Anthrozoology and Veterinary Practice—*Veterinarian Training and the Human-Animal Connection*

Cynthia Moss
Director, Amboseli Elephant Research Project, Nairobi, Kenya
Conservation and Environment—*Elephant Conservation and Welfare at the Amboseli Elephant Research Project*

Jim Motavalli
Editor, *E/The Environmental Magazine*, Norwalk, Connecticut
Conservation and Environment—*Conservation Medicine Links Human and Animal Health with the Environment*
Conservation and Environment—*Global Warming and the Spread of Disease*

Michael Mountain
President, Best Friends Animal Society, Kanab, Utah
Ethics and Animal Protection—*Best Friends Animal Society*

Alisa Mullins
Senior Writer, People for the Ethical Treatment of Animals, Norfolk, Virginia
Domestication—*The Wool Industry and Sheep*

Sarah Najor
Department of Psychology, University of Michigan, Ann Arbor, Michigan
Bonding—*Behavior of Animals Influences Human-Animal Interactions* (with Geoffrey E. Gerstner)

Nina Natelson
Founding Director, Concern for Helping Animals in Israel (CHAI), Alexandria, Virginia
Ethics and Animal Protection—*Israel and Animal Welfare*

Pradeep Kumat Nath
Founder and President, Visakha Society For Prevention of Cruelty to Animals, Andhra Pradesh, India
Culture, Religion, and Belief Systems—*Animals in India* [sidebar to *India's Holy Cows*]

Ruth C. Newberry
Associate Professor, Washington State University, Pullman, Washington
Living with Animals—*Pigs and Humans* (with Marek Špinka)

Michael Noonan
Professor of Biology and Psychology, Canisius College, Buffalo, New York
Living with Animals—*Killer Whales and Humans*

Barbara Noske
Research Fellow in Humanities and Social Sciences, University of Sydney, Australia
Culture, Religion, and Belief Systems—*Indigenous Cultures and Animals*
Ethics and Animal Protection—*Human-Animal Kinship for Animal Rightists and "Deep Greens"*

Siobhan O'Sullivan
PhD Candidate in Political Science, The University of Sydney, Sydney, Australia
Law—*Legislation: History (International) of Animal Welfare Policy*

Gard W. Otis
Professor of Environmental Biology, University of Guelph, Ontario, Canada
Bonding—*Discrimination between Humans by Honeybees* (with Hank Davis and Lisa Collis)

Robert A. Palmatier
Professor Emeritus of Linguistics, Western Michigan University, Kalamazoo, Michigan
Literature—*Metaphors about Animals*

Christopher M. Papouchis
Conservation Biologist, Mountain Lion Foundation, Sacramento, California
Living with Animals—*Mountain Lions and Humans*

Gary Patronek
Clinical Assistant Professor, Cummings School of Veterinary Medicine, Center for Animals and Public Policy, Tufts University, North Grafton, Massachusetts
Ethics and Animal Protection—*Hoarding Animals* (with Gary Patronek)

Emily Patterson-Kane
Animal Welfare Scientist, American Veterinary Medical Association, Schaumburg, IL.
Culture, Religion, and Belief Systems—*Cattle Mutilation*
Culture, Religion, and Belief Systems—*Totems and Spirit Guides*
Music, Dance, and Theater—*Music as a Shared Trait among Humans and Animals*
Research—*Laboratory Human-Animal Bonds*

Mauri Pesonen
Programmer, Finnish Game and Fisheries Research Institute, Joensuu, Finland
Animals at Work—*Dog and Human Cooperation in Hunting* (with Vesa Ruusila)

Anna Peterson
Professor of Religion, University of Florida, Gainesville, Florida
Culture, Religion, and Belief Systems—*Christian Theology, Ethics, and Animals* (with Samuel Snyder)
History—*Animals and the New World* (with Gavin Van Horn)
Human Perceptions of Animals—*Humanness and What It Means to Be a Human Animal* (with Lucas F. Johnston)

Brenda Peterson
Author, Journalist, and Teacher, Seattle, Washington
Ecotourism—*The Whale and the Cherry Blossom Festival: A Personal Encounter*

Dale Peterson
Author, Cambridge, Massachusetts
Ethics and Animal Protection—*Goodall, Jane* [sidebar: *The Significance of Jane Goodall's Chimpanzee Studies*]

Jessica Pierce
Independent Scholar, Longmont, Colorado
Sentience and Cognition—*Morality in Humans and Animals*

Aaron J. Place
Assistant Professor of Biology, Northwestern Oklahoma State University, Alva, Oklahoma
Culture, Religion, and Belief Systems—*Snakes as Cultural and Religious Symbols* (with Charles I. Abramson)

Anthony L. Podberscek
Postdoctoral Research Associate, University of Cambridge, Cambridge, UK
Animals as Food—*Dogs and Cats as Food in Asia*

Simone Pollo
Researcher in Moral Philosophy, Università "La Sapienza," Rome, Italy
Ethics and Animal Protection—*Biomedicine and Animals* (with Augusto Vitale)

Thomas G. Power
Professor of Human Development, Washington State University, Pullman, Washington
Play—*Human and Animal Play*

Harold "Wes" Pratt
Staff Scientist, Mote Marine Laboratory, Summerland Key, Florida
Living with Animals—*Sharks and Humans*

Frederick R. Prete
Instructor, Department of Biology, Northeastern Illinois University, Chicago, Illinois
Anthropomorphism—*The Myth of "Sexual Cannibalism" by the Praying Mantis*
Living with Animals—*Honeybee Society and Humans*

Dawn Prince-Hughes
Adjunct Professor of Anthropology, Western Washington University, Bellingham, Washington
Bonding—*Gorillas and Me: A Personal Journey*

Andrea Reynes
Journalist, Acton, Massachusetts
Animal Assistance to Humans—*Horse-Assisted Therapy: Reaching Troubled Young Women*

Frances Gates Rhodes
Associate Professor of English, Texas A&M International University, Laredo, Texas
Literature—*Children's Literature: Cats*
Literature—*Children's Literature: Horses*

Fabian Ritter
MEER e.V. (Mammals Encounters Education Research) Organization, Berlin, Germany
Conservation and Environment—*Whale Watching: A Sustainable Use of Cetaceans?*

Mim Eichler Rivas
Author, Hermosa Beach, California
Bonding—*The Horse "Beautiful Jim" and Dr. William Key: A Personal Essay*

Jill Robinson
Founder and CEO, Animals Asia Foundation, Hong Kong, China
Cruelty to Animals—*The Bear Bile Industry in China: A Personal Essay*

Terry L. Root
Senior Fellow at Woods Institute for the Environment and Professor of Biological Sciences, by courtesy, Stanford University, Stanford, California
Conservation and Environment—*Global Warming and Animals* [sidebar: *Global Warming and Oceans*]

Anthony L. Rose
President, The Biosynergy Institute, Palos Verdes Peninsula, California
Animals as Food—*Global Diversity and Bushmeat* (with Russell A. Mittermeier)
Biosynergy—*Biosynergy: A Personal Essay*

Nicole Rosmarino
Conservation Director, Forest Guardians, Santa Fe, New Mexico
Conservation and Environment—*Endangered Species Act*

David Rothenberg
Professor of Philosophy, New Jersey Institute of Technology, Newark, New Jersey
Music, Dance, and Theater—*Interspecies Music*

A. G. Rud
Associate Professor of Educational Studies, Purdue University, West Lafayette, Indiana
Ethics and Animal Protection—*Schweitzer, Albert*
Literature—*Melville, Herman*

Constance L. Russell
Associate Professor, Lakehead University, Thunder Bay, Canada
Ecotourism—*Ecotourism* (with Anne E. Russon)

Anne E. Russon
Professor, York University, Toronto, Canada
Ecotourism—*Ecotourism* (with Constance L. Russell)

Vesa Ruusila
Research Scientist, Finnish Game and Fisheries Research Institute, Joensuu, Finland
Animals at Work—*Dog and Human Cooperation in Hunting* (with Mauri Pesonen)

William Ellery Samuels
Director of Research and Education, People, Animals, Nature, Inc., Astoria, New York
Animal Assistance to Humans—*Animal-Assisted Interventions* (with Lieve Meers and Debbie Coultis)
Biosynergy—*Biophilia* (with Debbie Coultis and Lieve Meers)
Conservation and Environment—*Animal Conservationists* (with Susan Frey)
Education—*Nurturing Empathy in Children*
Sports—*Blood Sports and Animals* (with Lieve Meers and Debbie Coultis)

Clinton Sanders
Professor of Sociology, University of Connecticut, Storrs, Connecticut
Human Perceptions of Animals—*Social Construction of Animals* (with Arnold Arluke)

Constantine Sandis
Lecturer in Philosophy, Oxford Brookes University, Oxford, UK
Classification—*Classification of Animals*
Culture, Religion, and Belief Systems—*Animal Mummies in Ancient Egypt*
Culture, Religion, and Belief Systems—*Gandhi, Mohandas Karamchand (1869–1948)*
Human Perceptions of Animals—*Freaks—"Human-Animals"*
Media and Film—Planet of the Apes
Media and Film—*Superhero Animals*
Research—*Animals in Space*

Lisa Sarmicanic
Doctoral Student, University of Nevada, Las Vegas, Las Vegas, Nevada
Bonding—*Companion Animals*

Carol D. Saunders
Director of Conservation Psychology, Chicago Zoological Society, Brookfield, Illinois
Conservation and Environment—*Conservation Psychology*

Boria Sax
Director of Online Academic Services, Mercy College, Dobbs Ferry, New York
Culture, Religion, and Belief Systems—*Animals in Nazi Germany*
History—*The Ravens of the Tower of London*
Literature—*Metamorphosis*

Stephen Bede Scharper
Associate Professor, Centre for Environment, University of Toronto, and Department of Anthropology, University of Toronto at Mississauga
Conservation and Environment—*From Anthropocentrism to Anthropoharmonism*

James A. Serpell
Professor of Humane Ethics and Animal Welfare, University of Pennsylvania, Philadelphia, Pennsylvania
Culture, Religion, and Belief Systems—*Witchcraft and Animals*

Kenneth Shapiro
Psychologist, Animals and Society Institute, Washington Grove, Maryland
Education—*A History of Human-Animal Studies*

Rupert Sheldrake
Perrott-Warrick Scholar, Trinity College, Cambridge University, and Visiting Professor at the Graduate Institute, Milford, Connecticut
Communication and Language—*Telepathic Communication Systems between People and Animals*

Jo-Ann Shelton
Professor of Classics and Environmental Studies, University of California, Santa Barbara, California
Conservation and Environment—*Exotic Species*
History—*Animals in Ancient Roman Arenas*

Chris M. Sherwin
Senior Research Fellow in Animal Behaviour and Welfare, University of Bristol, Bristol, UK
Research—*Mice Experimentation and Laboratory Use*

Martha Sherwood
Research Associate, Department of Biology, University of Oregon, Eugene, Oregon
Conservation and Environment—*Extinction of Animals*
Health—*Animal Reservoirs of Human Disease*
Human Perceptions of Animals—*Perceptions of Animals in Medieval Europe*

Anne E. Silver
Graduate Student, York University, Glendon, Ontario, Canada
Bonding—*Discrimination between Humans by Gentoo Penguins* (Pygosceli papua papua/ellsworthii*)* (with Hank Davis and Celia Ackerman)

Con Slobodchikoff
Professor of Biology, Northern Arizona University, Flagstaff, Arizona
Living with Animals—*Prairie Dogs and Humans* (with Jennifer L. Verdolin)

Andrew T. Smith
Professor, School of Life Sciences, Arizona State University, Tempe, Arizona
Conservation and Environment—*Ecosystems and a Keystone Species, the Plateau Pika*

Douglas W. Smith
Wolf Project Leader, Yellowstone National Park, National Park Service, Yellowstone National Park, Montana
Conservation and Environment—*Wolf and Human Conflicts: A Long, Bad History*

Samuel Snyder
PhD Candidate, University of Florida, Gainesville, Florida
Culture, Religion, and Belief Systems—*Christian Theology, Ethics, and Animals* (with Anna Peterson)
Culture, Religion, and Belief Systems—*Indigenous Cultures, Hunting, and the Gifts of Prey*

Richard Sosis
Senior Lecturer in Anthropology, Hebrew University of Jerusalem, Jerusalem, Israel; Associate Professor of Anthropology, University of Connecticut, Storrs, Connecticut
Culture, Religion, and Belief Systems—*Rituals of Humans and Animals* (with Candace S. Alcorta)

Charles H. Southwick
Professor Emeritus of Biology, University of Colorado, Boulder, Colorado
Living with Animals—*Rhesus Monkeys and Humans*

Marek Špinka
Senior Researcher, Research Institute of Animal Production, Prague, Czechoslovakia
Living with Animals—*Pigs and Humans* (with Ruth C. Newberry)

H. Peter Steeves
Associate Professor of Philosophy, DePaul University, Chicago, Illinois
Children—*Feral Children*
Classification—*Species Concept*
Human Perceptions of Animals—*Cryptozoology (Bigfoot, the Loch Ness Monster, and Others)*

Christina Stern
Author and Adjunct Assistant Professor, City University of New York at LaGuardia Community College, Long Island City, New York
Ethics and Animal Protection—*The Enlightenment and Its Views of Animals*
Urban Animals—*Animals and Urbanism*

Gwyneth St. Francis
Artist, Pretoria, South Africa
Art—*Animals in Celtic Art*

Kristin L. Stewart
Department of Geography, Florida State University, Tallahassee, Florida
Geography—*Animal Geographies*
Zoos and Aquariums—*Marine Mammals and Aquariums*

Robert W. Sussman
Professor of Anthropology, Washington University, St. Louis, Missouri
Hunting, Fishing, and Trapping—*Humans as the Hunted* (with Donna Hart)

Ronald R. Swaisgood
Head, Applied Animal Ecology Division, Conservation and Research for Endangered Species, Zoological Society of San Diego, San Diego, California
Zoos and Aquariums—*Enrichment and Well-Being for Zoo Animals*

Paul S. C. Taçon
Professor, School of Arts, Griffith University, Queensland, Australia
Animals as Food—*Dogs in China May Be Food or Friend* (with Elly Maynard)

Michael L. Tan
Professor of Anthropology, University of the Philippines, Diliman, Quezon City, The Philippines
Animals as Food—*Dog Eating in the Philippines*

Daniel R. Tardona
Adjunct Faculty, University of North Florida, Jacksonville, Florida
Living with Animals—*Wildlife and Humans in the U.S. National Parks*

Clare Thomas
Doctoral Student, University of Maine, Orono, Maine
Animal Assistance to Humans—*Horse-Assisted Therapy: Psychotherapy with Horses*

Sydney Carroll Thomas
Associate Professor of Counselor Education, University of Maine, Orono, Maine
Rehabilitation of Animals—*Wild Bird Rehabilitation—Rare Intimacies: A Personal Essay*

Mary Thurston
Independent Scholar, Austin, Texas
Animals at Work—*Animals in War*
Culture, Religion, and Belief Systems—*Animal Burial and Animal Cemeteries*

Adrian Treves
Executive Director, COEX: Sharing the Land with Wildlife, Inc., Madison, Wisconsin
Conservation and Environment—*Conflicts between Humans and Wildlife*

Jacky Turner
Writer, Waterlooville, Hampshire, UK
Human Influences on Animal Reproduction—*Human Influences on Animal Reproduction*
Hunting, Fishing, and Trapping—*Fishing and Human Attitudes*

Linda M. Van Blerkom
Professor of Anthropology, Drew University, Madison, New Jersey
Health—*Humans, Viruses, and Evolution*

Gavin Van Horn
PhD Candidate, University of Florida, Gainesville, Florida
Culture, Religion, and Belief Systems—*Religion and Predators*
History—*Animals and the New World* (with Anna Peterson)

Jennifer L. Verdolin
PhD Candidate, Stony Brook University, Stony Brook, New York
Living with Animals—*Prairie Dogs and Humans* (with Con Slobodchikoff)

Augusto Vitale
Researcher in Animal Behaviour, Istituto Superiore di Sanità, Roma, Italy
Ethics and Animal Protection—*Biomedicine and Animals* (with Simone Pollo)

Carla Wakeman
Wildlife Rehabilitator, Running Springs, California
Rehabilitation of Animals—*Rehabilitating Wildlife*

Paul Waldau
Director, Center for Animals and Public Policy, Cummings School of Veterinary Medicine, Tufts University, North Grafton, Massachusetts
Culture, Religion, and Belief Systems—*Religion and Animals*
Law—*Animal Law*
Law—*Public Policy and Animals*

Traci Warkentin
PhD Candidate, Faculty of Environmental Studies, York University, Toronto, Canada
Ethics and Animal Protection—*Environmental Philosophy and Animals*
Literature—*Metaphors and the Treatment of Animals* [sidebar to *Metaphors in Constructing Human-Animal Relationships*]

Judith Ann Warner
Associate Professor of Sociology, Texas A&M International University, Laredo, Texas
Ethics and Animal Protection—*Horse Rescue*
Living with Animals—*Famous Horses*

Paul K. Wason
Director of Science and Religion Programs, John Templeton Foundation, West Conshohocken, Pennsylvania
Art—*Rock Art and Shamanism*
Culture, Religion, and Belief Systems—*Native American Vision Quests*
Culture, Religion, and Belief Systems—*Totemism*

Cristy Watkins
PhD Candidate, School of Natural Resources and Environment, University of Michigan, Ann Arbor, Michigan
Bonding—*Chimpanzee and Human Relationships* (with John Bock)

Bart Weetjens
Managing Director, APOPO, Morogoro, Tanzania
Animal Assistance to Humans—*Giant African Pouched Rats Saving Human Lives*

Zoe Weil
President and Head of Faculty, International Institute for Humane Education, Surry, Maine
Education—*Humane Education*

Deborah Wells
Senior Lecturer, School of Psychology, Queen's University, Belfast, Northern Ireland, UK
Bonding—*Dogs as Social Catalysts*

Harrington Wells
Associate Professor of Biology, University of Tulsa, Tulsa, Oklahoma
Health—*Rabies* (with Charles I. Abramson)
Research—*A Honeybee Model of Alcohol-Induced Behavior* (with Charles I. Abramson and Janko Bozic)

Françoise Wemelsfelder
Senior Research Scientist, Scottish Agricultural College, Edinburgh, UK
Enrichment for Animals—*Animal Boredom*

Hal Whitehead
Professor of Biology, Dalhousie University, Halifax, Nova Scotia, Canada
Conservation and Environment—*Whale and Dolphin Culture and Human Interactions*

Howard Whiteman
Associate Professor of Biological Sciences, Murray State University, Murray, Kentucky
Sports—*Animals as Sports Mascots* (with Susan Garnett)

Fred Whoriskey
Vice President of Research and Environment, Atlantic Salmon Federation, St. Andrews, New Brunswick, Canada
Hunting, Fishing, and Trapping—*Sport Fishing*

Pauline Williams
Associate Dean, Hartpury College, Hartpury, Gloucestershire, UK
Bonding—*Homelessness and Dogs* (with Heidi Leader)

George Wittemyer
NSF International Postdoctoral Fellow, Save the Elephants, Nairobi, Kenya
Conservation and Environment—*Elephants and Humans in Kenya* (with Renee Kuriyan)

Mary W. Wood
Librarian, UCD Center for Animal Alternatives Information, University of California, Davis, California
Education—*Information Resources on Humans and Animals*

Stephen Zawistowski
Executive Vice President, The American Society for the Prevention of Cruelty to Animals, New York, New York
Culture, Religion, and Belief Systems—*Francis of Assisi (1181/82–1226)*

Günther K. H. Zupanc
Professor of Neurobiology, School of Engineering and Science, International University of Bremen, Germany; and Section of Neurobiology, Division of Biological Sciences, University of California, San Diego, California
Living with Animals—*Fish and Humans* (with Marianne M. Zupanc)

Marianne M. Zupanc
Research Associate, School of Engineering and Science, International University of Bremen, Germany
Living with Animals—*Fish and Humans* (with Günther K. H. Zupanc)

Index

Note: Page numbers in **bold** represent main entries in the encyclopedia.